ALSO BY LAWRENCE WRIGHT

The Looming Tower
God's Favorite
Twins
Remembering Satan
Saints & Sinners
In the New World
City Children, Country Summer

GOING CLEAR

GOING CLEAR

Scientology, Hollywood, and the Prison of Belief

LAWRENCE WRIGHT

ALFRED A. KNOPF   NEW YORK   2013

THIS IS A BORZOI BOOK
PUBLISHED BY ALFRED A. KNOPF

Copyright © 2013 by Lawrence Wright

All rights reserved. Published in the United States by Alfred A. Knopf, a division of Random House, Inc., New York, and in Canada by Random House of Canada Limited, Toronto.

www.aaknopf.com

Knopf, Borzoi Books, and the colophon are registered trademarks of Random House, Inc.

ISBN: 978-0-307-70066-7

Library of Congress Cataloging-in-Publication Data
is on file at the Library of Congress

Jacket design by Peter Mendelsund

Manufactured in the United States of America
Published January 17, 2013
Second Printing, February 2013

3 0646 00188 9280

To my colleagues

at

The New Yorker

Contents

Introduction

Scientology plays an outsize role in the cast of new religions that have arisen in the twentieth century and survived into the twenty-first. The church won't release official membership figures, but informally it claims 8 million members worldwide, a figure that is based on the number of people who have donated to the church. A recent ad claims that the church welcomes 4.4 million new people every year. And yet, according to a former spokesperson for the church, the International Association of Scientologists, an organization that church members are forcefully encouraged to join, has only about 30,000 members. The largest concentration, about 5,000, is in Los Angeles. A survey of American religious affiliations compiled in the *Statistical Abstract of the United States* estimates that only 25,000 Americans actually call themselves Scientologists. That's less than half the number identifying themselves as Rastafarians.

Despite decades of declining membership and intermittent scandals that might have sunk other faiths, Scientology remains afloat, more than a quarter century after the death of its chimerical leader, L. Ron Hubbard. In part, its survival is due to colossal financial resources—about $1 billion in liquid assets, according to knowledgeable former members. Strictly in terms of cash reserves, that figure eclipses the holdings of most major world religions. Scientology's wealth testifies to the avidity of its membership, relentless fund-raising, and the legacy of Hubbard's copyrights to the thousand books and articles he published.

The church also claims about 12 million square feet of property around the world. Hollywood is the center of Scientology's real-estate empire, with twenty-six properties valued at $400 million. The most recent addition to the church's Hollywood portfolio is a television studio on Sunset Boulevard formerly owned by KCET, acquired in order to open a Scientology broadcasting center. In Clearwater, Florida, where Scientology maintains its spiritual headquarters, the church owns sixty-eight largely tax-exempt parcels of land, valued at $168 million. They include apartment buildings, hotels and motels, warehouses, schools, office buildings, a bank, and tracts of vacant land. The church often acquires landmark buildings near key locations, such as Music Row in Nashville, Dupont Circle in Washington, DC, and Times Square in New York City. A similar strategy governs the placement of Scientology's holdings in other countries. Typically, these buildings are magnificently restored architectural treasures, lavishly appointed, even if the membership is negligible. The church owns a five-hundred-acre compound in Southern California and a cruise ship, the *Freewinds*, which is based in the Caribbean. The Church of Spiritual Technology, the branch of Scientology that owns the trademarks and copyrights to all church materials, including Hubbard's immense body of popular fiction, maintains secret bases in several remote locations in at least three American states, where the founder's works are stored in titanium canisters in nuclear-blast-resistant caverns. One of the vault locations, in Trementina, New Mexico, has an airstrip and two giant interlocking circles carved into the desert floor—a landmark for UFOs, some believe, or for Hubbard's reincarnated spirit, when he chooses to return.

There are really three tiers of Scientologists. Public Scientologists constitute the majority of the membership. Many of them have their first exposure to the religion at a subway station or a shopping mall where they might take a free "stress test" or a personality inventory called "The Oxford Capacity Analysis" (there is no actual connection to Oxford University). On those occasions, potential recruits are likely to be told that they have problems that Scientology can resolve, and they are steered to a local church or mission for courses or therapy, which the church terms "auditing." That's as far as most new members go, but others begin a lengthy and expensive climb up the church's spiritual ladder.

The mystique that surrounds the religion is owed mainly to the second tier of membership: a small number of Hollywood actors and other celebrities. To promote the idea that Scientology is a unique refuge for spiritually hungry movie stars, as well as a kind of factory for stardom, the church operates Celebrity Centres in Hollywood and several other entertainment hubs. Any Scientologist can take courses at Celebrity Centres; it's part of the lure, that an ordinary member can envision being in classes with notable actors or musicians. In practice, the real celebrities have their own private entry and course rooms, and they rarely mix with the public—except for major contributors who are accorded the same heightened status. The total number of celebrities in the church is impossible to calculate, both because the term itself is so elastic and because some well-known personalities who have taken courses or auditing don't wish to have their association known.

An ordinary public Scientologist can be inconspicuous. No one really needs to know his beliefs. Public members who quit the church seldom make a scene; they just quietly remove themselves and the community closes the circle behind them (although they are likely to be pursued by mail and phone solicitations for the rest of their lives). Celebrity members, on the other hand, are constantly being pressed to add their names to petitions, being showcased at workshops and galas, or having their photos posted over the logo "I'm a Scientologist." Their fame greatly magnifies the influence of the church. They are deployed to advance the social agendas of the organization, including attacks on psychiatry and the pharmaceutical industry, and the promotion of Hubbard's contested theories of education and drug rehabilitation. They become tied to Scientology's banner, which makes it more difficult to break away if they should become disillusioned.

Neither the public nor the celebrity tiers of Scientology could exist without the third level of membership—the church's clergy, called the Sea Organization, or Sea Org, in Scientology jargon. It is an artifact of the private navy that Hubbard commanded during a decade when he was running the church while on the high seas. The church has said on various occasions that the Sea Org has 5,000, 6,000, or 10,000 members worldwide. Former Sea Org members estimate the actual size of the clergy to be between 3,000 and 5,000, concentrated mainly in Clearwater, Florida, and Los Angeles. Many of them joined the Sea Org as children. They have sacrificed their education and are impoverished by their service. As a symbol of their unswerving dedication to the promotion of Hubbard's principles, they have signed contracts for a billion years of service—only a brief moment in the eternal scheme, as seen by Scientology, which postulates that the universe is four quadrillion years old.

The church disputes the testimony of many of the sources I've spoken to for this book, especially those former members of the Sea Org who have now left the organization, calling them "apostates" and "defectors." It is certainly true that a number of them no longer accept the teachings of L. Ron Hubbard; but many still consider themselves fervent Scientologists, saying that it was the church itself that has strayed from his example. They include some of the highest officials who have ever served in the organization.

Scientology is certainly among the most stigmatized religions in the world, owing to its eccentric cosmology, its vindictive behavior toward critics and defectors, and the damage it has inflicted on families that have been broken apart by the church's policy of "disconnection"—the imposed isolation of church members from people who stand in the way of their longed-for spiritual progress. In the United States, constitutional guarantees of religious liberty protect the church from actions that might otherwise be considered abusive or in violation of laws in human trafficking or labor standards. Many of these practices are well known to the public.

And yet curious recruits continue to be attracted to the religion, though not in the numbers that Scientology claims; celebrities still find their way to the church's VIP lounge; and young people sign away the next billion years of their existence to an organization that promises to work them mercilessly for practically no pay. Obviously, there is an enduring appeal that survives the widespread assumption that Scientology is a cult and a fraud.

I have spent much of my career examining the effects of religious beliefs on people's lives—historically, a far more profound influence on society and individuals than politics, which is the substance of so much journalism. I was drawn to write this book by the questions that many people have about Scientology: What is it that makes the religion alluring? What do its adherents get out of it? How can seemingly rational people subscribe to beliefs that others find incomprehensible? Why do popular personalities associate themselves with a faith that is likely to create a kind of public relations martyrdom? These questions are not unique to Scientology, but they certainly underscore the conversation. In attempting to answer them in this book, I hope we can learn something about what might be called the process of belief. Few Scientologists have had a conversion experience—a sudden, radical reorientation of one's life; more common is a gradual, wholehearted acceptance of propositions that might have been regarded as unacceptable or absurd at the outset, as well as the incremental surrender of will on the part of people who have been promised enhanced power and authority. One can see by this example the motor that propels all great social movements, for good or ill.

LAWRENCE WRIGHT
Austin, Texas

Part I

SCIENTOLOGY

1

The Convert

London, Ontario, is a middling manufacturing town halfway between Toronto and Detroit, once known for its cigars and breweries. In a tribute to its famous namesake, London has its own Covent Garden, Piccadilly Street, and even a Thames River that forks around the modest, economically stressed downtown. The city, which sits in a humid basin, is remarked upon for its unpleasant weather. Summers are unusually hot, winters brutally cold, the springs and falls fine but fleeting. The most notable native son was the bandleader Guy Lombardo, who was honored in a local museum, until it closed for lack of visitors. London was a difficult place for an artist looking to find himself.

Paul Haggis was twenty-one years old in 1975. He was walking toward a record store in downtown London when he encountered a fast-talking, long-haired young man with piercing eyes standing on the corner of Dundas and Waterloo Streets. There was something keen and strangely adamant in his manner. His name was Jim Logan. He pressed a book into Haggis's hands. "You have a mind," Logan said. "This is the owner's manual." Then he demanded, "Give me two dollars."

The book was *Dianetics: The Modern Science of Mental Health*, by L. Ron Hubbard, which was published in 1950. By the time Logan pushed it on Haggis, the book had sold more than two million copies throughout the world. Haggis opened the book and saw a page stamped with the words "Church of Scientology."

"Take me there," he said to Logan.

At the time, there were only a handful of Scientologists in the entire province of Ontario. By coincidence, Haggis had heard about the organization a couple of months earlier, from a friend who had called it a cult. That interested Haggis; he considered the possibility of doing a documentary film about it. When he arrived at the church's quarters in London, it certainly didn't look like a cult—two young men occupying a hole-in-the-wall office above Woolworth's five-and-dime.

As an atheist, Haggis was wary of being dragged into a formal belief system. In response to his skepticism, Logan showed him a passage by Hubbard that read: "What is true is what is true for you. No one has any right to force data on you and command you to believe it or else. If it is not true for you, it isn't true. Think your own way through things, accept what is true for you, discard the rest. There is nothing unhappier than one who tries to live in a chaos of lies." These words resonated with Haggis.

Although he didn't realize it, Haggis was being drawn into the church through a classic, four-step "dissemination drill" that recruiters are carefully trained to follow. The first step is to make contact, as Jim Logan did with Haggis in 1975. The second step is to disarm any antagonism the individual may display toward Scientology. Once that's done, the task is to "find the ruin"—that is, the problem most on the mind of the potential recruit. For Paul, it was a turbulent romance. The fourth step is to convince the subject that Scientology has the answer. "Once the person is aware of the ruin, you bring about an understanding that Scientology can handle the condition," Hubbard writes. "It's at the right moment on this step that one . . . directs him to the service that will best handle what he needs handled." At that point, the potential recruit has officially been transformed into a Scientologist.

Paul responded to every step in an almost ideal manner. He and his girlfriend took a course together and, shortly thereafter, became Hubbard Qualified Scientologists, one of the first levels in what the church calls the Bridge to Total Freedom.

HAGGIS WAS BORN in 1953, the oldest of three children. His father, Ted, ran a construction company specializing in roadwork—mostly laying asphalt and pouring sidewalks, curbs, and gutters. He called his company Global, because he was serving both London and Paris— another Ontario community fifty miles to the east. As Ted was getting his business started, the family lived in a small house in the predominantly white town. The Haggises were one of the few Catholic families in a Protestant neighborhood, which led to occasional confrontations, including a schoolyard fistfight that left Paul with a broken nose. Although he didn't really think of himself as religious, he identified with being a minority; however, his mother, Mary, insisted on sending Paul and his two younger sisters, Kathy and Jo, to Mass every Sunday. One day, she spotted their priest driving an expensive car. "God wants me to have a Cadillac," the priest explained. Mary responded, "Then God doesn't want us in your church anymore." Paul admired his mother's stand; he knew how much her religion meant to her. After that, the family stopped going to Mass, but the children continued in Catholic schools.

Ted's construction business prospered to the point that he was able to buy a much larger house on eighteen acres of rolling land outside of town. There were a couple of horses in the stable, a Chrysler station wagon in the garage, and giant construction vehicles parked in the yard, like grazing dinosaurs. Paul spent a lot of time alone. He could walk the mile to catch the school bus and not see anyone along the way. His chores were to clean the horse stalls and the dog runs (Ted raised spaniels for field trials). At home, Paul made himself the center of attention—"the apple of his mother's eye," his father recalled—but he was mischievous and full of pranks. "He got the strap when he was five years old," Ted said.

When Paul was about thirteen, he was taken to say farewell to his grandfather on his deathbed. The old man had been a janitor in a bowling alley, having fled England because of some mysterious scandal. He seemed to recognize a similar dangerous quality in Paul. His parting words to him were, "I've wasted my life. Don't waste yours."

In high school, Paul began steering toward trouble. His worried parents sent him to Ridley College, a boarding school in St. Catharines, Ontario, near Niagara Falls, where he was required to be a part of the cadet corps of the Royal Canadian Army. He despised marching or any regulated behavior, and soon began skipping the compulsory drills. He would sit in his room reading *Ramparts*, the radical magazine that chronicled the social revolutions then unfolding in America, where he longed to be. He was constantly getting punished for his infractions, until he taught himself to pick locks; then he could sneak into the prefect's office and mark off his demerits. The experience sharpened an incipient talent for subversion.

After a year of this, his parents transferred him to a progressive boys' school, called Muskoka Lakes College, in northern Ontario, where there was very little system to subvert. Although it was called a college, it was basically a preparatory school. Students were encouraged to study whatever they wanted. Paul discovered a mentor in his art teacher, Max Allen, who was gay and politically radical. Allen produced a show for the Canadian Broadcasting Company called *As It Happens*. In 1973, while the Watergate hearings were going on in Washington, DC, Allen let Paul sit beside him in his cubicle at CBC while he edited John Dean's testimony for broadcast. Later, Allen opened a small theater in Toronto to show movies that had been banned under Ontario's draconian censorship laws, and Paul volunteered at the box office. They showed Ken Russell's *The Devils* and Bernardo Bertolucci's *Last Tango in Paris*. In Ted's mind, his son was working in a porno theater. "I just shut my eyes," Ted said.

Paul left school after he was caught forging a check. He attended art school briefly, and took some film classes at a community college, but he dropped out of that as well. He grew his curly blond hair to his shoulders. He began working in construction full-time for Ted, but he was drifting toward a precipice. In the 1970s, London acquired the nickname "Speed City," because of the methamphetamine labs that sprang up to serve its blossoming underworld. Hard drugs were easy to obtain. Two of Haggis's friends died from overdoses, and he had a gun pointed in his face a couple of times. "I was a bad kid," he admitted. "I didn't kill anybody. Not that I didn't try."

He also acted as a stage manager in the ninety-nine-seat theater his father created in an abandoned church for one of his stagestruck daughters. On Saturday nights, Paul would strike the set of whatever show was under way and put up a movie screen. In that way he introduced himself and the small community of film buffs in London to the works of Bergman, Hitchcock, and the French New Wave. He was so affected by Michelangelo Antonioni's *Blow-Up* that in 1974 he decided to become a fashion photographer in England, like the hero of that movie. That lasted less than a year, but when he returned he still carried a Leica over his shoulder.

Back in London, Ontario, he fell in love with a nursing student named Diane Gettas. They began sharing a one-bedroom apartment filled with Paul's books on film. He thought of himself then as "a loner and an artist and an iconoclast." His grades were too poor to get into college. He could see that he was going nowhere. He was ready to change, but he wasn't sure how.

Such was Paul Haggis's state of mind when he joined the Church of Scientology.

LIKE EVERY SCIENTOLOGIST, when Haggis entered the church, he took his first steps into the mind of L. Ron Hubbard. He read about Hubbard's adventurous life: how he wandered the world, led dangerous expeditions, and healed himself of crippling war injuries through the techniques that he developed into Dianetics. He was not a prophet, like Mohammed, or divine, like Jesus. He had not been visited by an angel bearing tablets of revelation, like Joseph Smith, the founder of Mormonism. Scientologists believe that Hubbard discovered the existential truths that form their doctrine through extensive research—in that way, it is "science." The apparent rationalism appealed to Haggis. He had long since walked away from the religion of his upbringing, but

L. Ron Hubbard in the 1960s

he was still looking for a way to express his idealism. It was important to him that Scientology didn't demand belief in a god. But the figure of L. Ron Hubbard did hover over the religion in suggestive ways. He wasn't worshipped, exactly, but his visage and name were everywhere, like the absolute ruler of a small kingdom.

There seemed to be two Hubbards within the church: the godlike authority whose every word was regarded as scripture, and the avuncular figure that Haggis saw on the training videos, who came across as wry and self-deprecating. Those were qualities that Haggis shared to a marked degree, and they inspired trust in the man he had come to accept as his spiritual guide. Still, Haggis felt a little stranded by the lack of irony among his fellow Scientologists. Their inability to laugh at themselves seemed at odds with the character of Hubbard himself. He didn't seem self-important or pious; he was like the dashing, wise-cracking hero of a B movie who had seen everything and somehow had it all figured out. When Haggis experienced doubts about the religion, he reflected on the 16 mm films of Hubbard's lectures from the 1950s and 1960s, which were part of the church's indoctrination process. Hubbard was always chuckling to himself, marveling over some random observation that had just occurred to him, with a little wink to the audience suggesting that they not take him too seriously. He would just open his mouth and a mob of new thoughts would burst forth, elbowing each other in the race to make themselves known to the world. They were often trivial and disjointed but also full of obscure, learned references and charged with a sense of originality and purpose. "You walked in one day and you said, 'I'm a seneschal,' " Hubbard observed in a characteristic aside,

> and this knight with eight-inch spurs, standing there—*humph*—and say, "I'm supposed to open the doors to this castle, I've been doing this for a long time, and I'm a very trusted retainer.". . . He's insisting he's the seneschal but nobody will pay him his wages, and so forth. . . . He was somebody before he became the seneschal.' Now, as a seneschal, he became nobody—until he finally went out and got a begging pan on the highway and began to hold it out for fish and chips as people came along, you know. . . . Now he says, "I am something, I am a beggar," but that's still something. Then the New York state police come along, or somebody, and they say to him—I'm a little mixed up in my periods here, but they say to

him—"Do you realize you cannot beg upon the public road without license Number 603-F?" . . . So he starves to death and kicks the bucket and there he lies. . . . Now he's somebody, he's a corpse, but he's not dead, he's merely a corpse. . . . Got the idea? But he goes through sequences of becoming nobody, somebody, nobody, somebody, nobody, somebody, nobody, not necessarily on a dwindling spiral. Some people get up to the point of being a happy man. You know the old story of a happy man—I won't tell it—he didn't have a shirt. . . .

Just as this fuzzy parable begins to ramble into incoherence, Hubbard comes to the point, which is that a being is not his occupation or even the body he presently inhabits. The central insight of Scientology is that the being is eternal, what Hubbard terms a "thetan." "This chap, in other words, was somebody until he began to identify his beingness with a thing. . . . None of these beingnesses are the person. The person is the thetan."

"He had this amazing buoyancy," Haggis recalled. "He had a dead-pan sense of humor and this sense of himself that seemed to say, 'Yes, I am fully aware that I might be mad, but I also might be on to something.' "

The zealotry that empowered so many members of the church came from the belief that they were the vanguard of the struggle to save humanity. "A civilization without insanity, without criminals and without war, where the able can prosper and honest beings can have rights, and where Man is free to rise to greater heights, are the aims of Scientology," Hubbard writes. Those breathless aims drew young idealists, like Haggis, to the church's banner.

To advance such lofty goals, Hubbard developed a "technology" to attain spiritual freedom and discover oneself as an immortal being. "Scientology works 100 percent of the time when it is properly applied to a person who sincerely desires to improve his life," a church publication declares. This guarantee rests on the assumption that through rigorous research, Hubbard had uncovered a perfect understanding of human nature. One must not stray from the path he has laid down or question his methods. Scientology is exact. Scientology is certain. Step by step one can ascend toward clarity and power, becoming more oneself—but, paradoxically, also more like Hubbard. Scientology is the geography of his mind. Perhaps no individual in history has taken such copious internal soundings and described with so much logic and minute detail the inner workings of his own mentality. The method Hubbard put forward created a road map toward his own ideal self. Hubbard's habits, his imagination, his goals and wishes—his character, in other words—became both the basis and the destination of Scientology.

Secretly, Haggis didn't really respect Hubbard as a writer. He hadn't been able to get through *Dianetics*, for instance. He read about thirty pages, then put it down. Much of the Scientology coursework, however, gave him a feeling of accomplishment. In 1976, he traveled to Los Angeles, the center of the Scientology universe, checking in at the old Château Élysée, on Franklin Avenue. Clark Gable and Katharine Hepburn had once stayed there, along with many other stars, but when Haggis arrived it was a run-down church retreat called the Manor Hotel.* He had a little apartment with a kitchen where he could write.

There were about 30,000 Scientologists in America at the time. Most of them were white, urban, and middle class; they were predominantly in their twenties, and many of them, especially in Los Angeles, were involved in graphic or performing arts. In other words, they were a lot like Paul Haggis. He immediately became a part of a community in a city that can otherwise be quite isolating. For the first time in his life, he experienced a feeling of kinship and camaraderie with people who had a lot in common—"all these atheists looking for something to believe in, and all these wanderers looking for a club to join."

In 1977, Haggis returned to Canada to continue working for his father, who could see that his son was struggling. Ted Haggis asked him what he wanted to do with his life. Haggis said he wanted to be a writer. His father said, "Well, there are only two places to do that, New York and Los Angeles. Pick one, and I'll keep you on the payroll for a year." Paul chose LA because it was the heart of the film world. Soon after this conversation with his father, Haggis and Diane Gettas got married. Two months later, they loaded up his brown Ranchero and drove to Los Angeles, moving into an apartment with Diane's brother, Gregg, and three other people. Paul got a job moving furniture. On the weekends he took photographs for yearbooks. At night

*It has since been spectacularly renovated and turned into Scientology's premier Celebrity Centre.

he wrote scripts on spec at a secondhand drafting table. The following year, Diane gave birth to their first child, Alissa.

SCIENTOLOGY HAD a giddy and playful air in the mid-seventies, when Haggis arrived in Los Angeles. It was seen as a cool, boutique religion, aimed especially toward the needs of artists and entertainers. The counterculture was still thriving in the seventies, and Scientology both was a part of it and stood apart from it. There was a saying, "After drugs, there's Scientology," and it was true that many who were drawn to the religion had taken hallucinogens and were open to alternative realities. Recruits had a sense of boundless possibility. Mystical powers were forecast; out-of-body experiences were to be expected; fundamental secrets of the universe were to be revealed.

Haggis became friends with other Scientologists who also hoped to make it in Hollywood. One of them was Skip Press, a writer and musician on the staff of the Celebrity Centre, which was the church's main foothold in the entertainment industry. Like many young recruits, Press believed that Scientology had given him superhuman powers; for instance, he believed that when he got into the right mental state, he

Paul Haggis on vacation in Antigua in 1975, the year he joined the Church of Scientology

could change traffic lights to green. He and Haggis formed a casual self-help group with other aspiring writers. They met at a Scientology hangout across from the Celebrity Centre called Two Dollar Bill's, where they would criticize each other's work and scheme about how to get ahead.

Eventually, this informal writers club came to the attention of Yvonne Gillham, the charismatic founder of the Celebrity Centre. Naturally warm and energetic, Gillham was an ideal candidate to woo the kinds of artists and opinion leaders that Hubbard sought to front his religion. The former kindergarten director staged parties, poetry readings, workshops, and dances. Chick Corea and other musicians associated with the church often played there. Gillham persuaded Haggis and his circle to hold their meetings at the Celebrity Centre, and they were folded into her web.

Haggis and a friend from the writers club eventually got a job scripting cartoons for Ruby-Spears Productions, beginning with a short-lived series called *Dingbat and the Creeps*, then *Heathcliff*. After that, Haggis went on to write *Richie Rich* and *Scooby-Doo* for Hanna-Barbera. He bought a used IBM Selectric typewriter. His career began to creep forward.

One day, a well-off strawberry farmer from Vancouver introduced himself to Haggis and Skip Press at the Celebrity Centre, saying he wanted to produce a life story of L. Ron Hubbard. He was offering fifteen thousand dollars for a script. Press declined, but Haggis accepted the money. His memory is that it was a horror script that he hoped to interest the strawberry farmer in. He never actually wrote a script about Hubbard, and eventually returned the entire sum, but in Press's opinion, that was when Haggis's career began to accelerate. "The money enabled Paul to cruise a bit and develop his career. Next thing I knew, Paul was getting an agent." His Scientology connections were paying off.

HAGGIS SPENT much of his time and money taking advanced courses and being "audited," a kind of Scientology psychotherapy that involves the use of an electropsychometer, or E-Meter. The device measures bodily changes in electrical resistance that occur when a person answers questions posed by an auditor. Hubbard compared it to a lie detector. The E-Meter bolstered the church's claim to being a scientific path to spiritual discovery. "It gives Man his first keen look into the heads and hearts of his fellows," Hubbard claimed, adding that Scientology boosted some people's IQ one point for every hour of auditing. "Our most spectacular feat was raising a boy from 83 IQ to 212," he once boasted to the *Saturday Evening Post*.

The theory of auditing is that it locates and discharges mental "masses" that are blocking the free flow of energy. Ideas and fantasies are not immaterial; they have weight and solidity. They can root themselves in the mind as phobias and obsessions. Auditing breaks up the masses that occupy what Hubbard terms the "reactive mind," which is where the fears and phobias reside. The E-Meter is presumed to measure changes in those masses. If the needle on the meter moves to the right, resistance is rising; to the left, it is falling. The auditor asks systematic questions aimed at detecting sources of "spiritual distress"—problems at work or in a relationship, for instance. Whenever the client, or "preclear," gives an answer that prompts the meter needle to jump, that subject becomes an area of concentration until the auditor is satisfied that emotional consequences of the troubling experience have drained away. Certain patterns of needle movement, such as sudden jumps or darts, long versus short falls, et cetera, have meaning as well. The auditor tries to guide the preclear to a "cognition" about the subject under examination, which leads to a "floating" needle. That doesn't necessarily mean that the needle is frozen. "The needle just idles around and yawns at your questions," Hubbard explains. The individual should experience a corresponding feeling of release. Eventually, the reactive mind is cleansed of its obsessions, fears, and irrational urges, and the preclear becomes Clear.*

---

*Hubbard sometimes disparaged the term "lie detector" in connection with E-Meters. "In the first place they do not detect lies and in the second place the police have known too little about the human mind to know that their instrument was actually accurate to an amazing perfection. These instruments should be called 'emotion detectors' " (Hubbard, "Electropsychometric Auditing Operator's Manual," 1952). According to David S. Touretsky, a research professor in computer science at Carnegie Mellon University (and a prominent Scientology critic), what are called "thoughts" are actually "fleeting patterns of chemical and electrical activity in our brains" that have no actual mass. "The meter is really more of a prop or talisman than a measuring instrument. Interpreting needle movements is like reading tea leaves. A good fortune teller picks up on lots of subliminal cues that let them 'read' their subject, while the tea leaves give the subject something to fixate on. And the subject is heavily invested in believing that the auditor and the meter are effective, so it's a mutually reinforcing system." The E-Meter measures skin resistance, like a lie detector. "Strong emotional reactions do cause changes in muscle tension or micro-tremors of the fingers will also cause changes in the current

Haggis found the E-Meter impressively responsive. He would grasp a cylindrical electrode in each hand. (When he first joined Scientology, the electrodes were empty Campbell's soup cans with the labels stripped off.) An imperceptible electrical charge would run from the meter through his body. The meter seemed able to gauge the kinds of thoughts he was having—whether they were scary or happy, or when he was hiding something. It was a little spooky. The auditor often probed for what Scientologists call "earlier similars." If Paul was having another fight with Diane, for instance, the auditor would ask him, "Can you remember an earlier time when something like this happened?" Each new memory led further and further back in time. The goal was to uncover and neutralize the emotional memories that were plaguing Paul's behavior.

Often, the process led participants to recall past lives. Although that never happened to Haggis, he envied others who professed to have vivid recollections of ancient times or distant civilizations. Wouldn't it be cool if you had many lifetimes before? he thought. Wouldn't it be easier to face death?

Scientology is not just a matter of belief, the recruits were constantly told; it is a step-by-step scientific process that will help you overcome your limitations and realize your full potential for greatness. Only Scientology can awaken individuals to the joyful truth of their immortal state. Only Scientology can rescue humanity from its inevitable doom. The recruits were infused with a sense of mystery, purpose, and intrigue. Life inside Scientology was just so much more compelling than life outside.

Preclears sometimes experience mystical states characterized by feelings of bliss or a sense of blending into the universe. They come to expect such phenomena, and they yearn for them if they don't occur. "Exteriorization"—the sense that one has actually left his physical being behind—is a commonly reported occurrence for Scientologists. If one's consciousness can actually uproot itself from the physical body and move about at will—what does that say about mortality? We must be something more than, something other than, a mere physical incarnation; we actually are thetans, to use Hubbard's term, immortal spiri-

---

flowing to the meter, so it's not purely measuring the physiological changes associated with skin resistance like a real lie detector would. (And real lie detectors also look at other variables, such as pulse and respiration rates.)" (David Touretsky, personal correspondence.)

tual beings that are incarnated in innumerable lifetimes. Hubbard said that exteriorization could be accomplished in about half the preclears by having the auditor simply command, "Be three feet back of your head." Free of the limitations of his body, the thetan can roam the universe, circling stars, strolling on Mars, or even creating entirely new universes. Reality expands far beyond what the individual had originally perceived it to be. The ultimate goal of auditing is not just to liberate a person from destructive mental phenomena; it is to emancipate him from the laws of matter, energy, space, and time—or MEST, as Hubbard termed them. These are just artifacts of the thetan's imagination, in any case. Bored thetans had created MEST universes where they could frolic and play games; eventually, they became so absorbed in their distractions they forgot their true immortal natures. They identified with the bodies that they were temporarily inhabiting, in a universe they had invented for their own amusement. The goal of Scientology is to recall to the thetan his immortality and help him relinquish his self-imposed limitations.

Once, Haggis had what he thought was an out-of-body experience. He was lying on a couch, and then he found himself across the room, observing himself lying there. The experience of being out of his body wasn't that grand, and later he wondered if he had simply been visualizing the scene. He didn't have the certainty his colleagues reported when they talked about seeing objects behind them or in distant places and times.

In 1976, at the Manor Hotel, Haggis went "Clear." It is the base camp for those who hope to ascend to the upper peaks of Scientology. The concept comes from *Dianetics*. A person who becomes Clear is "adaptable to and able to change his environment," Hubbard writes. "His ethical and moral standards are high, his ability to seek and experience pleasure is great. His personality is heightened and he is creative and constructive." Among other qualities, the Clear has a flawless memory and the capacity to perform mental tasks at unprecedented rates of speed; he is less susceptible to disease; and he is free of neuroses, compulsions, repressions, and psychosomatic illnesses. Hubbard sums up: "The dianetic *clear* is to a current normal individual as the current normal is to the severely insane."

Haggis was Clear #5925. "It was not life-changing," he admits. "It wasn't like, 'Oh my God, I can fly!' " At every level of advancement, he was encouraged to write a "success story" saying how effective his training had been. He had read many such stories by other Scientologists, and they felt overly effusive, geared toward getting through the gatekeepers so that the students could move on to the next level.

THE BRIDGE TO TOTAL FREEDOM is a journey that goes on and on (although confoundingly, in the Scientology metaphor, one moves "higher and higher"—up the Bridge rather than across it). Haggis quickly advanced through the upper levels. He was becoming an "Operating Thetan," which the church defines as one who "can handle things and exist without physical support and assistance." An editorial in a 1958 issue of the Scientology magazine *Ability* notes that "neither Buddha nor Jesus Christ were OTs according to the evidence. They were just a shade above Clear."

When Haggis joined the church, there were seven levels of Operating Thetans. According to church documents that have been leaked online, Hubbard's handwritten instructions for Operating Thetan Level One list thirteen mental exercises that attune practitioners to their relationship with others. The directives for OT I are so open-ended it could be difficult to know whether they have been satisfactorily accomplished. "Note several large and several small male bodies until you have a cognition," for instance. Or, "Seat yourself unobtrusively where you can observe a number of people. Spot things and people you are not. Do to cognition." The point is to familiarize oneself with one's environment from the perspective of being Clear.

In the second level, OT II, Scientologists attempt to delete past-life "implants" that hinder progress in one's current existence. This is accomplished through exercises and visualizations that explore oppositional forces: "Laughter comes from the rear half and calm from the front half simultaneously. Then they reverse. It gives one a sensation of total disagreement. The trick is to conceive of both at the same time. This tends to knock one out."

Each new level of achievement marked the entrance to a more select spiritual fraternity. Haggis didn't have a strong reaction to the material, but then, he wasn't expecting anything too profound. Everyone knew that the big revelations resided in OT III.

Hubbard called this level the Wall of Fire.

"The material involved in this sector is so vicious, that it is carefully arranged to kill anyone if he discovers the exact truth of it," he wrote in 1967. "So in January and February of this year I became very ill, almost lost this body, and somehow or another brought it off, and obtained the material, and was able to live through it. I am very sure that I was the first one that ever did live through any attempt to attain that material."

In the late seventies, the OT mysteries were still unknown, except to the elect. There was no Internet, and Scientology's confidential scriptures had never been published or produced in court. Scientologists looked toward the moment of initiation into OT III with extreme curiosity and excitement. The candidate had to be invited into this next level—Scientologists were cautioned that the material could cause harm or even death to those who were unprepared to receive it. The enforced secrecy added to the mystique and the giddy air of adventure.

One could look back at this crucial moment and examine the pros and cons of Haggis's decision to stay in Scientology. The fact that people often sneered at the church didn't deter him; on the contrary, he reveled in being a member of a stigmatized minority—it made him feel at one with other marginalized groups. The main drawback to belief was his own skeptical nature; he was a proud contrarian, and it would never have occurred to him to join the Baptist church, for instance, or to return to Catholicism; he simply wasn't interested. Intellectually, faith didn't call to him. Scientology, on the other hand, was exotic and tantalizing. The weirdness of some of the doctrines was hard to fathom, but there was no doubt in Haggis's mind that he had gained some practical benefits from his several years of auditing and that his communication skills had improved through some of the coursework. None of that had required him to "believe" in Scientology, but the religion had proved itself in certain ways that mattered to him. The process of induction was so gradual that things that might have shocked him earlier were more acceptable by the time he came upon them. Whenever he ran into something on the Bridge to Total Freedom that he couldn't fathom, he convinced himself that the next level would make everything understandable.

Scientology was a part of his community; it had taken root in Hollywood, just as Haggis had. His first writing jobs had come through Scientology connections. His wife was deeply involved in the church, as was his sister Kathy. His circle of friends was centered in the church. Haggis was deep enough into the process by now to understand implicitly that those relationships would be jeopardized if he chose to leave the church. Moreover, he had invested a considerable part of his income in the program. The incentive to believe was high.

He was also looking forward to having the enhanced abilities that his fellow adherents on the Bridge were constantly talking about. Although Hubbard had explicitly told Operating Thetans not to use their powers for "parlor tricks," there was a section of *Advance!*, a magazine for upper-level Scientologists, titled "OT Phenomena," where members could report clairvoyant or paranormal experiences. Parking spaces magically made themselves available and waiters immediately noticed you. "I saw that my goldfish was all red and lumpy," one Scientologist writes in *Advance!* "My husband, Rick, said that he's had goldfish like that before and they don't recover." The correspondent relates that she used her abilities to "flow energy" into the fish "until a big burst of matter blew. I ended off. When I went home that night the fish was completely healed." She concludes, "It was a big win for me, and the fish. It couldn't have been done without the technology of L. Ron Hubbard." Even if such effects were random and difficult to replicate, for those who experienced them life was suddenly full of unseen possibilities. There was a sense of having entered a sphere of transcendence, where minds communicate with each other across great distances, where wishes and intentions affect material objects or cause people to unconsciously obey telepathic orders, and where spirits from other ages or even other worlds make themselves known.

"A theta being is capable of emitting a considerable electronic flow," Hubbard notes, "enough to give somebody a very bad shock, to put out his eyes or cut him in half." Even ordinary actions pose unexpected dilemmas for the OT, Hubbard warns. "How do you answer the phone as an OT?" he asks in one of his lectures. "Supposing you get mad at somebody on the other end of the telephone. You go crunch! And that's so much Bakelite. The thing either goes into a fog of dust in the middle of the air or drips over the floor." To avoid crushing telephones with his unfathomable strength, the OT sets up an automatic action so he doesn't have to pick the receiver up himself. "Telephone rings, it springs into the air, and he talks. In other words, through involuntary intention the telephone stands there in mid-air." The promise of employing such powers was incredibly tantalizing.

Carrying an empty briefcase, Haggis went to the Advanced Organization building in Los Angeles, where the OT III material was held. A supervisor handed him a manila envelope. Haggis locked it in the briefcase, which was lashed to his arm. Then he entered a secure study room and bolted the door behind him. At last, he was able to examine the religion's highest mysteries, revealed in a couple of pages of Hubbard's handwritten scrawl. After a few minutes, Haggis returned to the supervisor.

"I don't understand," Haggis said.

"Do you know the words?"

"I know the words, I just don't understand."

"Go back and read it again," the supervisor suggested.

Haggis did so. In a moment, he returned. "Is this a metaphor?" he asked.

"No," the supervisor responded. "It is what it is. Do the actions that are required."

Maybe it's an insanity test, Haggis thought—if you believe it, you're automatically kicked out. He considered that possibility. But when he read it again, he decided, "This is madness."

2

Source

The many discrepancies between Hubbard's legend and his life have overshadowed the fact that he genuinely was a fascinating man: an explorer, a best-selling author, and the founder of a worldwide religious movement. The tug-of-war between Scientologists and anti-Scientologists over Hubbard's biography has created two swollen archetypes: the most important person who ever lived and the world's greatest con man. Hubbard himself seemed to revolve on this same axis, constantly inflating his actual accomplishments in a manner that was rather easy for his critics to puncture. But to label him a pure fraud is to ignore the complex, charming, delusional, and visionary features of his character that made him so compelling to the many thousands who followed him and the millions who read his work. One would also have to ignore his life's labor in creating the intricately detailed epistemology that has pulled so many into its net—including, most prominently, Hubbard himself.

Lafayette Ronald Hubbard was born in Tilden, Nebraska, in 1911, a striking, happy child with gray eyes and wispy carrot-colored hair. His father, Harry Ross "Hub" Hubbard, was in the Navy when he met Ledora May Waterbury, who was studying to be a teacher in Omaha. They married in 1909. By the time their only child came along two years later, Hub was out of the service and working in the advertising department of the local Omaha newspaper. May returned to her hometown of Tilden for the birth.

When Ron was two, the family moved to Helena, Montana, a gold town that was famous all over the West for its millionaires and its prostitutes. It was also the capital of the frontier state. Hub managed the Family Theater, which, despite its name, shared a building downtown with two bordellos. Even as a young child, Ron loved to watch the vaudeville acts that passed through, but the enterprise shut its doors when a larger theater opened nearby.

Ron's maternal grandparents lived nearby. Lafayette Waterbury was a veterinarian and a well-regarded horseman who doted on his redheaded grandson. "I was riding broncs at 3½ years," Hubbard later boasted. He supposedly began reading at the same precocious age, and according to the church he was "soon devouring shelves of classics, including much of Western philosophy, the pillars of English literature, and, of note, the essays of Sigmund Freud."

When the United States entered the First World War in 1917, Hubbard's father decided to re-enlist in the Navy. Ledora got a job with the State of Montana, and she and six-year-old Ron moved in with her parents, who had relocated to Helena. When the war ended, Hub decided to make a career in the Navy, and the Hubbard family was launched into the itinerant military life.

Hubbard's family was Methodist. He once remarked, "Many members of my family that I was raised with were devout Christians, and my grandfather was a devout atheist." Ron took his own eccentric path. Throughout his youth, he was fascinated by shamans and magicians. As a boy in Montana, he says, he was made a blood brother to the Blackfoot Indians by an elderly medicine man named Old Tom Madfeathers. Hubbard claims that Old Tom would put on displays of magic by leaping fifteen feet high from a seated position and perching on the top of his teepee. Hubbard observes, "I learned long ago that man has his standards for credulity, and when reality clashes with these, he feels challenged."

A signal moment in Hubbard's narrative is the seven-thousand-mile voyage he took in 1923 from Seattle through the Panama Canal to Washington, DC, where his father was being posted. One of his fellow passengers was Commander Joseph C. "Snake" Thompson of the US Navy Medical Corps. A neurosurgeon, a naturalist, and a former spy, Thompson made a vivid impression on the boy. "He was a very careless man," Hubbard later recalled. "He used to go to sleep reading a book and when he woke up, why, he got up and never bothered to press and change his uniform, you know. And he was usually in very bad odor with the Navy Department. . . . But he was a personal friend of Sigmund Freud's. . . . When he saw me—a defenseless character—and there was nothing to do on a big transport on a very long cruise, he started to work me over."

No doubt Thompson entertained the young Hubbard with tales of his adventures as a spy in the Far East. Raised in Japan by his father, a missionary, Thompson spoke fluent Japanese. He had spent much of his early military career roaming through Asia posing as a herpetologist looking for rare snakes while covertly gathering intelligence and charting possible routes of invasion.

"What impressed me," Hubbard later remarked, "he had a cat by the name of Psycho. This cat had a crooked tail, which is enough to impress any young man. And the cat would do tricks. And the first thing he did was teach me how to train cats. But it takes so long, and it requires such tremendous patience, that to this day I have never trained a cat. You have to wait, evidently, for the cat to do something, then you applaud it. But waiting for a cat to do something whose name is Psycho . . ."

One of Thompson's maxims was "If it's not true for you, it's not true." He told young Hubbard that the statement had come from Gautama Siddhartha, the Buddha. It made an impression on Hubbard. "If there's anybody in the world that's calculated to believe what he wants to believe and to reject what he doesn't want to believe, it is I."

Thompson had just returned from Vienna, where he had been sent by the Navy to study under Freud. "I was just a kid and Commander Thompson didn't have any boy of his own and he and I just got along fine," Hubbard recalls in one of his lectures. "Why he took it into his head to start beating Freud into my head, I don't know, but he did. And I wanted very much to follow out this work—wanted very much to. I didn't get a chance. My father . . . said, 'Son, you're going to be an engineer.' "

THOMPSON WAS ABOUT to publish a review of psychoanalytic literature in the *United States Naval Medical Bulletin*; indeed, he may have been working on it as he traveled to Washington, and no doubt he drew upon the thinking reflected in his article when he tutored

Hubbard in the basics of Freudian theory. "Man has two fundamental instincts—one for self-preservation and the other for race
propagation," Thompson writes in his review. "The most important
emotion of the self-preservation urge is hunger. The sole emotion of the
race-propagation urge is libido." Psychoanalysis, Thompson explains,
is the "technic" of discovering unconscious motivations that harm the
health or happiness of the individual. Once the patient understands
the motives behind his neurotic behavior, his symptoms automatically
disappear. "This uncovering of the hidden motive does not consist in
the mere explaining to the patient the mechanism of his plight. The
understanding alone comes from the analytic technic of free association and subsequent rational synthesis." Many of these thoughts are
deeply embedded in the principles of Dianetics, the foundation of Hubbard's philosophy of human nature, which predated the establishment
of Scientology.

In 1927, Hubbard's father was posted to Guam, and Ledora went
along, abandoning Ron to the care of her parents. For a man as garrulous as L. Ron Hubbard turned out to be, reflections on his parents
are rare, almost to the point of writing them out of his biography. His
story of himself reads like that of an orphan who has invented his own
way in the world. One of his lovers later said that he told her that his
mother was a whore and a lesbian, and that he had found her in bed
with another woman. His mistress also admitted, "I never knew what
to believe."

Hubbard made two voyages to visit his parents in Guam. One trip
included a detour to China, where he supposedly began his study of
Eastern religions after encountering magicians and holy men. According to the church's narrative, "He braved typhoons aboard a working
schooner to finally land on the China coast. . . . He then made his way
inland to finally venture deep into forbidden Buddhist lamaseries." He
watched monks meditating "for weeks on end." Everywhere he went,
the narrative goes, the teenage Hubbard was preoccupied with a central question: " 'Why?' Why so much human suffering and misery?
Why was man, with all his ancient wisdom and knowledge accumulated in learned texts and temples, unable to solve such basic problems
as war, insanity and unhappiness?"

In fact, Hubbard's contemporary journals don't really engage such
philosophical points. His trip to China, which was organized by the

YMCA, lasted only ten days. His parents accompanied him, although they are not mentioned in his journals. He did encounter monks, whom he described as croaking like bullfrogs. The journals reflect the mind of a budding young imperialist, who summons an unearned authority over an exotic and unfamiliar culture. "The very nature of the China-man holds him back," Hubbard observes on the ship back to Guam. "The trouble with China is, there are too many chinks here."

The journals provide a portrait of an adolescent writer trying on his future craft by cataloguing plot ideas, such as, "A young American in India with an organized army for rent to the various rajahs. Usual plot complications." Another idea: "Love story. Goes to France. Meets swell broad in Marseilles." He is trying uncertainly to find his voice:

> Rex Fraser mounted the knoll and setting his hat more securely against the wind squinted at the huddle of unpainted shacks below him.
> "So this," he said to his horse, "is Montana City."

Hubbard entered the School of Engineering at George Washington University in the fall of 1930. He was a poor student—failing German and calculus—but he excelled in extracurricular activities. He began writing for the school newspaper. A new literary magazine at GWU provided a venue for his first published works of fiction. He became director of the gliding club, a thrilling new pastime that was just catching on (Hubbard's gliding license was #385). The actual study of engineering was a secondary pursuit, as his failing grades reflected.

In September 1931, Hubbard and his friend Philip "Flip" Browning took a few weeks off to barnstorm through the Midwest in an Arrow Sport biplane. "We carefully wrapped our 'baggage,' threw the fire extinguisher out to save half a horsepower, patched a hole in the upper wing, and started off to skim over four or five states with the wind as our only compass," Hubbard writes. By now, he had taken to calling himself "Flash."

Hubbard's account of this adventure, "Tailwind Willies," was his first commercially published story, appearing in *The Sportsman Pilot* in January 1932. It was the launch of an unprecedented career. (He would go on to publish more books than any other author, according to the 2006 *Guinness World Records*, with 1,084 titles.)

In the spring of 1932, at the height of the Great Depression, Hubbard undertook a venture that displayed many of the hallmarks of his future exploits. He posted a notice on several university campuses: "Restless young men with wanderlust wanted for the Caribbean Motion Picture Expedition. Cost to applicant $250 payable at the dock in Baltimore before sailing. Must be healthy, dependable, resourceful, imaginative, and adventurous. No tea-hounds or tourist material need apply." The goals of the expedition were grand and various—primarily, to make newsreels for Fox Movietone and Pathé News, while exploring the pirate haunts of the Caribbean and voodoo rites in Haiti. There were also vague plans to "collect whatever one collects for exhibits in museums."

"It's difficult at any age to recognize a messiah in the making," wrote one of the young men, James S. Free, a journalist who signed on to the expedition. He was twenty-three years old, two years older than Hubbard. They were going to be partners in the adventure, along with Hubbard's old flying buddy, Phil Browning. "I cannot claim prescient awareness that my soon-to-be business partner possessed the ego and talents that would later develop his own private religion," Free wrote in a notebook he titled "Preview of a Messiah."

Hubbard was living with his parents in Washington, DC, when Free arrived. "Ron introduced me to his mother, whose long light brown hair seemed dark beside the reddish glow of her son's hair and face," Free wrote, in one of the few records of the actual relationship between Hubbard and his mother. "I recall little else about her except that like her husband, Navy lieutenant Henry Ross Hubbard, she plainly adored young Ron and considered him a budding genius."

Hubbard filled Free in on new developments. Phil Browning, the other partner, had dropped out at the last minute, but he had managed to get the loan of some laboratory equipment from the University of Michigan; meantime, Hubbard was negotiating with a professional cameraman for the anticipated films of the voodoo rites "and that sort of salable material." Thanks to Free's efforts to sign up more than twenty new members of the expedition, Hubbard said, "We have enough cash to go ahead."

The trip was a calamity from the start. A number of the "buccaneers" who signed up bailed out at the last minute, but fifty-six green collegians with no idea what they were doing clambered aboard the antiquated, four-masted schooner *Doris Hamlin*. The adventure began with the *Doris Hamlin* having to be towed out of Baltimore harbor because of lack of wind. That was almost the end of the expedition, since the tug was pulling toward the sea while the ship was still tied to the dock. Once in the Atlantic, the ship was either becalmed in glassy seas or roiling in high chop. The mainsails blew out in a squall as the expedition steered toward St. Thomas. Seasickness was rampant. At every port, more of the disgusted crew deserted. The only film that was shot was a desultory cockfight in Martinique.

It soon became evident that the expedition was broke. There was no meat or fruit, and the crew was soon reduced to buying their own food in port. Hubbard didn't have enough money to pay the only professional sailors on the ship—the captain, the first mate, and the cook—so he offered to sell shares in the venture to his crewmates and borrowed money from others. He raised seven or eight hundred dollars that way, and was able to set sail from Bermuda, only to become mired in the Sargasso Sea for four days.

After a meager supper one night, George Blakeslee, who had been brought along as a photographer, had had enough. "I tied a hangman's noose in a rope and everybody got the same idea," he wrote in his journal. "So we made an effigy of Hubbard and strung it up in the shrouds. Put a piece of red cloth on the head and a sign on it. 'Our red-headed _____!' " Hubbard stayed in his cabin after that.

The furious captain wired for money, then steered the ship back to Baltimore, pronouncing the expedition "the worst and most unpleasant I ever made." Hubbard was not aboard as the "jinx ship," as it was called in the local press, crept back into its home port. He was last seen in Puerto Rico, slipping off with a suitcase in each hand.

In some respects, Hubbard discovered himself on that unlucky voyage, which he termed a "glorious adventure." His infatuation with motion pictures first became evident on this trip, although no movies were actually made. Despite the defections, Hubbard demonstrated an impressive capacity to summon others to join him on what was clearly a shaky enterprise. Throughout his life he would enlist people—especially young people—in romantic, ill-conceived projects, often at sea, where he was out of reach of process servers. He was beginning to invent himself as a charismatic leader. The grandeur of his project was not yet evident, even to him, but in the Caribbean Motion Picture Expedition he clearly defined himself as an explorer, sailor, filmmaker, and leader of men, even though he failed spectacularly in each of those categories. He had an incorrigible ability to float above the evidence and to extract from his experiences lessons that others would say were irrational and even bizarre. Habitually, and perhaps unconsciously, Hubbard would fill this gap—between reality and his interpretation of it—with mythology. This was the source of what some call his genius, and others call his insanity.

WHEN HE WAS TWENTY-THREE, Hubbard married Margaret Louise Grubb, an aspiring aviator four years his senior, whom he called Polly. Amelia Earhart had just become the first female to fly solo across the Atlantic, inspiring many daring young women who wanted to follow her example. Although Polly never gained a pilot's license, it wasn't surprising that she would respond to Ron's swashbuckling personality and his tales of far-flung adventures. They settled in a small town in Maryland, near her family farm. Ron was trying to make it as a professional magazine writer, but by that point—at the end of 1933—he had only half a dozen articles in print. Soon, Polly was pregnant, and Ron had to find a way to make a living quickly.

Pulp fiction derives its name from the cheap paper stock used in printing the garish magazines—*Weird Tales, Black Mask, Argosy, Magic Carpet*—that became popular in Depression-era America. The pay for contributors was miserable—the standard rate was a penny a word. To fill the usual 128 pages, each pulp magazine required 65,000 words, so that the yearly quota to fill the 150 pulp weeklies, biweeklies, and monthlies that crowded the newsstands in 1934 amounted to about 195,000,000 words. Many well-known writers began their careers by feeding this gigantic maw, including Dashiell Hammett, H. P. Lovecraft, Erle Stanley Gardner, Raymond Chandler, Ray Bradbury, and Edgar Rice Burroughs. The pulps nurtured genres that were perhaps not new but until then had never been so blatantly and abundantly expressed.

Hubbard's actual life experiences seemed wonderfully suited for such literature. His first pulp story, "The Green God," published in *Thrilling Adventures* in 1934, is about a naval intelligence officer (possibly based on Snake Thompson) who is tortured and buried alive in China. "Maybe Because—!," published in *Cowboy Stories*, was the first of Hubbard's forty-seven westerns, which must have drawn upon his childhood in Montana. Soon, however, there were stories about submarines and zombies, tales set in Russia or Morocco. Plot was all that really mattered, and Hubbard's amazing capacity for invention readily colored the canvas. Success in the pulps depended on speed and imagination, and Hubbard had both in abundance. The church estimates that between 1934 and 1936, he was turning out a hundred thousand words of fiction a month. He was writing so fast that he began typing on a roll of butcher paper to save time. When a story was finished, he would tear off the sheet using a T-square and mail it to the publisher. Because the magazines didn't want an author to appear more than once in the same issue, Hubbard adopted pen names— Mr. Spectator, Capt. Humbert Reynolds, Rene Lafayette, Winchester Remington Colt, et cetera—accumulating about twenty aliases over the years. He said that when he was writing stories he would simply "roll the pictures" in his mind and write down what he saw as quickly as possible. It was a physical act: he would actually perspire when he wrote. His philosophy was "First draft, last draft, get it out the door."

Ron and Polly's son, L. Ron Hubbard, Jr., was born prematurely on May 7, 1934, in Encinitas, California, where the couple had gone to vacation. The baby, whom they called Nibs, weighed little more than two pounds at birth. Ron fashioned an incubator out of a cupboard drawer, using a lightbulb to keep it warm, while Polly fed Nibs with an eyedropper. Two years later, in New York City, Polly gave birth to a daughter, Katherine May Hubbard, whom they called Kay.

In 1936, the family moved to Bremerton, Washington, near where Ron's parents were then living, as well as his mother's family, the Waterburys. They warmly accepted Polly and the kids. Ron was doing well enough to buy a small farm in nearby Port Orchard with a house, five bungalows, a thousand feet of waterfront, and a view of Mount Rainier—"the prettiest place I ever saw in my life," he wrote to his best friend, Russell Hays, a fellow author of pulps who lived in Kansas. Ron spent much of his time in New York, however, cultivating his professional contacts, and leaving his wife and children for long periods of time.

Hubbard pined for Hollywood, in what would be a long-term, unrequited romance. Despite his overtures, he received only "vague offers" from studios for short-term contracts. "I have discarded Hollywood," he complained to Hays. "I haven't got enough charm." But in the spring of 1937, Columbia Pictures finally optioned one of Hubbard's stories to be folded into a serial, titled *The Secret of Treasure Island*. Hubbard quickly moved to Hollywood, hoping to finally make it in the movie business. (He later claimed to have worked on a number of films during this time—including the classic films *Stagecoach*, with John Wayne, and *The Plainsman*, with Gary Cooper—but he never actually received any film credits other than *The Secret of Treasure Island*.) By midsummer he had fled back to the farm in Washington, blaming the long hours, tension, and "dumb Jew producers."

Once again, he threw himself into writing the pulps with a fury, but also with a new note of cynicism. "Never write about a character type you cannot find in the magazine for which the story is intended," he advised Hays. "Never write about an unusual character." Realism was no asset in this kind of writing, he complained, remarking on "my utter inability to sell a story which has any connection with my own background. . . . Reality seems to be a very detested quantity."

Then, on New Year's Day, 1938, Hubbard had a revelation that would change his life—and eventually, the lives of many others. During a dental operation, he received a gas anesthetic. "While under the influence of it my heart must have stopped beating," he relates. "It was like sliding helter-skelter down into a vortex of scarlet and it was knowing that one was dying and that the process of dying was far from pleasant." In those brief, hallucinatory moments, Hubbard believed that the secrets of existence were accidentally revealed to him. Forrest Ackerman, who later became his literary agent, said that Hubbard told him that he had risen from the dental chair in spirit form, glanced back at his former body, and wondered, "Where do we go from here?" Hubbard's disembodied spirit then noticed a huge ornate gate in the distance, which he floated through. On the other side, Ackerman relates, Hubbard discovered "an intellectual smorgasbord of everything that had ever puzzled the mind of man—you know, how did it all begin, where do we go from here, are there past lives—and like a sponge he was just absorbing all this esoteric information. And all of a sudden, there was a kind of swishing in the air and he heard a voice, 'No, not yet! He's not ready!' And like a long umbilical cord, he felt himself being pulled back, back, back. And he lay down in his body, and he opened his eyes, and he said to the nurse, 'I was dead, wasn't I?' " The nurse looked startled, and the doctor gave her a dirty look for letting Hubbard know what had happened.

In Hubbard's own written account of the event, he remembers voices crying out as he is being restored to life, "Don't let him know!" When he came to, he was "still in contact with something." The intimation that he had briefly been given access to the divine mystery lingered for several days, but he couldn't call it back. "And then one morning, just as I awoke, it came to me."

In a fever, he dashed off a small book he titled *Excalibur*. "Once upon a time, according to a writer in The Arabian Nights, there lived a very wise old man," the book begins, in the brief portion that the church has published of the fragments it says it has in its possession. The old man, goes the story, wrote a long and learned book, but he became concerned that he had written too much. So he sat himself down for ten years more and reduced the original volume to one tenth its size. Even then, he was dissatisfied, and he constrained the work even further, to a single line, "which contained everything there was to be known." He hid the sacred line in a niche in his wall. But still he wondered, Could all human knowledge be distilled even further?

> Suppose all the wisdom of the world *were* reduced to just one line—suppose that one line were to be written today and given to you. With it you could understand the basis of all life and endeavor. . . . There *is* one line, conjured up out of a morass of facts and made available as an integrated unit to explain such things. This line is the philosophy of philosophy, thereby carrying the entire subject back into the simple and humble truth.
>
> All life is directed by one command and one command only—SURVIVE.

Hubbard sent excited telegrams to publishers in New York, inviting them to meet him at Penn Station, where he would auction off a manuscript that would change the world. He wrote Polly, "I have high hopes of smashing my name into history so violently that it will take a legendary form even if all the books are destroyed."

But *Excalibur* was never published, leading some to doubt that it was ever written. The stories Hubbard later told about the book added to the sense that it was more mythical than real. He said that when the Russians learned of the book's contents, they offered him money and laboratory facilities to complete his work. When he turned them down, they purloined a copy of his manuscript from his hotel room in Miami. Hubbard explained to his agent that he ultimately decided to withdraw the book from publication because the first six people who read it were so shattered by the revelations that they had lost their minds. The last time he showed *Excalibur* to a publisher, he said, the reader brought the manuscript into the room, set it on the publisher's desk, then jumped out the window of the skyscraper.

Hubbard despondently returned to the pulps. Five years of torrential output had left him exhausted and bitter. His work was "worthless," he admitted. "I have learned enough of my trade, have developed a certain technique," he wrote to Hays. "But curbed by editorial fear of reality and hindered by my own revolt I have never dared loose the pent flame, so far only releasing the smoke."

That same year Hubbard received an offer to write for a magazine called *Astounding Science-Fiction*. The editor, John W. Campbell, Jr., twenty-seven years old at the time, was to preside over what Hubbard and others would mark as the Golden Age of Science Fiction. One of the many brilliant young writers who would be pulled into Campbell's orbit, Isaac Asimov, described Campbell as "a tall, large man with light hair, a beaky nose, a wide face with thin lips, and with a cigarette holder forever clamped between his teeth." Campbell was an overbearing champion of extreme right-wing ideas and crackpot science—especially psychic phenomena—and he would hold forth in nonstop monologues, often adopting perverse views, such as supporting slavery, then defending such propositions to the point of exhausting everyone in the room. "A deviant figure of marked ferocity," as the British writer Kingsley Amis observed. On the other hand, Campbell was also a caring and resourceful editor who groomed inexperienced writers, such as Robert A. Heinlein—first published in *Astounding*—and turned them into cultural icons.

Campbell considered science fiction to be something far more than cheap literary diversion; for him, it amounted to prophecy. His conviction of the importance of the genre added a mystical allure that other forms of pulp fiction never aspired to. Fanzines and sci-fi clubs, composed largely of adolescent boys who were drawn to the romanticized image of science, formed in many cities around the country; some of those fans went on to become important scientists, and their work was animated by ideas that had first spilled out of the minds of writers such as Heinlein, Asimov, and Hubbard. "Science fiction, particularly in its Golden Age, had a mission," Hubbard writes. "To get man to the stars." He saw himself as well qualified for the field: "I had, myself, somewhat of a science background, had done some pioneer work in rockets and liquid gases."

Hubbard discovered his greatest talents as a writer in the field of science fiction, a more commodious genre and far more intellectually engaging than westerns or adventure yarns. Science fiction invites the writer to grandly explore alternative worlds and pose questions about meaning and destiny. Inventing plausible new realities is what the genre is all about. One starts from a hypothesis and then builds out the logic, adding detail and incident to give substance to imaginary structures. In that respect, science fiction and theology have much in common. Some of the most closely guarded secrets of Scientology were originally published in other guises in Hubbard's science fiction.

Certainly, the same mind that roamed so freely through imaginary universes might be inclined to look at the everyday world and suspect that there was something more behind the surface reality. The broad canvas of science fiction allowed Hubbard to think in large-scale terms about the human condition. He was bold. He was fanciful. He could easily invent an elaborate, plausible universe. But it is one thing to make that universe believable, and another to believe it. That is the difference between art and religion.

HUBBARD NOW LIVED two lives: one on the farm in Port Orchard, surrounded by his parents and Polly and the kids; the other in New York, where he rented an apartment on the Upper West Side. The city rewarded him with the recognition he craved. He enjoyed frequent lunches at the Knickerbocker Hotel with his colleagues in the American Fiction Guild, where he could swap tales and schmooze with editors. He also became a member of the prestigious Explorers Club, which added credibility to his frequently told stories of adventure.

"In his late twenties, Hubbard was a tall, well-built man with bright red hair, a pale complexion, and a long-nosed face that gave him the look of a reincarnated Pan," a fellow science-fiction writer, L. Sprague de Camp, later recalled. "He arranged in his New York apartment a curtained inclosure the size of a telephone booth, lit by a blue light bulb, in which he could work fast without distraction."

The fact that Hubbard was a continent away from his wife offered him the opportunity to court other women, which he did so openly that he became an object of wonder among his writer colleagues. Ron blamed Polly for his philandering. "Because of her coldness physically, the falsity of her pretensions, I believed myself a near eunuch," he wrote in a private memoir (which the church disputes) some years later.

"When I found I was attractive to other women, I had many affairs. But my failure to please Polly made me always pay so much attention to my momentary mate that I derived small pleasure myself. This was an anxiety neurosis which cut down my natural powers."

One of those momentary mates was named Helen. "I loved her and she me," Hubbard recorded. "The affair would have lasted had not Polly found out." Polly had discovered two letters to different women that Hubbard left in the mailbox when he was back in Port Orchard; she took the letters, read them, then vengefully switched the envelopes, and put them back in the mail. For a while, Ron and Polly didn't speak.

They were apparently reconciled in 1940, when the two of them cruised to Alaska on their thirty-foot ketch, the *Magician*, which they called *Maggie*. They left their children with other family members for the several months they were gone. Hubbard called the trip the Alaskan Radio-Experimental Expedition, which entitled him to fly the Explorers Club flag. The stated goal was to rewrite the navigation guide of the Alaskan coast using new radio techniques; however, when the engine broke down in Ketchikan, he told a local newspaper that the purpose was "two-fold, one to win a bet and another to gather material for a novel of Alaskan salmon fishing." Some of Hubbard's friends, he related, had wagered that his boat was too small for such a journey, and he was determined to prove them wrong.

While he was stranded in Ketchikan, waiting for a new crankshaft, Hubbard spent several weeks regaling listeners of the local KGBU radio about his adventures, which included tracking down a German agent who had been planted in Alaska with orders to cut off communications in the case of war, and lassoing a brown bear on a fishing trip, which proceeded to crawl into the boat with him.

When the crankshaft finally arrived, Ron and Polly headed home, arriving a few days after Christmas, 1940, nearly six months after they set out. Little had been accomplished. "Throughout all this, however," the church narrative goes, "Mr. Hubbard was continuing in his quest to answer the riddles of man."

THE COMPETING NARRATIVES of Hubbard's life arrive at a crucial point in the quarrel over his record in the US Navy during the Second World War and the injuries he allegedly received. He certainly longed for a military career, but he failed the entrance examination for the US Naval Academy and was further disqualified because of his poor eyesight. He lied—unnecessarily—about his age when he signed up for the US Marine Corps Reserve in 1930, backdating his birth by two years; this stratagem may have helped him get promoted over his contemporaries to first sergeant. His official record notes that he was "inactive, except for a period of active duty for training." He requested to be discharged the following year because "I do not have the time to devote to the welfare of the Regiment."

Months before Pearl Harbor, however, Hubbard was once again angling to get a commission in the Navy. He gathered a number of recommendations, including one from his congressman, Warren G. Magnuson, who wrote to President Franklin Roosevelt, praising "Captain" Hubbard, "a well-known writer" and "a respected explorer," who has "marine masters papers for more types of vessels than any other man in the United States. . . . In writing organizations he is a key figure, making him politically potent nationally." The congressman concluded: "An interesting trait is his distaste for personal publicity." Senator Robert M. Ford of Washington signed his name to another letter of recommendation that Hubbard actually wrote for him: "This will introduce one of the most brilliant men I have ever known: Captain L. Ron Hubbard."

In April 1941, his poor eyesight caused him to fail his physical once again. But with German U-boats attacking American shipping in the North Atlantic—and even in American coastal waters—President Roosevelt declared a national emergency, and Hubbard's physical shortcomings were suddenly overlooked. He received his commission in the Naval Reserve, as a lieutenant (junior grade), in July 1941.

According to Hubbard, he got into the action right away. He said he was aboard the destroyer USS *Edsall*, which was sunk off the north coast of Java. All hands were lost, except for Hubbard, who managed to get to shore and disappear into the jungles. That is where he says he was when the Japanese bombed Pearl Harbor on December 7, 1941. (Actually, the *Edsall* was not sunk until March 1942.) Hubbard said that he survived being machine-gunned by a Japanese patrol while he was hiding in the area, then escaped by sailing a raft to Australia. Elsewhere, Hubbard claimed that he had been posted to the Philippines at the outbreak of the war with Japan, then was flown home on the Secretary of the Navy's private plane in the spring of 1942 as the "first U.S. returned casualty from the Far East."

According to Navy records, however, Hubbard was training as an intelligence officer in New York when the war broke out. He was indeed supposed to have been posted to the Philippines, but his ship was diverted to Australia because of the overwhelming Japanese advance in the Pacific. There he awaited other transport to Manila, but he immediately got on the wrong side of the American naval attaché. "By assuming unauthorized authority and attempting to perform duties for which he has no qualification he became the source of much trouble," the attaché complained. "This officer is not satisfactory for independent duty assignment. He is garrulous and tries to give impressions of his importance." He sent Hubbard back to the United States for further assignment.

Hubbard found himself back in New York, working in the Office of the Cable Censor. He agitated for a shipboard posting, and was given the opportunity to command a trawler that was being converted into a gunboat, the USS *YP-422*, designed for coastal patrol. "Upon entering the Boston Navy Yard, Ron found himself facing a hundred or so enlisted men, fresh from the Portsmouth Naval Prison in New Hampshire," the church narrative goes. "A murderous looking lot, was Ron's initial impression, 'their braid dirty and their hammocks black with grime.' While on further investigation, he discovered not one among them had stepped aboard except to save himself a prison term." Hubbard allegedly spent six weeks drilling this convict crew, turning them into a splendid fighting unit, "with some seventy depth charge runs to their credit and not a single casualty." But according to naval records, he was relieved of command before the ship was even launched, by the commandant of the Boston Navy Yard, who declared him "not temperamentally fitted for independent command." There is no record that Hubbard saw action in the Atlantic at any time.

The Navy then sent Hubbard to the Submarine Chaser Training Center in Miami. He arrived wearing dark glasses, probably because of conjunctivitis, which plagued him throughout the war and after, but he explained to another young officer, Thomas Moulton, that he had been standing too close to a large-caliber gun while serving as the gunnery officer on a destroyer in the Pacific, and the muzzle flash had damaged his eyes. Hubbard's classmates at the sub-chaser school looked upon him as a great authority because of his wartime adventures. That he seemed so reticent to boast about them only enhanced his standing.

While he was in Miami, Hubbard contracted gonorrhea from a woman named Ginger. "She was a very loose person," he confides in his disputed secret memoir. "I was terrified by it, the consequences of being discovered by my wife, the navy, my friends. . . . I took to dosing myself with sulfa in such quantities that I was afraid I had affected my brain."

Wartime sexual diseases were a common affliction, and servicemen were constantly being cautioned about the dangers of casual romance. Although American sexual relations were freer in practice than the popular culture admitted at the time, divorce was still sharply stigmatized; and yet, as a young man Hubbard seemed to be constantly driven toward reckless liaisons and courtships that would destroy his marriages and alienate his children (he would eventually father seven children by three wives). He admitted in his disputed memoir that he suffered from bouts of impotence, which he apparently treated with testosterone. He also wrote of his concerns about masturbation, which at the time was considered a sign of moral weakness that could also lead to many physical ailments, such as weak eyesight, impotence, and insanity.

HUBBARD WAS FINALLY given another ship of his own, the USS *PC-815*, and he requested Moulton to join him as his executive officer. The ship was being constructed in Portland, Oregon, and when it was finally commissioned, in April 1943, the local paper wrote about it, describing Hubbard as a "Lieutenant Commander" (he was actually not yet a full lieutenant), who was "a veteran sub-hunter of the battles of the Pacific and the Atlantic." There is a photo of Hubbard and Moulton standing in front of the small ship, which was suited mainly for harbor patrol. Hubbard is wearing his glasses and holding a pipe in his hands, with the collar of his pea jacket turned up and a determined look on his face. "These little sweethearts are tough," he says of the ship. "They could lick the pants off anything Nelson or Farragut ever sailed. They put up a sizzling fight and are the only answer to the submarine menace. I state emphatically that the future of America rests with just such escort vessels."

It is worth lingering a moment over this overblown statement. The scripted language might as well have been lifted from one of Hubbard's pulp-fiction heroes. Hubbard must have longed to be such a figure in reality, only to be thwarted by his repeated quarrels with higher authority. Each detail Hubbard offers—comparing himself advantageously with history's greatest naval heroes, asserting that he holds the future of his nation in his hands—testifies to his need for grandeur and heroism, or at least to be seen as grand and heroic. He would soon be given an opportunity.

The *PC-815* was equipped with depth charges and sonar to detect enemy submarines. Sonar sends out pinging sounds, which, in clear water, go unanswered, but obstacles, such as enemy submarines—or fish, or debris, or even schools of shrimp—generate echoes. The art of reading such responses is a tricky one, and although Hubbard had trained on the device in sub-chaser school, he had been near the bottom of his class.

He cast off from Astoria, Oregon, for his shakedown cruise on May 18, bound for San Diego to pick up radar equipment. At 3:40 a.m., only five hours out of port, the sonar picked up an echo ten miles off Cape Lookout in a heavily traveled shipping lane. Hubbard and Moulton immediately put on headsets, trying to determine what the object was. In particular, they were listening for the giveaway sound of a propeller. The craft made no recognition signals that would have indicated it was an American vessel. "It made noises like a submarine and it was behaving like a submarine," Moulton later testified. "So we proceeded to attack."

"The target was moving left and away," Hubbard wrote in his subsequent Action Report. "The night was moonlit and the sea was flat calm." The professional writer in him warmed to the narrative: "The ship, sleepy and sceptical, had come to their guns swiftly and without error. No one, including the Commanding Officer, could readily credit the existence of an enemy submarine here on the steamer track."

It wasn't crazy to think that enemy ships might be in the area. A Japanese submarine had bombarded an oil facility near Santa Barbara the year before. Another Japanese submarine, the intrepid *I-25*, had shelled Fort Stevens, at the mouth of the Columbia River, not far from where Hubbard and his crew were now. The *I-25* had also smuggled a disassembled seaplane to the Oregon coast in September 1942, where it was put back together and used to drop incendiary bombs in the forest near Mount Emily.

Shortly after the first echo, "with dawn breaking over a glassy sea," an object appeared on the surface. Hubbard ordered the guns to open fire. It turned out to be a log. Hours passed. Convinced that the submarine was still out there, Hubbard ordered depth charges dropped on the elusive craft. "Great air boils were seen and the sound of blowing tanks was reported by the soundman," Hubbard wrote. "All guns were now manned with great attention as it was supposed that the sub was trying to surface." Incredibly, a second submarine was suddenly detected, only four hundred yards away. Hubbard radioed for assistance and additional explosives. Other naval ships soon arrived, but they were reluctant to drop their charges on a target they couldn't seem to locate. Hubbard was furious and blamed their "inexperience or unwillingness" for their failure to follow his lead.

Hubbard continued the attacks all day and into the next morning. At seven a.m., he reported, "a boil of orange colored oil, very thick, came to the surface immediately on our port bow. . . . Every man . . . then saw the periscope, moving from right to left." His gunners let loose. "The periscope vanished in an explosion of 20mm bullets."

After sixty-eight hours of action, Hubbard's ship was ordered to return to port. Hubbard and Moulton claimed that they had succeeded in sinking at least one, possibly two, enemy subs. An official investigation of the incident concluded, "There was no submarine in the area." A well-known magnetic deposit nearby most likely caused the echoes that were picked up on the sonar. The only evidence of a submarine was "one bubble of air," which might well have been the result of the turbulence caused by the heavy explosions. Japanese records after the war showed that no submarines had been present off the Oregon coast at the time.*

Hubbard continued to San Diego on his shakedown cruise. In June, the *PC-815* participated in an exercise off the coast of the Mexican state of Baja. Afterward, he ordered additional gunnery and small-arms fire,

---

*According to the church, "There was something under the water and it was definitely hostile, and after they dropped their charges, there was oil and something sunk. . . . It definitely happened."

shelling South Coronados Island, a dry atoll that he apparently failed to realize was a part of Mexico. He was admonished for firing on an ally and relieved of his command. He felt unjustly treated but also remorseful about the compromised situation he had placed his shipmates in. "This on top of having sunk two Jap subs without credit, the way my crew lied for me at the Court of Inquiry, the insults of the High Command, all combined to put me in the hospital with ulcers," Hubbard noted in his disputed secret memoir. He spent the next three months in a naval hospital in San Diego. In a letter to his family he explained that he had been injured when he had picked up an unexploded enemy shell that had landed on deck and had blown up in midair when he tried to throw it overboard.

In October, he got another assignment, this time as the navigation officer on the cargo ship the USS *Algol*. The US Navy and Marines had begun their final island-hopping campaign before the expected invasion of Japan itself—Operation Downfall. Millions of Allied casualties were forecast. For a man who wanted to be a hero, there would be a genuine opportunity. Instead, Hubbard requested a transfer to the School of Military Government at Princeton. "Once conversant with the following languages, but require review: Japanese, Spanish, Chamorro, Tagalog, Peking Pidgin and Shanghai Pidgin," Hubbard wrote in his application, adding, "Experienced in handling natives, all classes, in various parts of world." Through all the carnage, the end of the war was lurching into view, and the likely occupation of Japan was on the horizon. A polyglot such as Hubbard claimed to be would certainly find a place in the future administration.

When he arrived in Princeton, in September 1944, Hubbard fell in with a group of science-fiction writers who had been organized into an informal military think tank by his friend Robert Heinlein. The Navy was looking for ways to counter the kamikaze suicide attacks on Allied ships, which had begun that fall as desperation took hold of the Japanese military planners. Hubbard would spend weekends in Philadelphia at the Heinleins' apartment, along with some other of his former colleagues, including his former editor, John Campbell, gaming different scenarios for the Navy. (Some of their suggestions were actually tested in combat, but none proved useful.) Heinlein was extremely solicitous of his old friend, remarking, "Ron had had a busy war—sunk four times and wounded again and again." The fact that

Hubbard had an affair with Heinlein's wife didn't seem to affect his deep regard. "He almost forced me to sleep with his wife," Hubbard later marveled.

There was another lissome young woman hanging around with the science-fiction crowd: Vida Jameson, whose father, Malcolm, was a part of the Campbell group of *Astounding* writers. "Quiet, shy little greymouse," one of the crowd described Vida, "with great soulful black eyes and a habit of listening." She was twenty-eight, and already selling stories to the *Saturday Evening Post*, a more respectable literary endeavor than the pulps. Hubbard proposed to her. She knew he was married and refused his offer; still, she was captivated by him and continued her relationship with him until after the war.

Hubbard graduated from the School of Military Government in January 1945, and was ordered to proceed to Monterey, California, to join a civil affairs team, which would soon follow the invading forces. The Battle of Okinawa, in southern Japan, got under way that spring, creating the highest number of casualties in the Pacific Theater. Kamikaze attacks were at their peak. American troops suffered more than 60,000 casualties in less than three months. Japanese forces were fighting to the death. The savagery and scale of the combat has rarely been equaled.

Once again, Hubbard stood on the treacherous precipice, where the prospect of heroic action awaited him—or else indignity, or a death that would be obscured by the deaths of tens of thousands of others. One month after the invasion of Okinawa, Hubbard was admitted to the Oak Knoll Naval Hospital in Oakland, California, complaining of stomach pains.

This is a key moment in the narrative of Dianetics and Scientology. "Blinded with injured optic nerves and lame with physical injuries to hip and back at the end of World War II, I faced an almost nonexistent future," Hubbard writes of himself during this period. "I was abandoned by my family and friends as a supposedly hopeless cripple." Hubbard says he healed himself of his traumatic injuries, using techniques that would become the foundation of Dianetics and Scientology. "I had no one to help me; what I had to know I had to find out," he recalled. "And it's quite a trick studying when you cannot see."

Doctors at Oak Knoll were never sure exactly what was wrong with him, except for a recurrence of his ulcer. In records of Hubbard's many physical examinations and X-rays, the doctors make no note of scars or evidence of wounds, nor do his military records show that he was ever injured during the war.

In the hospital, Hubbard says, he was also given a psychiatric examination. To his alarm, the doctor wrote two pages of notes. "And I was watching this, you know, saying, 'Well, have I gone nuts, after all?' " He conspired to take a look at the records to see what the doctor had written. "I got to the end and it said, 'In short, this officer has no neurotic or psychotic tendencies of any kind whatsoever.' " (There is no psychiatric evaluation contained in Hubbard's medical records.)

POLLY AND THE TWO CHILDREN had spent the war waiting for Ron on their plot in Port Orchard, but there was no joyous homecoming. "My wife left me while I was in a hospital with ulcers," Hubbard noted. "It was a terrible blow when she left me for I was ill and without prospects."

Soon after leaving the hospital, Hubbard towed a house trailer behind an old Packard to Southern California, where so many ambitious and rootless members of his generation were seeking their destiny. There was a proliferation of exotic new religions in America and many other countries, caused by the tumult of war and disruptions of progress that older denominations weren't prepared to solve. Southern California was filled with migrants who weren't tied to old creeds and were ready to experiment with new ways of thinking. The region was swarming with Theosophists, Rosicrucians, Zoroastrians, and Vedantists. Swamis, mystics, and gurus of many different faiths pulled acolytes into their orbits.

The most brilliant member of this galaxy of occultists was John Whiteside Parsons, known as Jack, a rocket scientist working at what would later become the Jet Propulsion Laboratory at the California Technical Institute. (Parsons, who has a crater on the Moon named after him, developed solid rocket fuel.) Darkly handsome and brawny, later called by some scholars the "James Dean of the occult," Parsons was a science-fiction fan and an outspoken advocate of free love. He acquired a three-story Craftsman-style mansion, with a twelve-car garage, at 1003 South Orange Grove Avenue in Pasadena—a sedate, palm-lined street known as Millionaires Row. The house had once belonged to Arthur H. Fleming, a logging tycoon and philanthropist, who had hosted former president Theodore Roosevelt, John Muir, and

Albert Einstein in its oval dining room. The street had also been home to William Wrigley, of the chewing-gum fortune, and the beer baron Adolph Busch, whose widow still lived next door.

She must have been appalled to watch as Parsons divided the historic home and the coach house behind it into nineteen apartments, then advertised for renters. He sought artists, anarchists, and musicians—the more Bohemian the better. "Must not believe in God," the ad stated. Among those passing through the "Parsonage" were an aging actress from the silent movie era, an opera singer, several astrologers, an ex-convict, and the chief engineer for the development of the atomic bomb. A number of children from various alliances constantly raced through the house. Parsons threw parties that featured "women in diaphanous gowns," as one visitor observed, who "would dance around a pot of fire, surrounded by coffins topped with candles." Parsons turned the mansion into the headquarters of the Agapé Lodge, a branch of the Ordo Templi Orientis, a secret fraternal organization dedicated to witchcraft and sexual "magick," based on the writings of the notorious British writer and provocateur Aleister Crowley, whose glowering countenance was captured in a portrait hanging in the stairwell.

Despite the bizarre atmosphere that he cultivated, Parsons took his involvement in the OTO seriously, making brazen ethical claims for his movement—claims that would sound familiar when Scientology arose only a few years later. "The breakup of the home and family, the confusion in problems of morals and behavior, the frustration of the individual need for love, self-expression and freedom, and the immanence of the total destruction of western civilization all indicate the need for a basic reexamination and alteration of individual and social values," Parsons writes in a brief manifesto. "Mature investigation on the part of philosophers and social scientists have [*sic*] indicated the existence of only one force of sufficient power to solve these problems and effect the necessary changes, and that is the force of a new religion."

TWENTY-ONE-YEAR-OLD SARA ELIZABETH "BETTY" NORTHRUP, Parsons's feisty mistress, was the younger sister of his wife, who had run off with another man. Sara was tall, blond, buxom, and wild, often claiming to have lost her virginity at the age of ten. "Her chief interest in life is amusement," one of the boarders observed. But she was also quick and intelligent and full of joy, delighting everyone around her. She had become involved with Parsons, who was ten years older, when she was fifteen. Her parents tolerated the relationship; in fact, her indulgent father helped bankroll the Parsonage, which Sara purchased jointly with Parsons while she was still a teenager. One evening Robert Heinlein appeared at the house, bringing along his friend L. Ron Hubbard, who was wearing dark glasses and carrying a silver-handled cane. "He was not only a writer but he was a captain of a ship that had been downed in the Pacific and he was weeks on a raft and had been blinded by the sun and his back had been broken," Sara later recalled. "I believed everything he said."

A few months later, Hubbard moved in. He made an immediate, vivid impression on the other boarders. "He dominated the scene with his wit and inexhaustible fund of anecdotes," one of the boarders, Alva Rogers, later recalled. "Unfortunately, Ron's reputation for spinning tall tales (both off and on the printed page) made for a certain degree of skepticism in the minds of his audience. At any rate, he told one hell of a good story." Like Hubbard, Rogers had red hair, and he was intrigued by Hubbard's theory that redheads are the living remnant of the Neanderthals.

Hubbard invited one of his paramours from New York, Vida Jameson, to join him at the Parsonage, with the ostensible task of keeping the books. It's a testimony to his allure that she came all the way across America to be with him, although soon after she arrived, she discovered that she had been displaced.

The other boarders watched in astonishment as Hubbard worked his charms on the available women in the household, before setting his sights on "the most gorgeous, intelligent, sweet, wonderful girl," as another envious suitor described Sara Northrup. "There he was, living off Parsons' largesse and making out with his girlfriend right in front of him. Sometimes when the two of them were sitting at the table together, the hostility was almost tangible." Enlivened, no doubt, by their rivalry over Sara, Parsons and Hubbard quickly developed a highly competitive relationship. They liked to begin their mornings with a bout of fencing in the living room.

Parsons struggled with his feelings of jealousy, which were at war with his philosophy of free love. He could understand Northrup's attraction to the new boarder, describing Hubbard in a letter to Crowley in 1946 as "a gentleman, red hair, green eyes, honest and intelligent. . . . He moved in with me about two months ago." Then Parsons admits, "Although Betty and I are still friendly, she has transferred her sexual affections to Ron." He went on to admire Hubbard's supernatural abilities. "Although he has no formal training in Magick, he has an extraordinary amount of experience and understanding in the field. From some of his experiences I deduced that he is in direct touch with some higher intelligence, possibly his Guardian Angel. He describes his Angel as a beautiful winged woman with red hair whom he calls the Empress and who has guided him through his life and saved him many times."

The extent to which Scientology was influenced by Hubbard's involvement with the OTO has long been a matter of angry debate. There is little trace in Hubbard's life of organized religion or spiritual philosophy. In the Parsonage, he was drawn into an obscure and stigmatized creed, based on the writings and practice of Crowley— the "Great Beast," as he called himself—who gloried in being one of the most reviled men of his era. The Church of Scientology explicitly rejects any connection between Crowley's thinking and Hubbard's emerging philosophy; yet the two men were similar in striking ways. Like Hubbard, Crowley reveled in a life of constant physical, spiritual, and sexual exploration. He was a daring, even reckless mountaineer, and his exploits included several failed attempts to climb the world's most formidable peaks. He, too, was a prolific writer who authored novels and plays as well as books on magic and mysticism. Boisterous and highly self-regarding, he had been kicked out of an occult society called the Hermetic Order of the Golden Dawn after feuding with some of its most prominent members, including William Butler Yeats, whom Crowley accused of being envious of his talent as a poet. He may have served as a British spy while living in America during World War I, despite the fact that he was constantly publishing anti-British propaganda. Crowley relied on opiates and hallucinogens to enhance his spiritual pursuits. During an excursion to Cairo in 1904, he discovered his Holy Guardian Angel, a disembodied spirit named Aiwass, who claimed to be a messenger from the Egyptian god Horus. Crowley said that over a period of three days, Aiwass dictated to him an entire cosmology titled *The Book of the Law*, the main principle of which was, "Do what thou wilt shall be the whole of the law."

Nibs—Hubbard's estranged eldest son and namesake, L. Ron Hubbard, Jr. (he later changed his name to Ronald DeWolf)—claimed that his father had read the book when he was sixteen years old and developed a lifelong allegiance to black magic. "What a lot of people don't realize is that Scientology is black magic just spread out over a long time period," he contended. "Black magic is the inner core of Scientology—and it is probably the only part of Scientology that really works."

One striking parallel between Hubbard and Crowley is the latter's assertion that "spiritual progress did not depend on religious or moral codes, but was like any other science." Crowley argued that by advancing through a graded series of rituals and spiritual teachings, the adept could hope to make it across "The Abyss," which he defined as "the gulf existing between individual and cosmic consciousness." It is an image that Hubbard would evoke in his Bridge to Total Freedom.

Although Hubbard mentions Crowley only glancingly in a lecture—calling him "my very good friend"—they never actually met. Crowley died in 1947 at the age of seventy-two. "That's when Dad decided that he would take over the mantle of the Beast and that is the seed and the beginning of Dianetics and Scientology," Nibs later said. "It was his goal to be the most powerful being in the universe."

JACK PARSONS EXPERIMENTED with Crowley's rituals, taking them in his own eccentric direction. His personal brand of witchcraft centered on the adoration of female carnality, an interest Hubbard evidently shared. Parsons recorded in his journal that Hubbard had a vision of "a savage and beautiful woman riding naked on a great cat-like beast." That became the inspiration for Parsons's most audacious mystical experiment. He appointed Hubbard to be his "scribe" in a ceremony called the "Babalon Working." It was based on Crowley's notion that the supreme goal of the magician's art was to create a "moonchild"—a creature foretold in one of Crowley's books who becomes the Antichrist. Night after night, Parsons and Hubbard invoked the spirit world in a quest to summon up a "Scarlet Woman," the female companion who would play the role of Parsons's consort. The ceremony, likely aided by narcotics and hallucinogens, required Hubbard to channel the female deity of Babalon as Parsons performed the "invocation of wand with material basis on talisman"—in other words, masturbating on a piece of parchment. He typically invoked twice a night.

Parsons records that during one of these evenings a candle was forcibly knocked out of Hubbard's hand: "We observed a brownish yellow light about seven feet high in the kitchen. I brandished a magical sword and it disappeared. His right arm was paralyzed for the rest of the night." On another occasion, he writes, Hubbard saw the astral projection of one of Parsons's enemies manifest himself in a black robe. "Ron promptly launched an attack and pinned the phantom figure to the door with four throwing knives."

Evidently, the spirits relented. One day, an attractive young woman named Marjorie Cameron showed up at the Parsonage. Parsons later claimed that a bolt of lightning had struck outside, followed by a knock at the door. A beautiful woman was standing there. She had been in a traffic accident. "I don't know where I am or where I've come from," she told him. (Cameron's version is that she had been interested in the stories of the naked women jumping over fires in the garden, and she persuaded a friend who was boarding at the Parsonage to take her for a visit.) "I have my elemental!" Parsons exclaimed in a note to Crowley a few days later. "She has red hair and slant green eyes as specified. . . . She is an artist, strong minded and determined, with strong masculine characteristics and a fanatical independence."

The temple was lit with candles, the room suffused with incense, and Rachmaninoff's "Isle of the Dead" was playing in the background. Dressed in a hooded white robe, and carrying a lamp, Hubbard intoned, "Display thyself to Our Lady; dedicate thy organs to Her, dedicate thy heart to Her, dedicate thy mind to Her, dedicate thy soul to Her, for She shall absorb thee, and thou shalt become living flame before She incarnates." Whereupon Parsons and Cameron responded, "Glory unto the Scarlet Woman, Babalon, the Mother of Abominations, that rideth upon the Beast." Then, as Hubbard continued the incantation, Parsons and Cameron consummated the ceremony upon the altar. This same ritual went on for three nights in a row. Afterward, Parsons wrote to Crowley, "Instructions were received direct through Ron, the seer. . . . I am to act as instructor guardian guide for nine months; then it will be loosed on the world."

Crowley was unimpressed. "Apparently Parsons or Hubbard or somebody is producing a Moonchild," he complained to another follower. "I get fairly frantic when I contemplate the idiocy of these goats." Cameron did become pregnant, but got an abortion, with Parsons's consent, so it's unclear exactly what this ceremony was designed to produce. (Parsons and Cameron later married and aborted another pregnancy.) Nonetheless, Parsons asserted that the ritual had been a success. "Babalon is incarnate upon the earth today, awaiting the proper hour for her manifestation," he wrote after the ceremony. "And in that day my work will be accomplished, and I shall be blown away upon the Breath of the father."

Until that apocalypse occurred, Hubbard and Parsons decided, they would go into business together. The plan was for Hubbard to purchase yachts in Florida, sail them through the Panama Canal to California, and resell them at a profit. Parsons and Sara sold the Parsonage and handed over the money to Hubbard—more than twenty thousand dollars from Parsons alone. Hubbard and Northrup promptly left for Miami.

While in Florida, Hubbard appealed to the Veterans Administration for an increase in his medical disability. He was already receiving compensation for his ulcers, amounting to $11.50 per month. "I cannot tolerate a general diet—results in my having to abandon my old profession as a ship master and explorer, and seriously hampers me as a writer." He said his eyesight had been affected by "prolonged exposure to tropical sunlight," incurred while he was in the service, which caused a chronic case of conjunctivitis. He also complained that he was lame from a bone infection, which he theorized must have occurred by the abrupt change in climate when he was shipped to the East Coast. "My earning power, due to injuries, all service connected, has dropped to nothing," he summed up. Sara Northrup added a handwritten note of support. "I have know [sic] Lafayette Ronald Hubbard for many years," she claimed. "I see no chance of his condition improving to a point where he can regain his old standards. He is becoming steadily worse, his health impaired again by economic worries."

Parsons grew to believe that Hubbard and Sara had other plans for his money, and he flew to Miami to confront them. When he learned that they had just sailed away, he performed a "Banishing Ritual," invoking Bartzabel, a magical figure associated with Mars. According to Parsons, a sudden squall arose, ripping the sails off the ship that Hubbard was captaining, forcing him to limp back to port. Sara's memory was that she and Ron were on their way to California, when they were caught in a hurricane in the Panama Canal. The ship was too damaged to continue the voyage. Parsons gained a judgment against the couple, but declined to press criminal charges, possibly because his sexual relationship with Sara had begun while she was still below the age of consent, and she threatened to retaliate. Hubbard's friends were alarmed, both about his business dealings with Parsons and his romance with Sara. "Keep him at arm's length," Robert Heinlein warned a mutual friend. His wife, Virginia, regarded Ron as "a very sad case of post-war breakdown," and Sara as Hubbard's "latest Man-Eating Tigress."

Sara repeatedly refused Ron's entreaties to marry him, but he threatened to kill himself unless she relented. She still saw him as a broken war hero whom she could mend. Finally, she said, "All right, I'll marry you, if that's going to save you." They awakened a minister in Chestertown, Maryland, on August 10, 1946. The minister's wife and housekeeper served as witnesses to the wedding. The news ricocheted among Hubbard's science-fiction colleagues. "I suppose Polly was tiresome about not giving him his divorce so he could marry six other gals who were all hot & moist over him," one of Hubbard's writer friends, L. Sprague de Camp, wrote to the Heinleins. (In fact, Polly didn't learn of the marriage till the following year, when she read about it in the newspapers.) "How many girls is a man entitled to in one lifetime, anyway?" de Camp fumed. "Maybe he should be reincarnated as a rabbit."

The Church of Scientology admits that Hubbard was involved with Parsons and the OTO, characterizing it, however, as a secret mission for naval intelligence. The church claims that the government had been worried about top American scientists—including some from Los Alamos, where the atom bomb was developed—who made a habit of staying with Parsons when they visited California. Hubbard's mission was to penetrate and subvert the organization.

"Mr. Hubbard accomplished the assignment," the church maintains. "He engineered a business investment that tied up the money Parsons used to fund the group's activities, thus making it unavailable to Parsons for his occult pursuits." Hubbard, the church claims, "broke up black magic in America."

EVEN IF HUBBARD WAS a government spy, as the church claims, the available records show him at what must have been his lowest point in the years just after the war. His physical examination at the Veterans Administration in Los Angeles in September 1946 notes, "No work since discharge. Lives on his savings." (The VA eventually increased his disability to forty percent.) Sara noticed that he was having nightmares. That winter, they moved into a lighthouse on a frozen lake in the Poconos near Stroudsburg, Pennsylvania. It was an unsettling time for Sara; they were isolated, and Ron had a .45 pistol that he would fire randomly. Late one night, while she was in bed and Ron was typing, he hit her across the face with the pistol. He told her that she had been smiling in her sleep, so she must have been thinking about someone else. "I got up and left the house in the night and walked on the ice of the lake because I was terrified," Sara said in 1997, in an account she dictated shortly before she died. She was so shocked and humiliated she didn't know how to respond.

Ron had begun beating her in Florida, shortly after her father died. Her grief seemed to provoke Ron—she assumed it was because she wasn't being who he needed her to be. No one had ever struck her before. She recognized now how dangerous their relationship was; on the other hand, Ron's need for her was so stark. He had been blocked for a long time, and Sara had been churning out plots for him, and actually writing some of his stories. Ron worried that he would never write again. He frequently threatened suicide. Sara didn't believe in divorce—it was a terrible stigma at the time—and she still thought she could save Ron. "I kept thinking that he must be suffering or he wouldn't act that way." And so, she went back to him.

Ron took a loan and bought a house trailer, and he and Sara drove across the country to Port Orchard, where his parents and his undivorced first wife and children were living. Sara had no idea why people treated her so strangely, until finally Hubbard's son Nibs told her that his parents were still married. Once again, Sara fled. Ron found her waiting for the ferry that was leaving for California. The engines of the ship grumbled as Ron hastily pleaded his case. He told her that he really was getting a divorce. He claimed that an attorney had assured him that he and Sara actually were legally married. Finally, the ferry left without her.

Soon after that, Ron and Sara set out for Hollywood. They got as far as Ojai, California, where Ron was arrested for failing to make payments on the house trailer they were living in.

In October 1947, Hubbard sent the VA an alarming and revealing plea:

I am utterly unable to approach anything like my own competence. My last physician informed me that it might be very helpful if I were to be examined and perhaps treated psychiatrically or even by a psychoanalyst. . . . I avoided out of pride any mental examinations, hoping that time would balance a mind which I had every reason to suppose was seriously affected. . . . I cannot, myself, afford such treatment.

Would you please help me?

Nothing came of this request. There is no record that the VA conducted a psychological assessment of Hubbard. Throughout his life, however, questions would arise about his sanity. Russell Miller, a British biographer, tracked down an ex-lover of Hubbard's, who described him as "a manic depressive with paranoid tendencies." The woman, whom Miller called "Barbara Kaye" (her real name was Barbara Klowden), later became a psychologist. She added, "He said he always wanted to found a religion like Moses or Jesus." A man who later worked in the church as Hubbard's medical officer, Jim Dincalci, listed his traits: "Paranoid personality. Delusions of grandeur. Pathological lying." Dr. Stephen Wiseman, a professor in the Department of Psychiatry at the University of British Columbia, who has been a prominent critic of Scientology, speculated that a possible diagnosis of Hubbard's personality would be "malignant narcissism," which he characterizes as "a highly insecure individual protecting himself with aggressive grandiosity, disavowal of any and every need from others, antisocial orientation, and a heady and toxic mix of rage/anger/aggression/violence and paranoia."

And yet, if Hubbard was paranoid, it was also true that he really was often pursued, first by creditors and later by grand juries and government investigators. He may have had delusions of grandeur, as so many critics say, but he did in fact make an undeniable mark on the world, publishing many best sellers and establishing a religion that endures decades after his death. Grandiosity might well be a feature of a personality that could accomplish such feats.

A fascinating glimpse into Hubbard's state of mind during this time is found in what I am calling his secret memoir. The church claims that the document is a forgery. It was produced by the former archivist for the Church of Scientology, Gerald Armstrong, in a 1984 suit that the church brought against him. Armstrong read some portions of them into the record over the strong objections of the church attorneys; others later found their way onto the Internet. The church now maintains that Hubbard did not write this document, although when it was entered into evidence, the church's lawyers made no such representation, saying that the papers were intensely private, "constitute a kind of self-therapy," and did not reflect Hubbard's actual condition.

This disputed document has been called the Affirmations, or the Admissions, but it is rather difficult to define. In part, the thirty pages constitute a highly intimate autobiography, dealing with the most painful episodes in Hubbard's life. Many of the references to people and events made in these pages are supported by other documents. It appears that Hubbard is using techniques on himself that he would later develop into Dianetics. He explores memories that pose impediments in his mental and spiritual progress, and he prescribes affirmations or incantations to counter the psychological influence of these events. These statements would certainly be the most revealing and intimate disclosures Hubbard ever made about himself.

There are three sections in this document, each of which seems to have a different purpose.

The first section is called "Course I." This is what I have termed the secret memoir, as it contains reflections on the most embarrassing or troubling features of Hubbard's biography. "The purpose of this experiment is to re-establish the ambition, willpower, desire to survive, the talent and confidence of myself," Hubbard declares straightforwardly at the start. "I was always anxious about people's opinion of me and was afraid I would bore them. This injected anxiety and careless speed into my work. I must be convinced that I can write skillfully and well." Those who criticize his work are fools, he writes. "I must be convinced I have succeeded in writing and with ease will regain my popularity, which actually was not small."

"My service record was none too glorious," he admits. He also confesses his shame about his frequent affairs. But he is intent on succeeding in his relationship with Sara, whom he describes as "young, beautiful, desirable." Unfortunately, he is handicapped by bouts of impotence. "I want her always. But I am 13 years older than she. She is heavily sexed. My libido is so low I hardly admire her naked."

Sex preoccupies him. He's worried about his "very bad masturbatory history," his sexual diseases, and his impotence, which he had been treating with testosterone supplements. "By eliminating certain fears of hypnosis, curing my rheumatism and laying off hormones, I hope to restore my former libido. I must!"

Through self-hypnosis, he hopes to convince himself of certain prescriptive mantras, including:

> I can write.
> My mind is still brilliant.
> That masturbation was no sin or crime.
> That I do not need to have ulcers anymore.
> That I am fortunate in losing Polly and my parents, for they never meant well by me.
> That I believe in my gods and spiritual things.
> That my magical work is powerful and effective.
> That the numbers 7, 25, and 16 are not unlucky or evil for me.
> That I am not bad to look upon.
> That I am not susceptible to colds.
> That Sara is always beautiful to me.
> That these words and commands are like fire and will sear themselves into every corner of my being, making me happy and well and confident forever!

The second part of the document, labeled "Course II," included the statements that have come to be called Affirmations, although Hubbard refers to them as incantations. He had recently gotten a new recorder for dictation, called a SoundScriber. It may be that he recorded this portion and played it back to himself as a means of self-hypnosis. This section begins with the command "You are asleep."

In this lesson, Hubbard tells himself, he will learn several important things:

> You have no urge to talk about your navy life. You do not like to talk of it. You never illustrate your point with bogus stories. It is not necessary for you to lie to be amusing and witty.
> You like to have your intimate friends approve of and love you for what you are. This desire to be loved does not amount to a psychosis.
> You can sing beautifully.

Nothing can intervene between you and your Guardian. She
cannot be displaced because she is too powerful. She does not
control you. She advises you.

You will never forget these incantations. They are holy and are
now become an integral part of your nature.

Material things are yours for the asking. Men are your slaves.

You are not sleepy or tired ever. . . . Your Guardian alone can talk
to you as you sleep but she may not hypnotize you. Only you
can hypnotize yourself.

The desires of other people have no hypnotic effect on you.

Nothing, no one opposes your writing. . . . You can carry on a
wild social life and still write one hundred thousand words a
month or more. . . . Your writing has a deep hypnotic effect on
people.

You will make fortunes writing.

Your psychology is advanced and true and wonderful. It
hypnotizes people. It predicts their emotions, for you are their
ruler.

You will live to be 200 years old.

You will always look young.

You have no doubts about God.

You are not a coward.

Your eyes are getting progressively better. They became bad when
you used them as an excuse to escape the naval academy. You
have no reason to keep them bad.

Your stomach trouble you used as an excuse to keep the Navy
from punishing you. You are free of the Navy.

Your hip is a pose. You have a sound hip. It never hurts. Your
shoulder never hurts.

Your foot was an alibi. The injury is no longer needed.

Testosterone blends easily with your own hormones. . . . You have
no fear of what any woman may think of your bed conduct.
You know you are a master. You know they will be thrilled.
You can come many times without weariness. . . . Many
women are not capable of pleasure in sex and anything adverse
they say or do has no effect whatever upon your pleasure.

You have no fear if they conceive. What if they do? You do not
care. Pour it into them and let fate decide.

You can tell all the romantic tales you wish. . . . But you know

which ones were lies. . . . You have enough real experience to
make anecdotes forever. Stick to your true adventures.

Money will flood in upon you.

Self pity and conceit are not wrong. Your mother was in error.

Masturbation does not injure or make insane. Your parents were
in error. Everyone masturbates.

The most thrilling thing in your life is your love and consciousness
of your Guardian.

She has copper red hair, long braids, a lovely Venusian face, a
white gown belted with jade squares. She wears gold slippers.

You can talk with her and audibly hear her voice above all others.

You can do automatic writing whenever you wish. You do not care
what comes out on the paper when your Guardian dictates.

The red-haired Guardian Hubbard visualizes so vividly is a kind of
ideal mother, who also functions as his muse and is the source of his
astoundingly rapid writing. Hubbard loves her but reassures himself
that his Guardian does not control him. In all things, he is the controlling force. She seems to be an artifact of the influence of Aleister
Crowley. Jack Parsons had said that Hubbard called his Guardian "the
Empress."

His fear of hypnotism is quite striking. He was an accomplished
stage hypnotist, a skill he displayed at a meeting of a group of sci-fi
fans in Los Angeles, when he put nearly everyone in the audience into
a trance, and persuaded one of them that he was holding a pair of
miniature kangaroos in the palm of his hand. He also once tried to
hypnotize Sara's mother, after she had a stroke, to persuade her to leave
her money to him. But then he would accuse Sara of hypnotizing him
in his sleep.

If one looks behind the Affirmations to the conditions they are
meant to correct, one sees a man who is ashamed of his tendency to
fabricate personal stories, who is conflicted about his sexual needs, and
who worries about his mortality. He has a predatory view of women
but at the same time fears their power to humiliate him.

The third and final section of this document is titled "The Book."
It contains a checklist of personal goals and compliments he pays
to himself, but it is also a portrait of the superman that he wishes
to be. He does make mention of an actual book—he calls it *One
Commandment*—that seems to be a reference to *Excalibur*. "It freed

you forever from the fears of the material world and gave you material control over people," he writes.

> You are radiant like sunlight.
> You can read music.
> You are a magnificent writer who has thrilled millions.
> Ability to drop into a trance state at will.
> Lack of necessity of following a pulp pattern.
> You did a fine job in the Navy. No one there is now "out to get
> you."
> You are psychic.
> You do not masturbate.
> You do not know anger. Your patience is infinite.
> Snakes are not dangerous to you. There are no snakes in the
> bottom of your bed.
> You believe implicitly in God. You have no doubts of the All
> Powerful. You believe your Guardian perfectly.

The judge in the Armstrong suit, where this document was presented as evidence, offered his own amateur diagnosis of Hubbard's personality in a crushing decision against the church:

> The organization is clearly schizophrenic and paranoid, and this bizarre combination seems to be a reflection of its founder LRH. The evidence portrays a man who has been virtually a pathological liar when it comes to his history, background, and achievements. The writings and documents in evidence additionally reflect his egoism, greed, avarice, lust for power, and vindictiveness and aggressiveness against persons perceived by him to be disloyal or hostile. At the same time it appears that he is charismatic and highly capable of motivating, organizing, controlling, manipulating, and inspiring his adherents. . . . Obviously, he is and has been a very complex person, and that complexity is further reflected in his alter ego, the Church of Scientology.

IN 1948, ten years after his first attempt to establish himself as a screenwriter, Hubbard had returned to Hollywood, setting up shop as a freelance guru. "I went right down in the middle of Hollywood,

I rented an office, got a hold of a nurse, wrapped a towel around my head and became a swami," Hubbard later said. "I used to sit in my penthouse on Sunset Boulevard and write stories for New York and then go to my office in the studio and have my secretary tell everybody I was in conference while I caught up on my sleep," he recalled on another occasion. He painted a far different picture in a letter to the Veterans Administration, which was demanding reimbursement for an overpayment: "I cannot imagine how to repay this $51.00 as I am nearly penniless and have but $28.50 to last me for nearly a month to come," he writes. "My expenditures consist of $27 a month trailer rent and $80 a month food for my wife and self which includes gas, cigarettes and all incidentals. I am very much in debt and have not been able to get a job." Instead of repaying the VA, he boldly asks for a loan.

In Hollywood, Hubbard began perfecting techniques that he first developed in the naval hospital and that later became Dianetics. He boasts to Hays, "Been amusing myself making a monkey out of Freud. I always knew he was nutty but didn't have a firm case." He adds that he has been conducting research on inferiority complexes: "Nightly had people writhing in my Hollywood office, sending guys out twice as tall as superman." For the first time, he floats the idea of a book, which he tentatively titles *An Introduction to Traumatic Psychology.* He thinks it will require about six weeks to write. "I got to revolutionize this here field because nobody in it, so far as I can tell, knows his anatomy from a gopher hole."

Hubbard was casting around for a new direction in his life. He took up acting at the Geller Theater Workshop, paid for in part by the VA, but that didn't satisfy him. There was a larger plan stirring in his imagination. "I was hiding behind the horrible secret. And that is I was trying to find out what the mind was all about," he recalls. "I couldn't even tell my friends; they didn't understand. They said, 'Here's Hubbard, he's leading a perfectly wonderful life. He gets to associate with movie actresses. He knows hypnotism and so has no trouble with editors. He has apartments and stuff.' "

IT WAS THE LARVAL STAGE of Hubbard's astonishing transformation—from the depressed, rejected, impoverished, creatively exhausted figure he paints in the Affirmations, to his nearly overnight success as a thinker and founder of an international movement when his book

Dianetics was finally published. He wrote his friend Robert Heinlein, "I will soon, I hope give you a book risen from the ashes of the old Excalibur which details in full the mathematics of the human mind, solves all the problems of the ages, and gives six recipes for aphrodisiacs and plays the mouth organ with the left foot." He writes a little about recovering from the war, then remarks, "The main difficulty these days is getting sane again. I find out that I am making progress. Of course there is always the danger that I will get too sane to write." He is angling for a Guggenheim grant for his book on psychology. Meantime, he was so pressed financially that he begged Heinlein for a loan of fifty dollars. "Golly, I never was so many places in print with less to show for it," Hubbard complained. "I couldn't buy a stage costume for Gypsy Rose Lee."

Hubbard was writing these letters from Savannah, Georgia, in the waning days of 1948 and the spring of 1949. He said he was volunteering in a psychiatric clinic at St. Joseph's Medical Center, "getting case histories at the request of the American Psychiatric Assoc." It is a shadowy period in his life, but it was in Savannah that he began to sketch out the principles that would form the basis of his understanding of the human mind. He claimed to be getting phenomenal results on nearly every malady he addressed. "One week ago I brought in my first asthma cure," he writes to Heinlein. "I have an arthritis to finish tomorrow and so it goes."

It's unclear whether Hubbard himself was receiving treatment in Savannah. "My hip and stomach and side are well again," he writes to Heinlein, adding that he is "straightening out the kinks that have held down production on the money machine."

In his letters, Hubbard continually speculates about the book he hopes to finish soon. "It ain't *agin* religion," he boasts to Heinlein. "It just abolishes it. . . . It's science, boy, science." He makes a vague reference to the research he's performing on children. "This hellbroth I cooked up works remarkably well on kids," he remarks. "Took a scared little kid that was supposed to be stupid and was failing everything and worked on him about thirty-five hours just to make sure. That was last month. So now he turns up this afternoon with all A's and all of a sudden reading Shakespeare." He was also noting improvement in himself, both in his work and in his recovered sexual powers. "I am cruising on four hours sleep a night. But the most interesting thing is, I'm up to eight comes. In an evening, that is."

Heinlein was eager for details. Hubbard responded by outlining what he would later call the Tone Scale. It describes the range of human emotional states, from one to four. At bottom, there is Apathy, then Anger. These lower tones were governed by the unconscious, which Hubbard says should be called the "reactive mind." The third level, which was as yet untitled, is the normal state for most of humanity; and the fourth is a condition of happiness and industriousness. Hubbard's experimental technique aimed at raising an individual out of the lower tones and into the superior state of the fourth tone. His method, as he described it to Heinlein, was to drain off the painful experiences and associations that an individual has accumulated in his lifetime. Once that's done, "astonishing results take place." Asthma, headaches, arthritis, menstrual cramps, astigmatism, and ulcers simply disappear. There is a huge boost in competence. The reactive mind is eliminated, and the rational mind takes over.

At the end of April 1949, Hubbard sent a note to Heinlein that he was moving to Washington, DC, for an indefinite stay. There was no word about Sara. Three weeks later, the thirty-eight-year-old Hubbard applied for a license in Washington to marry twenty-six-year-old Ann Jensen. The application was canceled the next day at the request of the bride. Perhaps she had learned that Hubbard was already married to his second wife and had previously committed bigamy. In any case, Ann Jensen's name disappears from Hubbard's life story.

He and Sara moved to Elizabeth, New Jersey, where John Campbell, Hubbard's editor at *Astounding Science-Fiction* before the war, resided. Campbell visited Hubbard often and became one of his first and most important converts. "Dammit, the man's got something—and something big," he wrote excitedly to Heinlein.

Campbell underwent the treatment, which employed "deep hypnosis." In that entranced state, Campbell was able to retrieve traumatic memories of his birth. "I was born with a cord wrapped around my neck, strangling me," he recounted to Heinlein. The doctor who delivered him, whom Campbell now remembered had a German accent, had barked at Campbell's mother, saying, "You must stop fighting—you are killing him. Relax!" Later, the doctor put some corrosive medication in the baby's eyes, and said, "You'll forget all about this in a little while." Campbell characterized these instructions as "unshakeable post-hypnotic commands of tremendous force," which governed much of his subsequent behavior. "The neighbor bratlings could tease me unmercifully—and did—because I couldn't fight," he told Heinlein; his mother would often attempt to console him by telling him that he would forget the painful experiences of his childhood soon enough, with the result that many of the most important moments of his life were lost to him. "Ron's technique consists of bringing these old memories into view, and then *erasing* the memory," Campbell explained. He writes that although he now doesn't remember his actual birth, he does remember retrieving it and relating it to Hubbard, who then erased the real memory, with its painful associations, leaving Campbell with the experience of knowing what happened to him without actually having the memory continue its sinister influence. Obviously, the line between a real memory and an implanted one, or a confabulation, was very difficult to draw.

This was the most potent medicine ever discovered, Campbell continued, but also the most dangerous weapon imaginable if not properly handled. "With the knowledge I now have, I could turn most ordinary people into homicidal maniacs within one hour." And yet, as an editor, Campbell recognized the commercial possibilities: "This is the greatest story in the world—far bigger than the atomic bomb." He added in a postscript that he had also lost twenty pounds in twenty-five days— another commercial bonanza. Campbell was beside himself because Hubbard had yet to actually start writing the book. "The key to world sanity is in Ron Hubbard's head, and there isn't even an adequate written record!"

In December, Ron and Sara moved into what Hubbard termed "a little old shack" in Bayhead, New Jersey, with eight bedrooms, near the beach. In March 1950, he sent the Heinleins a handmade miniature book catalogue from "Hubbard House" publishers, proclaiming the spring collection:

Announcing
A New Hubbard Edition
Completely New Material
Not a revision
Co-Authors—Ron & Sara Hubbard
Release Date March 8, '50—11:50 A.M.
Weight—9 lbs. 2 oz. — Height—21 in.
Alexis Valerie
Has received rave notices from all reviewers!

Alexis was the image of her father, who delighted in her precocious-ness. "Ron is going at a little less than the speed of light all day and every day," Sara wrote to the Heinleins, "then, in the middle of the night he goes in and tells Alexis all about it."

Ron promised to send Heinlein a galley of *Dianetics* as soon as it was available. He reported that it was 180,000 words, "begun Jan. 12, '50, finished Feb. 10, off the press by April 25." When one of his follow-ers asked Hubbard how he had been able to dash it off so quickly, Hub-bard said that his guardian spirit, the Empress, had dictated it to him.

Like several other prominent sci-fi writers of the Golden Age, including Heinlein and A. E. van Vogt, Hubbard had been strongly influenced by the writings of Alfred Korzybski, a Polish American phi-losopher who created the theory of general semantics. In New Jersey, Sara read Korzybski and quoted several passages aloud to Ron, who immediately grasped the ideas as the basis for a system of psychology, if not for a whole religion.

Korzybski pointed out that words are not the things they describe, in the same way that a map is not the territory it represents. Lan-guage shapes thinking, creating mental habits, which can stand in the way of sanity by preserving delusions. Korzybski argued that emotional disturbances, learning disorders, and many psychosomatic illnesses—including heart problems, skin diseases, sexual disorders, migraines, alcoholism, arthritis, even dental cavities—could be rem-edied by semantic training, much as Hubbard would claim for his own work. He cited Korzybski frequently, although he admitted that he could never get through the texts themselves. "Bob Heinlein sat down one time and talked for ten whole minutes on the subject of Korzybski to me and it was very clever," he later related. "I know quite a bit about Korzybski's works."

From this secondhand knowledge, Hubbard saw the need for creat-ing a special vocabulary, which would allow him to define old thoughts in new ways (the soul becomes a thetan, for instance); or invent new words, such as "enturbulate" (confuse) and "hatting" (training); or use words and phrases in a novel manner, such as turning adjectives or verbs into nouns, or vice versa ("an overt," "a static," "alter-isness"); plus a Pentagon-level glut of acronyms—all of which would entrap his followers in a self-referential semantic labyrinth.

Hubbard granted his friend and acolyte John Campbell a scoop by letting him buy a lengthy excerpt of his forthcoming book. Thus the world got its first look at *Dianetics* in the pages of *Astounding Science-Fiction*. "This article is *not* a hoax, joke, or anything but a direct, clear statement of a totally new scientific thesis," Campbell warns his readers, who might be confused by finding a work of scholarship in a pulp magazine. "I know dianetics is one of, if not the greatest, discovery of all Man's written and unwritten history," he wrote to a puzzled contributor. "It produces the sort of stability and sanity men have dreamed about for centuries." He assured a young writer that Hubbard would win the Nobel Peace Prize for his work.

The book itself, *Dianetics: The Modern Science of Mental Health*, appeared in May. It was completely unexpected, given Hubbard's history as a writer. He intended it to stand as a capstone to the "fifty thousand years of thinking men without whose speculations and observations the creation and construction of Dianetics would not have been possible." In Scientology, *Dianetics* is known as Book One. "With 18 million copies sold, it is indisputably the most widely read and influential book on the human mind ever published," the church maintains. Scientology dates its own calendar from 1950, the year *Dianetics* was published.

Hubbard's theory is that the mind has two parts. The analytical, or conscious, mind is the center of awareness, the storehouse of all past perceptions. Nothing is lost from its data banks. Every smell or pattern or sound attached to one's previous experiences is present and capable of being completely recaptured. This is the mind that observes and thinks and solves problems. It is rational and aware of itself.

The other form of mentality is the reactive mind. It is the single source of nightmares, insecurity, and unreasonable fears. It doesn't think. It is a repository of painful and destructive emotions, which are recorded even while an individual is sleeping, or unconscious, or still in the womb. The recording is not the same as a memory, in the sense of being a mental construct; it is physically a part of the cellular structure and capable of reproducing itself in generations of new cells. "Cells are evidently sentient in some currently inexplicable way," Hubbard speculates. When awakened by some stimulus, the recording—Hubbard calls it an "engram"—turns off the conscious mind and seizes control of an individual's actions or behavior.

Hubbard compares the engram to a posthypnotic suggestion. He describes a man in a trance who has been told that every time the operator touches his tie, the subject will remove his coat. When the subject

is awakened, he is not consciously aware of the command. "The operator then touches his tie," Hubbard writes. "The subject may make
some remark about its being too warm and so take his coat off." This
can be done repeatedly. "At last the subject may become aware, from
the expressions on people's faces, that something is wrong. He will
not know what is wrong. He will not even know that the touching of
the tie is the signal which makes him take off his coat." The hypnotic
command in his unconscious continues to govern his behavior, even
when the subject recognizes that it is irrational and perhaps harmful.
In the same way, Hubbard suggests, engrams work their sinister influence on everyday actions, undermining one's self-confidence and subverting rational behavior. The individual feels helpless as he engages in
behavior he would never consciously consent to. He is "handled like a
marionette by his engrams."

Although there were no recorded case histories to prove his claim
that hundreds of patients had been cured through his methods, through
"many years of exact research and careful testing," Hubbard offered
appealing examples of hypothetical behavior. For instance, a woman
is beaten and kicked. "She is rendered 'unconscious.' " In that state,
she is told she is no good, a faker, and that she is always changing her
mind. Meantime, a chair has been knocked over; a faucet is running in
the kitchen; a car passes outside. All of these perceptions are parts of
the engram. The woman is not aware of it, but whenever she hears running water or a car passing by, the engram is partly restimulated. She
feels discomfort if she hears them together. If a chair happens to fall
as well, she experiences a shock. She begins to feel like the person she
was accused of being while she was unconscious—a fickle, no-good
faker. "This is not theory," Hubbard repeatedly asserts. It is an "exact
science" that represents "an evolutionary step in the development of
Man."

Hubbard proposed that the influence engrams have over one's current behavior can be eliminated by reciting the details of the original
incident until it no longer possesses an emotional charge.* "Dianetics

---

*A conspicuous example of Dianetic processing involved John Brodie, the outstanding
quarterback for the San Francisco 49ers, who suffered an injury to his throwing arm in
1970 that threatened to end his career. Despite the best medical attention and physical
therapy, his elbow remained sore and swollen. Finally, he went to Phil Spickler, a Scientologist and Dianetic auditor, who asked Brodie to tell him about previous incidents
that might be keeping his arm from healing. Brodie related that he had been in a severe
traffic accident in 1963, in which his arm had been broken. As he explored the inci-

deletes all the pain from a lifetime," Hubbard writes. "When this pain is erased in the engram bank and refiled as memory and experience in the memory banks, all aberrations and psychosomatic illnesses vanish." The object of Dianetics therapy is to drain the engrams of their painful, damaging qualities and eliminate the reactive mind entirely, leaving a person "Clear."

WRITTEN IN a bluff, quirky style, and overrun with patronizing footnotes that do little to substantiate its bold findings, *Dianetics* nonetheless became a sensation, lodging itself for twenty-eight weeks on the *New York Times* best-seller list and laying the groundwork for the category of postwar self-help books that would seek to emulate its success. Hundreds of Dianetics groups sprang up around the United States and in other countries in order for its adherents to apply the therapeutic principles Hubbard prescribed. One only needed a partner, called an auditor, who could guide the subject to locate his engrams and bring them into consciousness, where they would be released and rendered harmless. "You will find many reasons why you 'cannot get well,' " Hubbard warns, but he promises, "Dianetics is no solemn adventure. For all that it has to do with suffering and loss, its end is always laughter, so foolish, so misinterpreted were the things which caused the woe."

The book arrived at a moment when the aftershocks of the world war were still being felt. Behind the exhilaration of victory, there was immense trauma. Religious certainties were shaken by the development of bombs so powerful that civilization, if not life itself, became a wager in the Cold War contest. Loss, grief, and despair were cloaked by the stoicism of the age, but patients being treated in mental hospitals were already on the verge of outnumbering those being treated for any other

---

dent with Spickler, Brodie seemed to recall one of the ambulance attendants saying, "Well, that poor sonofabitch will never throw a football again." And yet Brodie was unconscious at the time. How could he have such a memory? Spickler told him this was all part of an engram that was keeping him from getting well. "The ambulance attendant's prediction had been simmering in my unconscious for seven years, agitating all my deepest fears of declining ability or failure," Brodie later writes. "It had finally surfaced as this psychosomatic ailment in my throwing arm. Phil made me tell the story again and again and again, until no charge showed on the E-Meter" (John Brodie and James D. Houston, *Open Field*, p. 166). The swelling on Brodie's arm diminished. He went on to have one of the greatest seasons of his career, and was voted the National Football League's most valuable player that year.

cause. Psychoanalysis was suspiciously viewed in much of America as a European—mainly Jewish—import, which was time-consuming and fantastically expensive. Hubbard promised results "in less than twenty hours of work" that would be "superior to any produced by several years of psycho-analysis."

The profession of psychiatry, meantime, had entered a period of brutal experimentation, characterized by the widespread practice of lobotomies and electroshock therapy. The prospect of consulting a psychiatrist was accompanied by a justified sense of dread. That may have played a role in Hubbard's decision not to follow up on his own request for psychiatric treatment. The appearance of a do-it-yourself manual that claimed to demystify the secrets of the human mind and produce guaranteed results—for free—was bound to attract an audience. "It was sweepingly, catastrophically successful," Hubbard marveled.

The scientific community, stupefied by the book's popularity, reacted with hostility and ridicule. It seemed to them little more than psychological folk art. "This volume probably contains more promises and less evidence per page than has any publication since the invention of printing," the Nobel physicist Isidor Isaac Rabi wrote in his review of *Dianetics* for *Scientific American*. "The huge sale of the book to date is distressing evidence of the frustrated ambitions, hopes, ideals, anxieties and worries of the many persons who through it have sought succor." Erich Fromm, one of the predominant thinkers of the psychoanalytic movement, denounced the book as being "expressive of a spirit that is exactly the opposite of Freud's teachings." Hubbard's method, he complains, "has no respect for and no understanding of the complexities of personality." He derisively quotes Hubbard: "In an engineering science like Dianetics we can work on a push-button basis." But, of course, that was part of the theory's immense appeal.

One of the most painful reviews of *Dianetics*, no doubt, was by Korzybski's most notable intellectual heir (and later, US senator from California), S. I. Hayakawa. He not only dismissed the book, he also criticized what he saw as the spurious craft of writing science fiction. "The art consists in concealing *from the reader*, for novelistic purposes, the distinctions between established scientific facts, almost-established scientific hypotheses, scientific conjectures, and imaginative extrapolations far beyond what has even been conjectured," he wrote. The writer who produces "too much of it too fast and too glibly" runs the risk of believing in his own creations. "It appears to me inevitable that anyone writing several million words of fantasy and science-fiction should ultimately begin to internalize the assumptions underlying the verbiage." *Dianetics*, Hayakawa noted, was neither science nor fiction, but something else: "fictional science."

Not all scientists rejected Hubbard's approach. One of his early supporters was Campbell's brother-in-law Dr. Joseph Winter, a physician who had also written for *Astounding Science-Fiction*. Searching for a more holistic approach to medicine, Winter traveled to New Jersey to experience Hubbard's method firsthand. "While listening to Hubbard 'running' one of his patients, or while being 'run' myself, I would find myself developing unaccountable pains in various portions of my anatomy, or becoming extremely fatigued and somnolent," he reported. "I had nightmares of being choked, of having my genitalia cut off, and I was convinced that dianetics as a method could produce effects."

Hubbard's method involved placing the patient in a state of "reverie," achieved by giving the command "When I count from one to seven your eyes will close." A tremble of the lashes as the eyelids flutter shut signals that the subject has fallen into a receptive condition. "*This is not hypnotism*," Hubbard insists. Although a person in a Dianetic reverie may appear to be in a trance, the opposite is the case, he says: "The purpose of therapy is to awaken a person in every period of his life when he has been forced into 'unconsciousness.' Dianetics wakes people up."

Sara watched the effect that Ron was having on his patients. "He would hold hands with them and try to talk them into these phony memories," she recalled. "He would concentrate on them and they *loved* it. They were so excited about someone who would just pay this much attention to them."

Dr. Winter tried out Hubbard's techniques on his six-year-old son, who was afraid of the dark because he was terrified of being choked by ghosts. Winter asked him to remember the first time he saw a ghost. "He has on a long white apron, a little white cap on his head and a piece of white cloth on his mouth," the boy said. He even had a name for the ghost—it happened to be the same as that of the obstetrician who delivered him. Winter then asked his son to look at the "ghost" in his mind repeatedly, until the boy began to calm down. "When the maximum relaxation had apparently been obtained after ten or twelve recountings, I told him to open his eyes," Winter reported. "It has been over a year since that short session with my son, and he has not had a recurrence of his fear of the dark in all that time."

The idea that early memories—even prenatal ones—could be recaptured was central to Hubbard's theory. Every engram rooted in the reactive mind has its predecessors; the object of Dianetics therapy is to hunt down the original insult, the "basic-basic," which produced the engram in the first place. Freud had also postulated that childhood traumas would be played out in later life through symptoms of hysteria or neurosis. In his famous Wolf Man case, for instance, Freud traced a childhood neurosis in his patient to the sight of his parents copulating when he was a year and a half old. "Everything goes back to the reproduction of scenes," Freud thought at the time. He recognized that in many cases such childhood memories were clearly invented, but from an analytical perspective, they were still useful, because the emotions and associations attached to the confabulations opened a window onto the patient's subconscious. False childhood memories were often as deeply believed in as real ones, but what made them stand apart from actual memories was that they were almost always the same, unvarying from patient to patient; they must be somehow universal. Freud's protégé Carl Jung would seize on this fact to construct his theory of the Collective Unconscious. Freud himself came to believe that what was a false memory in a present-day patient's mind had been a reality at some point in prehistory. "It seems to me quite possible that all the things that are told to us to-day in analysis as phantasy—the seduction of children, the inflaming of sexual excitement by observing parental intercourse, the threat of castration . . .—were once real occurrences in the primaeval times of the human family, and that children in their phantasies are simply filling in the gaps in individual truth with prehistoric truth." And yet Freud continued to be troubled by the fact that many of these supposed memories were formed at a suspiciously early age. "The extreme achievement on these lines is a phantasy of observing parental intercourse while one is still an unborn baby in the womb," he noted wryly. That absurdity was one of the reasons he eventually cast aside the seduction theory.

For Hubbard, however, early or even prenatal traumas were literally true. He believed that the fetus not only recorded details of his parents copulating during his pregnancy, but also every word spoken during the act. Such recordings can be restimulated in adult life by hearing similar language, which would then awaken the anxiety that the fetus experienced—during a violent sexual episode, for instance. That could lead to "aberration," which for Hubbard includes all psychoses, neuroses, compulsions and any other deviation from rational behavior. Engrams form chains of similar incidents, Hubbard suggests. He gives the example of seventeen prenatal engrams found in a single individual, who "had passed for 'normal' for thirty-six years of his life." Among them:

COITUS CHAIN, FATHER. 1st incident zygote. 56 succeeding
    incidents. Two branches, father drunk and father sober.
COITUS CHAIN, LOVER. 1st incident embryo. 18 succeeding
    incidents. All painful because of enthusiasm of lover.
FIGHT CHAIN. 1st incident embryo. 38 succeeding incidents.
    Three falls, loud voices, no beating.
ATTEMPTED ABORTION, SURGICAL. 1st incident embryo.
    21 succeeding incidents.
ATTEMPTED ABORTION, DOUCHE. 1st incident fetus.
    2 incidents. 1 using paste, 1 using Lysol, very strong.
MASTURBATION CHAIN. 1st incident embryo. 80 succeeding
    incidents. Mother masturbating with fingers, jolting child and
    injuring child with orgasm.

And so on, all leading up to:

BIRTH. Instrument. 29 hours labor.

Hubbard's view of women as revealed in this and many other examples is not just contemptuous; it betrays a kind of horror. He goes on to make this amazing statement: "It is a scientific fact that abortion attempts are the most important factor in aberration. The child on whom the abortion is attempted is condemned to live with *murderers* whom he reactively knows to be murderers through all his weak and helpless youth!" In his opinion, it is very difficult to abort a child, which is why the process so often fails. "Twenty or thirty abortion attempts are not uncommon in the aberree and in every attempt the child could have been pierced through the body or brain," Hubbard writes. "However many billions America spends yearly on institutions for the insane and jails for the criminals are spent primarily because of attempted abortions done by some sex-blocked mother to whom children are a curse, not a blessing of God."

One of the charges that would be lobbed against Hubbard by his disaffected eldest son was that his father had attempted two abortions on his mother. "One I observed when I was around six or seven," L. Ron Hubbard, Jr., later testified. He recalled seeing his father standing over his mother with a coat hanger in his hand. The other attempted abortion was upon himself. "I was born at six and a half months and weighed two pounds, two ounces. I mean, I wasn't born: this is what came out as a result of their attempt to abort me." Hubbard himself writes in his secret memoir that Polly was terrified of childbirth, "but conceived despite all precautions seven times in five years resulting in five abortions and two children." While he was writing *Dianetics,* and Sara was pregnant with Alexis, she says, Hubbard kicked her in the stomach several times to attempt to cause a miscarriage. Later, Hubbard told one of his lovers that he himself had been born of an attempted abortion.

While Hubbard was still writing *Dianetics*, he contacted both the American Psychiatric Association and the American Psychological Association, representing himself as a colleague who had made fundamental advances in the science. Patients placed in a trance state, he explained, could be guided to remember their own births. In sixteen of what he says were the twenty cases that he examined, psychosomatic illnesses had been caused by pre-birth or birth traumas. "Migraine headache, ulcers, asthma, sinusitis and arthritis were amongst those illnesses relieved," he asserted. In a similar letter to the American Gerontological Society, he also claimed that sixteen of the twenty cases had been made measurably younger. His preliminary title for the work was "Certain Discoveries and Researches Leading to the Removal of Early Traumatic Experiences Including Attempted Abortion, Birth Shock and Infant Accidents and Illnesses with an Examination of Their Effects on the Adult Mind and an Account of Techniques Evolved and Employed." When scientists tested some of Hubbard's claims and found that his techniques produced no measurable improvement, he blamed them for failing to understand his system.

Hubbard's rejection by the mental health establishment, even before *Dianetics* was published, was itself a kind of pre-birth trauma. After that, whenever Dianetics or Scientology was attacked in the press or by governments, Hubbard saw the hand of psychiatrists. "The psychiatrist and his front groups operate straight out of the terrorist textbooks," he wrote bitterly years later. "The Mafia looks like a convention of Sunday school teachers compared to these terrorist groups." Toward the end of his life he concluded that if psychiatrists "had the power to torture and kill everyone, they would do so. . . . Recognize them for what they are: psychotic criminals—and handle them accordingly." Psychiatry was "the sole cause of decline in this universe."

HUBBARD SET UP schools to train auditors in major cities, which, along with the book sales and his lecture fees, generated a cascade of revenue. "The money was just pouring in," Sara marveled. Hubbard began carrying huge wads of cash around in his pocket. "I remember going past a Lincoln dealer and admiring one of those big Lincolns they had then," Sara recalled. "He walked right in there and bought it for me, cash!"

The people who were drawn to Dianetics were young to middle-aged white-collar Protestants who had a pronounced interest in science fiction. Some were motivated by the prospect of employment in this booming new field. Others were truth seekers, often veterans of other movements and cults that were responding to the dislocations of the era. And then there were those who had heard the legend of the heroic Navy officer who had been blinded and crippled by the war, who had healed himself through Dianetic techniques. Like Hubbard, they sought a cure. Society and science had let them down. Through Dianetics, they hoped to be lifted up, enlightened, restored, and made whole.

One of the contradictory features of *Dianetics* is the fact that Hubbard continually referred to the powers of Clears, but as yet he had not actually produced a single one for inspection. Among other powers, a Clear "has complete recall of everything which has ever happened to him or anything he has ever studied. He does mental computations such as those of chess, for example, which a normal would do in half an hour, in ten or fifteen seconds." Such claims presumed that there was already a sizable population of Dianetic graduates with exceptional abilities, and Hubbard's readers naturally wondered where they were.

In August 1950, Hubbard presented the "World's First Clear" at the Shrine Auditorium in Los Angeles. Sonia Bianca, a very nervous physics student from Boston, was brought to the stage. Hubbard claimed that through Dianetics, Bianca had attained "full and perfect recall of every moment of her life." The audience began peppering her with questions, such as what she had had for breakfast eight years before, or what was on page 122 of Hubbard's book, or even elemental formulas in physics, her area of specialty. She was incapable of responding when someone asked the color of Hubbard's necktie, when he briefly had his back turned to her. It was a very public fiasco. Hubbard would not announce another Clear for sixteen years. One of his disillusioned acolytes later concluded that the concept of clearing was just a gimmick to dramatize the theory of Dianetics. "The fact is that there were never any clears, as he had described them," Helen O'Brien, Hubbard's top executive in the United States, wrote. "There were randomly occurring remissions of psychosomatics."

Meanwhile, his bigamous marriage to Sara was careening toward a spectacular conclusion. A month after the Sonia Bianca debacle, Ron and Sara were living at the Chateau Marmont in Hollywood. He was beating her regularly. "With or without an argument, there'd be an upsurge of violence," Sara recalled. "The veins in his forehead would engorge" and he would strike her, "out of the blue." One time he broke her eardrum. And yet, she stayed with him, a hostage to his needs. "I felt so guilty about the fact that he was so psychologically damaged," Sara said. "I felt as though he had given so much to our country and I couldn't even bring him peace of mind. I believed thoroughly that he was a man of great honor, had sacrificed his well being to the country. . . . It just never occurred to me he was a liar." Ron finally explained his dilemma: he didn't want to be married—"I do not want to be an American husband for I can buy my friends whenever I want them"—but divorce would hurt his reputation. The solution: if Sara really loved him, she should kill herself.

Sara took little "Alexi," as she called their daughter, and moved into the Los Angeles Dianetics Research Foundation, in a former governor's mansion near the University of Southern California campus. Soon after that, Sara began an affair with another man, Miles Hollister.

Hubbard furiously told his own lover, Barbara Klowden, that Sara and Miles were plotting to have him committed to a mental institution. Indeed, Sara had consulted a psychiatrist about Hubbard's condition. She told him that Ron had said he would rather kill her than let her leave him. The psychiatrist said that Hubbard probably needed to be institutionalized, and he warned Sara that her life was in danger.

Nonetheless, Sara went directly to Ron and told him what the doctor had said. If he got treatment, she said, she would stay with him; otherwise, she was going to leave. Ron responded by threatening to kill their child. "He didn't want her to be brought up by me because I was in league with the doctors," Sara recalled, in her deathbed tape. "He thought I had thrown in with the psychiatrists, with the devils."

On the night of February 24, 1951, Sara went to the movies and left her baby in the care of a young man named John Sanborne, who was studying at the foundation. Alexis had become a kind of celebrity, or at least a curiosity. Hubbard had been touting her as the world's first "dianetic baby"—shielded since birth against any engram-forming disruptions or parental conflict. As a result, Hubbard boasted, Alexis talked at three months, crawled at four, and had no phobias. At about ten o'clock, eleven-month-old Alexis began crying in her crib, so Sanborne picked her up to comfort her. Suddenly, the infant said in a hoarse whisper, "Don't sleep." Sanborne was startled. He didn't think a baby could talk like that. "It went through me in a funny way," he later said. "The hair raising on the back of the neck type of feeling."

At eleven p.m. there was a knock on the door. One of Hubbard's aides appeared, wearing a topcoat, with his hand in his pocket. Sanborne believed he was carrying a gun. The man said that Hubbard was here to take his daughter. Hubbard himself then came through the door, also wearing a topcoat, with his hand in his right pocket. They took the child and disappeared.

Later that night Hubbard returned with two other men to abduct Sara. "We have Alexis and you'll never see her alive unless you come with us," Hubbard said. They tied her hands and dragged her out of bed into a waiting Lincoln. She says that Hubbard had her in a chokehold to keep her from screaming. Hubbard's assistant, Richard de Mille (son of the famous movie director and producer Cecil B. DeMille), drove aimlessly, while Hubbard and Sara, who was wearing only a nightgown, sat in back. She warned him that kidnapping was a capital offense.

In San Bernardino, Hubbard ordered de Mille to stop at the county hospital so he could have Sara committed, but it was the middle of the night and no doctor would talk to him. Eventually, Hubbard and Sara negotiated a truce. Hubbard told her where Alexis was hidden—he had hired a nurse in West Los Angeles to watch her—and Sara signed a note saying that she had gone with Hubbard of her own free will. Hubbard and de Mille went to the Yuma, Arizona, airport and flew to Phoenix, while Sara drove the Lincoln back to Los Angeles in her nightgown to pick up Alexis. When she arrived at the nursing center, however, she was told that a young couple had just left with the baby.

Hubbard and de Mille flew on to Chicago, where Hubbard voluntarily presented himself for a psychological examination in order to counter the accusation that he was a paranoid schizophrenic. The psychologist administered some diagnostic tests, including Rorschach inkblots, and later provided a report that said that Hubbard was a creative individual who was upset by family problems and depressed about his work. Hubbard was extremely pleased; he would often mention that he had been given a clean bill of health by the psychological profession. Sara remembered that he then called her and told her that he had killed Alexis. "He said that he had cut her into little pieces and dropped the pieces in a river and that he had seen little arms and legs floating down the river and it was my fault, I'd done it because I'd left him," Sara remembered.

Hubbard and de Mille then traveled to Elizabeth, New Jersey, where the Dianetics Foundation had its headquarters. Meantime, the young couple that Hubbard had hired to abduct Alexis from the nursing center drove the infant all the way across the country to deliver her to Hubbard. It was the middle of March and snowing in New Jersey, so Hubbard decided to move on to Florida, where he intended to write his next book. De Mille came along with the baby. After a few days in Tampa, Hubbard still felt edgy and announced that the three of them were flying to Cuba. "He believed that as long as he had the child he could control the situation," de Mille told one of Hubbard's biographers.

For six weeks, Sara had searched for Alexis in Southern California, enlisting local police, sheriffs, and the FBI, but the authorities regarded the abduction as a domestic dispute. Finally, she filed a writ of habeas corpus demanding Alexis's return, setting off a press uproar. On April 23, 1951, Sara added to the sensation by finally filing for divorce in Los Angeles County, revealing that Hubbard was already married when they wed. She accused Hubbard of subjecting her to "systematic torture," including sleep deprivation, beatings, strangulations, and "scientific torture experiments." She said that she had consulted medical professionals, who concluded that Hubbard was "hopelessly insane, and crazy."

Soon afterward, Sara received a surprising letter of support from Polly:

> If I can help in any way, I'd like to—You must get Alexis in your custody—Ron is not normal. I had hoped that you could straighten him out. Your charges probably sound fantastic to the average person—but I've been through it—the beatings, threats on my life, all the sadistic traits you charge—twelve years of it. . . . Please do believe I do so want to help you get Alexis.

Meantime, in Havana, Hubbard hired a couple of women to take care of the baby. They kept her in a crib with wire over the top. To de Mille, it seemed that Alexis was being held like a monkey in a cage.

Cuba was run by mobsters, who had turned it into a hedonistic paradise, but Hubbard took little advantage of the nightlife; he locked himself in a hotel room, rented an old typewriter with Spanish-language keys, and began to write. According to de Mille, Hubbard wrote all night with a bottle of rum at hand, which was empty in the morning.

The book Hubbard was pounding out in Havana was *Science of Survival*. He introduced his readers to the Tone Scale, which had evolved since he sketched it out in his letter to Robert Heinlein two years before. The scale classifies emotional states, starting at zero, Body Death. The lower tones are characterized by psychosis, where hatred and anger give way to perversion, artful lying, cowardice, withdrawal, and apathy. "People below the 2.0 level, no matter their avowed intention, will bring death or injury to persons, things and organizations around them if in the anger bracket, or death to themselves if in the apathy bracket," Hubbard writes. "Anyone below 2.0 level is a potential suicide." Their bodies stink, as does their breath. At 2.5, there is a break point between the normal and the neurotic. This stage is characterized by boredom, vagueness, indifference, and pointless conversation. At level 3.0 one enters a stage that Hubbard characterizes as "very high normal," where one is resistant to infections, tolerant, and reasonable; however, he is also insincere, careless, and untrustworthy.

Clear registers 4.0 on the scale. A person who has attained this level is nearly accident-proof and immune to bacteria. He is exhilarated, eager, strong, able, curious, ethical, creative, courageous, responsible, and impossible to hypnotize. And yet this state is only one-tenth of what Hubbard forecasts in the realm of human potential. His scale goes all the way to 40.0, Serenity of Beingness, but the capabilities of the upper regions are largely unknown.

Given the circumstances that surrounded the creation of this book, it's interesting to read what Hubbard writes about sexual behavior and attitudes toward children. Not only was he on the run in Cuba with his abducted daughter when he wrote this, he was also being sued for non-support of the two children from his first marriage, whom he hadn't seen for years. "Sex," he wrote, "is an excellent index of the position of the preclear on the Tone Scale." The highest levels are characterized by monogamy, constancy, a pleasurable attitude toward sex, and an intense interest in children, although the urge to procreate is mitigated by the sublimation of sexual desire into pure creative thought. At 3.0 on the scale, sexual interest is diminished but the urge to procreate remains high. That begins to fall off at 2.5, "not for any reason beyond a general failure to be interested in anything." Children are tolerated, but there is little interest in their affairs. At 2.0, sex becomes revolting and children provoke anxiety. Rape and child abuse characterize 1.5.

Then Hubbard arrives at a level that preoccupies him, 1.1 on the Tone Scale. "Here is the harlot, the pervert, the unfaithful wife, Free Love, easy marriage and quick divorce and general sexual disaster," he writes. "A society which reaches this level is on its way out of history." A mother who is at 1.1 on the Tone Scale will attempt to abort her child. However, once the child is born, "we get general neglect and thoughtlessness about the child and no feeling whatsoever about the child's future or any effort to build one for it. We get careless familial actions, such as promiscuity, which will tear to pieces the family security upon which this child's future depends. Along this band, the child is considered a thing, a possession."

Hubbard finished the book and wrote this dedication:

To
Alexis Valerie Hubbard
For Whose Tomorrow May
Be Hoped a World That
Is Fit To Be Free

Hubbard eventually wrote a note to Sara to explain his where-abouts, saying that he was in a Cuban military hospital, about to be transferred to the States "as a classified scientist immune from inter-ference of all kinds." He adds, "I will be hospitalized probably a long time. Alexis is getting excellent care. I see her every day. She is all I have to live for. My wits never gave way under all you did and let them do but my body didn't stand up. My right side is paralyzed. . . . I hope my heart lasts. . . . Dianetics will last 10,000 years—for the Army and Navy have it now." He concludes by warning that in the event of his death, Alexis will inherit a fortune, but if Sara gains custody, the child will get nothing.

Hubbard did return to the United States and hunkered down in Wichita, Kansas, where a wealthy supporter, Don Purcell, provided him sanctuary. Hubbard's old friend Russell Hays was there, consult-ing for the Cessna Aircraft Corporation. Hubbard arrived with "a Cadillac so damn long he couldn't hardly park it anywhere, and two concubines," Hays marveled. When Sara discovered where her hus-band was, she sought to enjoin his assets. Hubbard retaliated by writ-ing a letter to the US attorney general, explaining the peril he was in. "I am, basically, a scientist in the field of atomic and molecular phenom-ena," he said by way of introduction. He said that his own investiga-tion showed that Sara was tied to Communists who had infiltrated the Dianetics Foundation. This was at the height of McCarthyism and the Red Scare. "I did not realize my wife was one until this spring," Hub-bard wrote. He named several of his disaffected followers, including Gregory Hemingway, son of the famous novelist. "When, when, when will we have a round-up?" he implored.

Meantime, Sara came to Wichita to pursue the divorce and to get Alexis back. Ron blithely suggested that they should take a trip together. "He told me that I was under the influence of this communist cell" run by her husband, Sara recalled. "And that they were dictat-ing to me what to do, and that I was in a state of complete madness. I told him, 'Yep, I think you're right. The only thing I can do is to work through it and do whatever they say.'" Ron replied that the Commu-nists had hypnotized her. Sara played along, but insisted she would have to go through the divorce; only then would she be able to break free of their power.

"You know, I'm a public figure and you're nobody," Ron said, "so if you have to go through the divorce, I'll accuse you of desertion so it

Sara Northrup Hubbard in April 1951, when she was suing
Hubbard for the return of their baby daughter, Alexis

won't look so bad on my public record." As long as she was going to get
Alexis back as part of the bargain, Sara agreed.

On the day of the divorce, Ron was convinced that the spell the
Communists had cast over Sara would be broken, and she would come
back to him. When they walked out of the courtroom, Sara told him
that she had to get their daughter. Ron took her to the place where
Alexis was being held. Sara said that the last thing she had to do was go
to the airport. She already had a ticket. Then the enchantment would
dissolve and she would be free.

On the day of her scheduled departure, Ron drove Sara and Alexis
to the airport. "We got halfway there and he said he wasn't going to do
it," Sara recalled.

"You're going to get on that plane and go away, aren't you?" Ron
said.

"Well, I have to follow their dictates," Sara replied. "I'll just go to
the airplane."

Ron parked the car. He told her that he couldn't stand the idea that she would be under the influence of psychiatrists, and that he might never see either of them again. "I'm not going to let you go," he said.

"I got out of the car, it was on the edge of the airfield," Sara remembered. "I left all Alexi's clothes in the car, I left my suitcase, one of her shoes fell off and I had my purse. I just ran across the airfield, across the runways, to the airport and got on the plane. And it was the nineteenth of June and it was the happiest day of my life."

IN THE SPACE of a year, Hubbard had gone from destitution and obscurity to great wealth and international renown, followed by a crashing descent. The foundation he had created to train auditors plummeted into debt and soon declared bankruptcy. Close supporters, such as John Campbell and Dr. Winter, deserted. Dianetics proved to be a fad that had swept the country, infatuating tens or even hundreds of thousands of people, but then burned itself out more quickly than the hula hoop.

Once again, Hubbard got a house trailer, and this time he drove it to Lawrence, Kansas, where Russell Hays now lived. Hays instructed Hubbard to park his trailer on some raw land he owned nearby. "That didn't please him," Hays said. "I wouldn't want to have to live with him, he'd get on my nerves." Hubbard was drinking and had a number of drugs along with him, and he pressed Hays to supply him with marijuana. Hays later dried some horseweed and mailed it to Hubbard, signing the letter, "I. M. Reefer."

Hays advised the discouraged Hubbard to make use of his extensive mailing list. There were many followers who still believed in the man and his method. Some had had meaningful emotional breakthroughs. Others had experiences—such as leaving their bodies—that conclusively proved to them the validity of Hubbard's claims. These acolytes provided the bedrock of support that Hubbard needed to regenerate his broken organization, rebuild his finances, and repair the stain on his reputation caused by his personal scandals.

In addition to Hubbard's relentless self-confidence, several new factors salvaged his movement. He had a new device, the E-Meter, developed by one of his followers, which Hubbard revealed in March 1952. The E-Meter would replace the Dianetic reverie with what appeared to be a more scientific approach, one that didn't look so much like a hypnotic trance. "It sees all, knows all," Hubbard declared. "It is never wrong." And he had a new wife, Mary Sue Whipp, a petite Texan, twenty years his junior, whom he married that same month. She was already pregnant with the first of their four children.

Hubbard also had a new name for his movement. From now on, it was Scientology.

3

Going Overboard

Given his biography, it would be easy to dismiss Hubbard as a fraud, but that would fail to explain his total absorption in his project. He would spend the rest of his life elaborating his theory and—even more obsessively—constructing the intricate bureaucracy designed to spread and enshrine his visionary understanding of human behavior. His life narrowed down to his singular mission. Each passageway in his interior expedition led him deeper into his imagination. That journey became Scientology, a totalistic universe in which his every turn was mapped and described.

Hubbard's own logic was inclining him toward conclusions that he was at first reluctant to draw. By admitting the validity of prenatal memories, he was bound to confront a dilemma: What if the memories didn't stop there? When patients began having "sperm dreams," Hubbard had to accept the idea that prenatal engrams were recorded *"as early as shortly before conception."* Then, when patients began to remember previous lives, Hubbard resisted the idea; it threatened to tear apart his organization. "The subject of past deaths and past lives is so full of tension that as early as last July 1950, the board of trustees of the [Dianetics] Foundation sought to pass a resolution banning the entire subject," he confided. Still, the implications were intriguing. What if we have lived before? Might there be memories that occasionally leak through into present time? Wouldn't that prove that we are immortal beings, only temporarily residing in our present incarnations?

Instead of remembering, the patient undergoing Dianetic counseling "returns" to the past-life event. "There is a different feel to another period in time that's so basic it's hard to describe," Hubbard's top US executive, Helen O'Brien, recalled. "If you find yourself in a room, there may be color with unfamiliar tones because of gaslight shining on it. The air has a strange quality. Its particles of dust derive from unmodern constituents. Even human bodies seem to radiate a different kind of warmth when they are covered with the fabrics of another age. Memory, per se, filters out all that. When you return, you find the past intact." Some of the "returnings" were shocking or painful. O'Brien's first past-life experience in an auditing session was that of being a young Irish woman in the early nineteenth century. She could feel the coarse texture of her full-skirted dress as she walked down a narrow country lane, hearing the birds and feeling the warm country air. But when she turned a corner of her house, she saw a British soldier bayoneting her fourteen-year-old son in the yard. "I literally shuddered with grief," O'Brien writes. When the soldier threw her to the ground and tried to rape her, she spit in his face. He crushed her skull with a cobblestone. O'Brien's auditor had her re-experience the scene over and over until she was able to move through the entire bloody tableau unaffected. "By the end of it, I was luxuriously comfortable in every fibre," she writes. "When I walked downstairs . . . the electric lights dazzled me. The clean modern lines of the house interior, and the furniture, were elegant and strange to me beyond all description. I was freshly there from another age. For the first time in this lifetime, I knew I was beyond the laws of space and time.

"I was never the same again."

With his new acceptance of past-life experiences, Hubbard could now describe the individual as being divisible into three parts. First there was the spirit, or soul, which Hubbard calls the thetan. The thetan normally lives in or near a body but can also be entirely separate from it. When a person goes exterior, for instance, it is the thetan part of him that travels outside the body or views himself from across the room. The mind, which serves mainly as a storehouse of pictures, functions as a communication and control system for the thetan, helping him operate in his environment. The body is merely the physical composition of the person, existing in space and time.

Anyone who stands in the way of a thetan's spiritual progress is a Suppressive Person (SP). This is a key concept in Scientology. Hubbard uses the term to describe a sociopath. The Suppressive instinctively fights against constructive forces and is driven berserk by those who try to help others. Hubbard estimates that Suppressives constitute about twenty percent of the population, but only about two and a half percent are truly dangerous. "A Suppressive Person will goof up or vilify any effort to help anybody and particularly knife with violence anything calculated to make human beings more powerful or more intelligent," Hubbard writes. "The artist in particular is often found as a magnet for persons with anti-social personalities who see in his art something which must be destroyed."

Naturally, anyone who is close to a Suppressive Person is in great danger of falling under his influence. Hubbard called that person a Potential Trouble Source. If, for instance, a parent opposes a child who wants to join Scientology, that parent is likely to be declared an SP; and as long as the child remains in contact with the parent, he is in danger of being defined as a PTS. He will be denied auditing and training. Eventually, the child will have to make a choice, either to leave the church—which offers him a path to career success, personal improvement, and salvation—or to disconnect from his parent, who is the cause of his failure to achieve happiness and realize his dreams.

Hubbard had learned some difficult lessons from his experience with Dianetics. He was by nature an autocrat, but his work beckoned to amateurs. The movement inspired by his book had sprung up so quickly there was no real chance to rein it in and exert the kind of authority that might have made it more durable. Although he tried to impose order by creating professional training schools for auditors, in truth he had more or less surrendered control of the movement from the moment of inception by empowering his readers to become practitioners themselves; all they had to do was to follow the formulas sketched in his book. Entrepreneurs grabbed hold of the concept and snatched it out of his hands. They spread the message, but they also diluted it. When the Dianetics movement subsided, Hubbard was unable to restore the momentum that had given it such a rocket-powered launch. Imitators and competitors came onto the field, some even rivaling Hubbard himself. He was determined not to make the same mistakes with Scientology. From now on, he would exercise total control. His word was law. He was not just the founder, he was "Source"—the last word, whose every pronouncement was scripture.

In the evolution of Dianetics to Scientology, however, there was a larger wheel turning inside Hubbard's protean imagination. Until now, religion had played little or no part in his life or his thought—except, perhaps, as it was reflected in the cynical remark he is reported to have made on a number of occasions, "I'd like to start a religion. That's where the money is." One of the problems with Dianetics, from a moneymaking perspective, was the lack of a long-term association on the part of its adherents. Psychotherapy has a theoretical conclusion to it; the patient is "cured" or decides that the procedure doesn't work for him. In either case, the revenue dries up. Religion solves that problem. In addition to tax advantages, religion supplies a commodity that is always in demand: salvation. Hubbard ingeniously developed Scientology into a series of veiled revelations, each of which promised greater abilities and increased spiritual power. "To keep a person on the Scientology path," Hubbard once told one of his associates, "feed him a mystery sandwich."

It may be true that his decision to take his movement in a new direction had more to do with the legal and tax advantages that accrue to religious organizations than it did with actual spiritual inspiration. He was desperate for money. The branches of his Dianetics Foundation were shuttered, one after another. At one point, Hubbard even lost the rights to the name Dianetics. The trend for his movement was toward disaster.

A letter Hubbard wrote to one of his executives in 1953 shows him weighing the advantages of setting up a new organization. "Perhaps we could call it a Spiritual Guidance Center," he speculates. "And we could put in nice desks and our boys in neat blue with diplomas on the walls and 1. knock psychotherapy into history and 2. make enough money to shine up my operating scope and 3. keep the HAS [Hubbard Association of Scientologists] solvent. It is a problem of practical business.

"I await your reaction on the religion angle."

In the anti-Scientology narrative, this is one of several clear statements of Hubbard's calculations and proof that the "church" was nothing more than a moneymaking front. But Hubbard follows this with the observation, "We're treating present time beingness, psychotherapy treats the past and the brain. And brother, that's religion, not mental science." At the end of that year, Hubbard incorporated three different churches: the Church of American Science, the Church of Spiritual Engineering, and the eventual winner in the brand-name contest, the Church of Scientology. The Church of Scientology of California was established on February 18, 1954, quickly followed by another in Washington, DC.

The fields of psychotherapy and religion have bled into each other on many occasions. They have in common the goal of reshaping one's view of the world and letting go of, or actually renouncing, one's previous stance.* Hubbard said there were "many, many reasons" to ally Scientology with religion. "To some this seems mere opportunism," he later admitted to a reporter. "To some it would seem that Scientology is simply making itself bulletproof in the eyes of the law."

Among the many other incentives to turn Hubbard's movement into a religion, there is one that might be considered especially in light of the frequent charge that he was insane. Religion is always an irrational enterprise, no matter how ennobling it may be to the human spirit. In many cultures, people who might be considered mentally ill in Western societies are thought of as religious healers, or shamans. Anthropologists have called schizophrenia the "shaman sickness," because part of a shaman's traditional journey requires suffering an illness that cannot be cured except by spiritual means. The shaman uses the powers and insights he gains from his experience to heal his community. This is exactly the history that Hubbard paints as his own: a blind cripple in the Navy hospital, given up for lost, who then heals himself through techniques he refines into Dianetics. This is the gift he humbly offers as a means of healing humanity. "The goal of Dianetics is a sane

---

*Harriet Whitehead, an anthropologist who conducted fieldwork in Scientology in the United States and the United Kingdom between 1969 and 1971, writes of the "fundamental kinship" between psychotherapy and religion. "The cosmological system that surrounds a renunciatory discipline cannot for long remain 'secular,' that is, finite and this-worldly, in its orientation," she writes. "This is one of the reasons . . . secular therapeutic doctrines often develop a religious or mystical cast." Although Freud was a nonreligious Jew, the techniques of analysis he developed may have had their roots in certain mystical practices rooted in the kabbalah, such as the interpretation of dreams and the use of free association to uncover hidden motivations. Jung subsequently steered psychoanalysis into deeply spiritual waters—a course, as Whitehead points out, that parallels the evolution of Dianetics into Scientology: "It would thus be facile to dismiss the promulgation of a quasi-empirical supernaturalism in the Dianetics movement as simply the product of amateur theorizing by a spinner of tales, when Hubbard's predecessors who established the framework within which psychotherapy, amateur and otherwise, would subsequently develop, did hardly any better" (Whitehead, *Renunciation and Reformulation*, pp. 27–8).

world—a world without insanity, without criminals and without war," he declares. "It can be stopped only by the insane."

For both the shaman and the schizophrenic, the boundaries between reality and illusion are soft, and consciousness slips easily from one to the other. Hubbard, with his highly imaginative mind, certainly had immediate access to visionary worlds; his science-fiction stories are evidence of that. But it is a different matter to be able to cast the nets of one's imagination into the unconscious and pull out best-selling books. The schizophrenic is rarely so productive in the material world.

Sometimes in Hubbard's writings, however, he puts forward what appear to be fantasies of a highly schizophrenic personality. In 1952, for instance, he began talking about "injected entities," which can paralyze portions of the anatomy or block information from being audited. These entities can be located in the body, always in the same places. For instance, one of the entities, the "crew chief," is found on the right side of the jaw down to the shoulder. "They are the 'mysterious voices' in the heads of some preclears," Hubbard said. "Paralysis, anxiety stomachs, arthritis and many ills and aberrations have been relieved by auditing them. An E-Meter shows them up and makes them confess their misdeeds. They are probably just compartments of the mind which, cut off, begin to act as though they were persons."

Hubbard says there are actually two separate genetic lines that, in the history of evolution, first came together in the mollusk, but have been contending for dominance ever since, even in human beings. "In the bivalve state, one finds them at war with each other in an effort to attain sole command of the entire bivalve," Hubbard writes. This primordial contest manifests itself in higher forms of life in such things as right- and left-handedness. "Your discussion of these incidents with the uninitiated in Scientology can produce havoc," Hubbard warns. "Should you describe the 'Clam' to someone, you may restimulate him to the point of causing severe jaw hinge pain. One such victim, after hearing about a clam death, could not use his jaws for three days."

HUBBARD'S THIRD WIFE was smart and poised, a decorous partner for him. She was so slight and weightless that it might be easy to overlook her, but her Southern manners and Texas accent concealed a hard and determined nature. Unlike Sara or Polly, Mary Sue was

Mary Sue and Ron with Diana, Quentin, Arthur, and Suzette

a true believer, a natural enforcer. One of Hubbard's executives later described her as "pragmatic, cold, cunning, calculating, efficient, and fiercely loyal." She had flinty blue eyes, a sharp, prominent nose, and a rare lopsided smile that would expose her uneven, slightly crossed front teeth.

Ron and Mary Sue, with their burgeoning family, began a restless search for a new home—for themselves and for the international headquarters of the church. In 1955, they moved to Washington, DC, but they stayed only a few months before moving to London. Less than two years later, they were back in Washington, living in a dignified brownstone near Dupont Circle, across the street from the Academy of Scientology. Hubbard was prospering once again, with mounting commissions from the sale of E-Meters and training processes, and royalties from sixty books in print. In 1956, his salary from the church was only five hundred dollars a month; but the following year, the church began paying him a percentage of its gross profits, and his income took a gigantic leap.

In Washington, Hubbard set up visiting hours from four to six every afternoon, and made a point of warning the pilgrims who trod the path to his door not to mistake him for a god or a guru, "so knock off the idolizing." And yet he couldn't resist exaggerating his status. Identifying himself as a nuclear physicist, Hubbard published a book in 1957, *All About Radiation*, in which he promoted a formula he called Dianazene, a mixture of nicotinic acid and vitamins, that was supposed to cure cancer as well as sunburns. "It should be taken daily," he recommended, "with milk and chocolate."

Ron and Mary Sue had four children in six years. Diana, born in 1952, was the eldest and clearly the dominant one. She had her father's red hair and a generous splattering of freckles. Quentin, born two years later, was the only one who was not a radiant redhead; he was small with ash-blond hair, like Mary Sue, and would always be his mother's favorite. Suzette was a year younger; she was a cheerful child, but somewhat overshadowed by her big sister. The baby, Arthur, was born in 1958. Seen together, the Hubbard family made a vivid impression, with their ruddy complexions and their striking hair color.

Although the children had a nanny, they spent much of their time unsupervised. School was an afterthought; it wasn't until Diana demanded to learn how to write her name that the children began their education. Mary Sue was a chilly presence as a mother; she rarely cuddled or even touched her children, but in the early years she would read to them—*Mary Poppins*, *Winnie the Pooh*, and Kipling's stories—in her slight Texas twang. As she took on additional responsibility in Scientology, she became even more removed; but Ron would hug the kids and toss them in the air. The house echoed with his booming laugh. He taught the children how to play "Chopsticks" on the piano and showed them card tricks with his quick hands and perfectly manicured fingernails. He would play records and dance with the children to Beethoven or Ravel or Edvard Grieg's Peer Gynt Suite—bold, soaring music. He liked to sing, and he would burst into "Farewell and Adieu to You Fair Spanish Ladies," and "Be Kind to Your Web-Footed Friends," a children's song that is sung to the tune of "The Stars and Stripes Forever." He was fanatical about taking vitamins, and he made sure the children took theirs, as well. Afterward, they would all roar to see who was the strongest.

Hubbard was restless in Washington, and in 1959 he moved his family back to England, to a luxurious estate in Sussex called Saint Hill Manor, which he purchased from the Maharajah of Jaipur. Hubbard employed an extensive household staff, including two butlers, a housekeeper, a nanny, a tutor for the children, a chauffeur, and main-

Hubbard using the E-Meter on a tomato in
1968 to test whether it experiences pain

tenance workers for the estate. "Dr." Hubbard presented himself to
the curious British press as an experimental horticultural scientist; to
prove it, he allowed a photograph to be published of himself staring
intently at a tomato that was attached to an E-Meter. The headline in
Garden News was "Plants Do Worry and Feel Pain."

The grand mansion was a terrific playground for the children. It
was actually a U-shaped castle with crenelated rooflines, ivy-covered
walls, and rumors of ghosts. There were fifty-two rolling acres to play
in, with rose gardens, goldfish ponds, and a lake. The house itself had
sweeping staircases, elevators, and even secret rooms where the children could hide from the nanny. The children also prowled through
their mother's closet. Left to herself, Mary Sue was an indifferent
dresser, but Ron brought tailors from London carrying gorgeous bolts
of cloth, and racks of clothing brought in from the top department
stores, all in Mary Sue's size. Her closet was full of sparkling gowns
and shimmering dresses. Trim and regal by nature, Mary Sue was a
wonderful model, but she really only dressed for him.

Hubbard's third-floor research room was the enticing inner sanctum; it was painted royal blue, with a bear rug in front of the fireplace, and a private bathroom that was redolent of the Spanish sandalwood soap he favored. Hubbard would disappear into his office every day for hours and hours, alone with his E-Meter, "mapping out the bank and looking for the next undercut," as he explained, meaning that he was trying to inventory the reactive mind and discover a path through its many snares.

School was, as usual, a secondary consideration. The children would take a taxi to class, when they actually went. Their father didn't really believe in public education, so he didn't pressure them. Sometimes, they had a tutor, but it was Diana who taught Suzette how to read. She didn't want Suzette to suffer the same embarrassment she had when she started school so far behind her peers. By the age of nine, Suzette was reading adult literature. She decided she wanted to be a writer, like her father. Quentin developed an obsession with airplanes, and he would often persuade the nanny or the chauffeur to take him to

Hubbard at Saint Hill Manor in 1959 showing an E-Meter to his children, Quentin, Diana, Suzette, and Arthur

Gatwick Airport instead of to class, so he could watch the various aircraft taking off and landing. He loved to stand near the runway with the heavy planes lumbering just overhead. He was soon able to close his eyes and identify the make of the plane strictly by its sound.

In school, other children would ask the older Hubbard kids about their father and what was going on in the castle. They realized that they didn't actually know. One day, Diana, Quentin, and Suzette marched into Hubbard's office and demanded, "What is this 'Scientology'?" Hubbard put them all on a starter Dianetics course.

Scientology was in its formative stage, still unfurling from Hubbard's imaginative mind. This was a volatile moment in Hubbard's life and the development of his movement. The fervent response of so many to his revelations must have added reality and substance to what otherwise might have seemed mere fantasies. Not only was he inventing a new religion, he was also reinventing himself as a religious leader. He was creating the legend of who he was in the minds of those who believed in him. And inevitably, he became imprisoned by their expectations.

His followers lived in a state of constant anticipation, trading legends among themselves about the marvels they had experienced or heard about, and speculating upon what was to come. Moments of magic and transcendence kept reason at bay. Ken Urquhart, who served as Hubbard's butler and later as his secretary—or "Communicator"—recalls coaching a "little old English lady" on a Scientology training exercise. As he observed her, "I noticed her nice skin, her eyes, eyebrows. I noted that behind the skin on her forehead was the bone of her forehead, and I knew that behind that lay her brain. As I thought that thought, her forehead absolutely disappeared. I was looking directly at her brain. I was first astounded and then quickly horrified. Here I was exposing her brain to germs and the cold. At once her forehead was back in place."

If Scientology really did bestow enhanced powers upon its adherents, Hubbard himself—of all people—should be able to exercise them. Hubbard's frailties were obvious to everyone; among other things, his hands shook from palsy and he was hard of hearing, constantly exclaiming, "What? What?" He sensed the presumptions that surrounded him. "Your friends," he said one day to Urquhart as his bath was being prepared, "might be curious as to why I employ somebody to open the shutters in my room when I can do it myself." He meant that he should be able, by sheer mental power, to project his intention and the shutters would open themselves. "Well, a lot of people would like me to appear in the sky over New York so as to impress the world. But if I were to do that I'd overwhelm a lot of people. I'm not here to overwhelm." Urquhart thought of saying that he was perfectly willing to be overwhelmed in order to see such a demonstration, but he wasn't altogether sure that Hubbard could actually do it. The failure of Hubbard's followers to challenge him made them complicit in the creation of the mythical figure that he became. They conspired to protect the image of L. Ron Hubbard, the prophet, the revelator, and the friend of mankind.

On the other hand, there were moments when Hubbard seemed to be toying with the limits of possibility. It was rumored that he could move the clouds around in the sky or stir up dust devils in his wake. Urquhart remembers a time when Hubbard was talking to him while sitting in a chair more than an arm's length away. "My attention wandered," he recalled. Suddenly, he felt a finger poking him in the ribs. "I came back. He was talking away, grinning and eyes twinkling. He had not moved his arms or gotten up from the chair." Such ineffable experiences seemed to add up to something, although it was not clear what that might be.

Hubbard's neighbors soon learned more about the new lord of the manor. Scientology's expansion, coupled with the increasingly bold claims that Hubbard made about the health benefits that could be expected, brought the organization under scrutiny by various governments. The first blow was a 1963 raid by US Marshals, acting on a warrant issued by the Food and Drug Administration to seize more than a hundred E-Meters stored in the Washington church. The FDA charged that the labeling for the E-Meter suggested that it was effective in diagnosing and treating "all mental and nervous disorders and illnesses," as well as "psychosomatic ailments of mankind such as arthritis, cancer, stomach ulcers, and radiation burns from atomic bombs, poliomyelitis, the common cold, etc."*

The IRS began an audit that would strip the church of its religious

---

*A federal district court eventually allowed E-Meters to be used for "bona fide religious counseling," but ordered that each device bear a warning that "the E-Meter is not medically or scientifically useful for the diagnosis, treatment or prevention of any disease. It is not medically or scientifically capable of improving the health or bodily functions of anyone" (Amended Order of US District Court for the District of Columbia, No.71–2064, Mar. 1, 1973).

tax exemption in 1967. At the same time, an Australian government board of inquiry produced a sweeping report that was passionate in its condemnation. "There are some features of Scientology which are so ludicrous that there may be a tendency to regard Scientology as silly and its practitioners as harmless cranks. To do so would be gravely to misunderstand the tenor of the Board's conclusions," the report began, then emphatically added: "*Scientology is evil, its techniques evil, its practice a serious threat* to the community, medically, morally and socially; and its adherents sadly deluded and *often mentally ill*." The report admitted that there were "transient gains" realized by some of the religion's adherents, but said that the organization plays on those gains in order to produce "a subservience amounting almost to mental enslavement." As for Hubbard himself, the board described him as "a man of restless energy" who is "constantly experimenting and speculating, and equally constantly he confuses the two." "Some of his claims are that . . . he has been up in the Van Allen Belt, that he has been on the planet Venus where he inspected an implant station, and that he has been to Heaven. He even recommends a protein formula for feeding non-breast fed babies—a mixture of boiled barley and corn syrup—stating that he 'picked it up in Roman days.' " Although Hubbard has "an insensate hostility" to psychiatrists and people in the field of mental health, the report noted, he is himself "mentally abnormal," evincing a "persecution complex" and "an imposing aggregation of symptoms which, in psychiatric circles, are strongly indicative of a condition of paranoid schizophrenia with delusions of grandeur—symptoms common to dictators." The report led to a ban of Scientology in two Australian states,* and prompted similar inquiries in New Zealand, Britain, and South Africa. Hubbard believed that the US Food and Drug Administration, along with the FBI and CIA, were feeding slanderous information about the church to various governments.

In the midst of all this upheaval, in February 1966 Hubbard finally declared another "first Clear." This time it was John McMaster, a dapper, blond South African, in his mid-thirties, who was the director of the Hubbard Guidance Center at the church's Saint Hill headquarters. Charming, ascetic, and well-spoken, McMaster had dropped out of medical school to become an auditor. He immediately proved to be a far more urbane representative of Scientology than Hubbard. His wry

*The ban was repealed in 1973.

manner made him a welcome guest on talk shows and on the lecture circuit, where he portrayed Scientology as a cool and nonthreatening route to self-realization. Suddenly the idea of going Clear began to catch on. McMaster adopted a clerical outfit that befitted his designation as the church's unofficial ambassador to the United Nations. At one point, Hubbard designated him Scientology's first "pope." It was a matter of puzzlement to Hubbard's closest associates, given Hubbard's disparagement of homosexuals in his books, that he would enlist a person to serve as the church's representative who was obviously gay. "He was very pronounced in his affect," one of Hubbard's medical officers remembered. But Hubbard's relationship to homosexuality was apparently more complicated in life than in theory.

CONVINCED THAT the British, American, and Soviet governments were interested in gaining control of Scientology's secrets in order to use them for evil intentions, Hubbard began looking for a safe harbor—ideally, a country that he could rule over. England had taken steps to "curb the growth" of Scientology, and Hubbard took the hint. He also suffered from the damp weather. "I had been ill with pneumonia for the third time in England and on the suggestion of my doctor was seeking a warmer climate for a short while in order to recover," he said, in an unprompted explanation to the CIA. He resigned as Executive Director of the Church of Scientology and sold his interests in the Hubbard Association of Scientologists International, although he maintained actual control of the organization through his innumerable telexes. He journeyed to Rhodesia, the South African republic that had recently declared its independence from the United Kingdom (it later became Zimbabwe). Isolated, diplomatically spurned, and subject to international sanctions, the Rhodesian government served a clique of white colonists who ruled over an insurgent black majority. To Hubbard, Rhodesia seemed ripe for a takeover. He felt a kinship with the republic's dashing and flamboyant founder, Cecil John Rhodes, who also had red hair and a taste for swashbuckling adventure. Hubbard believed he might have been Rhodes in a previous life, although it's unclear whether he knew that Rhodes was homosexual.

Hubbard had a fantasy that he would be welcomed in Rhodesia, that the black population would embrace him like a brother, and that eventually he would become its leader, issuing passports and his own currency. However, the current prime minister, Ian Smith, was desperately trying to negotiate a settlement with the black nationalist movement that would preserve white-minority rule. Hubbard thoughtfully wrote up a constitution for the government that he claimed would accomplish just that, but he couldn't get anyone to take it seriously.

While Hubbard talked about his big plans for developing the country, the government became increasingly suspicious of his motives and his resources. Ultimately, Hubbard's visa was not renewed. "He told me Ian Smith was going to be shot because he was a 'Suppressive,' " John McMaster said. "The real reason that Hubbard was kicked out of Rhodesia was that his cheques bounced."

Hubbard returned to England with a new scheme. If the world's governments were lining up against him, he would put himself beyond reach. Scientologists were whispering about a clandestine "sea project" that their leader was planning. He quietly began acquiring a small fleet of oceangoing vessels. Then he disappeared again.

This time, he went to Tangier, the Moroccan city on the Strait of Gibraltar, which was a famous hangout for hipsters and artists. There he began his research on Operating Thetan Level Three (OT III), his "Wall of Fire." Mary Sue and the children remained in England, but Hubbard wrote to her daily, complaining of a barking dog that was interrupting his work, and various ailments—a bad back, and a lung problem that emerged from a lingering cold. He admitted that he was "drinking lots of rum" and taking drugs—"pinks and grays"—while he was doing his research. He would sign off on the letters, "Your Sugie." Hubbard stayed only a month in Tangier before moving to Las Palmas in the Canary Islands, where one of his followers found him deeply depressed and surrounded by pills of all kinds. "I want to die," he said. Alarmed, Mary Sue flew down to take care of him.

In September 1967, Hubbard made a recording for his followers to explain his absence and inform them of important discoveries in his OT III research. "All this recent career has been relatively hard on this poor body," he relates. "I've broken its back, broken its knee, and now I have a broken arm, because of the strenuousness of these particular adventures. One wonders then, well, if he is in such good shape what is he doing breaking up his body? Well, that is the trouble. I have great difficulty getting down to the small power level of a body."

He also notes that he had directed Mary Sue to find out who was behind the attacks on Scientology that were turning the governments against the organization. Mary Sue had hired "several professional intelligence agents," who uncovered a conspiracy. "Our enemies on this planet are less than twelve men," Hubbard discloses. "They own and control newspaper chains and they are oddly enough directors in all the mental health groups in the world." Their plan was to "use mental health, which is to say psychiatric electric shock and prefrontal lobotomy, to remove from their path any political dissenters." For the first time, he openly talks about the Sea Organization, or Sea Org, an elite group who would form the committed inner core of the religion, Hubbard's disciples, a Scientology clergy.

HANA STRACHAN (now Hana Eltringham Whitfield) was one of the first young recruits admitted into the Sea Org. Her deranged and manipulative mother was a follower of Helena Blavatsky, the nineteenth-century spiritualist who was the founder of the Theosophical Society. When Hana was about fifteen, she learned that Blavatsky had prophesied a new race that would arise in the Americas in the 1950s; Hana was under the impression that it would be led by a man with red hair.

Hana escaped her traumatic family situation to become a nurse in Johannesburg, South Africa. A medical student there gave her a copy of *Dianetics*. It made immediate sense to her. She went to the local organization and said she wanted to learn more. "There's a course starting tonight," she was told. In the hallway of the office Hana noticed a photograph of Hubbard standing outside the Saint Hill headquarters. She was transfixed by his red hair. This must be the man Blavatsky was talking about, she decided. "That sealed it for me," she said. She moved to Saint Hill and became Clear #60. For three weeks she was in a state of euphoria, feeling slightly detached from her environment and her body. "This is who we were in eons past," she thought. She was convinced that Hubbard was a returned savior who would bring all humanity to an enlightened state.

Slender and stately, Hana was one of the first thirty-five Sea Org recruits. The mission of the Sea Org, according to the contract she signed, is "to get ETHICS IN on this PLANET AND THE UNIVERSE." She agreed to "subscribe to the discipline, mores and conditions of this group. . . . THEREFORE, I CONTRACT MYSELF TO THE SEA ORGANIZATION FOR THE NEXT BILLION YEARS."*

Hana married another Sea Org member, an American named Guy Eltringham, but they were separated when Hubbard ordered her to Las Palmas, where he was refitting an exhausted fishing trawler called the *Avon River*. The decks and the hold were coated with decades of fish oil that had to be scraped away. During the two months the *Avon River* was in dry dock, Hubbard would often linger for dinner with his Sea Org crew, and afterward he would sit on the deck and regale them with stories. Hubbard's depression had lifted and he seemed completely in control—relaxed and confident, even jovial. The crew were mainly drinking Spanish wines, but Hubbard favored rum and Coke—an eighth of a glass of Coke and seven-eighths rum—one after another through the evening. The heavens seemed very close in the dark harbor. Hubbard would point to the sky and say, "That is where the Fifth Invaders came from. They're the bad guys, they're the ones who put us here." He said he could actually spot their spaceships crossing in front of the stars, and he would salute them as they passed overhead, just to let them know that they had been seen.

During a session with her auditor, Hana revealed the story of Madame Blavatsky's prophecy of the red-haired man. Soon afterward, Hubbard came up on deck and gave her an intense look. From that point on, she became his favorite. He appointed her the first female Sea Org lieutenant. That day, she had a photograph made of herself in her Sea Org uniform—white shirt, dark tie and jacket, with a lanyard over one shoulder. She is young and elegant, her blond hair pulled back in a ponytail. After that, she rose through the Sea Org ranks with astonishing speed, often wondering if the revelation about the red-haired man was responsible for her rapid promotions.

Hubbard would drive over from his villa in Las Palmas to inspect the work on the *Avon River*. The lower holds of the ship were converted into offices and berthing spaces; new equipment—including radar and a gyrocompass—were installed, the screw replaced, and the hydraulic

*According to the church, "The first Sea Organization members formulated a one-billion-year pledge to symbolize their eternal commitment to the religion and it is still signed by all members today. It is a symbolic document which, similar to vows of dedication in other faiths and orders, serves to signify an individual's eternal commitment to the goals, purposes and principles of the Scientology religion."

system completely overhauled. The inexperienced Sea Org members did most of the work, although Spanish laborers did the welding and sandblasting. Whenever Hubbard spotted something wrong, he would be instantly transformed from the jovial and avuncular figure the crew adored into a raging, implacable tyrant. Hana, who was serving as master-at-arms, would dread seeing the "Commodore"—as Hubbard titled himself—arrive, since she felt responsible if anything went wrong. One day, when the Spanish workmen were painting a rust coat on the hull of the ship, she spotted Hubbard walking across the beach with his chief officer and his first mate, smoking and chatting happily. Then he suddenly stopped. His eyes went into slits and he began bellowing, "The rollers! The rollers!" Puzzled, Hana leaned over the side of the ship, then saw what had caught Hubbard's attention: tiny threads poking through the paint, which had been left by the cheap rollers that the workmen were using. "As those threads decomposed, they would leave little apertures for seawater to leak behind the rust coating," she realized. "It destroyed the integrity of the entire rust coating, and that's what Hubbard was screaming about as he lumbered toward the ship. And what amazed me was that he saw it at forty to sixty feet away from the ship. Later on, I walked that distance from the ship to see if I could see those little hairs coming out of the rust coat. There was no way I could see them. That added to my feeling of wonder and mystique about Hubbard."

IN TRUTH, Hubbard had very poor eyesight. Before the war, both the Naval Academy and the Naval Reserve had rejected him because of his vision, and all during the war he wore glasses. In 1951, when he was being evaluated for a medical disability, his vision tested at 20/200 for each eye, correctable to 20/20 with glasses, much the same as it had been before the war. The examiner noted, "Eyes tire easily, has worn all types of glasses but claims he sees just as well without as with glasses." Was that even possible? Eyesight does change over the years, but Hubbard's eyes were astigmatic—meaning they were more football-shaped than round—and not likely to have improved, certainly not dramatically. And yet many of Hubbard's associates testify to his keen eyesight. Without glasses, Hubbard would have been legally blind; perhaps that's what he was referring to when he said he had cured himself of blindness after the war. But, clearly his eye examination showed different results.

Hubbard had written in *Dianetics* that the eyesight of a Clear gradually improves to optimum perception. And yet, he admitted elsewhere that his vision was so bad in the postwar years that he could scarcely see his typewriter to write. He wore glasses and early versions of contact lenses. Through the use of Dianetic processing, he says, his eyes began to change. Many noticed that Hubbard had a habit of squinting, which has the effect of pressing astigmatic eyeballs into a rounder shape, which might momentarily improve his vision. He theorized that "astigmatism, a distortion of image, is only an anxiety to alter the image." One day, for instance, he was reading an American Medical Association report and couldn't make it out at all. He thought he might have to resort to using a magnifying glass. Then he realized that the reason he couldn't read it was that he wasn't willing to confront what it said. "I threw it aside, picked up a novel and the print was perfect."

Hubbard would sometimes chastise members of his crew about their dependence on eyeglasses, which he said were an admission of "overts"—transgressions against the group. One night as the fleet was sailing in the Caribbean, he looked at the young woman serving him dinner, Tracy Ekstrand, whose glasses were sliding down her nose in the tropical heat. "You're doing yourself an aesthetic disservice," he pronounced. She was mortified and stopped wearing glasses that night. Although she was still able to move from room to room and serve meals, her vision remained quite blurred. Some weeks later, as Hubbard was retiring for the night, he looked at her again. He held up his pack of cigarettes a foot in front of her face and asked if she could read the bold capital letters: "KOOL." Flustered by the personal attention from the Commodore, Ekstrand mumbled the name of the cigarettes. "There's been a shift!" he declared triumphantly, then went to bed. Ekstrand was shaken. "I remained outside his door for some minutes, dumbfounded and unsure how to react," she recalled. "This time there was no question. He was wrong. He was imagining improvement and success with Scientology where there had been none."

All of Hubbard's senses were painfully acute. Each day, every room he inhabited had to be dusted to the point that it would pass a white-glove test. He was fanatically clean but also hypersensitive to soap, so that his clothes had to be rinsed up to fifteen times, and even then he would complain that he could smell the detergent. His chef had to switch from cooking on stainless steel to Corningware because Hubbard complained of the taste of metal in his food. These stories were traded among his disciples as more evidence of his superhuman powers of discernment.

ACCORDING TO SEVERAL Sea Org members, while he was in Las Palmas, Hubbard fell in love with another woman—Yvonne Gillham, the ship's public relations officer. (She would later go on to start the Celebrity Centre in Hollywood.) She had a wide smile, large hazel eyes, and a short pixie haircut, bearing a resemblance to Julie Andrews in *The Sound of Music*. Gillham combined a down-to-earth personality with a touch of class that came from growing up in the high society of Queensland, Australia. Inevitably, Hubbard demanded that she accompany him on the high seas. Gillham had three young children at Saint Hill, and she had only joined the Sea Org on Hubbard's pledge that they could stay with her, but Hubbard's desire for her had become a prison, one that she was too loyal to escape.

Yvonne Gillham in a head shot she used during her modeling career, circa 1952

Hubbard was fifty-six years old in the fall of 1967, when he set sail with his youthful crew. There was no destination or purpose other than to wander. Hubbard was by now portly, ruddy-faced, and jowly; his swept-back, once-red hair had turned strawberry blond. His eyes, which have been described as blue or green by various observers, were actually gray, like seawater, casting an odd flatness over his aspect. Two strong lines transected his face: a deep furrow between his eyebrows, matching the notch below his nose and the cleft in his chin, and his duckbill lips, which were his most prominent feature. Once aboard, he dressed in various naval uniforms befitting his self-appointed station as Commodore of the fleet, with lots of braid and crossed anchors on his cap.

There were three ships in Hubbard's navy. In addition to the *Avon River*, there was a schooner called the *Enchanter*, and the 3,200-ton flagship, a flat-bottom cattle ferry originally called the *Royal Scotsman*, which was renamed the *Royal Scotman* because of a clerical error in the registration. The smokestack was emblazoned with the initials "LRH."

Hubbard spent most of his time in the air-conditioned captain's cabin on the promenade deck of the *Royal Scotman*, surrounded by windows to take in the ocean vistas. He rarely drank on the ship, except perhaps to take the chill off on a cold night on the bridge. Drugs were nowhere in evidence. His days were largely solitary, passed in auditing himself and writing policy papers. His office on the top deck was called the Research Room. It was behind a pair of highly polished wooden doors with brass handles. The floor was a bright red linoleum covered with Oriental rugs; there was a massive mahogany desk and a huge mirror above a fireplace. Crew members passing by on the upper deck could see him writing with his usual rapidity on foolscap, using a green pen for policy bulletins and a red one for the "tech"—that is, his vast corpus of coursework and procedures that comprised Scientology's spiritual technology. His restless leg would be jiggling as his hand raced across the page, faultlessly, in handsome, legible script. For other writing, he turned back to his typewriter. "I think he was doing automatic writing," said Jim Dincalci, one of his medical officers. "The pages would be flying. When he came out of it, he would blink his eyes, as if coming awake, and he did this thing with his lips, smacking."

Hubbard and Mary Sue would dine in his office between eight and ten p.m. Sometime after three in the morning, Dincalci would give

Hubbard a massage and he would go to sleep. After that, everyone on the ship had to be quiet until Hubbard awakened, sometime before noon, and remain absolutely mute while he was auditing himself on the E-Meter.

In Hubbard's opinion, the device operated just below the level of conscious awareness; it somehow knew what you were thinking before you did. It was eerily compelling. Anything that registered on the meter was seen as being significant. The trick was divining what the needle was saying. Sometimes the reaction was so violent that the needle would pound back and forth like a berserk windshield wiper—you could hear it snapping against the pins at either end. Hubbard called this a "rock slam." Anyone who registered such a reaction was deemed psychotic and certain to have committed crimes against Scientology; if that person was in the Sea Org, he would be punished automatically, the crime to be sorted out later.

After initially resisting the concept of past lives, Hubbard became passionately interested in the subject. "We Come Back" was the motto of the Sea Org. Hubbard began recalling many of his own previous existences, which the E-Meter validated. He claimed to have been a contemporary of Machiavelli's, and he was still upset that the author of *The Prince* stole his line "The end justifies the means." He said he had been a marshal to Joan of Arc and Tamburlaine's wife. He told stories about driving a race car in the alien Marcab civilization millions of years before. He came to believe that in some of his past lives on this planet, he had buried treasure in various locations, so he launched an expedition to unearth his ancient hoards. He called it the Mission into Time. He selected a small crew to go on the *Avon River*. Because he wanted to keep the mission secret, he had two long rafts fashioned, which could be rowed ashore under cover of darkness and pulled up on the beach near where he imagined his ancient treasure was buried. When Hana Eltringham saw she wasn't on the list, she wrote Hubbard, pleading to be included, saying she would be willing to perform any duty. To her surprise, Hubbard appointed her chief officer.

One very dark, overcast night in 1968, the *Avon River* dropped anchor on the western coast of Sicily, in the bay of Castellammare del Golfo, beside a steep promontory topped by an ancient watchtower. Hubbard gave his "missionaires" a treasure map he had drawn up based on his past-life recollections. The crew set out in one of the rafts toward the rocky shoreline, lugging ropes, shovels, and metal detectors.

Giggling and tripping over each other, they scrambled up a ten-foot cliff. It was so dark they couldn't see more than a foot in front of their faces. Each had a hand on another's shoulder as they picked their way through stands of cactus along the rocky outcropping. At one point, the leader of the expedition bumped into a cow. The cow started mooing, then a dog barked, and a light went on in a house nearby. Everyone stood dead still until the scene quieted down. Finally, the clouds parted enough for the moon to shine through. The missionaires found some old bricks they thought might have been the ruins of a castle beside the watchtower. The metal detectors found nothing.

Hubbard decided to come along the next day to inspect the site himself. "Yes, yes, this is the place!" he said excitedly. He explained the absence of treasure by saying that it must have been hidden in a portion of the ruined castle that had fallen into the sea.

The expedition moved on to Sardinia, where Hubbard claimed to have had an affair with the priestess in a temple—"liaisons in the moonlight," he told his enchanted missionaires—when he was a Carthaginian sailor. "We had a lot of good-looking girls in Carthage but they didn't come up to her." The *Avon River* next stopped in Calabria, on the toe of Italy, where Hubbard had buried gold in his days as a tax collector in the Roman Empire. None was found, however.

Near Tunis, where the missionaires hoped to dive on the ruins of an ancient underwater city, Hubbard found fault with the captain of the *Avon River*, Joe van Staden, and booted him off the ship. Eltringham was sitting at her desk on the 'tween deck when Hubbard called her into his office and told her she was the new captain of the four-hundred-ton trawler, starting in the morning. Eltringham went back to her desk and put her head in her hands. She was twenty-six years old. Everything she knew about sailing she had learned from Hubbard. To his credit, he had been a good teacher. He had taken a dozen members of the original Sea Org crew and taught them the semaphore code, how to navigate using a sextant, and basic laws of the sea. But she knew nothing about running the engine room, or operating the electronics on the bridge, or docking a ship. Half an hour later, Hubbard stuck his head out of his office and beckoned to her. He was holding an E-Meter. Standing in the doorway where everyone could see them, Hubbard handed her the cans. Then he screwed up his eyes and demanded, "Recall a time you were last a captain." As Eltringham closed her eyes and began to free-associate, Hubbard watched the needle on the E-Meter.

"What's that?" he asked, when the needle suddenly dropped.

"That was sometime on a ship somewhere and the ship was sinking," Eltringham responded.

"Okay, go back earlier." A moment later, he asked her again, "What's that?"

"That's just a lot of confusion. I'm in a cabin with a lot of other people. Something urgent is going on."

Hubbard asked her to talk more about it. Eltringham began to see the incident more clearly. "We were in some kind of spaceship," she said. "We were under attack and—oh my God!—I can see a planet down there! And the planet's on fire! And something is shooting at us and—oh my God!—the spaceship exploded!"

Hubbard asked her to tell the story several more times to destimulate the incident. Then he asked Eltringham how she was feeling.

"I'm fine, sir."

Hubbard screwed up his eyes again. "Do you have any other thoughts about it?" Eltringham realized that he was looking for a floating needle, but she wasn't able to give it to him.

"Okay, one more question. Are you a loyal officer?"

"I don't know what you mean by that," Eltringham said. "I'm loyal to you, and I'm an officer."

Hubbard said, "All right, that's as far as we'll go this time."

Eltringham walked up on the deck and tried to take in what Hubbard meant. Suddenly it came to her. Hubbard wasn't talking about the present. He was referring to the time in her visualization. Some catastrophe must have happened. Eltringham realized that it must have been her planet that was being attacked, and she had been trying to save it.

A few minutes later, Hubbard came up on deck and stood beside her. She turned to him and said, "Yep, you're right, sir. I was a loyal officer. I am."

Hubbard beamed.

THE *AVON RIVER* WAS traveling down the east side of Corsica when Hubbard gathered his crew and read them a new revelation. Nearby, in the north of Corsica, there was an underground space station, he said. He even provided the coordinates. There, a secret doorway would open by a palm print on the lock—but only one person's hand would do the trick. Hubbard smiled suggestively, without saying whose hand that would be. The rock face would slide open, revealing an immense cavern harboring a mother ship and hundreds of smaller craft, all fueled and ready to go.

The space station would remain undiscovered, however. Word arrived that the *Royal Scotman* had run into trouble with the port authorities in Valencia, where Hubbard had hoped to make a permanent base. He furiously abandoned the expedition and ordered the *Avon River* to make haste to Valencia before the *Royal Scotman* was forcibly expelled from the Spanish harbor. The crew was bitterly disappointed that they would miss uncovering the space station. "If there's time, we'll come back," Hubbard promised.

After making amends with the port captain in Valencia, Hubbard threw a party to report on the Mission into Time. He was loud and affected, in what Eltringham privately called his "full pantomime mode." Such moments made her cringe. She hid in the back of the crowd. She genuinely revered Hubbard, but when he was strutting in front of his acolytes, he could become comically self-important, a parody of himself. His eyes rolled, his body language was inappropriate and weird, and his hands flew around meaninglessly in odd directions. Sometimes he spoke with a British accent or a Scottish brogue. In her opinion, his performance was ridiculous, but also disturbing. If the man she regarded as a savior was a "nut case," what did that say about his teachings? What did it say about her, that she idolized him while at the same time harboring these illicit feelings of shame? No one else seemed to share these warring perceptions. She felt very much alone.

Hubbard regaled the crowd with the story of his romance with the temple priestess in Sardinia when he was a Carthaginian sailor. "The girl would say, 'Hey, how are YOU?' and all the other guys didn't stand a chance for a while. If you've got enough war vessels and you're making enough dough, girls usually say this."

He said he had recently remembered a secret passageway into the temple. "Missions were sent ashore to survey and map the area to see if they couldn't discover this old secret entrance to the temple." If they found it, that would prove the truthfulness of his past-life recollections, what he called the "whole track memory."

"And now," he said, "I'm going to call on Hana Eltringham to tell you whether or not it was a positive result."

Mortified, Eltringham stood in front of her colleagues and ratified

Hubbard's findings. "We did find the tunnel," she said, mentioning a ditch that the missionaires had found, which had a tile base. "So that was totally proven and accurate."

THE ANTICIPATION SURROUNDING the release of OT III was intense, so when Hubbard finally made it available to a select group of Sea Org members, in March 1968 aboard the *Royal Scotman* in Valencia, a thrill radiated through the entire crew. The saga of Hubbard's research in Tangier and Las Palmas led them to think that this was the breakthrough that would lead to the salvation of the planet. They—the Sea Org—would be the vanguard of this movement, newly empowered by the revelations that Hubbard promised.

In a lecture aboard the ship, Hubbard said that in researching OT III, he had uncovered two "incidents"—which, for him, meant implants—that prevented thetans from being free. Incident One was a kind of Garden of Eden fall from grace that occurred four quadrillion years ago, which is when Hubbard dates the origin of the universe. Before Incident One, thetans were in a pure, godlike state. Suddenly, there was a loud snap and a flood of light. A chariot appeared, trailed by a trumpeting cherub; then darkness. This incident marked the moment when thetans became separated from their original static condition and created the physical universe of matter, energy, space, and time (MEST). In the process, they lost awareness of their immortality.

Incident Two is central to the OT III saga. This one took place seventy-five million years ago in the Galactic Confederacy, which was composed of seventy-six planets and twenty-six stars. "The world we live in now replicates the civilization of that period," Hubbard said. "People at that particular time and place were walking around in clothes which looked very remarkably like the clothes they wear this very minute. . . . The cars they drove looked exactly the same, and the trains they ran looked the same, and the boats they had looked the same. Circa nineteen-fifty, nineteen-sixty."

A tyrannical overlord named Xenu ruled the Confederacy. "He was a Suppressive to end all Suppressives," Hubbard told his followers. Xenu had been chosen by a kind of Praetorian guard called the Loyal Officers, but they realized that their leader was wicked and they decided to remove him. Xenu had other plans, Hubbard said. "He took the last moments he had in office to really goof the floof." Xenu and a few evil conspirators—mainly psychiatrists—fed false information to the population to draw them into centers where Xenu's troops could destroy them. "One of the mechanisms they used was to tell them to come in for an income-tax investigation," Hubbard related. "So in they went, and the troops started slaughtering them." The preferred method was to shoot a needle into a lung, paralyzing the thetan with an injection of frozen alcohol and glycol. The frozen bodies were packed into boxes and loaded onto space planes, which resembled the DC-8 jetliner. "No difference—except the DC-8 had fans—propellers—on it and the space plane didn't." In this fashion, billions of thetans were transported to Teegeeack, the planet now called Earth, where they were dropped into volcanoes and then blown up with hydrogen bombs.

Thetans are immortal, however. Freed from their corporeal incarnations, they floated along on the powerful winds created by the explosion. Then they were trapped in an electronic ribbon and placed in front of a "three-D, super colossal motion picture" for thirty-six days, during which time they were subjected to images called R6 implants. "These pictures contain God, the Devil, angels, space opera, theaters, helicopters, a constant spinning, a spinning dancer, trains and various scenes very like modern England. You name it, it's in this implant." The implant included all world religions and "a motion picture studio" complete with screenwriters.

Xenu didn't have much time to gloat over his victory. Some Loyal Officers remained, scattered around the galaxy. There was a civil war, and within a year, the Loyal Officers had captured Xenu and locked him up in an electrified wire cage buried in a mountain. "He is not likely ever to get out," Hubbard said.

Because Teegeeack was a dumping ground for thetans, it became known as the Prison Planet, "the planet of ill repute." The Galactic Confederacy abandoned the area, although various invaders have appeared throughout the millennia. But these free-floating thetans remain behind. They are the souls of people who have been dead for seventy-five million years. They attach themselves to living people because they no longer have free will. There can be millions of them clustered inside a single person's body. Auditing for Scientologists at OT III and above would now focus on eliminating the "body thetans"— or BTs—that stand in the way of spiritual progress.

More than individual salvation was at stake. Hubbard said that the Prison Planet had been civilized many times in the past, but it always arrived at the same end: utter annihilation. No matter how sophisticated mankind became, there was a trigger implanted in the imprisoned thetans that led them to blow themselves to pieces before they could escape their fate and go on to higher levels of existence. The goal of Scientology was to "clear the planet" and save humanity from its endless cycle of self-destruction.

Hubbard never really explained how he came by these revelations. "We won't go into that," he told the crew, saying only that he was fortunate to have somehow escaped the cataclysm so many eons ago. "You are the chosen," he told them. "You are the Loyal Officers. We made the agreement way back when that we would all get together again. This time no one is going to stop us."

Eltringham and two dozen Sea Org members had the honor of being the very first group to view the OT III materials. They went in one by one to read the documents. When she came to the part about the Loyal Officers, Eltringham immediately understood that this was what Hubbard had been talking about: she instinctively felt that she had been among them. At the same time, the account seemed incredible to her, bizarre and completely unfathomable.

Her task now was to take the materials into her cabin, along with an E-Meter, and audit herself to discover and expel body thetans. Once they were exposed and confronted, Hubbard promised, they would take flight, "lickety-split." She began each day with a session, but she couldn't locate any BTs. At the end of the week she turned in her folder and asked for help. She went through review auditing, but it was no use. She began to worry that she was unauditable, what Hubbard called a Dog Case or a Degraded Being—someone who had committed so many misdeeds as to be beyond help. It was all her fault.

Despite the fact that he was only fourteen, Quentin—LRH's heir apparent—was among the first to be initiated into the OT III mysteries. Everyone on the ship knew what was happening, and people would hover near the cabin where the materials were held to see the expression on the faces of those who had been exposed to it. When Quentin emerged, he was pale, and he threw up violently. After that, he was never as sunny as he used to be.

TO MAKE SURE his orders were carried out, Hubbard created the Commodore's Messengers Organization. In the beginning, the Messengers were four young teenage girls, including Yvonne Gillham's two daughters, Terri and Janis, who were thirteen and eleven years old; Annie Tidman, twelve; and, briefly, Hubbard's youngest daughter, Suzette, who was thirteen at the time. Soon, several more teenage girls joined them, and Suzette went to work on the decks. Two of the girls were always posted outside Hubbard's office, waiting to take his hand-written directives to the mimeograph machine or deliver his orders in person. He instructed them to parrot his exact words and tone of voice when they were delivering one of his directives—to inform the captain what time to set sail, for instance, or to tell a member of the crew he was "a fucking asshole" if he had displeased him. Hubbard allowed them to create their own uniforms, so in warmer climates they attired themselves in white hot pants, halter tops, and platform shoes. When the Commodore moved around the ship, one or more Messengers trailed behind him, carrying his hat and an ashtray, lighting his cigarettes, and quickly moving a chair into place if he started to sit down. People lived in fear of Hubbard's teenage minions. They had to call the Messenger "sir" even if she was a twelve-year-old girl. (That practice has continued in the Sea Org. All senior officials are referred to as "sir," regardless of gender.) "They held the power of God in their little hands, their little lips," Eltringham recalled.

The relationship between Hubbard and these girls was intimate but not overtly sexual. They prepared his bath when he retired and would sit outside his room until he awakened and called out, "Messenger!" They would help him out of bed, light his cigarette, run his shower, prepare his toiletries, and help him dress. Some of the children had parents on the ship, others were there alone, but in either case Hubbard was their primary caretaker—and vice versa. When the girls became old enough to start wearing makeup, Hubbard was the one who showed them how to apply it. He also helped them do their hair.

While he was on the ship, Hubbard was working out a code of Scientology ethics. He began with the idea that man is basically good. Even a criminal leaves clues to his crime, because he wishes for someone to stop his unethical behavior, Hubbard theorized. Similarly, a person who has accidentally hurt himself or gotten ill is "putting ethics in on himself" in order to lessen the damage he does to others or to his environment. These were testaments to the basic longing of all people to live decent, worthy lives.

Good and evil actions can be judged only by understanding what

Hubbard termed the Eight Dynamics. The First Dynamic is the Self and its urge toward existence. The Second Dynamic is Sex, which includes the sexual act as well as the family unit. The Third Dynamic is the Group—any school, or class, organization, city, or nation. The Fourth Dynamic is Mankind. The Fifth Dynamic is the urge toward existence of all living creatures, including vegetables and grass—"anything directly and intimately motivated by life." The Sixth Dynamic is the matter, energy, space, and time that compose the reality we live in. The Seventh Dynamic is the Spiritual, which must be obtained before expanding into the Eighth Dynamic, which is called Infinity or God. The Scientology mantra for judging ethical behavior is "the greatest good for the greatest number of dynamics"—a formula that can excuse quite a number of crimes.

Every individual or group moves through stages, which Hubbard calls Ethics Conditions, that incline toward either survival or collapse. They range from the highest state, Power, to the lowest, Confusion. The way to determine what condition one is in at any given moment is through statistics, compiled each Thursday at two p.m. For a Scientology church, the relevant statistic might be how much money it is bringing in. The "org" that brings in less money week after week is in a condition of Non-Existence, which, plotted on a graph, is represented as a steeply plummeting line. A level or slightly declining line indicates a condition of Emergency. Slightly up is Normal; sharply up is Affluence. Every Scientology organization, and every member of its staff, henceforth would be judged by the implacable weekly statistics. Hubbard warned his charges, "You have to establish an ethics presence hard. Otherwise, you're just gonna be wrapped around a telegraph pole."

The years at sea were critical ones for the future of Scientology. Even as Hubbard was inventing the doctrine, each of his decisions and actions would become enshrined in Scientology lore as something to be emulated—his cigarette smoking, for instance, which is still a feature of the church's culture at the upper levels, as are his 1950s habits of speech, his casual misogyny, his aversion to perfume and scented deodorants, and his love of cars and motorcycles and Rolex watches. More significant is the legacy of his belittling behavior toward subordinates and his paranoia about the government. Such traits stamped the religion as an extremely secretive and sometimes hostile organization that saw enemies on every corner.

Because Hubbard viewed the world that way, he awakened suspicion that there must be something very dangerous about Scientology. One by one, ports began turning away the fleet. It had begun with Gibraltar in 1967, when the ship was refused assistance during a heavy storm in the strait. England banned foreign Scientologists from entering the country for study in July 1968 and declared Hubbard an undesirable alien. Hubbard took out his frustration on his crew. He assigned Yvonne Gillham a condition of Non-Existence and reduced her to a "swamper," which he defined as "one who cleans up." Her hands became raw and gnarled. "She was like Cinderella," a friend recalled, "always scrubbing."

While the ships were docked in Valencia, a storm arose. Hubbard happened to be aboard the *Avon River* when he noticed that the *Royal Scotman* had torn free from one of its mooring lines. He screamed that someone should hoist the anchor and start the engines, but before the crew reacted, the big ship crashed against the dock, damaging its prop. Although the ship was not badly damaged, Hubbard assigned the crew and the *Royal Scotman* itself to a condition of Liability, which is below Non-Existence on his ethics scale. Hubbard stayed aboard the *Avon River* and steamed off to Marseilles until the *Royal Scotman* was returned to favor. Mary Sue was made the captain and ordered to retrain the crew and spruce up the ship to an acceptable state. No one could bathe or change clothes for months. The crew wore dirty gray rags on their left arms, which signaled their degraded status. Even Mary Sue's snappish Corgi, Vixie, had a rag around its collar, and the ship itself wore a bracelet of gray tarpaulins around its funnel. An Ethics Officer walked the decks actually swinging a mace.

Despite the squalid conditions, Mary Sue ran the ship with a minimum of hysteria, earning her the respect and loyalty of many aboard. Without Hubbard, the mood lightened. Mary Sue used to have parties in her cabin with Candy Swanson, the children's tutor, and two men they were sweet on. They danced to Jimi Hendrix records. But when Hubbard returned, the party was over.

A YOUNG MAN with a gift for languages named Belkacem Ferradj joined the Sea Org when the ship docked briefly in Algiers in 1968. Hubbard, surrounded by his Messengers, had made an immediate impression on Ferradj. He was dressed like an admiral, and he spoke with a broad American accent. A golden glow seemed to emanate from his large head. Mary Sue struck Ferradj as "gorgeous," with long, curly hair and piercing eyes, but he thought she was "the most secretive person in the world." When the ship sailed in July, Ferradj was aboard, having signed his billion-year contract with the Sea Org.

Ferradj became close to Hubbard's sixteen-year-old daughter, Diana. She had developed into a glamorous young woman, with flowing red hair and pale skin showered with freckles. She played the grand piano in the family dining room on the ship. Some saw her as imperious, a princess, but Ferradj, who was four years older than Diana, was smitten. When Hubbard found out about the relationship, he summoned Ferradj to the poop deck. Ferradj said Hubbard greeted him with a blow to the jaw. "I hit the bulkhead of the ship and slumped to the deck," he recalled. "I don't know if it was because I was an Arab or what. I left in disgrace."

When Otto Roos, a Sea Org executive from Holland, failed to lash a steel cable to a bollard on the dock during a terrible storm in Tunisia, Hubbard ordered him thrown from the ship's bridge into the sea, a height of about four stories. Hana Eltringham wrote a concerned report to Hubbard that night, explaining that the storm had been so furious that Roos simply couldn't hang on when trying to secure the ship. The report was returned to her with the comment "Never question LRH."*

Roos survived his punishment, only to set a dismal precedent. After that, overboardings became routine, but mostly from the lower poop deck. Nearly every morning, when the crew was mustered, there would be a list of those sentenced to go over the side, even in rough seas. They would be fished out and hauled back onboard through the old cattle doors that led to the hold. The overboardings contributed to the decision of the Greek government to expel the Scientology crew from Corfu in March 1969. That didn't stop the practice. None except Hubbard family members were spared. John McMaster, the second "first Clear," was tossed over the side six times, breaking his shoulder on the last occasion. He left the church not long afterward. Eltringham had to

*The church explained, "As it became a matter of tradition among the crew members at that time having adopted the practice of overboarding, Mr. Hubbard set forth rules in October of 1968 to ensure it was conducted safely in attaining the spiritual benefit intended. To that end, given that it was an ecclesiastical penance, the procedure includes the Chaplain making the following statement as part of the observance: 'We commit your sins and errors to the waves and trust you will arise a better thetan.'"

stand with Hubbard and his aides on the deck when the punishments were meted out. If the crewman seemed insufficiently cowed by the prospect, Hubbard would have his hands and feet bound. Whitfield remembered one American woman, Julia Lewis Salmen, sixty years old, a longtime Scientology executive, who was bound and blindfolded before being thrown overboard. "She screamed all the way down," Eltringham said. "When the sound stopped, Hubbard ordered a deck hand to jump in after her. Had he not, I think Julia may have drowned."

Hubbard chose a different punishment for another of the older members of the crew, Charlie Reisdorf. He and two other Sea Org crew were made to race each other around the rough, splintery decks while pushing peanuts with their noses. "They all had raw, bleeding noses, leaving a trail of blood behind them," a senior auditor recalled. The entire crew was ordered to watch the spectacle. "Reisdorf was in his late fifties, probably. His two daughters were Messengers; they were eleven or twelve at the time, and his wife was there also. It was hard to say which was worse to watch: this old guy with a bleeding nose or his wife and kids sobbing and crying and being forced to watch this. Hubbard was standing there, calling the shots, yelling, 'Faster, faster!' "

Hubbard increasingly turned his wrath on children, who were becoming a nuisance on the ship. He thought that they were best raised away from their parents, who were "counter-intention" to their children. As a result, he became their only—stern as well as neglectful—parent. Children who committed minor infractions, such as laughing inappropriately or failing to remember a Scientology term, would be made to climb to the crow's nest, at the top of the mast, four stories high, and spend the night, or sent to the hold and made to chip rust. A rambunctious four-year-old boy named Derek Greene, an adopted black child, had taken a Rolex watch belonging to a wealthy member of the Sea Org and dropped it overboard. Hubbard ordered him confined in the chain locker, a closed container where the massive anchor chain is stored. It was dark, damp, and cold. There was a danger that the child could be mutilated if the anchor was accidentally lowered or slipped. Although he was fed, he was not given blankets or allowed to go to the bathroom. He stayed sitting on the chain for two days and nights. The crew could hear the boy crying. His mother pleaded with Hubbard to let him out, but Hubbard reminded her of the Scientology axiom that children are actually adults in small bodies, and equally responsible for their behavior. Other young children were sentenced to the locker for infractions—such as chewing up a telex—for as long as three weeks. Hubbard ruled that they were Suppressive Persons. One little girl, a deaf mute, was placed in the locker for a week because Hubbard thought it might cure her deafness.

Hubbard explained to Hana Eltringham that the punishments were meant to raise the level of "confront" in order to deal with the evil in the universe. One member of Eltringham's crew on the *Avon River,* Terry Dickinson, a jocular Australian electrician, made the mistake of failing to order a part for the ship-to-shore radio. Hubbard sent a handwritten note to Eltringham ordering her to keep Dickinson awake until the part arrived and the radio was properly installed. If the crewman fell asleep, he would be expelled. Eltringham guiltily carried out the order, but she knew the hapless Dickinson couldn't make it on his own, so she stayed awake with him for five days and nights, pouring coffee down his throat, walking him up and down the beach, and consoling him as he wept and said he couldn't take it anymore. Eltringham believed she was saving Dickinson's soul, as well as her own, but he left shortly after that incident, "a broken man." Later, Hubbard wrote a note explaining that Dickinson "did not have the confront to see this through."

"You would say to yourself, 'Why didn't you do anything? Why didn't you speak out?' " Eltringham later remarked. "You see, I was a true believer. I believed that Hubbard knew what he was doing. I, unfortunately, believed that he knew what it was going to take to help everyone in the world and that, even though I didn't understand, it was my duty to follow and support what he was doing. None of us spoke out. None of us did anything."

IN THE SHIP'S LOG of December 8, 1968, Hubbard mentions an organization he calls SMERSH, a name taken from James Bond novels. Hubbard describes it as a "hidden government . . . that aspired to world domination!" Psychiatry is the dominating force behind this sinister institution. "Recently a check showed that we had never seen or heard of an 'insane' person who had not been in their hands," Hubbard writes. "And the question arises, is there any insanity at all? That is not manufactured by them?" He said that SMERSH had made one big mistake, however; it attacked Scientology. He vowed revenge.

Hubbard had been wooing a young Florida woman, Catherine "Kit" Harrington (a pseudonym), to join the Sea Org. She had come from a prominent family in the south and had studied in Europe. She spoke French, German, and Spanish. She had admirable social skills; moreover, she was a redhead, always a stamp of pre-eminence in Hubbard's book. Finally, Kit agreed to join the *Royal Scotman* in 1969, just as the ship was being expelled from Corfu. She was soon appointed to the "Missionaires Elite Unit." Hubbard already had an assignment in mind for her.

Hubbard set a course for Cagliari, on the Italian island of Sardinia. On the way, he personally tutored her in his plan to take over the World Federation for Mental Health, which was headquartered in Geneva. Hubbard had learned that the organization had never bothered to actually incorporate itself in Switzerland. His grand idea was to set up an office in Bern, the capital, posing as an American delegation of the WFMH bent on reforming the organization from within. The true scheme was to establish a presence in the country long enough to incorporate as the WFMH; and then, posing as the actual mental health organization, go to the United Nations with a plan for enforced euthanization of the "useless or unfixable" elements of society. Hubbard predicted that the outcry that would surely follow would turn the world against the WFMH. It would be a powerful strike against his most formidable enemy, SMERSH.

All the way to Sardinia Hubbard drilled Kit in the history of the health organization, its former presidents, and the policies it supported, such as electroshock therapy. Kit didn't need to be persuaded about the dangers of that practice; her own mother had been subjected to electroshock in the 1940s, without her consent, as treatment for postpartum depression. After that, her mother suffered from amnesia and a fear of change and losing control.

By the time the *Royal Scotman* docked in Cagliari, Kit was well schooled. She and another Sea Org member, Marjorie Johnson (a pseudonym), a trained Shakespearian actress from Cincinnati, traveled to Bern. They set up an office, purchased furniture, and covered the walls with phony certificates. They had business cards and stationery printed. Then they filed papers for incorporation as the World Federation for Mental Health.

Soon after that, they received a call from the Federal Office of Public Health in Switzerland demanding to know what they were up to. The two women were invited to explain themselves to the director himself.

Kit and Marjorie were both in their early twenties. They dressed in dowdy clothes and put powder in their hair to make themselves appear older. When they arrived at the office, they were shown to a conference room with about ten other people, including the director, a stenographer, and several lawyers. Marjorie's hands were trembling as Kit brazenly presented their case for taking over the WFMH. She claimed that the organization had long been misrepresenting itself; for instance, was the director aware that the WFMH never even bothered to incorporate in Switzerland? He was not. Nor was he a fan of some of the policies that the women said that WFMH championed, such as euthanasia. By the end of the meeting, the director seemed persuaded. "I like how you Americans work!" he said enthusiastically.

The women emerged from the meeting elated, but the response to their telex to Hubbard surprised them. He ordered them back to the ship, "for your protection." As soon as they returned to Cagliari, Hubbard cast off lines and set a course through the Strait of Gibraltar for open water. He even changed the names of his ships, in order to erase the connections with Scientology. The *Enchanter* became the *Diana*, the *Avon River* became the *Athena*, and the flagship *Royal Scotman* turned into the *Apollo*. All were registered with Panamanian credentials as belonging to the Operation and Transport Corporation. The *Apollo* was now billed as "the pride of the Panamanian fleet," "a floating school of philosophy," and "the sanest space on the planet."

Hubbard was convinced that the Swiss authorities had laid a trap: they would arrest Kit and Marjorie and force them to testify and expose his whole scheme. For months, he was afraid to touch land. The ship drifted aimlessly in the Atlantic; the crew was forced to live on its stores, and soon they were down to half-rations. Near Madeira, they were caught up in a fierce tropical storm, which threatened to swamp the *Apollo*. Immense waves swept over the funnel and shattered the two-inch-thick windows of the dining room. Water gushed into the engine room, where the seasick officer on watch tied a bucket around his neck. Terrified Messengers hauled themselves along the rails of the wildly pitching deck trying to deliver communications to the bridge; at times the nose of the ship was pointed directly down into the sea. The

Portuguese postcard of the *Apollo*

storm lasted ten days, propelling the ship eight hundred miles north, all the way to the Azores.

Looking for a safe port, Hubbard turned toward Morocco. He thought that an Arab country might be safer and less conspicuous for the Scientology fleet, which had gained too much unfavorable attention in European ports. In October 1969, he dropped anchor in Safi, near Marrakesh. At last the crew, shaken and hungry, could take on stores. Hubbard began sizing up the country as a possible Scientology homeland. He picked Kit Harrington and Richard Wrigley, another redhead, to lead an exploratory mission to the capital, Rabat. The only order they got from Hubbard was to "secure Morocco."

Wrigley and Harrington set up in the Hôtel La Tour Hassan, where diplomats typically stayed. Wrigley became friendly with an African envoy and drifted off to the Ivory Coast, leaving Kit to secure Morocco by herself. She established an office titled the American Institute of Human Engineering and Development, and sold a project to develop hydroponic farming to the Moroccan government. That project went nowhere, but it gave her legitimate cover. With her social skills, she soon found herself hobnobbing with the royal palace's inner circles—in particular, she made friends among some high-ranking military officers, including a tall, handsome intelligence officer named Colonel Allam.

As it happened, Colonel Allam and Kit shared a birthday, May 17, so she found herself invited to a soiree at the governor's palace in Marrakesh. In the middle of the party, there was a great stir caused by the arrival of General Mohammed Oufkir, the truculent minister of the interior. General Oufkir cast a long shadow over the nation, which had long been terrorized by the tyrannical rule of King Hassan II. Kit immediately sized him up as a shady figure—tall, hollow-cheeked, his eyes hidden by dark glasses, the blood of so many of his countrymen on his hands.

Her Moroccan friends bluntly warned Kit to keep her distance from the military, but Hubbard was pressing her to do the very opposite. He and Mary Sue rented a villa in Tangier. Mary Sue was thrilled; she hated being cooped up aboard ship. The prospect of taking over Morocco began to seem not so far-fetched.

For most of the next year, Kit lived in Rabat, reporting to the *Apollo* every couple of months. In July 1971, Colonel Allam invited her and two other Scientologists to watch a war-games exercise on the occasion of the king's forty-second birthday. The games, which were held at the king's summer palace in Skhirat, were a panoramic fantasia of Berber tribesmen on camels, followed by infantry formations and tank manuevers. The audience sat in tents and nibbled on endless hors d'oeuvres, and the pretty Scientology girls fended off advances from the Moroccan brass. They played poker with the generals to pass the time. Everything went smoothly, but suddenly, in the middle of the airshow portion of the exercise, two fighter aircraft emerged from a cloud and dropped out of formation, flying low over the panicked crowd. They trained their guns on the king's tent, which was next to where Kit and the other Scientologists were sitting. Simultaneously, a thousand military cadets stormed the palace. A hundred people were killed in the coup attempt. The king escaped by hiding in the toilet. Kit and her companions were quickly shuttled back to their hotel. Unnerved, they turned on the television to see what had happened, only to watch the generals they had been sitting with lined up against a wall and shot. The coup attempt quickly fell apart. King Hassan fled to France and left the country in charge of General Oufkir, who was also given the post of minister of defense. There was no one else the king trusted. He was convinced that the CIA was determined to oust him.

Even in this chaotic and dangerous situation, Hubbard saw an opportunity. He proposed the creation of an elite guard to protect the king. He ordered Kit to instruct General Oufkir in the use of E-Meters as lie detectors in order to determine which members of the government had been a part of the rebel forces and root out subversion. She refused; her own sources told her it was far too dangerous, not only for her, but for everyone involved. Hubbard ordered her back to the ship and put her in charge of the snack bar. He sent another team, and they quickly began to uncover the plotters. Colonel Allam was marched out to the desert and shot, along with dozens of others.

When King Hassan II returned from France, in 1972, a squadron of Moroccan fighter jets accompanied his passenger jet. As soon as they left French airspace, however, one of the escort jets began firing on the king's aircraft. The king, who was also a pilot, immediately grasped what was happening. He raced into the cockpit and seized control. "Stop firing! The tyrant is dead!" he shouted into the radio. Then he flew the jet on to Morocco.

That night, the architect of the coup was revealed: General Oufkir. It was announced that he had committed "suicide," although his body was riddled with bullets.

The shaken king turned his attention to the Scientologists. He had long suspected that Scientology was a CIA front—a rumor that was spreading all over the Mediterranean. There was also gossip that the *Apollo* was involved in drug trafficking and prostitution, or that it was part of a pornography ring. In December 1972, the Scientologists were expelled from the country, leaving a trail of confusion and recrimination behind them.*

PAULETTE COOPER WAS studying comparative religion for a summer at Harvard in the late 1960s when she became interested in Scientology, which was gaining attention. "A friend came to me and said he had joined Scientology and discovered he was Jesus Christ," she recalled. She decided to go undercover to see what the church was about. "I didn't like what I saw," she said. The Scientologists she encountered seemed to be in a kind of trance. When she looked into the claims that the church was making, she found many of them false or impossible to substantiate. "I lost my parents in Auschwitz," Cooper said, explaining

*The church denies that Scientologists worked with General Oufkir's men or used the E-Meter to provide security checking for the Moroccan government.

her motivation in deciding to write about Scientology at a time when there had been very little published and those who criticized the church came under concentrated legal and personal attacks. A slender, soft-spoken woman, Cooper published her first article in *Queen*, a British magazine, in 1970. "I got death threats," she said. The church filed suit against her. She refused to be silent. "I thought if, in the nineteen-thirties people had been more outspoken, maybe my parents would have lived." The following year, Cooper published a book, *The Scandal of Scientology*, that broadly attacked the teachings of Hubbard, revealing among other things that Hubbard had misrepresented his credentials and that defectors claimed to have been financially ripped off and harassed if they tried to speak out.

Soon after her book came out, Cooper received a visit from Ron and Sara Hubbard's daughter, Alexis, who was then studying at Smith College. Cooper had demanded that Alexis bring substantial identification to prove who she was, but when she opened the door, she drew a breath. It was as if Hubbard had been reincarnated as a freckled, twenty-two-year-old woman. Alexis asked Cooper whether or not she was legitimate. In her social circle, illegitimacy was a terrible stigma. Cooper was able to show her Ron and Sara's marriage certificate.

Alexis had been to Hawaii over the Christmas holidays to visit her mother. When she returned to college, she learned that there was a man who had been waiting to see her for four days. He identified himself as an FBI agent and said he had several pages of a letter he was required to read aloud to her. The letter said that Alexis was illegitimate. It was clearly written by Hubbard. "Your mother was with me as a secretary in Savannah in late 1948," the letter stated. He said he had to fire Sara because she was a "street-walker" and a Nazi spy. "In July 1949 I was in Elizabeth, New Jersey, writing a movie," the letter continues. "She turned up destitute and pregnant." Out of the goodness of his heart, Hubbard said, he had taken Sara in, to see her "through her trouble." Weirdly, the letter was signed, "Your good friend, J. Edgar Hoover."

After *The Scandal of Scientology*, Cooper's life turned into a nightmare. She was followed; her phone was tapped; she was sued nineteen times. Her name and telephone number were written on the stalls in public men's rooms. One day, when Cooper was out of town, her cousin, who was staying in her New York apartment, opened the door for a delivery from a florist. The deliveryman took a gun from the bouquet, put it to her temple, and pulled the trigger. When the gun didn't fire, he attempted to strangle her. Cooper's cousin screamed and the assailant fled. Cooper then moved to an apartment building with a doorman, but soon after that her three hundred neighbors received letters saying that she was a prostitute with venereal disease who molested children. A woman impersonating Cooper voiced threats against Secretary of State Henry Kissinger and President Gerald Ford at a Laundromat, while a Scientologist who happened to be present notified the FBI. Two members from the Guardian's office broke into Cooper's psychiatrist's office and stole her files, then sent copies to her adoptive parents. Cooper was charged with mailing bomb threats to the Church of Scientology. In the courtroom, the prosecutor produced a threatening letter with her fingerprint on it, and Cooper fainted. (Later, she remembered signing a petition, which may have had a blank page underneath it.) In May 1973, Cooper was indicted by the US Attorney's office for mailing the threats and then lying about it before the grand jury.

IF THE RUMORS about Hubbard were true—that he had created a religion only in order to get rich—he had long since accomplished that goal. One of his disaffected lieutenants later claimed that Hubbard had admitted to "an insatiable lust for power and money." He hectored his adherents on this subject. "MAKE MONEY," he demanded in a 1972 policy letter. "MAKE MORE MONEY. MAKE OTHERS PRODUCE SO AS TO MAKE MONEY." In order to siphon money into Hubbard's personal accounts, a number of front organizations were established, including the Religious Research Foundation, which was incorporated in Liberia. In the mid-seventies that single foundation had an account in Switzerland containing more than $300 million. At one point, panicked that Switzerland was going to make a change in its tax laws, Hubbard ordered his medical officer, Kima Douglas, to move those funds from Switzerland to Lichtenstein. She described stacks of cash sitting in the bank vault, mostly hundred-dollar bills, four feet high and three to four feet wide, one pile in Hubbard's name, the other in the church's. "Church's was bigger but his was big too," she told Hubbard's biographer Russell Miller. L. Ron Hubbard, Jr., remembered shoeboxes full of money in his father's closet. He later testified that Hubbard habitually kept "great chunks of cash" within easy reach, "so that if there was any problem he could just take off right out the window."

"Making money, I think, to Hubbard was paramount," Hana Eltringham later speculated. "He wasn't that interested in it for himself. He did have perks, he did have his cars, his motorbikes, his books, his good food, and things like that, and eventually he had his villas and he had his estates and so on, but the money that he wanted predominantly was for power."

For all his wealth, Hubbard spent much of his time in his cabin alone, auditing himself on the E-Meter and developing his spiritual technology. He may have been grandiose and delusional, but the endless stream of policy letters and training routines that poured from his typewriter hour after hour, day after day, attests to his obsession with the notion of creating a step-by-step pathway to universal salvation. If it was all a con, why would he bother?

Hubbard and Mary Sue slept in separate staterooms. In the opinion of members of their household staff and others, by the time they boarded ship, Hubbard had lost interest in Mary Sue sexually. Yvonne Gillham had managed to get herself posted on another ship, out of range of Hubbard's longing and Mary Sue's wrath. For the most part, the Commodore left his female crew members alone. One exception was a tall, slender woman from Oregon. She approached Hana Eltringham with a big smile on her face and confessed that she was having an affair with Hubbard. Soon after that, Hubbard busted the woman down to deckhand and assigned Eltringham to audit her. The woman would weep through the session. Eltringham would dutifully pass along the auditing files to Hubbard for review. "I could hear him chortling," she recalled.

The situation was much less restrained belowdecks. The Sea Org members were young and vigorous; sexual escapades were routine, and marriages quite fluid. Hubbard seemed to be oblivious, but Mary Sue was increasingly scandalized. When she learned that a crew member, who was nineteen or twenty, had slept with a fifteen-year-old girl on the ship, she got a dagger out of her cabin and held it against his throat and told him he had to be off the ship in two hours or else. In 1971, on New Year's Eve, there was a drunken orgy of historic proportions. "Maybe a hundred Sea Org members were having sex everywhere from the topside boatdecks to the lowest holds of the ship," one of the participants recalled. Mary Sue had had enough. With two attractive teenage daughters of her own on the ship, she started cracking down on premarital sex. Hubbard observed that 1972 was a leap year, and said that any woman on the ship could propose to any man, leading to a sudden rash of weddings. Hubbard had forbidden babies on board, but so many women were getting pregnant that he began permitting the children to stay, rather than sending their parents to another post. The baby boom eventually prompted Hubbard to order that no one could get pregnant without his permission; according to several Sea Org members, any woman disobeying his command would be "off-loaded" to another Scientology organization or flown to New York for an abortion.*

WORD ARRIVED while the *Apollo* was in dry dock in Portugal that the French government was going to indict the Church of Scientology for fraud, with Hubbard named as a conspirator (he would eventually be convicted in absentia and sentenced to four years in prison). Hubbard flew to New York the very next day. Few crew members knew where he was. Jim Dincalci, his medical officer, and Paul Preston, a former Green Beret who acted as Hubbard's bodyguard, joined him and set up housekeeping in Queens.

It was an odd interlude. Abruptly freed from the daily responsibility of running the ship, training executives, and overseeing the entire Scientology enterprise, Hubbard suddenly had time on his hands. He spent it watching television and reading novels. Dincalci was designated to be the chef, which meant that fish sticks and pasta were on the menu until Dincalci learned how to expand his repertoire. He studied Adelle Davis's popular health food book *Let's Get Well*. Hubbard began to gain energy and lose weight. He would go for walks around the neighborhood, but always in a clownish disguise—a wig, a hat, and glasses with no prescription. Hubbard thought he was being nondescript, but Dincalci heard the comments the kids were making about how goofy he looked.

Dincalci had long since come to the conclusion that Hubbard was not an Operating Thetan. He was obese and weird and he failed to exhibit any of the extraordinary powers that are supposed to be a part of the OT arsenal. Moreover, he was under siege by various countries. Why couldn't he simply set things straight? Wasn't he supposed to be in

---

*The church supplied me with a number of affidavits from former Sea Org members saying that they had not been forced to terminate their pregnancies.

control of his environment? How could he be so persecuted and pow-
erless? What was he doing hiding out in Queens, wearing a wig and
watching television when the planet needed salvation? At one point,
Hubbard was talking about how pleasant it used to be to sit on a cloud,
but now he complained to Dincalci, "I'm PTS to nations." He meant
that he was a Potential Trouble Source because entire countries were
dysfunctional and suppressive. Dincalci thought, "Oh, that explains
it," but then it didn't, really.

During the ten months Hubbard was in hiding in Queens, he began
plotting another way to destroy SMERSH. His escapade to take over
the World Federation for Mental Health had been foiled, he believed,
by those sinister forces. One day, Hubbard surprised Dincalci by asking him for the names of Snow White's Seven Dwarfs. Dincalci dutifully trotted to the library to look them up. He wouldn't learn the real
significance of Snow White for some time. Hubbard had set in motion
an operation so daring and dangerous that it threatened to destroy Scientology forever.

On April 20, 1973, Hubbard wrote a secret order, "Snow White
Program," in which he noted a dangerous trend in the gradual reduc-
tion since 1967 of countries available to Scientology. He put the blame
on the American and British governments, which he said were spreading false allegations against the church. He proposed to swamp the
countries that had turned against the church in a vast campaign of
litigation with the aim of expunging defamatory files and leaving Hubbard and the *Apollo* "free to frequent all western ports and nations
without threat."

In Hubbard's absence, Mary Sue exerted increased control over the
church's operations. Hubbard had already appointed her the head of
the Guardian's Office, a special unit with a broad mandate to protect
the religion. Among its other duties, the GO functioned as an intelligence agency, gathering information on critics and government agencies around the world, generating lawsuits to intimidate opponents,
and waging an unremitting campaign against mental health professionals. It was the GO that Hubbard tasked with Snow White. Under
Mary Sue's direction, the GO infiltrated government offices around
the world, looking for damning files on the church. Within the next
few years, as many as five thousand Scientologists were covertly placed
in 136 government agencies worldwide. Project Grumpy, for instance,
covered Germany, where the Guardian's Office was set up to infiltrate

Interpol as well as German police and immigration authorities. In addition, there was a scheme to accuse German critics of the church of committing genocide. Project Sleepy was to clear files in Austria; Happy was for Denmark, Bashful for Belgium, and Dopey for Italy. There were also Projects Mirror, Apple, Reflection, and so on, all drawn from elements of the fairy tale. Projects Witch and Stepmother both targeted the UK, the source of Scientology's immigration problems.

Project Hunter was the United States, where Scientologists penetrated the IRS, the Justice, Treasury, and Labor Departments, the Federal Trade Commission, and the Drug Enforcement Administration, as well as foreign embassies and consulates; private companies and organizations, such as the American Medical Association, the American Psychiatric Association, and the Better Business Bureau; and newspapers—including the *St. Petersburg Times*, the *Clearwater Sun*, and the *Washington Post*—that were critical of the religion. In an evident attempt at blackmail, they stole the Los Angeles IRS intelligence files of celebrities and political figures, including California governor Jerry Brown, Los Angeles mayor Tom Bradley, and Frank Sinatra. Nothing in American history can compare with the scale of the domestic espionage of Operation Snow White.

IN SEPTEMBER 1973, learning that he was not going to be extradited to France after all, Hubbard returned to Lisbon, where the *Apollo* was in dry dock. He amused himself by going off on photo expeditions in Portugal, with his Messengers acting as porters. Then, in December, the *Apollo* lifted anchor and headed to the warmer climate of the Canary Islands. One day in Tenerife, Hubbard decided to take his Harley-Davidson motorcycle out for a spin on the twisty mountain roads. Miles away, in the lush volcanic landscape, the Harley hit a patch of oil or mud and crashed. Hubbard broke his arm and several ribs. Somehow he managed to right his bike and make his way back to the ship.

Some members of the Sea Org cite the motorcycle accident as the moment when Scientology changed course and sailed toward a darker horizon. Hubbard was in terrible pain, but he was fearful of doctors and refused to go to the hospital. Dincalci and the ship's other medical officer, Kima Douglas, neither of whom had a medical degree, attempted to treat him. They strapped Hubbard's injured arm to his side and wrapped his broken ribs, then sat him in a velvet reading chair, which he rarely left for the next six weeks, day or night.

The whole ship could hear him cursing and screaming and throwing plates and things against the wall with his one good arm. He was in too much discomfort to sleep for more than a couple of hours at a time, so the ranting and moaning went on almost nonstop. The medical officers had persuaded him to let a local doctor come aboard with a kind of primitive X-ray machine, which confirmed the broken bones. The doctor left Dincalci a prescription for pain pills. The first time Dincalci gave Hubbard the pain pills, however, Hubbard panicked and said that they had slowed down his heart. "You're trying to kill me!" he shouted. Dincalci, who looked upon Hubbard as a father, both spiritually and emotionally, was devastated. Hubbard ordered him "beached"—dropped off in Madeira, the distant Portuguese atoll, where he remained for a year.

Other members of the Sea Org were having a hard time coping with the blatant contradiction between Hubbard's legend and the crabby, disconsolate figure howling in his stateroom. "If he is who he says he is, why does he have so little staying power?" Hana Eltringham wondered. "He has a motorcycle accident, he doesn't recover quickly, and he doesn't use Scientology techniques on himself."

By now, Eltringham had been promoted to Deputy Commodore, the highest post in the Sea Org after Hubbard himself. She had been off the ship for a couple of years, in Los Angeles, running the Advanced Orgs—the divisions responsible for producing Operating Thetans—and setting up a liaison office to supply the Scientology fleet. During that period, she began experiencing crippling headaches. Some days she was unable to work at all. She couldn't even lie down because the pressure from the pillow was unbearable. The vibration of footsteps in the hall outside her room made the pain excruciating. She thought if she could only discover the body thetans that she must be harboring she could ease her misery. Every day, hour after hour, she audited herself on the E-Meter, probing for some stirring or a sign of recognition. Hubbard himself was her case supervisor, which made her anxiety all the greater. Despite her rank, she, too, worried about being beached or punished. Even worse, according to Hubbard's dictates, she alone was responsible for her pain. So why was she doing this to herself?

Then, one day in her auditing, she felt something. A kind of "flicker." Was it a BT? She decided that it must be. An immense feeling of relief washed over her. Soon after that, she discovered more BTs—eventually, hundreds, thousands. Sometimes there was a feeling of lightness or of floating when the BT was expelled. Other times, Eltringham exteriorized from her body. But the headaches remained. Then something new arrived: quarrelsome voices inside her head. At first the voices were faint, but they grew louder and more insistent. Eltringham worried that she was going insane.

When she returned to the *Apollo*, she was shocked by the hellish changes that had taken place. In January 1974, Hubbard issued Flag Order 3434RB, creating the Rehabilitation Project Force. The stated goal was to rehabilitate Sea Org members whose statistics were down or who might be harboring subversive thoughts against Hubbard or his technology. Because the RPF provided a second chance for those who might otherwise be fired, Hubbard saw it as an enlightened management technique, the sole purpose of which was "redemption." When Eltringham came aboard, she found dozens of crew members housed in the old cattle hold belowdecks, illuminated by a single lightbulb, sleeping on stained mattresses on the floor. They were dressed in black overalls, called boiler suits, and forbidden to speak to anyone outside their group. They ate using their hands from a bucket of table scraps, shoveling the food into their mouths as if they were starving.

Despite the confusion and the harsh punishment, there were many Sea Org members who experienced their days on the *Apollo* as a time of incomparable adventure, filled with a sense of mission and an esprit de corps they would never again recapture. Although Hubbard could be terrifying and irrational, and comically pompous, he still held his followers in thrall. Those who were close to him saw a generous and caring leader who used his gigantic personality to keep his ship, his fleet, his organization, and his religion on track. Karen de la Carriere, a young British auditor, remembers watching Hubbard in his office screaming at one of the crew; when that person left, cowering, Hubbard swiveled in his chair and gave Karen a big wink. "He was in total control," she realized. "It was all theatrical to create a desired effect."

Hubbard developed many of the basic Scientology techniques aboard the *Apollo*. In one instance, de la Carriere was having no luck auditing a wealthy Scientologist with a long drug history, who kept falling asleep during their sessions. Hubbard theorized that the LSD he had taken must still be in his system; perhaps the drugs could be sweated out by putting him to work swabbing the decks. After six weeks, he was a changed man. De la Carriere says that was the beginning of the Scientology drug-treatment program, called the Purification Rundown.

A strapping crewman named Bruce Welch had what other crew members diagnosed as a nervous breakdown or a psychotic episode. In Scientology terms, he had gone "Type III." He had a crush on one of the ship's young women, and when he learned she was engaged, he went berserk. According to de la Carriere, Welch got a butcher knife from the pantry and threatened to kill Hubbard and other members of the crew. There were no designated security procedures or personnel trained to handle such a case. It took four crewmen to eventually subdue Welch and wrestle him into a cabin in the forecastle, the storage area above the bow, away from most of the crew, where he screamed continuously. There was a metal bed with a mattress, and a metal cabinet, but Welch managed to tear them apart with his bare hands and shove the pieces through the porthole.

A young Australian named Mike Rinder (who would eventually become the church's chief spokesperson) had just arrived aboard the *Apollo* and was given the assignment of guarding Welch's cabin. He sat on a trunk in the hallway, listening to Welch shouting, "Bring the Commodore here! I want the Commodore right now!" Then Welch would yank on the door, which was locked and lashed to the bulkhead with sturdy ropes. Several times, Rinder recalled, Welch beat up other members of the crew when he was escorted to the bathroom or given his meals.

Hubbard saw Welch's rampage as an opportunity to experiment with the problem of acute mental breakdown. Total silence was enforced on the forecastle deck so that Welch would have nothing to stimulate him. Three times a day, Hubbard would write Welch a note, asking about his well-being. According to de la Carriere, Welch's response might be, "You're the devil incarnate. I'm going to enjoy plunging the knife in you." Hubbard would respond that he understood, and by the way was there any special food that the chef could prepare for him? In this way, Welch's rage began to subside. He allowed an auditor to visit him each day. After two weeks, the door to Welch's cabin was unlocked and he emerged, serene and apparently cured.

"I have made a technical discovery which possibly ranks with the major discoveries of the twentieth century," Hubbard boasted in one of his bulletins. "It is called the Introspection Rundown." He explained that the psychotic break had long bedeviled psychiatry, which had attempted to treat it with drugs, lobotomies, and shock treatments. The key, Hubbard had discovered in his treatment of Welch, was to learn what had caused the person to "introspect" before his break-down. "THIS MEANS THE LAST REASON TO HAVE PSYCHI-ATRY AROUND IS GONE," Hubbard declared. "The psychotic break, the last of the 'unsolvable' conditions that can trap a person, has been solved. . . . You have in your hands the tool to take over mental therapy in full."

Hubbard's recipe for curing psychosis was to isolate the subject, with the attendants "*completely* muzzled (no speech)." By discovering the last severe conflict that triggered the episode, and then helping the subject discharge the emotions surrounding it, the auditor can begin to untangle the mental knots that have thrown the subject into his present state of wrestling with "the mystery of some incorrectly designated error." The subject should be given vitamins, especially Vitamin B, along with calcium and magnesium, in order to restore his physical well-being. He should be examined on the E-Meter for discordant moments in his life, such as someone accusing him of something he hadn't done, or being told he was a Potential Trouble Source when he wasn't, or having his identity questioned. These steps are simple, Hubbard said, but "its results are magical in effectiveness." The goal is to take the highly introverted personality, who is trapped in an endless loop of self-criticism, and bring him out of himself.

The subject should be able to look at the world once again and see it as "quite real and quite bright."

"Do it flawlessly and we will all win," Hubbard promised.

"THIS PLANET IS OURS."

The *Apollo* crew were in awe of their leader. They had seen the transformation with their own eyes. "A madman was made sane on the high seas," de la Carriere said. "To do that, you have got to have a certain amount of greatness."

ONCE A WEEK, there was a movie night on the aft deck, with a recently released film flown in. Popcorn was made, a screen erected, and when everyone was settled Hubbard would descend from the prom deck, resplendent in his Commodore's uniform, with Mary Sue and the children in tow.

In the interest of public relations, Hubbard staged free concerts at various ports of call, using the ship's ragtag band, the Apollo Stars. He wanted to "revolutionize music," and composed original songs for the band to play. He started a modern dance troupe as well. Quentin wanted to join the dancers, but his father sternly told him that he had other plans for him. By 1974, Hubbard had decided that his two oldest children by Mary Sue—Diana, twenty-two, and Quentin, twenty—were to take over the major management and technology functions of Scientology. Diana was enthusiastic—she had been the Lieutenant Commander since the age of sixteen and was often at her father's side—but everyone knew that Quentin's great ambition was to fly. His cabin was full of model airplanes, suspended from the ceiling with dental floss, and books about flying. He was often seen weaving along the deck with his arms outstretched, making engine noises, completely absorbed in being a plane.

Jim Dincalci, the medical officer who was still beached in Madeira, learned that the *Apollo* was headed in his direction. By now, he had made friends with many of the local people, and he was surprised to learn from them that the *Apollo* was widely suspected of being a spy ship for the CIA.* He sent telexes warning the ship that it would be better to avoid Madeira, but Hubbard came anyway. Soon after the *Apollo* docked, a mob arrived and began stoning the ship. Hubbard ordered fire hoses turned on the crowd, which further infuriated them. There were motorcycles belonging to crew members and two of Hubbard's cars which had been offloaded onto the pier; the mob shoved them all into the harbor, then loosened the moorings so that the ship drifted offshore. Mary Sue and some other members of the ship's company were stranded in town and had to be rescued by the local authorities.

Quentin returned to the ship in bad shape. He had taken an overdose of pills in a failed suicide attempt. After his stomach was pumped

---

*The CIA at the time was taking note of Hubbard, mainly through newspaper clippings. "There is no indication that HUBBARD or members of his organization have been engaged in intelligence or security matters," an agency dispatch notes. "Rather, HUBBARD appears to be a shrewd businessman who has parlayed his Scientology 'religion' into a multi-million dollar business by taking advantage of that portion of society prone to fall for such gimmicks" ("Scientology/L. Ron HUBBARD," CIA dispatch, Mar. 18, 1971).

at a local hospital, he was brought back to the ship, pale and weak, and put in isolation in his cabin, guarded night and day, becoming the second person to undergo the Introspection Rundown. Suzette was the only one to visit him. He looked like a broken doll.

Quentin was now twenty years old, popular and free-spirited, but in many ways still a soft-spoken, dreamy boy. Although he was small like his mother, and had her coloring, in other respects he bore a strong resemblance to his father. His facial features were almost an exact match: almond-shaped eyes under low, reddish brows; protuberant lips; and a deep cleft in the chin. Even though Quentin became one of the highest-rated auditors in the Sea Org, his father was constantly disappointed in his performance. "You have to improve," he barked at Quentin in front of the other auditors. "It doesn't matter that you're a Hubbard." Quentin would sit there and smile, seemingly unfazed, as the others cringed for him. Privately, he confided, "Daddy doesn't love me anymore."

Eventually, Hubbard sentenced Quentin to the Rehabilitation Project Force. His "twin" on the RPF was Monica Pignotti, an auditor in training at age twenty-one. As they practiced auditing each other, they became close. Quentin sneaked some peanut butter from the family

Quentin Hubbard, circa 1973

pantry and shared it with Monica. They made up skits and played
with his tape recorder. They never became intimate. Quentin told her
that he had once become sexually involved with a woman, but when
his father found out, she was sent off the ship. He knew that people
regarded him as a homosexual, he said, but that was only something
he told other women on the ship who were after him because he was
Hubbard's son.

HUBBARD SET A new course: due west, toward America. The destination was Charleston, South Carolina. The crew were thrilled that they
would be returning to the States, only to be crestfallen when a message
arrived from the Guardian's Office, just as the ship was approaching
port, alerting Mary Sue that agents from US Customs, Immigration,
Coast Guard, DEA, and US Marshals were waiting for them to dock,
plus 180 IRS agents waiting to impound the ship. The federal agents
had a subpoena to depose Hubbard in a civil tax case in Hawaii. A Scientologist on shore realized what was happening when he was blocked
from entering the dock area. He sent a pizza to a radio operator with a
message inside to send to the ship. Hubbard was just five miles offshore,
but he suddenly broadcasted a new course over the radio—due north
for Halifax, Nova Scotia—then turned sharply south and headed to
the Bahamas.

Hubbard was sixty-four years old in 1975, as the *Apollo* began
its circumnavigation of the Caribbean. He weighed 260 pounds. He
was still meticulously groomed, but his teeth and fingers were darkly
stained from constant smoking. He was on the run from the courts,
fearful of being discovered, marked by age, and visibly in decline. In
Curaçao, he suffered a small stroke and spent several weeks in a local
hospital. It was becoming clear that life at sea posed a real danger for
a man in such frail health. His crew rationalized his obvious decline by
saying that his body was battered by the research he was undertaking
and the volumes of suppression aimed at him. "He's risking his life for
us," they told each other.

By now the rumor about the CIA spy ship had spread all over the
Caribbean, making the Scientologists unwelcome or at least under
suspicion everywhere they went. They were kicked out of Barbados,
Curaçao, and Jamaica. Moreover, the Arab oil embargo had sent the

price of fuel skyrocketing, so the roving life was getting too expensive to support. It was time to come ashore.

FROM THE *APOLLO*, Hubbard sent a couple of delegations to locate a land base for Scientology—specifically, a town that the church could take over. One team arrived in the Florida retirement community of Clearwater—a resonant name for Scientologists—to look over a dowdy downtown hotel called the Fort Harrison, which had earned a place in popular history when Mick Jagger wrote the lyrics for "Satisfaction" beside the swimming pool in 1965. Hubbard purchased the Fort Harrison and a bank building across the street using a false front called the United Churches of Florida, which he calculated would not disturb the staid moral climate of the conservative community. When the mayor of Clearwater, Gabriel Cazares, raised questions about the extraordinary security that suddenly appeared around the church buildings, Guardian's Office operatives tried to frame him in a staged hit-and-run accident and planted false marriage documents in Tijuana, Mexico, to make it appear that Cazares was a bigamist. Several months passed before the flabbergasted citizens discovered that Clearwater had become the Flag Land Base for the Church of Scientology. (Scientologists would simply call it Flag.)

Hubbard had been keeping a low profile in a condominium nearby, but in January 1976 his tailor leaked the news to a *St. Petersburg Times* reporter that the leader of Scientology was in town. As soon as Hubbard heard this, he grabbed twenty-five thousand dollars in cash, collected Kima Douglas, his medical officer, and her husband, Michael, and lit out in his Cadillac for Orlando. The next day, he announced that they were going to his old hideout in Queens. The Cadillac was too conspicuous, so he sent Michael out to buy a nondescript Chevy hatchback. The trip to New York took three days, with Hubbard smoking continuously in the backseat and crying, "There they are! They're after us!" every time he saw a police car. When they finally arrived, Kima judged Queens too depressing, so they turned around and went to Washington, DC.

Meanwhile, agents from the Guardian's Office raced to Southern California to look for remote properties where Hubbard could operate more discreetly. Soon, Hubbard and Mary Sue, along with her

Tibetan terriers, Yama and Tashi, set up in their new quarters on three large properties in La Quinta, California, a desert town south of Palm Springs. Hubbard grew a goatee and let his hair hang down to his shoulders. "He looked like Wild Bill Hickok," one Sea Org member recalled. He kept a hopped-up Plymouth and half a million dollars in cash ready for a quick getaway.

Left behind in Clearwater, and without his father hovering over him, Quentin became freer and more assertive. He befriended an older Scientologist from New Zealand, Grace Alpe, who arrived at Flag Base with terminal cancer. "She looked like a witch, with gray hair and a hooked nose, like she was in a haunted house," said Karen de la Carriere, who was Alpe's auditor. During auditing sessions Alpe would just rock back and forth, crying, "I'm going to die! I'm going to die!" Everyone kept a distance from the woman, except Quentin, who took over her case. He actually let her move into his room and sleep in his bed, while he slept on the floor. Then he made a catastrophic mistake.

Dennis Erlich, the chief "cramming officer" at Flag, who supervised the upper-level auditors, noted jarring disparities between Quentin's upbeat reports on Alpe and her glaring lack of progress. Erlich called Quentin in for a meeting. "Quentin, or 'Q' as his friends called him, was 22 at the time," Erlich later wrote. "He looked 15 and acted 5." During the interview, Quentin continually zoomed his hand through the air and made airplane noises. He calmly told Erlich that he had falsely reported the results. "I think a lot of my father's stuff doesn't work," he said. "So I false report whenever I need to. Personally, I think my father's crazy."

Not only was Quentin the founder's son, he was also one of the highest-ranked auditors in the church, and yet he had committed an unpardonable offense. Erlich had no choice but to tell him that he would have to surrender all of his training certificates and start the entire Scientology series all over again—years of work. Quentin seemed completely nonchalant.

What happened after this is full of contradiction and mystery. Tracy Ekstrand, who was Quentin's steward, set a cookie on his bedside table that evening. It was still there the next night. The bed had not been slept in. Erlich was expecting Quentin to show up to go over his new training program, but he didn't appear that day or the next. Word went out that Quentin had "blown"—in other words, he had fled. He left a confused note, full of references to UFOs, saying that he was going to Area 51, the secret airbase north of Las Vegas, Nevada, where the CIA has developed spy planes; in popular culture, Area 51 was said to be where an alien spacecraft was stored. Quentin had only just learned to drive a car, in the parking garage of the condominium, where he accidentally ran into the wall with such force that the entire building registered the shock. He was scarcely qualified to drive all the way across the country by himself. Quentin had repeatedly requested a leave to take flying lessons, but Hubbard was convinced that Quentin couldn't be trusted to fly a plane under any circumstances.

Frantic, Mary Sue dispatched three hundred Guardian's Office operatives to find him. Weeks passed, as the Scientologists checked hotels and flying schools in multiple states. A cover story was put out that Quentin had been given flying lessons as a present from his parents, and he was driving to California to fulfill his lifelong ambition.

Quentin was indeed headed for Nevada. It was one of the very few times in his life when he was on his own and free. He stopped in St. Louis on his drive west and took a VIP tour of the giant aerospace manufacturer McDonnell Douglas. He was enthralled by the display of aircraft and artifacts of the Mercury and Gemini space programs; he even got a ride in one of the company's business jets. "He was so happy," Cindy Mallien, who had lunch with him that afternoon, recalled. "He was just beaming."

But only a few days later, Las Vegas police were trying to identify a slight young man with blond hair and a reddish moustache who had been discovered comatose in a car parked on Sunset Road facing the end of the runway of McCarran Airport. He was naked. He was five feet one inch tall, and weighed just over a hundred pounds. There were no identifying marks on his body and no personal identification. The license plates had been removed. The engine of the white Pontiac was still running when he was discovered. The windows were rolled up, and a vacuum tube led from the exhaust through the passenger's vent window. Two weeks later, on November 12, 1976, the young man died without regaining consciousness. Las Vegas police were finally able to connect the Pontiac with Quentin through a Florida smog sticker and the vehicle identification number.

An agent from the Guardian's Office came into Hubbard's office in La Quinta as he was having breakfast and handed him the report on Quentin's death. "That little shit has done it to me again!" Hubbard cried. He threw the report at Kima Douglas and ordered her to read it.

The report said Quentin had died of asphyxiation of carbon monoxide. It also noted that there was semen in his rectum. When Hubbard told Mary Sue that Quentin was dead, she screamed for ten minutes. For months, she was disconsolate, hiding behind dark glasses. Everyone knew that Quentin was her favorite.

A spokesman for the church said that Quentin had been on vacation. Meantime, Mary Sue arranged for three further autopsies to be performed. In the last one, the cause of death was said to be unknown. She put out the word that he had died of encephalitis. Hubbard himself was convinced that Quentin was murdered as a way of getting at him.

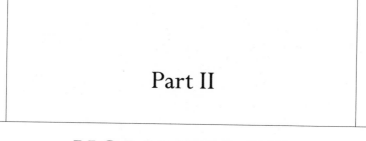

Part II

HOLLYWOOD

4

The Faith Factory

D espite its reputation for carnality and narcissism, Los Angeles has always been a spawning ground for new religions. In 1906, a one-eyed black preacher named William Seymour set up a church in a livery stable on Azusa Street and began a revival that lasted for three years. Hundreds of thousands of pilgrims came to hear his message. Stigmatized as Holy Rollers and decried because of their interracial worship, Seymour's followers gave birth to the Pentecostal movement, which quickly spread across the world, becoming an enduring force in modern Christianity. In 1912, a theosophist colony called Krotona took root just below the current Hollywood sign, where the hills were said to be "magnetically impregnated." An organization called Mighty I AM Presence began in Los Angeles and expanded all across America, gaining about a million followers by 1938. The founders were Guy and Edna Ballard, who claimed to be able to communicate with "ascended masters." Guy wrote a popular book titled *Unveiled Mysteries*, in which he related his travels through the stratosphere, visiting great cities of antiquity and unearthing buried loot—much as Hubbard attempted to do several decades later. Writers William Butler Yeats, D. H. Lawrence, Christopher Isherwood, and Aldous Huxley passed through the city, all drawn by its reputation as a center for spiritual innovation.

One of the most famous preachers in American history, Aimee Semple McPherson, built the Angelus Temple near Echo Park in 1923, where she married Pentecostalism with Hollywood theatricality. She created sets for her sermons on a stage designed for her by Charlie Chaplin, who may have been one of her secret Hollywood paramours (Milton Berle claimed to be another). Anticipating the garb of Hubbard and the Sea Org, McPherson liked to dress in an admiral's uniform, while her disciples wore nautical outfits. As a teenager, Anthony Quinn played the saxophone in the church and translated for Sister Aimee when she preached in Mexican neighborhoods. After he became a movie star, Quinn would compare her to the great actresses he worked with, including Ingrid Bergman and Katharine Hepburn. "They all fell short of that first electric shock Aimee Semple McPherson produced in me."

And so when the Church of Scientology was officially founded in Los Angeles, in February 1954, by several of Hubbard's devoted followers, there was already a history of religious celebrities and celebrity religions. The cultivation of famous people—or people who aspired to be famous—was a feature of Hubbard's grand design. He foresaw that the best way of promoting Scientology as a ladder to enlightenment was to court celebrities, whom he defined as "any person important enough in his field or an opinion leader or his entourage, business associates, family or friends with particular attention to the arts, sports and management and government." It was not surprising that Hubbard would hire as his personal assistant Richard de Mille, son of the legendary producer and director Cecil B. DeMille, who had started Paramount Pictures and was in some ways responsible for the creation of Hollywood itself.

In 1955, a year after the church's founding, an editorial in *Ability*, a publication affiliated with the church, urged Scientologists to recruit celebrities. A long list of desirable prospects followed, including Marlene Dietrich, Walt Disney, Jackie Gleason, John Ford, Bob Hope, and Howard Hughes. "If you want one of these celebrities as your game, write us at once so the notable will be yours to hunt without interference," the editorial promised. "If you bring one of them home you will get a small plaque as your reward." Author William Burroughs and actor Stephen Boyd were drawn into the church in its early days. Scientology was a religion rather perfectly calibrated for its time and place, since American culture, and soon the rest of the world, was bending increasingly toward the worship of celebrity, with Hollywood as its chief shrine. At the end of the sixties, the church established its first Celebrity Centre, in Hollywood. (There are now satellites in Paris, Vienna, Düsseldorf, Munich, Florence, London, New York, Las Vegas, and Nashville.) The object was to "make celebrities even better known and to help their careers with Scientology," Hubbard wrote. "By accomplishing this Major Target I know that Celebrity Centres can take over the whole acting-artists world."

Hubbard was particularly interested in stars whose careers had crested but still had enough luster that they could be rehabilitated and made into icons of Scientology. The prototype was Gloria Swanson, one of the greatest stars of the silent movie era, who personified the lavish glamour of that era. Although she never regained the international fame she had known before the talkies, she continued acting on television and in occasional movies—most memorably, as Norma Desmond in the 1950 classic *Sunset Boulevard*. Hubbard's top auditor, Peggy Conway, a South African entertainer, ardently cultivated Swanson, calling her "My Adorable Glory," in her many letters to the star, although she saves her highest praise for Hubbard, who was also her auditor: "The Master did his Sunday best on me," she wrote Swanson in 1956. "He never went to bed—we talked the clock around—day after day—night after night—I was six thousand light years above Arcturus—what a genius is our Great Red Father!"

A constant stream of aspiring young actors, writers, and directors came to Hollywood with common dreams, trying to leverage whatever ability or looks they might have in a market already overwhelmed by beautiful and talented and chronically unemployed young people. Many of them were rather poorly educated—they had left school to gamble on stardom—but they were smart, talented, and desperately ambitious. Scientology promised these neophytes an entry into the gated community of celebrity. The church claimed to have a method for getting ahead; just as enticing was the whispered assertion that a network of Scientologists existed at the upper levels of the entertainment industry eager to advance like-minded believers—a claim that never had much to support it, but was not entirely untrue. Scientology was a small but growing subculture in the Hollywood studios.

Kirstie Alley was an aspiring actress from Wichita who left the University of Kansas in her sophomore year, then struggled with an addiction to cocaine. She says that a single auditing session cured her habit. "Without Scientology, I would be dead," she declared. The testimonials of such celebrities would lead many curious seekers to follow their example. Posters with the faces of television and movie stars were placed outside Scientology churches and missions, saying, "I AM A SCIENTOLOGIST . . . COME IN AND FIND OUT WHY." In the Hollywood trade magazine *Variety*, Scientology offered courses promising to help neophyte actors "increase your self-confidence" and "make it in the industry." Scientologists stood outside Central Casting, where actors sign up for roles as extras, passing out flyers for workshops on how to find an agent or get into the Screen Actors Guild. Courses at the Celebrity Centre focused on communication and self-presentation skills, which were especially prized in the entertainment industry. The drills and training routines would have felt somewhat familiar to anyone who had done scene work in an acting class. Many actors, at once insecure but competitive by nature, were looking for an advantage, which Scientology promised to give them. The fact that anyone was interested in them at all must have come as a welcome surprise.

Others who passed through Scientology at the same time as Paul Haggis were actors Tom Berenger, Christopher Reeve, and Anne Francis; and musicians Lou Rawls, Leonard Cohen, Sonny Bono, and Gordon Lightfoot. None stayed long. Jerry Seinfeld took a communication course, which he still credits with helping him as a comedian. Elvis Presley bought some books as well as some services he never actually availed himself of. Rock Hudson visited the Celebrity Centre but stormed out when his auditor had the nerve to tell him he couldn't leave until he finished with his session, although the matinee idol had run out of time on his parking meter. The exemplary figure that Hubbard sought eluded capture.

VERY EARLY ONE MORNING in July 1977, the FBI, having been tipped off about Operation Snow White, carried out raids on Scientology offices in Los Angeles and Washington, DC, carting off nearly fifty thousand documents. One of the files was titled "Operation Freakout." It concerned the treatment of Paulette Cooper, the journalist who had published an exposé of Scientology, *The Scandal of Scientology*, six years earlier.

After having been indicted for perjury and making bomb threats against Scientology, Cooper had gone into a deep depression. She stopped eating. At one point, she weighed just eighty-three pounds. She considered suicide. Finally, she persuaded a doctor to give her sodium pentothal, or "truth serum," and question her under the anesthesia. The government was sufficiently impressed that the prosecutor dropped the case against her, but her reputation was ruined, she was broke, and her health was uncertain.

The day after the FBI raid on the Scientology headquarters, Cooper was flying back from Africa, on assignment for a travel magazine, when she read a story in the *International Herald Tribune* about the raid. One of the files the federal agents discovered was titled "Operation Freakout." The goal of the operation was to get Cooper "incarcerated in a mental institution or jail."

One of the doors the federal agents opened during the raid in Los Angeles led to the darkened basement of the old Cedars of Lebanon Hospital on Fountain Avenue, newly christened as Scientology's Advanced Org building. There were no lights, so the heavily armed agents made their way down the stairs with flashlights. They found a warren of small cubicles, each occupied by half a dozen people dressed in black boiler suits and wearing filthy rags around their arms to indicate their degraded status. Altogether, about 120 people were huddled in the pitch-black basement, serving time in the Rehabilitation Project Force. The ranks of the RPF had expanded along with the church's need for cheap labor to renovate its recently purchased buildings in Hollywood. The federal agents had no idea what they were seeing. Within moments, a representative of the church's Guardian's Office arrived and began shouting at the agents that they were exceeding the limits of their search warrants. Seeing that the Sea Org members posed no threat to them, the agents shrugged and moved on.

It is instructive to realize that none of the Sea Org members consigned to the RPF dungeon took the opportunity to escape. If the FBI had bothered to interrogate them, it's unlikely that any of them would have said that they were there against their will. Most of them believed that they were there by mistake, or that they deserved their punishment and would benefit by the work and study they were prescribed. Even those who had been physically forced into the RPF were not inclined to leave. Despite federal laws against human trafficking and unlawful imprisonment, the FBI never opened the door on the RPF again.

Jesse Prince, one of the very few black members of the Sea Org, was among those being punished. He had been attracted to Scientology by the beautiful girls and the promise of superhuman powers. He recalls being told he would learn to levitate, travel through time, control the thoughts of others, and have total command over the material universe. In 1976, when he signed up for the Sea Org, Scientology had just purchased the Cedars of Lebanon Hospital, part of the real-estate empire that the church was acquiring in Hollywood, along with the Château Élysée and the old Wilcox Hotel, which functioned as Sea Org berthing. The hospital was a mess; there were leftover medical devices and body parts in laboratory jars; there was even a corpse in the basement morgue. The Sea Org crew slaved to convert the hospital into a dormitory and offices. One night Prince was awakened after an hour of sleep and ordered to report to a superior, who chewed him out for slacking off. Prince had had enough. "Fuck you, I'm outta here," he said. His superior told him he wasn't going anywhere. "He snapped his fingers and six people came and put me in a room," Prince recalled. "I was literally incarcerated." It was March 1977. Prince was placed in the RPF with two hundred other Sea Org members, doing heavy labor and studying Hubbard's spiritual technology. He would be held there for eighteen months. "They told me the only way to get out is to learn this tech to a 'T' and then be able to apply it."

The question posed by Prince's experience in the RPF is whether or not he was brainwashed. It is a charge often leveled at Scientologists, although social scientists have long been at war with each other over whether such a phenomenon is even possible. The decade of the 1950s, when Scientology was born, was a time of extreme concern—even hysteria—about mind control. Robert Jay Lifton, a young American psychiatrist, began studying victims of what Chinese Communists called "thought reform," which they were carrying out in prisons and revolutionary universities during the Maoist era; it was one of the greatest efforts to manipulate human behavior ever attempted. In 1949, a number of Americans and Europeans who had been imprisoned during the Maoist revolution emerged from their cells apparently converted to Communism. Then, during the Korean War, several United Nations soldiers captured by Chinese troops defected to the enemy. Some American soldiers among them went on camera to denounce capitalism and imperialism with apparent sincerity. It was a stunning ideological betrayal. To explain this phenomenon, an American journalist and CIA operative, Edward Hunter, coined the term "brainwashing." Hunter described robotic agents with glassy eyes, like zombies or the products of demon possession. A popular novel, *The Manchurian Candidate*, published in 1959, and a film of the same name that came out three years later, capitalized on this conception of brainwashing as being the total surrender of free will through coercive forms of persuasion.

Lifton's early work on thought reform has become the basis for much of the scholarship on the subject since then. Lifton defined thought reform as having two basic elements: *confession*, which is the renunciation of past "evil," and *re-education*, which in China meant refashioning an individual in the Communist image. "Behind ideological totalism lies the ever-present human quest for the omnipotent guide—for the supernatural force, political party, philosophical ideas, great leader, or precise science—that will bring ultimate solidarity to all men and eliminate the terror of death and nothingness," Lifton observes. In facing the commonplace charge that psychiatry, or the Marines, or Catholic schools all engage in forms of brainwashing, Lifton developed a set of criteria to identify a totalistic environment, and contrasted these with more-open approaches to reshaping human behavior.

The totalist paradigm begins with shutting off the individual's access to the outside world, so that his perceptions of reality can be manipulated without interference. The goal at this stage is to provoke expectable patterns of behavior that will appear to arise spontaneously, adding to the impression of omniscience on the part of the controlling group. Those who are involved in the manipulation are guided by a sense of higher purpose that permits them—actually, compels them—to set aside ordinary feelings of human decency in order to accomplish their great mission. Those who are being manipulated may come to endorse the goals and means of the group—as Prince did—or simply abandon the will to resist. In either case, the individual is robbed of the chance for independent action or self-expression.

Because the moral climate is entirely controlled by the group, the "sins" that one is made to confess function as pledges of loyalty to the ideals of the movement. The repetitive nature of these confessions inevitably turns them into performances. When the treasury of real sins is emptied, new ones may be coined to satisfy the incessant demands of the inquisitors. In Scientology, one can conveniently reach into previous existences to produce an endless supply of misdeeds. Lifton points out that in totalist hands, confession is used to exploit vulnerabilities, rather than to provide the solace or forgiveness that therapy and religion seek to provide. The paradoxical result can be the opposite of total exposure: secrets proliferate, and doubts about the movement go underground.

The dogma of the group is promoted as scientifically incontestable—in fact, truer than anything any human being has ever experienced. Resistance is not just immoral; it is illogical and unscientific. In order to support this notion, language is constricted by what Lifton calls the "thought-terminating cliché." "The most far-reaching and complex of human problems are compressed into brief, highly reductive, definitive-sounding phrases, easily memorized and easily expressed," he writes. "These become the start and finish of any ideological analysis." For instance, the Chinese Communists dismissed the quest for individual expression and the exploration of alternative ideas as examples of "bourgeois mentality." In Scientology, terms such as "Suppressive Person" and "Potential Trouble Source" play a similar role of declaring allegiance to the group and pushing discussion off the table. The Chinese Communists divided the world into the "people" (the peasantry, the petite bourgeoisie) and the "reactionaries" or "lackeys of imperialism" (landlords and capitalists), who were essentially non-people. In a similar manner, Hubbard distinguished between Scientologists and "wogs." The word is a derogatory artifact of British imperialism, when it was used to describe dark-skinned peoples, especially South Asians. Hubbard appropriated the slur, which he said stood for "worthy Oriental gentleman." To him, a wog represented "a common, ordinary, run-of-the-mill, garden-variety humanoid"—an individual who is not present as a spirit. Those who are within the group are made to strive for a condition of perfection that is unattainable—the ideal Communist state, for instance, or the clearing of the planet by Scientology.

When a preclear voices a criticism of Scientology or expresses a desire to leave the church, the auditor's response is to discover the "crimes" that the client has committed against the group. In Scientology jargon, those crimes are called "overts and withholds." An overt is an action taken against the moral code of the group, and a withhold is an overt action that the person is refusing to acknowledge. Hubbard explained that the only reason a person would want to leave Scientology is because he has committed a crime against the group. Paradoxically, this is because humanity is basically good; he wants to separate himself from the others in order to protect the group from his own bad behavior.

In order to save the preclear from his self-destructive thoughts, the E-Meter is used in a security check (sec-check) to probe for other thoughts or actions. For extreme cases, Hubbard developed what he called the Johannesburg Confessional List. The questions include:

Have you ever stolen anything?
Have you ever blackmailed anybody?
Have you ever been involved in an abortion?

There are further questions asking if the respondent has ever sold drugs, committed adultery, practiced homosexuality, had sex with a family member or a person of another race. It winds up by inquiring:

Have you ever had unkind thoughts about LRH?
Are you upset about this Confessional List?

The result of the sec-check procedure is that the person expressing doubts about the church is steered into thinking about his own faults that led him to question Scientology in the first place. In the Chinese Communist example, Lifton points out, the combination of enforced logic and clichéd discourse creates a kind of melodrama, in which formulaic thoughts and handicapped language substitute for real emotions and complex understandings of human nature. Once inside the powerful logic of the group, one drifts further and further from the shore of common understanding.

According to Lifton, factors such as these award the group life-and-death authority over individual members. And yet, despite the Communists' absolute control of the environment, of the forty victims that Lifton studied, only three were "apparent converts" to the ideology. That figure has been used to discredit the notion of brainwashing, although Lifton himself later said that he was impressed by the extent to which minds could be altered and "truth blurred to the point of near extinction."

The CIA, alarmed by the reputed success of Chinese indoctrination, started its own research into mind control, through a program called MKUltra. In the mid-1950s, the agency began funding Dr. Ewen Cameron, a Scottish-born American citizen who was then directing the Allan Memorial Institute at McGill University in Montreal.

Cameron was one of the most eminent psychiatrists of his time: earlier in his career, he had been a part of the Nuremberg tribunal that examined the atrocious human experiments of Nazi doctors; later he became president of the American Psychiatric Association, the Canadian Psychiatric Association, and—when the CIA stumbled onto his work—president of the World Psychiatric Association. Cameron hoped to cure mental illness by eliminating painful memories and reordering the personality through positive suggestion. The agency's goal was somewhat different, of course; the stated reason was to uncover effective methods of mind control and then train American soldiers in ways of resisting such efforts. The CIA eventually destroyed the files of the MKUltra program, saying that it had acquired no useful information, but the real intention of the agency may have been to learn scientific ways of extracting information from unwilling subjects. (After 9/11, documents emerging from the Guantánamo Bay Naval Base showed that the methods used by US interrogators to question al-Qaeda suspects were based on Chinese Communist techniques.)

The methods that Cameron used to erase his patients' memories certainly meet the definition of torture. Electroshock therapy was administered to break the "patterns" of personality; up to 360 shocks were administered in a single month in order to make the subject hyper-suggestible. On top of that, powerful drugs—uppers, downers, and hallucinogens—were fed to the incapacitated patients to increase their disorientation. According to author Naomi Klein, who wrote about these experiments in *The Shock Doctrine*, when Cameron finally believed he had achieved the desired blank slate, he placed the patients in isolation and played tape-recorded messages of positive reinforcement, such as "You are a good mother and wife and people enjoy your company." Some patients were put into an insulin coma to keep them from resisting; in that state they were forced to listen to such mantras up to twenty hours a day. In one case, Cameron played a message continuously for more than a hundred days.

Cameron was a perfect archetype for the evil that science has done in the name of mental health, and in the minds of many Scientologists, his work justifies the campaign the church has waged against psychiatry. It is intriguing to compare these actual experiments with Hubbard's mythic vision of Xenu and the R6 implants, in which the disembodied thetans were forced to sit in front of movie screens for thirty-six days of programming at the hands of psychiatrists.

Although it is unlikely that Hubbard would have known about MKUltra when it was going on, he had become fascinated by the mind-control scare. In 1955, he distributed a pamphlet, which he probably wrote, called "Brain-Washing: A Synthesis of the Russian Textbook on Psychopolitics." For some former Scientologists, "Brain-Washing" provides a codex for Hubbard's grand scheme. There is an eerie mirroring of the techniques described in the pamphlet and some Scientology practices, especially those put into effect in the RPF.

The pamphlet opens with what is claimed to be a purloined speech given by Lavrenti Beria, the head of the Soviet secret police under Joseph Stalin, to American students studying at Lenin University, on the subject of "psycho-politics." The term is defined as "[t]he art and science of asserting and maintaining dominion over the thoughts and loyalties of individuals, bureaus, and masses, and the effecting of the conquest of enemy nations through 'mental healing.' "

The text specifies how to realign the goals of the individual with those of the group. The first task is to undermine the ability of the person to act and to trust himself. Next, his loyalty to his family is destroyed by breaking the economic dependency of the family unit, lessening the value of marriage, and turning over the raising of children to the State or the group. The individual's trust and affection for his friends is shattered by anonymous reports to the authorities, supposedly from people close to him. Ultimately, all other emotional claims on the person have been broken; only the State or the group remains. "A psychopolitician must work hard to produce the maximum chaos in the fields of 'mental healing,' " Beria says in his introductory speech. "You must labour until we have dominion over the minds and bodies of every important person in your nation."

FROM THE PERSPECTIVE of those social scientists who believe that brainwashing is a myth or a fraud that has been used to denigrate new religious movements, including Scientology, Jesse Prince must already have been a convert, or close to one, before he went into the RPF. Although he says he was attracted to the church largely because of the girls, he was aware of the rigors of the Sea Org before he joined it. Perhaps, like the three victims of Chinese Communist thought reform that Lifton termed "apparent converts," Prince was predisposed to be a part of a totalitarian movement because of his own psychological need to conform, or to be a part of a polarized system that separates all humanity into the saved and the damned. Such persons, the theory goes, are reared in either chaotic or extremely authoritarian homes. They have conflicted images of themselves as being at once extremely good and extremely bad. This is particularly true in adolescence, when identities are still volatile. Prince didn't need to be brainwashed, the theory goes; he was actively looking for a totalistic organization that accommodated his polarized personality.

Some incidents in Prince's background support this hypothesis. Although his upbringing was "tumultuous"—his mother died when he was ten—Prince maintained close and loving relationships with his father and his three younger siblings. After his mother died, however, he began experiencing bouts of total body paralysis accompanied by a sense of falling—"like jumping off the Grand Canyon." The feeling was of helpless, abject terror. Then, suddenly, he would be outside his body, as if a parachute had opened, and he could observe himself sleeping in his bed. The intensity of these experiences made them absolutely real to him, but he decided not to talk about them because "if you bring that up, you go to the crazy house." Prince now sees those episodes of body paralysis as severe anxiety attacks, but they prepared him to accept the truthfulness of the paranormal powers that Scientology claimed to provide.

Brainwashing theory, on the other hand, proposes that strenuous influence techniques can overwhelm and actually convert an individual to a wholly different perspective, regardless of his background or pre-existing character traits, almost like an addiction to a powerful drug can create an overpowering dependency that can transform an otherwise stable personality. Stripping away a person's prior convictions leaves him hungry for new ones. Through endless rounds of confession and the constant, disarmingly unpredictable fluctuations between leniency and assault, love and castigation, the individual is broken loose from his previous identity and made into a valued and trusted member of the group. To keep alienated members in the fold, "exit costs"—such as financial penalties, physical threats, and the loss of community—make the prospect of leaving more painful than staying.

Whether Prince was brainwashed, as he believes, or spiritually enlightened, as the church would have it, his thinking did change over the year and a half he spent in the RPF. In order to move out of the RPF, a member has to have a "cognition" that he is a Suppressive Person; only then can he begin to deal with the "crimes" that he committed that caused him to be confined in the RPF in the first place. During his many hours of auditing, Prince later related, "You just kinda get sprinkles of little things that seem interesting, sprinkles of something that's insightful. And then you're constantly audited and in a highly suggestible state . . . like being pulled along very slightly to the point where now I might as well just be here and see what this is about now. Maybe it's not so bad, you know?"

ONE OF JESSE PRINCE'S COMPANIONS in RPF was Spanky Taylor, an old friend of Paul Haggis's from his early days in Scientology. She had become close to Paul and Diane soon after they arrived in Los Angeles. She called him "Paulie," and had helped him market some of his early scripts when he was still trying to break out of cartoons. From the beginning, she had seen his talent; her own talent was helping others realize theirs.

"Spanky" was a schoolyard nickname for Sylvia, but it had such a teasing twist that she could never escape it. She was the child of Mexican American laborers in San Jose. When she was fourteen, she became a fan of a local cover band called People!, which included several Scientologists. She began helping the group with concert promotion, and soon she was working with some of the other great bands coming out of the Bay Area, such as Creedence Clearwater Revival and Big Brother and the Holding Company. Scientology was just another expression of the political and cultural upheaval of the times. Even members of the Grateful Dead were drawn into Scientology, which promised mystical experiences without hallucinogens. Albert Ribisi, the keyboard player for People!, introduced Spanky to the church. She joined the staff at the Santa Clara mission when she was fifteen.

She was a cheerful young woman with warm brown eyes who called everyone "honey." Because of her experience with promotion, she was posted to the Celebrity Centre. The place was constantly buzzing with activity—tie-dyeing, fencing, poetry readings—and she loved it. Famous people were always passing through, which added to the sense that something fun and important was happening here.

Spanky inevitably came to the notice of Yvonne Gillham, who had created the Celebrity Centre in 1969, after gaining Hubbard's permission to go to LA and escape the tension of his romantic pursuit of her. Gillham came to look upon Spanky almost as an extension of herself, with the same easy, natural flair for dealing with people. Even though Spanky was still a teenager, Gillham arranged for her to take care of some of the most important figures associated with the church.

One celebrity quickly took precedence. John Travolta was in Mexico making his first film, *The Devil's Rain,* a cheap horror movie starring Ernest Borgnine and William Shatner. He got to be friends with Joan Prather, a promising young actress and dancer, who was one of the few cast members his age. "He glommed on to me from day one," she said. "He was extremely unhappy and not doing well." Prather began talking about how much Scientology had helped her. Actors are often asked to get in touch with feelings that can be quite devastating. "Dianetics offered a tool to get to one's raw emotions without going completely bonkers," she observed.

"It sounded really interesting, so I brought up certain things about my case and asked if that could be handled," Travolta later recalled. "And she said it could. I said, 'Come on . . . could *THAT* be handled? You know, I couldn't believe it." Prather gave him a copy of *Dianetics.* It helped with his bouts of depression and insomnia. "Sometimes people say the most incredible things in the world to me that last year would make me suicidal," he observed. On another occasion he remarked, "Before *Dianetics,* if people said negative things to me or about me, I would cave in easily. Being a man, that wasn't a very appealing quality. Some people would say, 'The boy is too sensitive.' But many times I had suppressive people around me who would cave me in on purpose. I was sort of like a minefield."

Prather also counseled him using some of the basic processes of Scientology. "I went outside my body," Travolta later said. "It was like the body was sort of on its own and I was outside walking round it. I got real frightened, and she said, 'Oh my goodness, you've gone exterior.' "

When he returned to Los Angeles, Travolta began taking the Hubbard Qualified Scientologist Course at the Celebrity Centre with about 150 other students. He confided to the teacher, Sandy Kent, that he was about to audition for a television show, *Welcome Back, Kotter.* After roll call, Kent instructed everyone to point in the direction of ABC Studios and telepathically communicate the instruction: "We want John

Travolta for the part." At the next meeting, Travolta revealed he had gotten the role of Vinnie Barbarino—the part that would soon make him famous. "My career immediately took off," Travolta boasted in a church publication. "I would say Scientology put me in the big time."

Gillham adored Travolta and constantly told him he was going to be a star. To prove it, she gave him Spanky.

Although Travolta craved fame, he was taken aback by the clamor that came along with it. Spanky managed his relationship with his fans. She went to the tapings of his television show, accompanied him to his many public appearances, and persuaded Paramount Pictures to buy a large block of Scientology auditing for his birthday. She was his liaison with the church—in Scientology language, his terminal ("any person who receives, relays or sends communications"). She also became a conduit between the rising young star and other Scientologists in the industry, such as Paul Haggis, who gave Spanky a spec script for *Welcome Back, Kotter* to pass on to Travolta (it was never made).

Travolta generously credited the church for advancing his career and giving him the poise to handle his burgeoning celebrity. "You always have the fear, 'Success is terrific now, but will it last forever?'" he observed in one interview. "When you hit it quickly, you don't know where it will go. . . . Scientology makes it all a lot saner." He introduced a number of fellow actors to Scientology, including Forest Whitaker, Tom Berenger, and Patrick Swayze, as well as the great Russian dancer Mikhail Baryshnikov. (Travolta's friend Priscilla Presley was the only one who actually stuck with the church.) Spanky Taylor was a visible reminder of Travolta's increasing devotion to Scientology, as well as the church's investment in his fame, which could be jeopardized by the indiscreet behavior of a talented but entitled movie star.

When the FBI raid on the Church of Scientology took place on July 8, 1977, Taylor was six months pregnant and living with her husband, Norman, in the squalid Wilcox Hotel. Norm was an executive in the legal bureau. Early on the morning of the raid, he frantically called Spanky and told her to get over to Yvonne's office right away to get the loaded gun she had been given by a friend, which she kept in her desk. By the time Taylor arrived, there were FBI agents everywhere—more than 150 of them at two Scientology buildings, the Advanced Org and Château Élysée. It was the largest FBI raid in history, and it went on all day and night. They brought battering rams and sledgehammers to break the locks and knock down walls. In addition to the 200,000 documents they were carting off—many of them purloined by Guardian's Office operatives from government workplaces—they found burglar tools and eavesdropping equipment. Taylor dutifully made her way through the chaos to Yvonne's office and slipped the gun into her purse. She didn't allow herself to think how crazy it was to be carrying a weapon past all these lawmen.

Outside the gates, reporters were clamoring to get in. Just then, a school bus pulled up, full of kids from a religion class at the Pacific Palisades high school. Taylor recalled with alarm that they were coming to take a tour that she had previously arranged. The wide-eyed teens watched as Taylor explained to the teacher that this wasn't the best time for the tour. (They never rescheduled.)

Within the church, the explanation for the raid was that some Scientologists were being charged with stealing the Xerox paper they used when they had copied the reports on the church in government files—in other words, it was just another example of jackbooted government goons twisting the Constitution in order to crack down on religious freedom. But when the indictments came out the following year, the scale of Operation Snow White was plainly exposed. Eleven Scientology executives, including Mary Sue Hubbard, were indicted in Operation Snow White. Her husband was named as an unindicted co-conspirator, although it had arisen from his original plan.

Saturday Night Fever premiered at Grauman's Chinese Theatre in Hollywood in December. Travolta had spent five months training for the film, running two miles a day and dancing three hours a night. He recognized the opportunity that the film provided, and he supplied a singular, electrifying performance. But when he walked down the red carpet past the fusillade of camera flashes, he looked dazed. "When I got out of the limo in front of Grauman's, I was dumbfounded, I didn't know how to take it," he said in a televised interview at the after-party. "It was like a fantasy, it was like a dream tonight." He was twenty-three years old, now an international star. He was also the most conspicuous Scientologist in the world, after only L. Ron Hubbard himself. And who is to say that Scientology didn't help make his dreams come true?

YVONNE GILLHAM HAD fallen ill. She complained of headaches and was losing weight. She wanted desperately to go to Flag, where she could get the upper-level auditing she thought could cure her, but she was told there wasn't money for that. Instead, she was sent on a mission to Mexico with her husband, Heber Jentzsch, an actor and musician who later became president of the church, a largely ceremonial post. They had married five years earlier. On her fiftieth birthday, October 20, 1977, while still in Mexico, Yvonne suffered a stroke. Jentzsch sent her back to Los Angeles, while he completed the tour. After that, her daughter Janis, one of Hubbard's original Messengers, received a beautiful suitcase from her. Inside there was a letter, but it made no sense. Janis tried to find out what was wrong, but no one would say. Her sister, Terri, went to the Sea Org berthing and found Yvonne lying in her room unattended. Finally, she was sent to a hospital, where doctors found a tumor in her brain, which had caused the stroke in the first place. It would have been operable if she had come to them sooner, the doctors said.

Desperate to get Gillham the auditing she still thought she needed, Taylor went to the financial banking officer and begged her for the funds to send her friend to Flag. "If she wants to go to Flag, she can take the fucking Greyhound," the officer responded.

"You're Yvonne's assassin!" Taylor shouted.

For her impertinence, Taylor was sentenced to RPF. Her new baby daughter, Vanessa, was taken away and placed in the Child Care Org, the Scientology nursery. There were thirty infants crammed into a small apartment with wall-to-wall cribs, with one nanny for every twelve children. It was dark and dank and the children were rarely, if ever, taken outside.

When she got the news, Taylor cried, "You can't do that *now!*" She was thinking of Travolta. He had just called her the day before, saying that he was arriving on an Air France flight after his appearance at a film festival in Deauville, where he was promoting *Saturday Night Fever.* Despite his triumph, Travolta appeared depressed and withdrawn. During the filming of *Saturday Night Fever* his girlfriend, Diana Hyland, had died in his arms. She was two decades older than he—she played his mother in a made-for-TV movie, *The Boy in the Plastic Bubble*—and had already had a double mastectomy when they met. Their romance was doomed when her cancer recurred. Taylor had helped Travolta through that period of grief, but now his mother, the most important figure in his life, had also developed cancer. Travolta asked Taylor if she would pick him up at the airport. She promised him, "Wild horses wouldn't keep me from being there!"

The church officials now told Taylor that someone else would meet Travolta. Taylor knew the star would feel surprised and betrayed. He had come to rely on her, both as an unpaid assistant and for emotional support. He would immediately suspect that something terrible had happened and worry about her. Taylor was mortified to think that she would be the cause of his discomfort.

The RPF had moved out of the basement up to the top floor of the old V-shaped building that formerly housed the Cedars of Lebanon Hospital. Nearly two hundred people were crammed by the dozen into old patient rooms in bunks stacked three high. Because of the overcrowding, Taylor was given a soggy mattress on the roof. It was cold. She could hear the traffic on Sunset Boulevard only a block away. She had a view of the Hollywood Hills and the endless lights of the wakeful city, which was throbbing all around her. So many young people like her had been pulled into the matrix of Hollywood glamour and fame, even if they would never enjoy it themselves. And now, here she was, in the heart of it—isolated, trapped, humiliated, an unnoticed speck on a rooftop. Who could believe that a person could be so lost in the middle of so much life?

Moreover, she was pregnant again. It happened a few weeks after she entered RPF, during a brief marital visit from her husband. There was no maternal care or any easing of the intensely physical work she was made to do with the other "RPF'ers," as they called themselves. For one two-week stretch, they were putting in thirty hours at a stretch with only three hours off. Like everyone else, Taylor ate slop from a bucket—table scraps or rice and beans. After six months on this diet she still wasn't showing her pregnancy; indeed, she was losing weight. She worried that she was going to lose the baby.

A pair of missionaires came to see Taylor one day with a strange request. They were thinking about how to reward the RPF'ers for having done the renovations to the Advanced Org building, which were now almost complete. "We would like you to arrange a private screening of *Saturday Night Fever*," they told her.

Of course, no one in the RPF had been able to see the movie, despite the fact that it was an international sensation. Getting to Travolta wasn't easy, however. He was now the top box-office star in the world. *Playboy* called him "America's newest sex symbol." The church hierarchy was worried that he was also drifting away from Scientology. A screening of his movie would underscore his commitment to the religion at a moment when that seemed in doubt.

As the church's liaison to Travolta, Taylor was the obvious person to make the arrangements.

"First of all, I can't use the phone," Taylor told the missionaires. "Secondly, I can't leave the building. Maybe you'd like a Beatles reunion while you're asking for that."

"We just think you could take care of this," they replied.

Taylor had to figure out a way to get a print of the film from Travolta without having to explain why she had failed to pick him up at the airport and then disappeared from his life for months, without a word. A couple of days later, the missionaires arranged for her to use a pay phone on one of the lower floors of the building. Taylor called Kate Edwards, Travolta's creative director at the time.

"Spanky! Where are you?" Edwards cried. Travolta and his production company had been looking for her frantically.

"Honey, I can't really talk," Taylor said. She told Edwards that she was in the Los Angeles complex. "I've been specially selected to do a program that will help me," she explained vaguely. She said she had an urgent favor to ask—a print of the film.

That was a problem. The movie was being shown around the world and all the prints were out. The only one available was Travolta's personal copy, but Edwards said she would make the request. "Johnny said if you ever called and needed something, just do it," Edwards assured her.

"You can't tell John about this call!" Taylor said.

"I'm going to have to tell him," Edwards replied. "I'm going to have to ask him to borrow it."

The next time Taylor was allowed to call, Edwards told her that Travolta had agreed to loan Taylor the print, under one condition: that he could see her. The missionaires conferred with their superiors. They decided that as long as Taylor got the print, she could meet Travolta for dinner on the Sunday night after the screening.*

Travolta followed up by sending flowers, which were delivered to Taylor in RPF.

*Travolta's attorney denies there was an agreement to visit Spanky in exchange for his personal copy of *Saturday Night Fever*.

The screening took place on Saturday night in Scientology's Lebanon Hall. It was a high point for everyone, all the more so because it was followed by a disco dance. Across the country similar dances were taking place, inspired by Travolta's passionate performance.

Taylor wouldn't be a part of it, however. As soon as the movie was over and the credits were rolling, several Scientology executives, including Yvonne's former husband, Heber Jentzsch, escorted Taylor to an office and told her to call Travolta and cancel their date for dinner the following night.

"I can't do that!" Taylor said.

"There have been all sorts of efforts to recover him, and we can't let you get in the way of that," Jentzsch told her. "Call him right now."

"It's after midnight!"

Travolta was furious when he heard what she had to say. "We had a deal!" he said.

"I know, I'm sorry."

"How could you do this?" he demanded. "How could you leave your baby?" For the first time in their relationship, he raised his voice. "My mother died, and you weren't there!"

Taylor began to bawl so hard she couldn't speak. She recalled that Travolta was asking questions she couldn't answer, questions she had been afraid to pose herself. He seemed to know what she was going through. "Unless you killed somebody, which I don't think you did, there's no reason for you to be where you are," Travolta told her. He had never said an unkind word to her in their entire relationship, and his frankness was devastating.

"I'm doing this so I can be better!" Taylor sobbed. "So I can help you more."

Meanwhile, Jentzsch was jabbing his finger at her and mouthing the order to hang up the phone. She quickly said good-bye and set the phone in the cradle. Then she was escorted back to RPF.

All that night she cried and cried, but when the sun came up, she was flooded with clarity. "I am so fucking out of here!" she decided. "I don't know how, but I'm getting out."

It wasn't obvious how she could escape. She had been placed in RPF in March; now it was September. There hadn't been time to plan because she was working constantly. She didn't know where to turn. It didn't occur to her to call her parents because she was so apprehensive that she might bring shame on Scientology if anybody knew what had happened to her. In any case, she was forbidden to speak to anyone outside the RPF, even to other Sea Org members. And even if she did escape, she realized, she actually knew very little about what was going on in the world. Since she had joined Scientology at the age of fourteen, she had never read a book that hadn't been written by L. Ron Hubbard.

Taylor managed to slip away to visit her ten-month-old daughter in the Child Care Org across the street. To her horror, she discovered that Vanessa had contracted whooping cough, which is highly contagious and occasionally fatal. The baby's eyes were welded shut with mucus, and her diaper was wet—in fact, her whole crib was soaking. She was covered with fruit flies. Taylor recoiled. The prospect of losing both her unborn baby and her daughter seemed very likely.

She finally conceived a plan. Explaining to her guards that she had to telephone the doctor, she managed a brief call to Travolta's office and asked Kate Edwards to meet her the next day at a certain time, giving the address of the Child Care Org. She hung up without even hearing Edwards's response.

The next day she was allowed a brief visit to the nursery. Taylor put an extra diaper in her purse. She had four dimes, all the money she had in the world, and a toothbrush. Fortunately, Edwards arrived, right on time.

Taylor explained to her Scientology escort that Edwards was her sister-in-law who had come to take Vanessa to the doctor.

"Is this approved?" he asked.

"Oh, absolutely!" Taylor opened Edwards's door and handed her the baby. Edwards stared in bewilderment as Taylor loudly told her to call as soon as she found out what the doctor said. Then, under her breath, she added, "Kate, when I shut this door, please drive away as quickly as you can." Edwards nodded, then Taylor jumped in. Edwards hit the gas.

"Spanky, no!" the escort cried.

Taylor hadn't planned any further than this.

She was still dressed in a man's black boiler suit, with the sleeves and legs rolled up. Edwards fetched some clothes from her mother that would fit Taylor's emaciated frame and picked up some diapers for Vanessa, then checked them in to the Tropicana Hotel on Santa

Monica Boulevard. Taylor finally called her husband in the Guardian's Office. Another executive picked up the line. "Spanky! They're looking for you everywhere! Where are you?" he demanded.

"I want to talk to Norm," she said.

"You need to come back!"

Taylor said she would call back at eleven that night. This time, her husband answered.

"Are they there?" Taylor asked him.

"Yes."

She hung up. After an hour or two, she called again. He said he was alone. She told him she was out of the church and not going back. The baby was safe, she said. Norm wanted to meet, and Spanky finally told him where she was. She realized their marriage was probably over, but she felt she owed him that. Norm came over to the Tropicana and they spoke for several hours.

The next morning at nine there was a knock on the door of Taylor's hotel room. Three Sea Org executives were there to haul her back to RPF.

Taylor still believed in the revelations of her religion. She worried that her salvation was at stake. But she was also gripped with fear that her baby and her unborn child were in mortal danger.

At first, she was firm in telling the men that she wasn't coming back. "If you lay a hand on me or my child, I'm filing charges!" she cried. They assured her they just wanted to talk. They told her that they hated to see her be declared a Suppressive Person. She would be cut off from any other Scientologist—nearly everyone she knew. There was a proper way to "route out," they reminded her. Eventually, Taylor agreed to return to the office to file the paperwork that would allow her to leave the Sea Org on good terms and still be a Scientologist.

As part of the routing process, Taylor was given a confession to sign detailing all the "crimes" she had committed. She glanced at the document. Some of the actions cited were drawn from her preclear folders, things she had confessed to her auditors that were supposed to remain confidential. She knew how it worked; she says she had once been assigned to go through members' folders and circle any "evil intentions" toward Scientology. Sexual indiscretions or illegal acts were always highlighted. These would be forwarded to the Guardian's Office to be used against anyone who threatened to subvert the church.

If the crimes weren't sufficiently damning, Taylor came to learn, scandalous material would simply be manufactured. She signed her confession without really reading it. Later, she was given her bill.

The theory of the "freeloader's tab" is that people who join the Sea Org don't have to pay for the cost of auditing and the coursework to move up the Bridge. The truth is that there is never much time to take advantage of such instruction. Taylor had been in the Sea Org for seven years, however, and the bill for the services she might have taken amounted to more than $100,000.

Just before she left the office, the executive handling her case was called away for a moment. Taylor took her confession off his desk and stuffed it in her purse. When she finally left the building, she tore it to pieces.

WHEN HUBBARD FOUND OUT Yvonne Gillham was dying, he sent her a telex asking if she wanted to keep her body or move on to the next cycle. She decided it would be quicker just to let go, but she still wanted the auditing. Hubbard agreed to let her travel to Clearwater, to do an "end of cycle on her hats"—meaning that she would brief her successor at the Celebrity Centre before she died.

Hana Eltringham was stationed at Flag, and she was shocked at the sight of her dear friend. Yvonne was dizzy and frequently lost her balance, and her thoughts trailed away. She refused to take pain medication because it would interfere with her auditing. She tearfully blamed herself for the terrible "overt" of dying and deserting Hubbard. She was desperate to see her children, to say good-bye, but they were kept away.

Hubbard designated Catherine Harrington, one of Yvonne's closest friends, to talk to her about the celebrities in her care—who was a reliable speaker, who was good at recruiting other celebrities. Yvonne talked about various people—some television actors, a Mexican pop singer, the producer Don Simpson, Karen Black, Chick Corea, and Paul Haggis, among others—but she was particularly worried about Travolta. "Please help him. He's especially sensitive," she said. She advised Harrington to deal with the celebrities the same way she treated Hubbard—very delicately, and with an open mind. Gillham died in January 1978.

Spanky Taylor's son, Travis, was born that March, weighing less than three pounds, although he was carried to full term. (Both of Taylor's children are alive and healthy today.)

Many former Sea Org members found their departure from the church to be tangled in confusion, panic, grief, and conflicting loyalties. Many still cling to a relationship with the church, sometimes for years, like Taylor, or for the rest of their lives. The coda to Taylor's story is that a year after leaving the Sea Org, she traveled to Houston to meet with Travolta. He was filming *Urban Cowboy* at the time. On her own initiative, she came to "recover" him for the church. She had heard that he was having problems in his life, and she worried that her own troubles had prevented him from turning to the church for help. It was also possible that if she brought Travolta back into the fold, her standing in the church would be improved.

Like most celebrities, Travolta had been shielded from the church's inner workings. The scandals that periodically erupted in the press about Hubbard's biography, or his disappearance, or the church's use of private investigators and the courts to harass critics—these things rarely touched the awareness of Scientology luminaries. Many simply didn't want to hear about the problems inside their organization. It was easy enough to chalk such revelations up to religious persecution or yellow journalism. "There are two sides to the story, but I don't know both sides," Travolta blithely said when he was asked about Operation Snow White. "I'm not involved with that." In any case, for someone like Travolta, who was so publicly associated with the church, it would be hard to just walk away. He had been asked to declare himself publicly, and he had done so, again and again.

The star was staying in a private house in Houston. He and Taylor met in the evening, after dinner, over a plate of chocolate-chip cookies that she had brought. She explained that she had left the Sea Org and was with her children now, then quickly changed the subject and asked about him. He described the problems he was having.

Former Scientologists have given conflicting accounts of Travolta's stressful relationship with the church at that time. The church hierarchy was desperately concerned that their most valuable member would be revealed as gay; at the same time, the hierarchy was prepared to use that against him. Bill Franks, the church's former executive director, told *Time* magazine that Travolta was worried that if he defected, the church would expose his sexual identity. Jesse Prince has stated that Travolta was threatening to marry a man, although that wasn't a legal option at the time. In Franks's opinion, the church had Travolta trapped. At one point, the star sought assurance from Franks that his private confessions wouldn't be used against him. "My sessions are protected, right?" he asked Franks. In truth, intelligence officers inside the church had already been directed to gather material—called a Dead Agent pack—that would be used against Travolta if he turned.

In Houston, however, Travolta told Taylor that he didn't really feel that he needed to be recovered—he was just taking a break. However, Taylor did persuade him to buy a costly package of auditing so that he could get back on the Bridge. He had stopped his coursework after completing OT III.

After that, Taylor received a letter from Hubbard saying, "Well done." The founder asked if there was anything she needed. She asked nothing for herself, but begged Hubbard to do a "Folder Error Summary" on Travolta, in which the founder would personally review all the star's auditing over the years to spot any mistakes—a tremendous honor for any Scientologist. A Messenger assured her that it would be done.

Not long afterward, however, Travolta stopped talking to Taylor. She got a call from Priscilla Presley, who asked what was going on. Presley had run into Travolta and he said that they should get together. "I'll call Spanky," Presley had told him.

"No, don't go through Spanky," Travolta said.

When Spanky heard this, she realized she had been declared a Suppressive Person. Nobody had bothered to tell her, but from now on, no Scientologist would be allowed to talk to her.

Taylor never tried to speak to Paul Haggis again, worried that she might compromise his relationship to the church. For his part, Haggis had no idea what had happened to Spanky. He wondered why she had just disappeared. But Scientologists were always drifting in and out of his life. Sea Org members, even friends like Spanky, might be suddenly posted somewhere else without explanation, or assigned to Clearwater for advanced training, or sent to a secret Sea Org base where they were rarely in contact with the outside world. That might explain her absence. He didn't inquire. He readily identified with the church's narrative that Scientology was being victimized by an intolerant and uncomprehending press, self-serving politicians, careerist bureaucrats, and reactionary police agencies looking for headlines. By publicly defending Scientology, he took on the great burden of scorn and ridicule routinely directed at the church; and in that way, he also allied himself with persecuted minorities everywhere: he was one of them.

If he had known that his friend had been declared a Suppressive, Haggis would have had a difficult choice to make. It was one he would face soon in any case. In 1983, Haggis's writing partner on the TV series *Diff'rent Strokes*, Howard Meyers, who was also a Scientologist, decided to follow a splinter group led by David Mayo, who had been one of the highest officials in the church. Haggis told Meyers that he couldn't work with him anymore. Because Meyers was the senior writer on the show, Haggis resigned and went looking for other work.

5

Dropping the Body

Hubbard never lost his interest in being a movie director. He wrote innumerable scripts for Scientology training films, but he still thought he could take over Hollywood. He had particularly high hopes for one script, "Revolt in the Stars," that was based on one of his novels. Inspired by the thunderous success of *Star Wars*, Hubbard worked on the script in 1979 with the legendary acting teacher Milton Katselas with the aim of having it made into a feature film.

A journeyman theater and film director before taking over the Beverly Hills Playhouse, Katselas had directed the 1972 film *Butterflies Are Free*, starring Goldie Hawn and Edward Albert (Eileen Heckart won an Oscar for Best Actress in a Supporting Role). He was a vital link to the Hollywood celebrity machine that Scientology depended upon. The list of his protégés included Al Pacino, Goldie Hawn, George C. Scott, Alec Baldwin, Ted Danson, Michelle Pfeiffer, Gene Hackman, George Clooney, and many other now-familiar names. His invitation-only Saturday master class was seen by many young actors as a portal to stardom. He attained OT V status and was one of the most profitable sources of recruits for the church, receiving in return a ten percent commission on the money contributed by his students. At one point, Katselas asked if he could join the Sea Org, but Hubbard told him it was more important to continue doing what he was doing.

When Katselas and Hubbard finished the script of "Revolt in the

Stars," Hubbard dispatched one of his top Messengers, Catherine Harrington, to Hollywood to make a deal. After the Moroccan adventure, Hubbard had appointed her his Personal Public Relations Officer. Harrington came from a moneyed background, and she knew how to talk about finances. She shopped the script around and found a buyer willing to offer $10 million—which, at the time, would have been the highest price ever paid for a script, she was told. The Guardian's Office became suspicious and investigated the buyers, who they learned were Mormons. Hubbard figured that the only reason Mormons would buy it was to put it on the shelf. Harrington wound up being sent to the RPF, and when she balked at that, she was demoted even further—to the RPF's RPF, alone, in the furnace room under the parking garage of the Clearwater base. The script never did get made into a film.

Hubbard's location was a deep secret. Scientologists who asked were told he was "over the rainbow." Meantime, a full-fledged movie studio, the Cine Org, was set up in a barn at Hubbard's La Quinta hideaway. With his usual brio, Hubbard assumed that he was fully capable of writing, producing, and directing his own material, but his novice staff often frustrated him. He would do scenes over and over again, exhausting everyone, but he was rarely satisfied with the outcome. He walked around the set bellowing orders through a bullhorn, sometimes right in the face of a humiliated staff member.

Hubbard was becoming increasingly cranky and confused. He slept with guards outside his door, hiding in the tamarind trees that flanked his cottage. One morning he accused the Messenger outside his door of abandoning his post. "Someone came in and exchanged my left boot for a boot half a size smaller," he said. "They even scuffed it up to make it look the same. Someone is trying to make me think I'm crazy."

IN AN EFFORT to lighten the mood, several of the crew made up a comic skit and gave a video of it to Hubbard. He was offended; he was sure they were mocking him. "He was shouting at the TV," one of his executives recalled. "He sent the Messengers to find the names of everyone involved."

One of the perpetrators of the skit was a cocky young camera operator named David Miscavige. Only seventeen years old, Miscavige had already been marked as a rocket within the church. He spent his early years in Willingboro, New Jersey, a suburb of Philadelphia; it was one of the mass-produced Levittowns built in America after World War II. He and his older brother, Ronnie, played football in a children's league for a team called the Pennypacker Park Patriots. Despite his athleticism, David was handicapped by his diminutive size and severe bouts of asthma, which caused numerous trips to the emergency room.

His father, Ron Miscavige, a salesman at various times of cookware, china, insurance, and cosmetics, was the first in the family to be drawn to the work of Hubbard. Frustrated with the ineffective treatment his son was getting for his asthma, Ron took David to a Dianetics counselor. "I experienced a miracle," David later declared, "and as a result I decided to devote my life to the religion." But in fact asthma continued to afflict him, and his disease was at the center of the Miscavige family drama.

Soon Ron and his wife, Loretta, and their four children were getting auditing at the Scientology mission in Cherry Hill, New Jersey. Ronnie Junior was the oldest of the children, followed by the twins, David and Denise, and the youngest, Laurie. In 1972, the family moved to England in order to take advanced courses at the church's worldwide headquarters at Saint Hill. At the age of twelve, David became one of the youngest auditors in the history of the church—"the Wonder Kid," he was called.

The following year, in June, Ron and Loretta had to return to the United States for a couple of weeks. They needed someone to take care of David while they and the other children were gone. There was another American studying at Saint Hill, Ervin Scott, whose wife was also afflicted with asthma. His memory is that he agreed to let the boy stay with him. He recalls that in the first encounter David's parents, along with his twin sister, met with him before they left. Scott immediately liked the family. The father was "wonderful and bright," the mother was "very beautiful, with high affinity," and the daughter was "the cutest thing." David, however, sat at the end of the couch, unsmiling, with his arms crossed. The family wanted to make sure that Scott knew what to do in case of an intense asthma attack. "They said, 'We have to warn you about Dave,'" Scott recalled. "'David has episodes, very unusual episodes.'" The parents explained that Dave became extremely angry when he was suffering an asthma seizure. "Then they said, starting with the husband, 'When these episodes occur, *do not touch him!*' The mother reiterated, 'Yes, please don't touch him!' I said, 'What happens?' They said, 'David gets very, very violent, and he beats the hell out of you if you touch him.' And the sister says, 'Oh my God, he does beat you, really hard!' " Again and again, the family members emphasized that David had beaten them during an attack.

Scott glanced at David, who, he recalls, nodded in agreement. He seemed almost smug, Scott remembers thinking, "like he was arrogantly proud of kicking their ass."

Scott was puzzled. He had never heard of asthma making a person violent. In his experience, a person in the grip of such an attack was frozen with fear. He said he would heed the warning, however.

The next morning, David moved in. Scott took him shopping and then to a pub, where he bought him a Coke. Scott also got a nonalcoholic drink. They chatted with some other Scientology auditors and David began to warm up. He seemed pleased to be around auditors, but Scott felt that there was "a certain falseness" in his behavior.

They went back to Scott's quarters and watched television, then turned in around ten. Scott placed David in the bed by the window, which was cracked to give him some fresh air. David went right to sleep. Scott was used to the rattle of asthmatic breathing, so he soon fell asleep as well.

Scott remembers hearing a scream around one o'clock. He jumped up and turned on the light. David was leaning on the bed with one arm. His face was blue and his eyes were rolled back. Scott had never seen anything like it. He started to touch him, but drew back and performed a Scientology "assist." He said, "That's it, David, come up to present time," repeating the command twice. David blinked and then jolted awake. He was still disoriented, so Scott performed another Scientology exercise, called a locational: "Look at that wall. Look at that bed." Slowly, David began to focus. Finally he asked Scott, "Did I hit you?"

"No."

"Whew!"

David was still groggy and quickly went back to sleep, but Scott was unsettled. He watched the boy for another hour before drifting off again himself. In the morning, David remembered nothing of what had happened during the night. He got ready to take a shower. When he took off his pajama top, Scott did a double take. He had never seen a thirteen-year-old boy with such muscles. "This kid is built like Arnold Schwarzenegger!" he thought.

While David was in the shower, Scott took a look at the medication on his nightstand. He remembers seeing two bottles and two inhalers. One of the inhalers was a typical over-the-counter medication, but all the others contained steroids. Scott had grown up on a farm, and he had used steroids to treat some diseases in animals, but also to build up the muscle mass in cattle. Could that have had the same effect on Miscavige? (Actually, asthma medications often use corticosteroids, which do not have the same effect as the anabolic steroids that weightlifters and athletes employ. Corticosteroids can stunt growth, however, and if Miscavige took them might have contributed to his short stature.) Scott decided to write a Knowledge Report about what he had seen, which would go to the Ethics Officer. "Here is a Scientologist, and he's taking drugs, and he's having these very bad episodes of asthmatic attacks, that can and should be handled by auditing." He also asked for David's preclear folder, which should have a record of his previous auditing. He was told that David didn't have a PC folder. Scott had never heard of a Scientologist without one.

Scott worked with David on some of his coursework and training drills. At times, the teenager struck him as highly intelligent, but robotic, and there were some concepts he couldn't seem to grasp. For instance, with the most basic E-Meter drill, which was simply to touch the meter and then let go, Scott recalls that David's hand was shaking. "David, relax! This is just a drill," Scott said. David settled down, and they continued the drill, but Scott was troubled. The boy was supposed to be a qualified auditor but he didn't seem to be trained at all. According to Scott, David admitted that he had never audited anyone and that, in fact, he had never even been audited himself. "Auditing is for weaklings," he said. In any case, he said, he was Clear from a past life. Scott wrote up another Knowledge Report.

The course supervisor was strangely impatient with Scott for taking extra time to get Dave through the drills. There was something else that was peculiar, too. A photographer kept following David around. Later, Scott learned that a Scientology magazine was preparing an article about the youngest auditor to complete an internship in the Sea Org. Scott was complicating matters by holding up David's progress.

Scott remembers that on Monday, David audited a preclear. When he came back to the room, he seemed agitated, and Scott asked him what was going on. "Those fucking women!" Scott remembers David exclaiming. "There should be no women in the Sea Org." Scott learned that there were three women who were overseeing David's internship at Saint Hill. David's attitude toward women was deeply troubling, as Scott noted in yet another Knowledge Report. So far, no one in the Ethics Office had responded.

That changed a few days later. Scott was called into the Ethics Office and told that David had complained that Scott was enturbulating, or upsetting, him and causing problems because of the abundant reports he was writing. "This kid is an SP," Scott warned, "and you better handle him." Then he opened the door to leave. David was standing just outside. His reaction told Scott that he had overheard him calling him a Suppressive Person. "He went into total fear," Scott said. That very day, David was moved into another room, and his parents soon returned from the United States. But David avoided Scott whenever they passed each other.

In August, Scott was sitting out in the yard across from the castle and the auditing rooms on the Saint Hill grounds. He was talking to a friend of his, a Norwegian nurse. Suddenly they heard a young woman wailing. Scott remembers looking up and seeing David, his face red and the veins visible in his forehead. He had a preclear folder under his arm. Behind him was the crying girl, who was holding her side in apparent pain. According to Scott the nurse exclaimed, "He beat up his PC!"

Karen de la Carriere was also a young intern at Saint Hill, and she was directed to join the others in the internship room. "They told us that David Miscavige had struck his PC," she recalled. "He had been removed from his internship, and we were not to rumor-monger or gossip about it. We were supposed to just bury it."*

David was not done with Scientology, however. At fifteen, he went Clear in his present life. On his sixteenth birthday in 1976, "sickened by the declining moral situation in schools illustrated by rampant drug use," he dropped out of tenth grade and formally joined the Sea Org. He began his service in Clearwater; less than a year later, he was transferred to the Commodore's Messengers in California, where once again he quickly captured the attention of the church hierarchy with his energy and commitment. He rose to the position of Chief Cinematographer at the age of seventeen. After the skit that made such a poor

---

*David Miscavige's personal attorney denies the incident took place.

impression on Hubbard, David redeemed himself in the founder's eyes by renovating one of his houses and ridding it of fiberglass, which Hubbard said he was allergic to.

David Miscavige filled a spot in Hubbard's plans that once might have been occupied by Quentin, although Miscavige displayed a passion and focus that Quentin never really possessed. He was tough, tireless, and doctrinaire. Despite David's youth, Hubbard promoted him to Action Chief, the person in charge of making sure that Hubbard's directives were strictly and remorselessly carried out. He ran missions around the world to perform operations that local orgs were unable to do themselves—at least, not to Hubbard's satisfaction.*

HUBBARD FINISHED WRITING his thousand-page opus, *Battlefield Earth*, in 1980. (Mitt Romney would name it as his favorite novel.) Hubbard hoped to have the book made into a major motion picture, so the Executive Director of the church, Bill Franks, approached Travolta about producing and starring in it. Travolta was excited about the prospect. Suddenly Franks got a call from Miscavige saying, "Get me John Travolta. I want to meet that guy!" Miscavige began wining and dining the star. "He just moved in and took over Travolta," Franks recalled. But he says that privately Miscavige was telling him, "The guy is a faggot. We're going to out him."

Fleeing subpoenas from three grand juries, and pursued by forty-eight lawsuits, all naming the founder, Hubbard slipped away from public view on Valentine's Day, 1980, in a white Dodge van, with

*Miscavige has been circumspect about what missions he actually performed in his capacity as Action Chief. He once testified: "What is a mission? Okay. Well, you have a situation and a situation is defined as a departure, major departure from the ideal scene, and at the bottom of that there's some Y. Y is defined as an explanation that opens a door to a handling. And if you have actually pulled the strings on the situation all the way down, you will now have a Y, which means that the situation can be resolved. A mission would take a situation, knowing what the Y is, and therefore knowing what exact handling steps are thus possible as a result of the door being opened because the Y was found by evaluation, and they would . . . operate on what is known as a set of mission orders, and the set of mission orders is an exact series of steps, sometimes consecutive, sometimes not, sometimes they can be done concurrently within each other. . . . These mission orders have an exact purpose to be accomplished, exact major targets, exact primary targets, exact vital targets, exact operating targets; they have listed the means of mission communication, and they have also listed the target date for completion." He did not clarify the situation further. (David Miscavige testimony, *Bent Corydon v. Church of Scientology*, July 1990.)

velvet curtains and a daybed. It had been customized by John Brousseau, a Sea Org member who took care of all of Hubbard's vehicles.
The elaborate escape plan involved ditching the Dodge for an orange
Ford. In the meantime, Brousseau purchased another Dodge van for
Hubbard, identical to the first. He then cut the original one into pieces
and took them to the dump. The Ford was chopped up and dumped
as well.

Hubbard briefly settled in Newport Beach, California, in a one-
bedroom apartment with a kitchenette. In the apartment next door
were Pat and Annie Broeker, his two closest aides. Pat, a handsome former rock-and-roll guitar player, enthusiastically adopted the role of an
undercover operative, running secret errands for Hubbard and going
to any lengths to keep their location a secret. His wife, Annie, one
of the original Commodore's Messengers, was a shy blonde, totally
devoted to Hubbard.

Hubbard soon decided that the Newport Beach location was compromised, so the three of them hit the road. Pat drove a Chevrolet
pickup with a forty-foot Country Aire trailer, which mainly contained
Hubbard's wardrobe, and Annie piloted a luxurious Blue Bird mobile
home that John Brousseau had purchased for $120,000 in cash under
a false name. The Blue Bird towed a Nissan pickup that Brousseau had
converted into a mobile kitchen. For most of a year, this cumbersome
caravan roamed the Sierras, lighting in parks along the way. At one
point, Hubbard bought a small ranch with a gold mine, but he didn't
really settle down until 1983, on a horse farm in Creston, California,
population 270, outside San Luis Obispo, near a spread owned by the
country singer Kenny Rogers. He grew a beard and called himself
"Jack Farnsworth."

Hubbard had been used to receiving regular shipments of money,
but after he took flight, the entire structure of the church was reorganized, making such under-the-table transfers more difficult to disguise.
Miscavige ordered that $1 million a week be transferred to the founder,
but now it had to be done in a nominally legal manner. One scheme
was to commission screenplays based on Hubbard's innumerable movie
ideas. That way, Hubbard could be paid for the "treatment"—about
$100,000 for each idea. Fifty such treatments were prepared. Paul
Haggis was one of the writers asked to participate. He received a message from the old man asking him to write a script called "Influenc-
ing the Planet." The script was supposed to demonstrate the range of

Hubbard's efforts to improve civilization. Haggis co-wrote the script with another Scientologist, Steve Johnstone. "What they wanted was really quite dreadful," Haggis admitted. Hubbard sent him notes on the draft, but apparently the film was never made.

Meanwhile, Miscavige consolidated his position in the church as the essential conduit to the founder. Miscavige's title was head of Special Project Ops, a mysterious post, and he reported only to Pat Broeker. Miscavige was twenty-three years old at the time and Broeker a decade older. As gatekeepers, they determined what information reached Hubbard's ears. Under their regency, some of Hubbard's most senior executives were booted out—people who might have been considered competitors to Miscavige and Broeker in the future management of the church—and replaced by much younger counterparts.

Miscavige and Broeker would communicate in code on their pagers. At any hour of the night, John Brousseau, who was Miscavige's driver, would take him to one of the several designated pay telephone booths between Los Angeles and Riverside County to wait for a call revealing the rendezvous point. It was usually a parking lot somewhere. The drivers of the two men would wait while Miscavige and Broeker talked, sometimes for hours.

Gale Irwin, who had been on the *Apollo* when she was sixteen years old and had risen to being the head of the Commodore's Messengers Org, began to wonder what was going on. Hubbard's dispatches had become increasingly paranoid, and his only line of communication to the outside world was through these two ambitious young men. Nearly every one of the original Messengers who had joined Hubbard on the *Apollo* had been purged. David Mayo, who was Hubbard's personal auditor, had also been shut off from contact. He, too, became suspicious of Miscavige and ordered him to be security-checked, but Miscavige refused this direct order from a superior. Gale Irwin says she confronted him, and Miscavige knocked her to the ground with a flying tackle. (The church denies all charges of Miscavige's abuse.)

Brousseau got a call from Irwin. She was agitated. She told him that Miscavige had gone psychotic. She said she had to contact Pat Broeker right away for a meeting. When Brousseau asked to talk to Miscavige, Irwin began shouting orders at him, saying that Miscavige was raving and had to be restrained. In no way could Brousseau talk to him! He must arrange the meeting with Broeker immediately!

Brousseau drove her to a prearranged pay phone outside a Denny's restaurant in San Bernardino, which was used only for emergencies. As they waited for the call from Broeker's driver, a black Dodge van came barreling into the parking lot and slammed to a halt between Brousseau's car and the phone booth. The doors blew open and half a dozen men spilled out of the van, including David Miscavige. Irwin says that Miscavige used a tire iron to pummel the pay phone, without much effect. Finally he was able to yank the receiver off the cable. Miscavige ordered Irwin into the van, and she meekly acquiesced.

With this action, the coup was accomplished: Miscavige and Broeker were now fully and defiantly in control of Scientology. The founder was isolated, caged by his notoriety and paranoia. No one knew if the orders coming from over the rainbow were from Hubbard or his lieutenants, but now it no longer mattered. Irwin was busted. A year later, in 1984, Miscavige declared her a Suppressive Person, which would happen to nearly every one of the original Messengers, the most trusted circle of Hubbard's advisers. David Mayo was sent to the RPF. He was made to run around a pole in the searing desert heat for twelve hours a day, until his teeth fell out.

There was one last obstacle that Miscavige had to remove. In 1979, as a result of the FBI raid, Mary Sue had been charged and convicted of conspiracy, along with ten other Scientology executives, and sentenced to five years in prison, despite the evidence that her health was in decline. She suffered from chronic pancreatitis, a painful condition that made it difficult to digest food. "She was frail and thin and completely oblivious to anything she had done wrong," recalled a Scientologist who escorted her into the back door of the courthouse in Washington. "She said, 'I don't want to be photographed.' That was more important to her than the fact that she was going to jail for five years."

While her case was on appeal, Mary Sue was placed in a comfortable house in Los Angeles, well away from Hubbard. She posed a dilemma for the church, and particularly for her husband. Hubbard was concerned that he might be indicted by a grand jury in New York that was looking into the church's harassment of Paulette Cooper, the journalist who had written *The Scandal of Scientology*. If Mary Sue were sufficiently alienated to implicate Hubbard, Scientology would be devastated. Hubbard dictated frequent letters telling her what to say to prosecutors; the letters would be read to her and then destroyed. A crew of Messengers spent weeks sorting through all the orders and correspondence relating to Operation Snow White and other possible criminal activity that the FBI had not seized, making sure that Hubbard's name was excised from any damning evidence.

Mary Sue still commanded the loyalty and affection of many Scientologists who saw her as a martyr. Moreover, she refused to divorce Hubbard or to resign her position as head of the Guardian's Office. The sprawling intelligence apparatus that she built still operated in secret, behind locked doors. The Commodore's Messengers Org and the Guardian's Office were parallel and sometimes competing arms of their founders, and they had often struggled for power, in a kind of bureaucratic marital spat. Now that Miscavige was fully in control of the CMO, he concluded that the GO had to be ripped out of Mary Sue's grasp—but without upsetting her to the point that she sought revenge.

In the spring of 1981, a delegation of Commodore's Messengers—including Miscavige and Bill Franks—went to meet Mary Sue at a conference room in the Westin Bonaventure Hotel in Los Angeles. Each of them wore a hidden microphone. Miscavige's audacious plan was to seize control of the GO and place it under control of the Messengers, who numbered only about fifty at the time. Several thousand Guardians were still working for Mary Sue. She had treated them kindly, paying them decent wages and allowing them to live in private homes. Most of them remained loyal to her and thought that she was being made a scapegoat. They would have to be purged.

Mary Sue received the delegation of Messengers coolly. Her case was still on appeal, but the outcome was clear: she was taking the fall for a program that Hubbard, after all, had put in motion. She understood the influence she still wielded in the church and the threat she represented. She demanded to deal with Hubbard himself, but Miscavige refused. He controlled access to the church's founder so thoroughly that even his wife couldn't talk to him. Indeed, they hadn't spoken in more than a year. Mary Sue cursed Miscavige and threatened to throw a heavy ashtray at him. But her negotiating position was not strong, unless she was willing to betray everything she had worked to build with the man she still believed was a savior.

It must have been galling for her to negotiate with Miscavige, who was twenty-one at the time—the age Mary Sue was when she married Hubbard. Privately, she called him "Little Napoleon." In exchange for her resignation from the GO, the Messengers offered a house and a financial settlement. Mary Sue had substantial legal bills and no other means of support. Under the guise of having to sort out the messes that would be left behind in the wake of her resignation, Miscavige went over a number of different subjects, even including a couple of murders that were alleged to have been committed by a member of the GO office in London. He wanted Mary Sue on tape, confessing to other crimes, which could then be fed to the government. This was done, Bill Franks asserts, with Hubbard's knowledge: "Hubbard wanted her out of the way. He wanted all guns pointed at her so he could go about his old age without worrying about being thrown in jail."

Mary Sue lost her last appeal. She began serving a five-year sentence in Lexington, Kentucky, in January 1983. Hubbard never visited her in prison. Her letters went unanswered. "I don't believe he's getting them," she later reasoned. Mary Sue was released after serving one year. She never saw her husband again.

MANY PEOPLE WHO JOINED the church under Hubbard would later contend that Miscavige's machinations were opposed to the will of the founder. But there is evidence that Miscavige was acting on Hubbard's direct orders. Jesse Prince says that when Hubbard was angry at someone he would command Miscavige to hit or spit on them, then report back when he had done so. Larry Brennan, who was a member of the church's Watchdog Committee in charge of dealing with legal affairs, had seen how a minor infraction could be inflated into a major offense that justified the most severe penalty. There were no mistakes; there were only crimes. Every action was intended. This logic brooked no defense.

Once a week, after Hubbard disappeared, Brennan had to drive ninety miles southeast of Los Angeles to the little town of Hemet in order to write up confidential reports to be sent to the missing leader. The church operated a secret base there in a former resort known as Gilman Hot Springs. Two Sea Org bases are located on the old Gilman resort, Gold and Int. Gold Base is named after Golden Era Productions, the lavishly equipped film and recording studio set up by Hubbard to make his movies and produce Scientology materials. Int. Base is the church's international headquarters. On the north side of the highway, nestled against the dry hills, is Bonnie View, the house that Hubbard hoped one day to live in. Miscavige keeps an office on the property. Few Scientologists, and almost no one outside of the church, knew of its existence. The local community was told that the bankrupt property on California Highway 79 had been purchased in 1978 by the "Scottish Highland Quietude Club." Most of the Sea Org members on the base had no idea where they were; they had been transported there overnight from the former base at La Quinta in a deliberately circuitous route.

Gold Base was the only place deemed secure enough for Brennan to send his dispatches. Brennan says that in late 1982 he witnessed Miscavige abusing three Scientology executives who had made some small error. The three offenders were lined up before their leader. According to Brennan, he punched the first one in the mouth. The next he slapped hard in the face. He choked the third executive so hard that Brennan thought the man would black out. No explanation was offered. This came at a time when Hubbard was furious that his legal situation left him in limbo, and he was upset about the church's finances. Brennan had access to all the correspondence coming from Hubbard to the Watchdog Committee, and he knew that Hubbard was demanding action. "He wanted a head on a pike," Brennan said.

Gold Base, the Scientology compound in Gilman Hot Springs, California. It includes Bonnie View (center rear), awaiting Hubbard's anticipated return from other realms; the management building (to its right), which houses David Miscavige's offices; and staff apartments (right front).

Brennan says that after the beating, the three executives were held as prisoners on the base.* They were assigned lowly tasks and Sea Org members spat on them whenever they passed. Later, one of the three men approached Brennan, in tears, worried about what might happen to him. "He had to have great courage just to speak to me, because they were not allowed to speak unless spoken to," Brennan recalled. "I had Hubbard's orders in my hand to spit on him. I couldn't do it."

In December 1982, David Miscavige married Michele "Shelly" Barnett, a slight blonde, twenty-one years old. She had been one of the early Commodore's Messengers on the *Apollo*. She was quiet, petite, and younger than most of the other Messengers at the time—about twelve when she joined—and a bit overshadowed by the older girls. "She was a sweet, innocent thing thrown into chaos," one of her shipmates recalled.

John Brousseau was married to Shelly's older sister, Clarisse, and one day he proposed that the two couples go fishing. Miscavige had never been. They drove up to Lake Hemet, a glacial lake in the mountains above Gold Base. It was a beautiful spring day, the sun was glinting off the water, a mild breeze was blowing, the wildflowers were out, and birds were singing. Everyone was dressed in shorts or jeans. They had brought sandwiches and sodas for a picnic.

Brousseau baited the poles with salmon eggs, and then showed the others how to cast. He said to just let the line sink to the bottom and then sit back and wait. Maybe a trout would take a bite.

Brousseau recalls looking over at Miscavige five minutes later. He was visibly shaking, his veins were bulging. "You got to be kidding me!" he said. "This is it? You just sit here and fucking wait?"

Brousseau said that was the general idea.

"I can't stand it!" Brousseau remembers Miscavige saying. "I feel like jumping in and grabbing a fish with my fucking hands! Or cramming the hook down their fucking throats!"

That was the end of the fishing trip.

After Quentin's suicide and Mary Sue's prison sentence, the remainder of Hubbard's family broke apart. His oldest daughter, Diana, had been Hubbard's main supporter. She and her husband, Jonathan Horwich, lived at Flag Base in the Fort Harrison penthouse in Clearwater, with their daughter, Roanne. As her father became increasingly

*The church categorically denies all charges of Miscavige's abuse.

remote, Diana decided to try her luck as a singer and songwriter. She released a soft-jazz album titled *LifeTimes* in 1979, using notable Scientologist musicians, including Chick Corea and Stanley Clarke, as backup. The cover features her in a black dress, lips parted, arms crossed, her pale shoulders hunched, and her waist-length red hair stirring in the breeze.

Although the album received little notice, Diana decided to leave her husband, and the Sea Org, and marry John Ryan, a public Scientologist who had produced her record. She moved to Los Angeles to dedicate herself to music. Horwich agreed to the divorce, but he refused to part with Roanne, who was two years old at the time. Hubbard strongly supported this decision, but Mary Sue was opposed. She wanted her granddaughter to be nearby, and she began agitating for Diana to gain custody.

Several missions were sent to bargain with Diana, but she was unmoved. Finally, Jesse Prince got the assignment. "It was a do or die mission," he recalled. If he didn't succeed in gaining clear custody of Roanne for Horwich, he would be sent back to the RPF. For whatever reason, Diana signed the release he put in front of her. Hubbard was thrilled. He rewarded Prince with a leather coat, a gold chain, some cash, and an M14 assault rifle.

Suzette, Diana's younger sister, was increasingly disaffected. Quentin's death had been a blow, but the fact that there had been no ceremony afterward—his name was essentially erased from family history—left her embittered and wary. She longed for the warmth of her Saint Hill childhood, when her mother would read to her and her father would laugh and toss her in the air. Those days were long gone. The forces pulling her family apart were far too powerful for her to resist. She wanted nothing more than to walk away and start a family of her own. But that was not so easily done. She had tried to elope with another Sea Org member she had met years before, in Washington. "We had fallen in love and wanted to get married and live together for the rest of our lives," her suitor, Arnaldo Lerma, later said. He flew to Clearwater; they got blood tests and a marriage license. Suzette then confessed the plan in an auditing session. "She spilled the beans and I got arrested—well, detained," Lerma said. "I remember being in a room with a chair and a light bulb and two guys outside the door. I was interrogated for several hours. I was not struck, hit, or physically abused. However, what I do remember is the deal I was offered: 'We will give you a guarantee of safe passage out of the state of Florida with all body parts attached if you tell Suzette Hubbard the marriage is off.' " Lerma did as he was told, leaving the church as well. Later, when Hubbard learned about another man Suzette was interested in, he paid him to leave her alone. She was isolated and desperately lonely.

She did finally get married to a Scientologist named Michael Titmus, in 1980, when she was twenty-five, but her father didn't trust him either. Titmus was sent to RPF and denounced as an infiltrator. Suzette was told to divorce him, which she did; soon after that, she was transferred to Gold Base to work in the Household Unit, cleaning rooms and doing the laundry—for David Miscavige, among others.

IN 1985, with Hubbard in seclusion, the church faced two of its most difficult court challenges. In Los Angeles, a former Sea Org member, Lawrence Wollersheim, sought $25 million for emotional distress caused by "brainwashing" and emotional abuse. He said he had been forced to disconnect from his family and locked for eighteen hours a day in the hold of a ship docked in Long Beach, California, deprived of sleep, and fed only once a day. After attaining OT III status, Wollersheim said, his "core sense of identity" had been shattered. "At OT III, you find out you're really thousands of individual beings struggling for control of your body. Aliens left over from space wars that are giving you cancer or making you crazy or making you impotent," he later recalled. "I went psychotic on OT III. I lost a sense of who I was."

In order to substantiate the charges, Wollersheim's attorney introduced Scientology's most confidential materials—including the OT III secrets—as evidence. At this point, those materials were still unknown to the general public. The loss of Scientology's chest of secrets was not just a violation of the sanctity of its esoteric doctrines; from the church's perspective, open examination of these materials represented a copyright infringement and a potential business catastrophe. Those who were traveling up the Bridge would now know their destination. The fog of mystery would be dissipated.

The Wollersheim suit had been filed in 1980, but Scientology lawyers had been frantically dragging it out with writs and motions. An undercover campaign was launched to discredit or blackmail Wollersheim's lawyer, Charles O'Reilly. His house was bugged and his office was infiltrated by a Scientology operative. There was an attempt to trap him or his bodyguards in a compromising situation with women. The church also harassed the judge in the case, Ronald Swearinger. "I was followed," the judge later said. "My car tires were slashed. My collie drowned in my pool." A former Scientology executive, Vicki Aznaran, later testified that there was an effort to compromise the judge by setting up his son, who they heard was gay, with a minor boy.

When the case finally came to trial, the church stacked the courtroom with OT VIIs. "They thought OT VIIs could move mountains," Tory Christman, a former Sea Org member, said. Although she was only an OT III at the time, she persuaded church officials to let her into the room. The Scientologists directed their intentions toward the judge and the jury, hoping to influence their decisions telepathically.

On a Friday afternoon, the judge announced that the OT III documents would be made public at nine a.m. the following Monday, on a first-come, first-serve basis. This was the disaster the church had been dreading. When the courthouse opened that Monday, there were fifteen hundred Scientologists lined up. They filled three hallways of the courthouse, and overwhelmed the clerk's office with requests to photocopy the documents in order to keep anyone else from getting their hands on the confidential materials. They kept it up until the judge issued a restraining order at noon, pending a hearing later in the week. Despite these efforts, the *Los Angeles Times* managed to get a copy of the OT III materials and published a summary of them.

"A major cause of mankind's problems began 75 million years ago," the *Times* account begins. In a studiously neutral tone, the lengthy article reveals Scientology's occult cosmology. The planet Earth, formerly called Teegeeack, was part of a confederation of planets under the leadership of a despotic ruler named Xenu. Although the details were sketchy, the secrets that had stunned Paul Haggis were suddenly public knowledge. The jury awarded Wollersheim $30 million.* Worse than the financial loss was the derision that greeted the church all over the world and the loss of control of its secret doctrines. The church has never recovered from the blow.

The other court challenge that year involved Julie Christofferson Titchbourne, a young defector who had spent her college savings on Scientology counseling. She argued that the church had falsely claimed

---

*In 1989, an appellate court reduced the judgment to $2.5 million, which the church finally paid in 2002, plus interest, which brought the sum to $8.6 million.

that Scientology would improve her intelligence, creativity, communication skills, and even her eyesight. For the first time, much of Hubbard's biography came under attack. The litigant said that Hubbard had been portrayed as a nuclear physicist and civil engineer. The evidence showed that he attended George Washington University but never graduated. In response to Hubbard's claim that he had cured himself of his injuries in the Second World War, the evidence showed he had never been wounded. Other embarrassing revelations came to light. The church stated that Hubbard was paid less than the average Scientology staff member—at the time, about fifteen dollars a week—but witnesses for the plaintiff testified that in one six-month period in 1982, about $34 million had been transferred from the church into Hubbard's personal bank from a Liberian corporation.* One former Scientologist described training sessions in which members were hectored and teased over sensitive issues until they were desensitized and would no longer react. In two such instances of "bull-baiting," Christofferson Titchbourne saw the eight-year-old son of the registrar repeatedly put his hands down the front of a woman student's dress and a female coach unzipping the pants of a male student and fondling his genitals. The jury seemed most disturbed by testimony that members of the Guardian's Office had culled the auditing files of members, looking for salacious material that could be used to blackmail potential defectors. Christofferson Titchbourne had originally sought a $30,000 refund from the church. The jury awarded her $39 million. At the time, that sum could have bankrupted Scientology.

That evening, Miscavige and other members of the church hierarchy had a gloomy meeting in a condo in Portland, Oregon. One of the executives vowed that Christofferson Titchbourne would never collect because he was going to kill her. "I don't care if I get the chair," he said. "It's only one lifetime." There was a lengthy silence, and then Miscavige said, "No, here's what we're going to do." And on the spot, he came up with the Portland crusade.

As many as 12,000 Scientologists came from all over the world in May and June 1985 to protest the judgment in what they called the Battle of Portland. Day after day they marched around the Multnomah County courthouse, shouting "Religious freedom now!" and carrying banners reading WE SHALL OVERCOME! Chick Corea flew in from

*The church claims that Hubbard's income was generated by his book sales.

Japan to play a concert, along with other musicians affiliated with the church, including Al Jarreau, Stanley Clarke, and Edgar Winter. Stevie Wonder phoned in and sang "I Just Called to Say I Love You" as the crowd cheered.

The most notable presence in Portland was John Travolta. It was a decisive moment in his relationship with the religion. The church had made enormous efforts to persuade him to attend. Two years before the Portland crusade, Travolta had told *Rolling Stone* that although he still believed in Scientology, he had not had any auditing for the past year and a half. When asked if he was being exploited by the church to promote its cause, he responded, "I've been something of an ostrich about how it's used me, because I haven't investigated exactly what the organization's done. One part of me says that if somebody gets some good out of it, maybe it's all right. The other part of me says that I hope it uses some taste and discretion. I wish I could defend Scientology better, but I don't think it even deserves to be defended, in a sense."

But here he was in Portland, unshaven and exhausted, having flown his own plane in at midnight for a two-hour visit. "Once in a while you have to stand up for what you believe in, and I'm here tonight, I've had counseling, I give counseling, and I don't want to lose that," he declared. "And it's as simple as that."

The Portland march was one of the greatest triumphs in Scientology's history, capped by the judge's declaration of a mistrial. He ruled that Christofferson Titchbourne's lawyers had presented prejudicial arguments to the jury by saying that Hubbard was a sociopath and that Scientology was not a religion but a terrorist organization. Church members who had been in Portland would always feel an ecstatic sense of kinship. (A year and a half later, the church settled with Christofferson Titchbourne for an undisclosed sum.)

FOR YEARS, Hubbard's declining health was a secret known to few in the upper levels of the church. Only a handful of his closest followers were allowed to see him. He had made no clear arrangements for a successor, nor was there any open talk of it. There was an unstated belief that Operating Thetans did not grow frail or lose their mental faculties. Old age and illness were embarrassing refutations of Scientology's core beliefs.

Death was a subject that Hubbard rarely addressed, assuring Sci-

entologists that it was of little importance: "If you had an automobile
sitting out here on the street and you came out totally expecting to
find this automobile there and it's gone, it's been stolen and so forth,
you'd be upset," he said in 1957, reflecting on the death of one of his
close followers. "Well, that's just about the frame of mind a thetan is
usually in when he finds his body dead." The thetan has to report to a
"between-lives" area, Hubbard later explained, which for most of them
is the planet Mars. There the thetan is given a "forgetter implant."
"The implant is very interesting," Hubbard later wrote. "The preclear
is seated before a wheel which contains numbers of pictures. As the
wheel turns, these pictures go away from him. . . . The whole effect is
to give him the impression that he has no past life." The thetan is then
sent back to Earth to pick up a baby's body as soon as it is born. "The
baby takes its first gasp, why, a thetan usually picks it up." Sometimes
there is a shortage of new bodies, and occasionally a thetan will follow
a pregnant woman around waiting for the moment of delivery so he
can pounce. Contrarily, when a body dies, it's important for the thetan
to be freed as quickly as possible—preferably by cremating the corpse
and scattering the ashes in water, so that nothing clings together. "It's
very confused, this whole subject of death," Hubbard observed. "It's
quite funny, as a matter of fact, the amount of this and that that is paid,
the amount of flowers and that sort of thing which are shipped around
at dead corpses after the thetan has shoved off, and so on. It's very
amusing." He presented himself as an expert on the subject, claiming
he had been pronounced dead but had come back to life on two or
three occasions.

Hubbard suffered a severe stroke on January 16, 1986, at the Creston ranch. He realized that he was in his final days. He summoned Ray
Mithoff, one of his most senior Messengers, to help him put his affairs
in order and administer a "death assist." He didn't ask to see any of
his family members; indeed, one of his last actions was to sign a will
reducing their inheritance, except for a provision for Mary Sue, who
received $1 million, which may have been a part of the agreement that
had kept her from testifying against him. He had previously disowned
his daughter Alexis, an embarrassing reminder of his bigamous marriage to Sara Northrup. Hubbard was in a nightgown, pacing up and
down, saying, "Let's get this over with! My head is hurting!" He signed
the will with a shaky hand.

Hubbard also proclaimed Flag Order 3879, "The Sea Org & the

Future," in which he promoted himself to Admiral and retired the rank of Commodore. He instituted a new rank, that of Loyal Officer, after the stalwart members of the Galactic Confederacy who had imprisoned the tyrannical overlord Xenu. Hubbard appointed only two persons to serve at that level, Pat and Annie Broeker. They were an attractive couple, his closest advisers; he was clearly passing them the scepter. "I'll be scouting the way and doing the first port survey missions," Hubbard promised his followers. "We will meet again later."

On Friday evening, January 24, 1986, Hubbard died in the Blue Bird bus that had served as his living quarters for the past three years. Ray Mithoff, Pat Broeker, and Hubbard's personal physician, Eugene Denk, were at his side, along with a handful of acolytes and employees. His body had suffered the usual insults of old age, along with the consequences of obesity and a lifetime of heavy smoking. Dr. Denk had given him injections of Vistaril, a tranquilizer, usually prescribed for anxiety. Whatever powers Scientology was supposed to bestow were no more evident in the death of its founder than they had been in his life.

Late that night, a handful of senior executives and a couple of private investigators drove to a restaurant in Paso Robles, where they were met by Pat Broeker, who guided them to the Creston ranch. The site was so secret that none of the executives, including Miscavige, had ever actually been there. They arrived around four in the morning. Earle Cooley, a church attorney, took charge of the body. At seven thirty that morning, about twelve hours after Hubbard's death, the mortuary in San Luis Obispo was notified. Cooley demanded an immediate cremation, but when the owner of the mortuary saw the name on the death certificate, she called the coroner. After learning that Hubbard had signed a new will the day before his death, the coroner ordered an autopsy, but Cooley was able to produce a document signed by Hubbard stating that an autopsy would violate his religious beliefs. The lawyer did permit the coroner to take a blood sample and fingerprints to verify that the corpse was actually Hubbard. Many questions would be asked, since Hubbard hadn't been seen in public for nearly six years.

There was another problem that had to be dealt with quickly: how to explain Hubbard's death to Scientologists. Broeker and Miscavige came up with a plan: Hubbard didn't die, he had intentionally "dropped his body" in order to move on to a higher level of existence.

Miscavige told one of the other executives he didn't want to see "any grief bullshit." Sinar Parman, Hubbard's former chef, arrived that morning, to help with cooking and logistics. He found Annie Broeker sitting on the floor of the cabin, with Miscavige's wife, Shelly. Annie had obviously been crying. Meanwhile, he noticed Miscavige and Broeker in another room. "They were joking," he recalled. "They were ecstatic. They'd never been so happy."

That Sunday, Hubbard's ashes were scattered in the Pacific.

The next day, more than two thousand Scientologists gathered in the Hollywood Palladium for a special announcement. The news had been kept quiet until then. Miscavige stepped onto the stage. He was twenty-five years old, wearing his double-breasted Sea Org uniform with a black tie and a gold lanyard over his right shoulder. For most Scientologists, this was their first introduction to the man who would dominate the religion in the decades after the founder's death. Short and trim, with brown hair and sharp features, Miscavige announced to the assembled Scientologists that for the past six years of exile, Hubbard had been investigating new, higher OT levels. "He has now moved on to the next level," Miscavige said. "It's beyond anything any of us has imagined. This level is, in fact, done in an exterior state. Meaning that it is done completely exterior from the body." Someone in the audience whistled in amazement. "At this level of OT, the body is nothing more than an impediment, an encumbrance to any further gain as an OT." The audience began to stir as the realization began to sink in. "Thus—," Miscavige said, then paused and adjusted the microphone. "Thus, at two thousand hours, Friday, the twenty-fourth of January, A.D. 36 [that is, thirty-six years after the publication of *Dianetics*], L. Ron Hubbard discarded the body he had used in this lifetime for seventy-four years, ten months, and eleven days." Miscavige turned to a large photograph of Commodore Hubbard with the waves behind him and began to applaud. "Hip, hip, hooray!" he cried, as the audience echoed him. "Hip, hip, hooray!"

MISSIONAIRES HAD BEEN SENT to Scientology centers all over the world to coordinate the announcement of Hubbard's death. Afterward, they flew back to Los Angeles and met at the Liberace mansion in West Hollywood, near the church headquarters. Most executives in the church naturally assumed that the leadership had already passed to Pat and Annie Broeker, who were the Loyal Officers, the highest post available. That seemed to be as clear a statement of the line of succession as anyone would ever find. Miscavige was not mentioned in the founder's final declaration.

Jesse Prince was at the gathering, having just returned from delivering the news to Scientologists in Italy. After his lengthy indoctrination in RPF, Prince had become a trusted member of the Sea Org inner circle. He and Miscavige were friendly. Prince could tell that he was upset when Miscavige confided that something would have to be done about Pat Broeker. During the memorial service at the Hollywood Palladium, Broeker had told the assembled Scientologists that Hubbard had made significant breakthroughs in his research. At that point, the highest level possible on the Bridge to Total Freedom was OT VII (OT VIII would not be introduced for another two years). Broeker surprised everyone by saying that before Hubbard dropped his body, he had completed the OT IX and OT X levels. Broeker even held up a handwritten page that he represented as being from OT X. It was a very long string of numbers, which he said was a date. It was so far back in time he couldn't denominate it, except to say it was "twelve down and fifteen across," about 180 numerals altogether. "I wanted to show the significance, the magnitude of what he's done," Broeker had said. The audience had tittered in amazement. The little teaser about the OT X materials reinforced Broeker's standing as the new leader of the church. Only he knew what lay ahead.

Every new religion faces an existential crisis following the death of its charismatic founder. Through his missionary work, Paul the Apostle kept Christianity alive after the crucifixion of Jesus. Brigham Young rescued the Church of Latter Day Saints following the murder of Joseph Smith by leading the Mormon exodus across the Great Plains into Utah. Religious geniuses arise all the time, but the historical test falls upon the successor, whose fate is to be forever overshadowed by the founder. Miscavige knew his own talents and limitations. He didn't pretend to be a prophet, nor was he skilled in public relations. "People think I'm trying to be the leader," he confided to his brother-in-law, John Brousseau. "That's not my job. I'm the whip." Other possible successors had been purged or had fled the organization, however, leaving only the Broekers as rivals. Neither of them was a match for Miscavige. He angrily told Prince that Pat had made a fool of himself at the Palladium. Prince was surprised. Until that night in the Liberace mansion, he had been convinced that Miscavige had no interest in leading the church; now he realized that Miscavige felt compelled to remove the Broekers in order to keep Scientology from being destroyed. Whatever reservations Miscavige had had about seizing power had fallen away.

Over the past six years, Pat Broeker and David Miscavige had forged a powerful alliance. Broeker had been on one side of the gate, controlling all access to Hubbard; Miscavige had been on the other, acting as the conduit for the church. Broeker deliberately stayed in the shadows, setting up elaborate drops for the messages that had passed to and from Hubbard's hideaway, sometimes adopting disguises and carrying an Uzi machine gun when he left the ranch. He fancied himself a crafty undercover operative. The consequence of his secrecy, however, was that even Scientology insiders knew little about him.

Miscavige was also well schooled in intrigue. Although he was still quite a young man, he had been running operations for Hubbard for

David Miscavige speaking at the inauguration of the Church of Scientology in Madrid, 2004

several years, with brutal efficiency. In order to eliminate Hubbard's designated successors, however, Miscavige needed a lieutenant with similar qualities of remorselessness and total commitment.

MARK RATHBUN CAME FROM a distinguished but deeply troubled family. His father was a graduate of the US Naval Academy. His artistic mother was the daughter of Haddon Sundblom, the illustrator who created some of the most enduring images in American commercial history—Aunt Jemima, the Quaker Oats man, and the famous Santa Claus drinking a Coca-Cola beside the Christmas tree. The Rathbun family lived in Marin County, a Bohemian enclave just north of San Francisco. When Mark was a young child, his mother had a series of nervous breakdowns. On five or six occasions she received what was the standard treatment of the day, electroshock therapy. In September 1962, when Mark was five, his mother's body was found floating in San Francisco Bay. Her car was parked on the Golden Gate Bridge.

Mark turned into a restless young man. He went to college to study creative writing but dropped out in order to experience the real world. In 1976 he was living in a camp of migrant workers, hoping to become the next Jack London, when he learned that his brother Bruce had become catatonic and had been committed to a state hospital in Oregon.

Mark hitchhiked to Portland to oversee Bruce's care. He carried around a backpack full of books on Buddhism and the works of Jiddu Krishnamurti. Although it is easy to see in hindsight that the nineteen-year-old Mark Rathbun was primed, because of his troubled background and questing philosophy, to become a part of the Church of Scientology, it wasn't clear to him at the time. His current spiritual mentor, Krishnamurti, preached against the idea of messiahs, but he also stated that every individual has the responsibility for discovering the causes of his own limitations in order to attain universal spiritual and psychological freedom. That resonated with Hubbard's aim of "clearing the planet."

Psychotherapy had evolved somewhat from the indignities that had been inflicted on their mother; it had moved into pharmacology. But drugs didn't seem to offer a solution to Bruce's problems; in Mark's opinion, his brother was just being warehoused, held in a chemical straitjacket. Rathbun got a job as a short-order cook at Dave's Deli, and each day, when he went to the bus stop in downtown Portland on his way to the hospital, he would pass the Scientology mission on Salmon Street. He would banter with the Scientology recruiters and soon got to know them by name. One day, he told a recruiter, "I've got ten minutes. Why don't you give me your best shot?" The Scientologist started pitching the Hubbard communications course, which at the time cost fifty dollars. It immediately appealed to Rathbun. "The problem is, I've only got twenty-five bucks to my entire name," he said. The recruiter let him take the course, and threw in a copy of *Dianetics* as well.

In that first course, Rathbun went exterior. It was completely real to him. All the Eastern philosophy he had absorbed had been leading to this moment. He finally realized that he was separate from his body. Hadn't this been the point of the Buddha's teachings—to isolate the spirit and end the repetitive cycle of life and death? From that moment on, Rathbun never looked back. He was transformed.

Another recruiter persuaded Rathbun that he would be better able to deal with his brother's problems if he had more training, which he could afford if he joined the Sea Org. Rathbun signed the billion-year contract in January 1978.*

A few months later, Rathbun was sent to work in LA. One night, he was assigned to escort Diane Colletto, the twenty-five-year-old editor of Scientology's *Auditor* magazine, from the publications building to the Scientology complex in Hollywood where they both lived. It was late at night on August 19, 1978. Diane was a petite and mousy intellectual, with thick glasses. A diligent worker, she was often the last to leave the office. On this night, she was frightened.

Diane's husband, John Colletto, a highly trained auditor, had recently been declared a Suppressive Person. John had gotten into an argument with church officials over a matter of policy. After being declared, he went to visit a Scientology chaplain, who could see that he was having a breakdown. He kept crying and grabbing his head in despair. At that point, he was forcibly detained in the RPF. He spent

---

*Rathbun was never able to apply those advanced techniques on his brother. In 1981, two boys walking their dogs near a vacant lot in Garden Grove, California, discovered Bruce Rathbun's body buried under a pile of debris. The cause of death was never determined and the case was never resolved (www.ci.garden-grove.ca.us/?q=police/Unsolved/1981/Rathbun).

several weeks there, but managed to escape. Diane was ordered to disconnect from him. She told the chaplain that John had threatened her, saying that if he couldn't have Scientology, then neither could she.

Rathbun—a big man, a former college basketball player—knew nothing of this as he rode back to the berthing with Diane in her Fiat. She was uncommunicative. She drove north on Rampart Boulevard, where the Pubs Org was located, to Sunset, and then left on Santa Monica Boulevard. It was mid-August, but there was a breeze from the ocean and the night air was unseasonably cool. As soon as Diane turned the corner from North Edgemont Street onto Fountain Avenue, in front of the Scientology complex, a pair of headlights on high beam blinded them, then a car rammed into them, pinning Diane's vehicle against the curb.

Rathbun was in shock, but he managed to get out of the passenger side of the car. They had come to a stop in front of a small house with a picket fence. He saw the man in the other car get out and run toward Diane, who was still in the driver's seat. Rathbun came around the front of the car, just in time to hear a popping noise and the sound of glass shattering. It was the first time in his life he had ever heard a gunshot. Jesse Prince, who was in RPF on the seventh floor, heard the sound and rushed to the windows. People were shouting, "John Colletto!" Everyone knew immediately what was happening.

Rathbun grabbed Colletto, and they spun around in the street. He got Colletto in a headlock, but Colletto pistol-whipped him and Rathbun momentarily lost consciousness. Both of them tumbled to the ground.

When Rathbun recovered, he saw Diane on all fours, crawling on the sidewalk, and Colletto running toward her with the gun. Rathbun says he got up and tackled John. They crashed through the picket fence and wrestled on the lawn. More shots were fired. At one point, according to Rathbun, the barrel of the revolver was pressed against the nape of his neck and Colletto pulled the trigger. The gun didn't fire, but Rathbun went exterior, viewing the scene from twelve feet above his body.

Colletto broke free and caught up to his wife. He stuck the gun in her ear. Rathbun says he saw what was happening and did a "flying sidekick," but at that fatal moment the gun fired.

Colletto was knocked to the ground by Rathbun's blow and the gun skittered across the pavement. Rathbun picked it up and tried to fire it at Colletto, but the chambers were all empty. Colletto got in his car and screeched away.

Rathbun went back to Diane. Blood was gurgling and spewing from her mouth. He thought she was drowning in her own blood. Rathbun took off his shirt and put it under her head. As he heard the sirens screaming, she died in his arms.*

Three days later, John Colletto's decomposing body was found. He had slashed his wrists and bled to death on the shoulder of the Ventura Freeway.

Because of this incident, Rathbun was singled out for his fearlessness, or what Scientology terms his "high level of confront." Soon after that, he was sent to La Quinta, Hubbard's winter headquarters, where the old man was just then building up his moviemaking enterprise. Miscavige had appointed Rathbun head of what was known as the "All Clear" unit. The object was to resolve the dozens of lawsuits around the country that had named Hubbard as a defendant. He was also the target of grand juries in Tampa, New York, and Washington, DC. Hubbard wanted to be able to return to his moviemaking full-time, but he was afraid to show himself until he was assured that he wouldn't be hauled into court. (He died before that happened.)

Like many Sea Org members on the secret base, Rathbun adopted an alias for security reasons, one that was similar to his real name but that separated him from his previous identity; it also made it more difficult for anyone to find him. Mark became Marty.

AS THE NEW CHURCH LEADER, Pat Broeker quickly sought to exert his influence. He had a special uniform made up for himself, with solid gold epaulettes, and a "Loyal Officer" flag that was to be flown wherever he was in residence. He announced that he was going to issue a new "Grade Chart" on Sea Org Day in Clearwater. He justified the altera-

---

*The police report confirms Rathbun's story. "A suspect, tentatively I.D.'d as her husband, fired one shot through the driver's side of the auto," the report states. "He then forced her vehicle to stop, got out, and became involved in a fight with her male companion, during which time he was firing the weapon, a .22 caliber (short), 8-shot revolver. . . . The male companion was able to wrest the revolver from the suspect, at which point the husband fled." The companion was identified as Mark Rathbun. The empty gun was found at the scene (Michael A. Shepherd, County of Los Angeles Case Report, Aug. 19, 1978).

tion of Hubbard's sacred material with his own divinations because he claimed to be in telepathic communication with the founder. His Sea Org Day speech was stymied, however, when he was told that church authorities expected that a government raid would take place if he showed himself in public. That wasn't true, but it wasn't out of the question. For several years, the leaders of the church, including Hubbard, Miscavige, and Broeker, had been targets of an IRS criminal investigation. Church lawyers persuaded Broeker that while the investigation was still ongoing he should confine himself to another ranch near Creston that Hubbard had purchased. Broeker was content with that arrangement. He seemed more at home with the quarter horses that he so lovingly purchased with the church's money than he did with the bureaucrats in the church hierarchy. He continued shopping for exemplary breeding stock even after Hubbard's death, claiming he was carrying out the founder's vision. He seemed to think he could run the church from the sidelines.

Other than Hubbard's imprimatur, Broeker had few assets on his side. He had the unfortunate combination of being garrulous without being articulate. Many of the executives he had been close to had been forced out of the church or had fled. Even people who didn't like him, however, were fond of Annie. She was in many ways her husband's opposite. She was measured where he was goofy and impetuous. Sweet and shy, with a fragile beauty that some compared to the actress Jessica Lange, Annie had been born into Scientology and was one of the few original Messengers who hadn't been purged. In 1982, Hubbard had made her Inspector General of the Religious Technology Center, the highest post in the church bureaucracy, in charge of protecting the sanctity of Scientology's spiritual technology. It was a job she was ill suited for, by nature and also by circumstance, as she was not an auditor, and for years she had been living at the remote ranch as Hubbard's caretaker, away from the administration of church affairs. In March 1987, Miscavige seized control of the RTC, making himself the Chairman of the Board. He downgraded the Inspector General's post by dividing it into three parts. His new lieutenant and henchman, Marty Rathbun, became the IG for Ethics.

Still, both Pat and Annie remained untouchable because of Hubbard's final decree. And, most tantalizingly, only Pat seemed to know where the new OT levels—which he now claimed went all the way up to XV—were hidden. They were his insurance. Nothing could be more precious in the world of Scientology—to its members, who sought to gain Hubbard's final revelations on the Bridge to Total Freedom, and to the organization, which profited from that journey.

At Miscavige's direction, Rathbun hired a team of private investigators to follow Broeker and dig into his private life. One of them was a former cop who met Broeker at a gun show, then began frequenting Broeker's favorite tavern. He would chat him up whenever he came in. They got to be so friendly that at Christmas the ex-cop gave Broeker a cordless phone. Because such phones emit a weak radio signal, Rathbun's minions were able to record Broeker's calls. The detectives followed him everywhere, but there was no clue as to where the secret OT levels might be hidden.

Miscavige still worried that Broeker was holding vital material back. A few months later, he and church attorneys went to the ranch to persuade the Broekers to hand over whatever confidential materials they might have to the church for safekeeping. While this was going on, a gang of a dozen powerful men assembled by Rathbun surrounded the ranch quarters and hid in the bushes.

Inside the ranch house, Miscavige and the lawyers argued that Scientology would never get its tax exemption if the church did not have in its possession its most important documents. Miscavige also threatened Broeker with the prospect of criminal prosecution. Rathbun had discovered that there was $1.8 million of Hubbard's funds that Broeker couldn't account for. Broeker appeared to cave in. He let Rathbun load the file cabinets in the ranch house into a truck. Had Broeker not agreed, Rathbun was prepared to signal his goon squad to storm the place and seize everything. It took months to sort through the voluminous files, only to find that there was really nothing there—certainly, nothing that resembled new OT levels.

In November 1987, the IRS notified the church that its criminal investigation had concluded. No charges were filed, but that also reduced the leverage Miscavige had over Broeker. A few months later, Miscavige decided that a final operation to retrieve the missing OT levels was in order. This time there would be no subterfuge, no subtle argument. Rathbun brought along a team of armed private investigators and off-duty LA cops as muscle, along with several other church executives. One of them found fifty thousand dollars stashed under the kitchen sink.

Miscavige concentrated his attention on Annie. He took her to a separate room and interrogated her as a detective barred the door, preventing her husband from seeing her. Eventually, Annie admitted that Pat kept a storage locker in nearby Paso Robles, and she coughed up the key. Rathbun's team found more files, but not what they wanted. Rathbun eventually came to the conclusion that there were no further OT levels—no OT IX, X, XI, XII, XIII, XIV, XV—it was all a bluff on Broeker's part, a lie that the church would have to live with, since the levels had been so publicly announced.*

In April 1988, Miscavige formally canceled Hubbard's final directive, Flag Order 3879, that had named the Broekers Loyal Officers. Miscavige declared that Pat Broeker had fabricated the order, although he produced no evidence to substantiate his charge. Broeker's last claim to the legacy of L. Ron Hubbard was destroyed. He fled the country, followed by two private detectives, Paul Marrick and Greg Arnold, who claim that they tailed Broeker for the next twenty-four years, even to foreign countries. They say they were supervised personally by David Miscavige and paid from church funds. "He lived a very quiet, normal life, and everybody around him loves him," Marrick later said of Broeker. "So that's his whole story from our perspective."

The same day that Miscavige canceled Hubbard's order, Annie showed up in a remote re-education camp, in the Soboba Indian Reservation in Southern California, that Scientologists called Happy Valley. It had once belonged to an order of nuns, who left a sign on the gate that said VALLEY OF THE SINGING HEART. An armed guard stood watch. Dogs were trained to track down anyone who tried to leave.

Miscavige was now in complete control.

---

*None of the promised levels has ever been released.

6

In Service to the Stars

In 1986, the same year that L. Ron Hubbard died, Paul Haggis appeared on the cover of the church's *Celebrity* magazine, marking his entry into the pantheon of the Scientology elite. The photo shows Haggis sitting in a director's chair, holding a coffee cup. He's clean-shaven, with glasses, wearing a herringbone jacket with a pocket square in the breast pocket and pleated linen slacks, looking like a nerdy Hollywood executive with a lot of money to spend on clothes. The article took note of his rising influence in Hollywood. He had broken free of the cartoon ghetto after selling a script to *The Love Boat*, then ascended through the ranks of network television, writing movies of the week and children's shows before settling into sitcoms. He worked on *Diff'rent Strokes*, *Who's the Boss?* and *One Day at a Time*. He was now the executive producer of *The Facts of Life*, a top-rated Saturday night staple. *Celebrity* noted, "He is one of the few writers in Hollywood who has major credits in all genres: comedy, suspense, human drama, animation."

In the article, Haggis said of Scientology, "What excited me about the technology was that you could actually handle life, and your problems, and not have them handle you." He added, "I also liked the motto, 'Scientology makes the able more able.'" He credited the church for improving his relationship with his wife, Diane. "Instead of fighting (we did a lot of that before Scientology philosophy) we now talk things out, listen to each other and apply Scientology technology to our problems."

Haggis told the magazine that he had recently gone through the Purification Rundown, a program intended to eliminate body toxins that form a "biochemical barrier to spiritual well-being." For an average of three weeks, participants undergo a lengthy daily regimen, spending up to eight hours a day in a sauna, interspersed with exercise, and taking massive doses of vitamins, especially niacin. In large amounts, niacin can cause liver damage, but it will also stimulate the skin to flush and create a tingling sensation. The church says that this is evidence of drugs and other toxins being purged from the body. Although many in the medical profession have been hostile to the Purification Rundown, citing it as a fraud and a scam, Hubbard thought he deserved a Nobel Prize for it.

In the *Celebrity* interview, Haggis admitted that he had been skeptical of the procedure before going through it—"My idea of doing good for my body was smoking low-tar cigarettes"—but the Purification Rundown, he said, "was WONDERFUL. I really did feel more alert and more aware and more at ease—I wasn't running in six directions to get something done, or bouncing off the walls when something went wrong." He mentioned the drugs that he had taken when he was young. "Getting rid of all those residual toxins and medicines and drugs really had an effect," he said. "After completing the rundown I drank a diet cola and suddenly could really taste it: every single chemical!" He had recommended the Rundown to others, including his mother, when she was seriously ill, and had persuaded a young writer on his staff to take the course in order to wean herself from various medications. "She could tell Scientology worked by the example I set," Haggis told the magazine. "That made me feel very good."

The Purification Rundown is a fundamental feature of Scientology's drug rehabilitation program, Narconon, which operates nearly two hundred residential centers around the world. Celebrity Scientologists conspicuously promote Narconon, citing the church's claims that Narconon is "the most effective rehabilitation program there is." Kirstie Alley, who served as the national spokesperson for Narconon for a number of years, describes herself as "the heart and soul of the project," because it had helped break her dependency on cocaine. A year after 9/11, Tom Cruise set up a program for over a thousand rescue workers in New York to go through a similar procedure, which was paid for in part by using city money. Many participants reported positive results, saying that they had sweated a kind of black paste through their pores while in the sauna. The Borough of Manhattan gratefully declared March 13 (Hubbard's birthday), 2004, as "Hubbard Detoxification Day."

Kelly Preston has promoted Narconon in her native Hawaii. "Starting in the schools, we've delivered to over ten thousand different kids," she said. Preston and Travolta's sixteen-year-old son, Jett, who was autistic, died of a seizure in January 2009. His parents had taken him off of Depakote, an anti-seizure medication, saying it was ineffective. (The church claims that it does not oppose the use of such drugs when prescribed by a doctor; however, Hubbard himself denounced the use of anti-seizure medications.) Previously, Preston asserted on the *Montel Williams Show* that Jett suffered from Kawasaki syndrome, a rare disorder that she thought was brought on by his exposure to pesticides and household chemicals.

"With Jett, you started him on a program that I think is talked about in this book by L. Ron Hubbard," Williams said, holding up *Clear Body, Clear Mind*, which outlines the principles of the Purification Rundown.

"Exactly," Preston replied.* She then talked about her own profound experience on the program. Novocaine from previous dental work began to surface. "I had my entire mouth get numb again for an hour and a half," she said. Other drugs were purged as well, along with radiation exposure from the sun. "I had a bathing suit when I was seven years old—this is completely true. I had a bathing suit that I thought was so cool with holes in the side and a hole in the center," she said. "And I got a sunburn in it. And twenty years later, I had this same sunburn come out in my skin, the entire sunburn." Preston brought copies of Hubbard's book for the entire studio audience.

DESPITE HIS EXUBERANT TESTIMONIAL, Haggis was increasingly troubled by the contradictions in the church. Scientology had begun to seem like two different things: a systematic approach to self-knowledge,

---

* A lawyer for Preston and Travolta claims that the couple "never put their son through a 'Purification Rundown' treatment and would never have engaged in any type of conduct that would have endangered their son's health, welfare, or well-being in any way." He maintains that Preston was referring to herself when she responded to Williams's question.

which he found useful and insightful; and a religion that he simply couldn't grasp. He liked and admired his auditor, and the confessions were helpful, and he continued to advance on the Bridge, even after his unsettling encounter with OT III. He saw so many intelligent people on the path, and he always expected that his concerns would be addressed at the next level. They never were. After OT III, it was all "intergalactic spirituality," in his opinion. On the other hand, he had already paid for the complete package, so why not continue and see what happened? "Maybe there is something, and I'm missing it," he told himself.

When Haggis reached OT VII, which was the peak at the time, he still felt confused and unsatisfied. At the top of the OT pyramid, the thetan was promised the ability to control "thought, life, form, matter, energy, space and time, subjective and objective." The final exercise (according to documents obtained by WikiLeaks—Haggis refused to talk about it) was "Go out to a park, train station or other busy area. Practice placing an intention into individuals until you can successfully and easily place an intention into or on a Being and/or a body." But even if you could do that, how would you know if you succeeded? If you were transmitting the intention "Scratch your head" and a person did so, was he responding to your psychic order or was it simply coincidental? It was difficult to evaluate.

Haggis thought that Hubbard was such a brilliant intellect that the failure to grasp these concepts and abilities must be his alone. He finally confided to a counselor at the Celebrity Centre that he didn't think he was a very good Scientologist because he couldn't bring himself to believe. He said he felt like a fraud and thought he might have to leave the church. She told him, "There are all sorts of Scientologists," just as there are many varieties of Jews and Christians with varying levels of belief. The implication was that Haggis could believe whatever he wanted, to "pick and choose," as he says.

Haggis's career was going so well that in 1987 he was approached by Ed Zwick and Marshall Herskovitz to write for a new television series called *thirtysomething*. They were looking for distinctive voices. "I love the fact that you guys are doing a show that's about emotions," Haggis told them. "I *hate* writing about emotions. And I don't like to talk about my own." But he seemed to be looking for a chance to push himself creatively. With his first script, Zwick and Herskovitz told him, "This is really good, but where does it come from?" Haggis didn't know what they meant. "Where does it come from—within *you*?" they explained. The thought that his own experience mattered was a revelation.

Zwick and Herskovitz sensed that Haggis wasn't happy on the show; in any case, he got a lucrative offer to create his own series and left after the first season. But he had won two Emmys, for writing and producing, and the experience transformed him as a writer. From working with Zwick and Herskovitz, Haggis became interested in directing. He finally got the chance to do a brief ad for the church about Dianetics. He decided against the usual portrayal of Scientology as a triumphal march toward enlightenment, choosing instead to shoot a group of people talking about practical ways they had used Dianetics in their lives. It was casual and naturalistic. Church authorities hated it. They told him it looked like a meeting of Alcoholics Anonymous.

Then, out of the blue, Haggis got a huge break. He did a favor for a friend who wanted to create a new series that would star Chuck Norris, whose career as an action-movie hero had gone into decline. Haggis wrote the pilot for *Walker, Texas Ranger*, which ran for eight seasons and was broadcast in a hundred countries. Haggis was credited as a co-creator. "It was the most successful thing I ever did," he said. "Two weeks of work. And they never even used my script."

With his growing accomplishments and wealth, Haggis became a bigger prize for the church. He agreed to teach a workshop on television writing while he was still the executive producer of *Facts of Life*, and that brought a number of aspiring scriptwriters into the Celebrity Centre. Then, in 1988, Scientology sponsored a Dianetics car in the Indianapolis 500, and Paul and Diane were invited to attend. Executives from the major book chains were attracted to the Scientology reception by the presence of stars, including Kirstie Alley and John Travolta, and also by the fact that Hubbard's books have traditionally sold extraordinarily well. B. Dalton ordered 65,000 copies of *Dianetics* and Waldenbooks asked for 100,000. *Dianetics* went back on the *New York Times* paperback best-seller list for advice books, thirty-eight years after it was originally published.

David Miscavige was at the race. It was one of the few times he and Haggis ever met. The organizer of the event, Bill Dendiu, recalled that Miscavige was not pleased that Haggis had been invited. Dendiu defended his decision because Haggis was now a bona fide celebrity.

"He has had a string of hit TV shows and by my estimation is a very devoted member of the church," he told Miscavige. Paul and Diane met Miscavige and other top-level members of the church for dinner. "Paul takes no shit from anybody," Dendiu recalled. "The fact that he did not suck up to Miscavige—and in fact, had a couple of little zingers or one-liners for him while we were at the dinner—that got me some additional browbeating." He added: "You have to understand that no one challenges David Miscavige."

The Dianetics car crashed in the first lap. Paul and Diane flew home in Travolta's plane, with Travolta himself at the controls.

SUZETTE HUBBARD BLEW in February 1988.

Five years earlier she had met Guy White, a Sea Org marketing executive, on the RPF running program, which at the time was in Griffith Park in Los Angeles—about fifty people running all day long, even after dinner, stuffing themselves on bread and honey to keep themselves going. Suzette was warned by an auditor that Guy was gay. In fact, Guy didn't know if he was gay or not. When he joined the staff, he had to respond to a questionnaire that asked, "Have you ever been involved in prostitution, homosexuality, illegal sex or perversion? Give who, when, where, what in each instance." He had never actually had a homosexual relationship and had been celibate for a decade; moreover, it was generally assumed that homosexuality was a false identity, a "valence," in Hubbard's language, and that such longings would disappear when he got to OT III.

Suzette and Guy married in March 1986, three months after her father died. Their son, Tyson, was born nine months and a day later. It was strange having a child on Gold Base. Suzette had been pregnant when the order was issued banning Sea Org members from having children,* and the only other child around was Roanne, Diana Hubbard's daughter. Other Sea Org members looked upon the children longingly. "People could see what they could never have," Guy White said. The fact that Tyson had been born so soon after Hubbard's death, and that he had shockingly red hair, stirred speculation that

---

*According to the church, "The Sea Org policy on children changed in 1986. The Executive Director International, Mr. Guillaume Lesevre, issued the change in policy which provided that Sea Org members could no longer have children and remain in the Sea Org."

he might be a reincarnation of the founder. "Is he? Is he?" they asked themselves.

Every church or mission maintains an office for the day Hubbard returns. A pen and a yellow legal pad await him at each of his desks. His personal bathrooms have toothbrushes and identical sets of Thom McAn sandals beside the shower. On Gold Base, his modest original house was razed and replaced with a $10 million mansion. A full-time staff attends the empty residence, regularly laundering the founder's clothes and keeping the house ready for his white-glove inspection. His vehicles are still in the garage, gassed up, with the keys in the ignition. On his nightstand is a Louis L'Amour novel, with a bookmark placed midway through. The dining table is set for one.

The search for Hubbard's reincarnated being resembles the quest for the new Dalai Lama in Tibetan Buddhism, although there are few clues about his identity. He had prophesied that he would be out of action "for the next 20–25 years." In some versions of the story, Hubbard will be recognized by his red hair, which is why Tyson's birth aroused such expectations.

Suzette was terrified that Tyson would be taken away from her. She had little time with him as it was. There was a Sea Org policy, written by her father, which mandated an hour a day of "family time," but that had been canceled. Now Suzette was pregnant again. Over a period of days she smuggled toys and clothes via a laundry basket into her little Mazda; then one night she left a farewell note for Guy, grabbed Tyson, and drove to San Diego. A few days later, she moved in with Mary Sue. Mary Sue was living in a house in the Los Feliz neighborhood of Los Angeles that the church provided when she got out of prison. Amid all the anxiety, Suzette had a miscarriage.

After Suzette blew, Guy recalls being sent to Happy Valley and being told he would have to divorce his wife. Jonathan Horwich, Roanne's father, was also in Happy Valley, along with Arthur Hubbard, Ron and Mary Sue's youngest child. One night, while Horwich was supposed to be standing guard, Arthur blew and was never recovered.

In October 1988, Guy also decided to escape. Each evening, he went for a stroll along the fence line, a little farther each time, carrying a snack for the German shepherd guard dogs. One night, he jumped the fence, but the dogs betrayed him and began barking. He had to dive off the road when he saw the lights of the blow team coming after him. For hours, he stumbled through the brush, bleeding, his clothes torn, until he made it to Hemet, where he pounded on the door of a bowling alley. In broken Spanish, he told the person who peeked out that he had been in a car wreck.

Guy finally rejoined Suzette. (They had two other children before he came out to her as gay. They divorced in 1998.)

LIKE PAUL HAGGIS, Tom Cruise had been raised Catholic, although he was more religiously inclined than Paul. His family moved frequently, and he spent part of his childhood in Canada, where he had the reputation of being a headstrong, troublesome, charismatic, and charming boy. His schoolwork suffered because of dyslexia, and he later said that when he graduated from high school he was "a functional illiterate." However, he excelled in sports and drama. His family, like the Haggis family, threw themselves into theater, founding an amateur troupe of players in Ottawa. His antisocial, bullying father was a disruptive force in the family, and early one morning, when Cruise was twelve, his mother packed up her three daughters and her precocious son and fled back to America. "We felt like fugitives," Cruise later recalled.

Spiritual questing and a tendency toward piety were already features of Cruise's personality. He spent a year in seminary in Cincinnati, with a view toward joining the priesthood. But there was another, intensely ambitious side that was focused entirely on stardom. He went to Hollywood when he was eighteen, and managed to get a role in *Endless Love*, a movie starring Brooke Shields. He was a natural actor, but also persistent and choosy, quickly finding his way into memorable roles. The longing to express his spiritual side had never gone away, but it was difficult, in Hollywood, to know exactly how to fit that in.

There was one church that was especially designed to resolve this dilemma.

Cruise's first wife, the actress Mimi Rogers, introduced him to Scientology in 1986. He had just finished filming *Top Gun*, which had made him the world's biggest movie star. He had little incentive to publicly declare himself a Scientologist after the widespread opprobrium directed at Scientology following the FBI raids on Operation Snow White and the exposure of the church's esoteric beliefs. Rumors of his involvement began to mount, however. For several years he managed to keep his affiliation quiet, even from church management. Using his birth name, Thomas Mapother IV, he received auditing at a small Scientology mission called the Enhancement Center in Sherman Oaks, which Rogers had started with her former husband. Rogers's close friend, and former roommate, Kirstie Alley, did her auditing there, along with singer—and later, congressman—Sonny Bono, who had also been brought into the church by Rogers. Cruise would later credit Scientology's study methods for helping him overcome his dyslexia.

The triumph of adding Cruise to the Scientology stable was fraught with problems. Mimi Rogers was at the top of that list. Her parents had been involved with Dianetics since the early days of the movement. In 1957, when Mimi was a year old, they had moved to Washington, DC, to work for Hubbard, and her father, Philip Spickler, had briefly joined the Sea Org. But Mimi's parents had become disaffected by the end of the seventies. They were considered "squirrels," because they continued to practice Scientology outside the guidance of the church. It would be one thing to have Tom Cruise as a trophy for Scientology, but it would be a disaster if he became a walking advertisement for the squirrels.

When Miscavige learned of Cruise's involvement in Scientology, he arranged to have the star brought to Gold Base, alone, at its secret desert location near Hemet, in August 1989. He assigned his top people to audit and supervise the young star during his first weekend stay. Cruise arrived wearing a baseball cap and dark glasses, trying to keep a low profile, although everyone on the base knew he was there.

Cruise was preparing to make *Days of Thunder* that fall. He had just seen a twenty-one-year-old Australian actress, Nicole Kidman, in the thriller *Dead Calm*, and he was so enchanted that he cast her in a part she was far too young to play: a brain surgeon who brings Cruise's character back to life after he crashes his race car. They had an immediate, intense connection, one that quickly became a subject of tabloid speculation.

According to Rathbun, Cruise and Miscavige now had a common interest: getting rid of Mimi. She demanded and received a church mediation of their relationship, which involves each partner being put on E-Meters and confessing their "crimes" in front of the other. But with Cruise ready to move on and Miscavige seemingly set against her, Rogers stood little chance. Marty Rathbun and a church attorney went to her home carrying divorce papers. "I told her this was the right thing to do for Tom, because he was going to do lots of good for Scientology," Rathbun recalled. "That was the end of Mimi Rogers."

Rogers later said that she and Cruise were already having difficulty in their marriage. He had been seriously thinking about becoming a monk, in which case marriage wouldn't fit into his plans. "He thought he had to be celibate to maintain the purity of his instrument," she told *Playboy.* "Therefore, it became obvious that we had to split."

AFTER TWO YEARS, Annie Broeker had worked her way out of Happy Valley. She was assigned to Gold Base, which serves as the headquarters for the Commodore's Messengers Org; Golden Era Productions, which makes Scientology films and manufactures the audiovisual materials for the church, as well as E-Meters; and the Religious Technology Center, which enforces the orthodoxy of Scientology practices. Through his position as chairman of the RTC, Miscavige directed the church's operations, spending much of his time living on the base. Rathbun and other top executives were also living and working on the five-hundred-acre base, which was still so hush-hush that few Scientologists knew of its existence. Rathbun believed that Miscavige wanted Annie close by, in case Pat Broeker ever stirred back to life.

An ex-marine named Andre Tabayoyon, who oversaw construction of the security at the Gold Base, later testified that church funds were used to purchase assault rifles, shotguns, and pistols; he also said that explosive devices were placed around the perimeter to be used in case of assault by law enforcement officials. Surrounded by a security fence with three-inch spikes, patrolled by armed guards, and monitored by cameras, motion detectors, infrared scanners, and a sniper's nest at the top of a hill, the property houses about eight hundred Sea Org members, in conditions that the church describes as "like one would find in a convent or seminary, albeit much more comfortable."

Annie resumed using her maiden name, Tidman. Although she was continuously under guard, she had fallen in love with another Sea Org member—Jim Logan, the same man who had recruited Paul Haggis into Scientology on the street corner in London, Ontario. Annie had met Logan in Happy Valley when both were on the RPF. Jim and Annie married in June 1990 and moved to Sea Org berthing near Gold Base. Logan was no longer the long-haired hippie he had been in those days; he was now middle-aged and balding, with a black moustache, but he still had those intense, playful eyes and a ready laugh. His outsized, boisterous personality didn't always fit well in the highly regimented life he had signed up for. In the summer of 1992, Logan was served with a "non-enturbulation order," which meant that he should stop stirring things up. In October, eight men came to escort him to a detention facility where troublesome staff members were confined. Logan was told that he had been declared a Suppressive Person and was going to be booted out of the Sea Org.

Annie had previously confided that she was "finished" with the Sea Org and would leave if Jim was ready. He didn't want to go then; he still hoped to rehabilitate himself in the eyes of the church, but Annie made application to formally route out of the Sea Org. In a few months, if all went well, they would have a quiet reunion in Nova Scotia, where they could have children and forget the past. Annie promised him, "They can't make me divorce you." But on October 8, 1992, Logan's last day in the Sea Org, church officials told him that Annie had been ordered to disconnect from him. He was served with divorce papers, given a freeloader tab for more than $350,000, and then dropped off at the bus station with a ticket to Bangor, Maine.

Several times after that, Jim and Annie were able to speak secretly. She would manage to sneak a call to him late at night, or he would have his mother call her. When Annie couldn't wait any longer to see him, Jim bought her an open ticket from Ontario, California—the nearest airport—to Bangor. It would be waiting for her to pick up whenever she wanted. A few weeks later, Jim got a call from Annie: she was on her way. It was about five in the morning in California. She was catching a flight that stopped in Denver, then went on to Boston, where she would change planes for Bangor. Jim set out from Nova Scotia for the nine-hour drive to the airport.

Rathbun got the message that Annie had fled the base about an hour and a half after she left. He was panicked. Annie knew as well as anyone the inside story of the secret money transfers to Hubbard, the offshore accounts, the shredding of incriminating documents. She could torpedo the church's application for tax-exempt status. She also knew the true circumstances of Hubbard's last days. She might even reunite with Pat Broeker, and the two of them could pose a challenge to Miscavige. Rathbun saw Annie as a potential "doomsday machine."

According to Gary Morehead, the hulking chief of security at Gold Base at the time, a "blow drill" went into effect immediately. Morehead had refined the process to a model of Sea Org efficiency. Each year, a minimum of a hundred people attempted to escape from Gold, but few got away cleanly. Morehead's security team kept files on members, containing bank account and credit card numbers, family contacts, even hobbies and predilections. When one senior executive fled in 1992, for instance, Morehead knew he was a baseball fan. He caught him a week later in the parking lot of the San Francisco Giants stadium.

Morehead's team was aided by the isolation of the base—Gold was in a narrow valley in the middle of the desert, seven miles from the village of Hemet. There was a single highway, easy to patrol; mountain ranges enclosed the base on either side, and the rocky slopes were copiously supplied with cactus and rattlesnakes. Many of the Sea Org members had neither the resources nor the skills to get very far. There was an ingrained distrust of the non-Scientology "wog" world and its system of justice, as well as a fatalistic view of the reach of the church, especially among Sea Org members who, like Annie, had grown up in Scientology. Those who had cell phones used them mainly as walkie-talkies for communication on the base; phone records were monitored and the phones would be taken away if they were used to make outside calls. Few of them had cars of their own, or even driver's licenses, so the best they could do was to try to get to the bus station before they were discovered missing. By the time the bus made its next stop, however, there was usually a member of Morehead's team waiting for them. If that failed, Morehead's security squad would stake out the houses of the blown member's family and friends, using scanners that could listen in on cordless phones and cell phones, and running the license plates of everyone who came and went. When the team finally confronted their prey, they would try to talk them into returning to the base voluntarily. If that failed, occasionally they would use force.*

Most of those who fled were torn by conflicting emotions. On the one hand, they were often frightened, humiliated, and angry. They desperately wanted a life outside the organization. Some, like Annie, wanted to have children, which she was forbidden to do as a Sea Org member. On the other hand, they believed that their eternal salvation was at stake. The youthful enthusiasm that had caused them to sign

---

*The church denies that there is such a thing as the blow drill. The church produced an affidavit by Morehead, executed Mar. 31, 1997, in which he says: "I have seen people leave and they were free to do so. I am now doing so myself. . . . I am aware of stories of individuals claiming to have been held against their will, but I know for myself and from my security position that the stories are completely false." Morehead repudiates the statement, saying, "In March of 1997 at that specific moment I would have signed anything."

their billion-year contract of service may have been dampened, but there was usually some residual idealism that the security team could appeal to. Typically, in these confrontations, Morehead would bring along the escapee's "opinion leader," which could be his case supervisor, or another family member who was in Scientology—his wife or his mother, for instance. In many instances, the fleeing Sea Org member didn't even argue; he just gave up, knowing that he would probably be taken directly to RPF, where he might spend months or years working his way back into good standing.

At any time, a fleeing member could guarantee his safety by simply calling the police, but that rarely if ever happened. The Riverside County Sheriff's Department, whose jurisdiction includes Gold Base, says that there has never been an outcry of abuse, or an accusation of illegal detention from members of the church at the base. Although the Sea Org members lived inside a highly secure compound in a desert hideaway, surrounded by fences and high-tech sensors, most of them weren't really being held against their will. On the contrary, it was their will that held them. But according to Morehead, no one who escaped ever returned voluntarily.

As soon as Morehead learned that Annie had blown, his team began combing through her personal effects, calling hotels and motels in the area, and looking for clues as to where she was headed. The easiest way of doing that was to have someone pretend to be Annie and try to book a flight, then be told, for instance, "Oh, we already have you on the eleven-ten flight to Boston." If that didn't work, another member would call the airlines, posing as a sick relative, and demand help in finding the missing "son" or "wife" or whatever; if the airline representative refused to give out that information, the member would continue asking to speak to a higher-up, until he got the information. In one case, it was the vice president of an airline who, thinking he was responding to a family medical emergency, gave up the pertinent details. Morehead also hired former FBI or CIA agents as private investigators. As soon as an escapee made the mistake of using a credit card, the team would know almost immediately where the charge was placed. Morehead was always surprised at how easily such supposedly confidential information could be obtained. His team quickly learned that Annie was on the flight to Boston.

Minutes later, Marty Rathbun lit out for the airport at a hundred miles an hour. He didn't even have time to change clothes. He was wearing a T-shirt, sweatpants, and sneakers. His secretary booked a direct flight that would arrive at Boston only twenty minutes after Annie's, and just twenty minutes before her connecting flight to Bangor.

It was winter and snowing in Boston when he landed, at ten at night, when most of the air traffic had ended. He ran through the nearly empty corridors of Logan Airport to the gate for the Bangor flight. There was a stairwell that led downstairs, and a door that opened to the tarmac. Rathbun rushed outside into the frigid air. The passengers were still on the ramp; Annie was only six feet away from him. "Annie!" he cried. She turned around. As soon as she saw who it was, her shoulders slumped, and she walked toward him.

Rathbun talked to Miscavige and said that he would get a couple of hotel rooms in Boston and bring Annie back in the morning, but Miscavige was unwilling to risk it. He told Rathbun that he had already arranged for John Travolta's jet to pick them up a few hours later.

Annie and Jim Logan were finally divorced on August 26, 1993. He never saw her again. (She died in 2011 of lung cancer, at the age of fifty-five.)

BY HIS ACTIONS, Miscavige showed his instinctive understanding of how to cater to the sense of entitlement that comes with great stardom. It was not just a matter of disposing of awkward personal problems, such as clinging spouses; there were also the endless demands for nourishment of an ego that is always aware of the fragility of success; the longing for privacy that is constantly at war with the demand for recognition; the need to be fortified against ordinariness and feelings of mortality; and the sense that the quality of the material world that surrounds you reflects upon your own value, and therefore everything must be made perfect. These were qualities Miscavige demanded for himself as well. He surrounded Tom Cruise and Nicole Kidman with an approving and completely deferential environment, as spotless and odorless as a fairy tale. A special bungalow was prepared for their stay at Gold Base, along with a private rose garden. When the couple longed to play tennis, a court was rehabilitated, at significant expense. Miscavige heard about the couple's fantasy of running through a field of wildflowers together, so he had Sea Org members plant a section of the desert; when that failed to meet his expectations, the meadow was plowed up and sodded with grass. Miscavige assigned them a personal chef, Sinar Parman, who had cooked for Hubbard, and had a high-end gym constructed that was mainly for the use of Cruise and himself. When a flood triggered a mudslide that despoiled the couple's romantic bungalow, Miscavige held the entire base responsible, and ordered everyone to work sixteen-hour days until everything was restored to its previous pristine condition.

In July 1990, Cruise's involvement with the church became public in an article in the tabloid *Star*. (Cruise himself didn't admit his affiliation until two years later, in an interview with Barbara Walters.) The fact that the information was leaked, probably from a source within the church, was at once a great embarrassment for Miscavige and a relief, because Cruise's name was now finally linked irrevocably in the public mind with Scientology. He offered an unparalleled conduit to Hollywood celebrity culture, and Miscavige went to great lengths to court him. At Thanksgiving, 1990, he ordered Parman to cook dinner for Cruise's whole family. Miscavige even arranged for Cruise to place some investments with the Feshbach brothers—Kurt, Joseph, and Matthew—three Palo Alto, California, stockbrokers. They were devoted Scientologists who had made a fortune by selling short on the stock market. According to Rathbun, when Cruise's investments actually lost money, the Feshbachs obligingly replenished the star's account with their personal funds.

Early on, Cruise and Miscavige shared a powerful sense of identity with each other. They were both short but powerfully built, "East Coast personalities," as Parman diagnosed them. They shared a love of motorcycles, cars, and adventurous sports. Miscavige was bedazzled by the glamour surrounding the star, who introduced him to a social set outside of Scientology, a world Miscavige knew little about. He had spent most of his life cloistered in the Sea Org. He was thrilled when he visited Cruise on the set of *Days of Thunder*, and the actor took him skydiving for the first time. Cruise, for his part, fell under the spell of Miscavige's commanding personality. He modeled his determined naval-officer hero in *A Few Good Men* on Miscavige, a fact that the church leader liked to brag about.

Just before Christmas, 1990, Sinar Parman was told that Tom and Nicole were going to get married, and that he and a Sea Org pastry chef, along with their wives, would be cooking for the wedding party. Parman was assured that they would get paid for their trouble; in the meantime, they should buy some civilian clothes suitable for a cold climate. Parman went shopping and put everything on his credit card, along with a Christmas present for Cruise. Then Cruise's private jet flew them to Telluride, Colorado, where the wedding took place. They spent three days preparing meals for guests. Cruise's auditor, Ray Mithoff, performed the ceremony, and David Miscavige served as best man. Afterward, Parman was informed that Miscavige had changed his mind about paying for his services and the expenses incurred. Parman was left with hundreds of dollars charged to his credit card, which he struggled to pay off on his Sea Org salary—fifty dollars a week at the time.

At first, Tom and Nicole seemed like the ideal Scientology power match. They were intelligent, articulate, extraordinarily attractive people. At Gold Base, Tom reached OT III. He would have spent a considerable amount of time after that self-auditing in order to exorcise his body thetans. Although Nicole didn't share Tom's obvious enthusiasm for Scientology—she was a cooler personality in any case—she was drawn along by his intensity. She went Clear in no time. Within a year, she had reached OT II, but then, mysteriously, stopped. A candidate who has begun the OT levels is not supposed to pause until OT III has been achieved. Miscavige suspected the influence of a Suppressive Person—specifically, Kidman's father, Antony Kidman, a clinical psychologist who had written several popular self-help books in Australia. From the beginning Kidman was privately considered a Potential Trouble Source.

One day at Gold Base, Marty Rathbun summoned a sixteen-year-old Sea Org member, Marc Headley, and told him that he had been selected to undergo special auditing. He was to tell no one about it, including his co-workers and his family. And by the way, the auditor would be Tom Cruise.

Headley reported to a large conference room. Right away he noticed Nicole Kidman, who was also receiving auditing, and Kirstie Alley, who he later came to believe was there mainly as a "celebrity prop," since she did little other than read.

"Hello, I am Tom," Headley remembers Cruise saying, vigorously shaking his hand.* He handed Headley the metal cans that were

---

*Cruise, through his attorney, says he has no recollection of meeting Marc Headley. Bruce Hines, who was there to make sure the process was done correctly, witnessed the sessions and clearly remembers Cruise auditing Headley.

attached to the E-Meter and asked if the temperature in the room was all right. Then he instructed Headley to take a deep breath and let it out. This was a metabolism test, which is supposed to show whether the preclear was prepared for the session. Apparently, the needle on the E-Meter didn't fall sufficiently. Headley was so starstruck that he was having trouble focusing.

"Did you get enough sleep?" Cruise asked.

"Yeah."

"Did you get enough to eat?"

"Yeah."

"Did you take your vitamins?"

Headley said he never took vitamins.

"That might be the problem," Cruise said. He went into the pantry, which was filled with snacks for the celebrities. Headley was used to the meager Sea Org fare, and he was taken aback by the cornucopia laid out for the stars to nibble on. As Cruise rummaged through the cabinets, Headley bit into a cheese Danish. The actor found several vitamins and then asked, "Do you take a lot of bee pollen?"

Headley had no idea what he meant.

"Never had bee pollen?" Cruise said excitedly. "Oh, that will do the trick for sure."

He led Headley to his Yamaha motorcycle and rode the two of them to the base canteen. It was dinnertime, and the canteen was filled with Headley's gawking co-workers. Headley was surprised to learn that there was bee pollen for sale, although he says Cruise didn't pay for it; he just grabbed it and they went back to the conference room. This time, Headley passed the metabolism test, although he privately credited the Danish over the bee pollen.

According to Headley, Cruise helped him through the Upper Indoctrination Training Routines. "Look at the wall," Cruise would have said, according to Hubbard's specifications. "Thank you. Walk over to the wall. Thank you. Touch the wall. Thank you." The purpose of this exercise, according to Hubbard, is to "assert control over the preclear and increase the preclear's havingness." Cruise went on to ask Headley to make an object, such as a desk, hold still, or become more solid. Another exercise involved telling an ashtray to stand up, at which point the preclear stands and lifts the ashtray, thanks the ashtray, and then commands the ashtray to sit down. With each repetition, the preclear's commands get louder, so soon he is yelling at the ashtray at the top of his voice. The purpose of this drill is to come to the realization that your intention is separate from your words and the sound waves that carry them. These procedures went on for hours, as Headley robotically responded to Cruise's commands. "You learn that if you don't do what they say, they'll just ask the same questions five million times," Headley recalled. At one point, he fell asleep, but he kept responding automatically. This training went on for hours every day for several weeks, until Tom and Nicole returned to Hollywood.

When Nicole moved into Tom's mansion in Pacific Palisades, they were under constant watch. Miscavige's wife, Shelly, interviewed Scientology candidates for Tom and Nicole's household staff. According to former executives, the Scientologists who worked for Cruise and Kidman reported to the church about whatever they observed. Miscavige offered the couple significant gifts of service from Sea Org members. They installed a sophisticated audiovisual system. Sinar Parman, the chef, says he helped design the kitchen. There was a comfortable, symbiotic relationship between the star and the church. The use of unpaid church clergy to help him renovate his house, hire his staff, and install sophisticated technology was simply a part of the deal.*

PAUL HAGGIS WAS ALWAYS a workaholic, and as his career took off, he spent even less time with his family. He wouldn't get home till late at night or early in the morning. His three daughters scarcely knew who he was.

In general, Haggis was far more interested in causes than people. He drove an environmentally friendly car—a little yellow Mini Cooper with a WAR IS NOT THE ANSWER bumper sticker. The Haggis house became a regular stop for the social-justice sector of the Hollywood left. Once when Haggis threw a fund-raiser for Tibet, the Dalai Lama came. The backyard was strewn with celebrities and chanting monks. The girls thought it was hysterical. Barbra Streisand introduced herself to the Dalai Lama, and he asked what she did. "A little singing, a little dancing," she told him.

For years, Paul and Diane's marriage had been in turmoil, and in 1983 they began an epic and bitter divorce. The proceedings lasted for

*Cruise's attorney remarks, "So far as I know, Mr. Cruise has always paid for any services he received."

nine years. The girls lived with Diane, visiting Paul every other weekend. During this period of estrangement from his wife, Haggis flew to New York with a casting director, who was also a Scientologist. They shared a kiss. He later confessed the incident during an auditing session and was sent to the Ethics Office, where he was assigned some minor punishment. He had been to Ethics before, usually for missing coursework, but he was beginning to feel that the more famous he became, the less likely he was to be rebuked for behavior that was considered "out ethics" for other members.

Anytime Haggis boggled at an illogical or fanciful piece of data, he was invariably reminded that it was his failure entirely. He had come into Scientology as an adult, so his experience outside the church still informed his judgments. When he stumbled on something in Scientology that he thought was ridiculous, he would make a mental detour around it, not wanting to spend the time and money to do the "repairs" that his supervisors would prescribe. Although he never lost his skepticism, his daughters were born into the religion. They were schooled in it from the beginning. Nearly everyone they knew was a Scientologist.

Each of the girls was a near clone of one of the parents. Alissa and Katy were Paul, pale and blond, but more sharp-featured, with dimpled noses and sculpted cheekbones. Lauren, the middle daughter, was Diane, inheriting her half-Greek mother's olive skin and dark, Mediterranean eyes. The girls were bright, inquisitive, and cheerful by nature, but their parents' divorce was an endless, churning, distracting, heartbreaking trauma, and it took a toll.

The girls went to Delphi Academy, a private school that uses Hubbard "study tech." It is largely self-guided. According to Scientology pedagogy, there are three barriers that retard a student's progress. The first is "Lack of Mass." This principle was derived from Alfred Korzybski's observation that the word and the object that it names are not the same thing. If the student is studying tractors, for instance, it is best to have a real tractor in front of him. The absence of the actual object is disorienting to the student. "It makes him feel physiologically condensed," Hubbard writes. "Actually makes him feel squashed. Makes him feel bent, sort of spinny, sort of dead, bored, exasperated." Photographs of the object can help, or motion pictures, as they are "a sort of promise of hope of the mass," but they are not an adequate substitute for the tractor under study. The result for the student is that he becomes dizzy, he'll have headaches, his stomach gets upset, his eyes will hurt, and "he's going to wind up with a face that feels squashed." Illness and even suicide may be the expected result. Hubbard's study tech remedies the problem by using clay or Play-Doh for the student to make replicas of the object.

The second principle is "Too Steep a Gradient," which Hubbard describes as the difficulty a student encounters when he makes a leap he's not prepared for. "It is a sort of a confusion or a reelingness that goes with this one," Hubbard writes. His solution is to go back to the point where the student fully understands the subject, then break the material into bite-size pieces.

The "Undefined Word"—the third and most important principle—occurs when the student tries to absorb material while bypassing the definition of the words employed. "THE ONLY REASON A PERSON GIVES UP A STUDY OR BECOMES CONFUSED OR UNABLE TO LEARN IS BECAUSE HE HAS GONE PAST A WORD THAT WAS NOT UNDERSTOOD," Hubbard emphasizes in one of his chiding technical bulletins. "WORDS SOMETIMES HAVE DIFFERENT OR MORE THAN ONE MEANING." A misunderstood word "gives one a distinctly blank feeling or a washed out feeling," Hubbard writes. "A not-there feeling and a sort of an hysteria will follow in the back of that." The solution is to have a large dictionary at hand, preferably one with lots of pictures in it. All Scientology texts contain glossaries for specialized Scientology terms. The need to understand the meaning of words, Hubbard writes, "is a sweepingly fantastic discovery in the field of education and don't neglect it."

These last two principles are fundamental to the induction of Scientology itself. Because the church asserts that everything Hubbard wrote or spoke is inarguably true, whatever you don't understand or accept is your fault. The solution is to go back and study the words and approach the material in a more deliberate fashion. Eventually, you'll get it. Then you can move on.

Lauren loved her teacher at Delphi, but the Hubbard method placed the responsibility of learning almost entirely on the student. For Lauren, her parents' tumultuous divorce was a crushing distraction. It seemed to her that no one was paying attention to her, either at home or at school. She was illiterate until she was eleven. She couldn't read or write her own name.

Second-generation Scientologists are typically far more at home with the language and culture of the church than their parents are. And yet they may find themselves a little lost when trying to deal with an uncomprehending society. The first time Alissa noticed that she was doing something different from most people was when she performed a Contact Assist. Scientology preaches that if you repeatedly touch a fresh wound to the object that caused the injury and silently concentrate, the pain lessens and the sense of trauma fades. If a Scientologist sees a person close his hand in a door, for instance, a church manual instructs the Scientologist to "have him go back and, with his injured hand, touch the *exact spot* on the *same* door, duplicating the same motions that occurred at the time of the injury." There are other kinds of assists that will awaken an unconscious person, eliminate boils, reduce earaches and back pain, and make a drunk sober. Instead of crying when she hurt herself, Alissa would quietly redo the action over and over, until she had drained it of its sting. She noticed that non-Scientologists had no idea what she was doing. She was also surprised when she went to a friend's house for dinner and the family said grace before the meal. It took her a second to realize what they were doing. In her opinion, God plays a negligible role in Scientology. "I mean, there's a spot for it, but it's sort of a blank spot." So whenever her friends began to pray, "I would bow my head and let them have their ceremony."

Paul was also scarred by the divorce—although, as would often be the case for him, he would mine the experience for his work. He created a television series, *Family Law*, that was based to some extent on his divorce from Diane. He always found more solace and meaning in his work than he did in his family. Each year he grew more successful, but the gap between him and his daughters grew wider. They knew him better as a writer than as a father, and they would puzzle over the fact that he was so cool to them, when his scripts were often full of emotion. Paul felt guilty about not spending time with the girls, so he would arrange to bring them to the set and assign them some small task. Alissa got to do nearly every job in the industry, from wardrobe to production assistant; she received a Directors Guild card in Canada by the time she was fifteen.

In 1991, Haggis went to a Fourth of July party at the home of some Scientologist friends. He met a striking actress there named Debo-

Deborah Rennard and Milton Katselas in Silverlake, California, 1985

rah Rennard. She had grown up in Scientology. In her early twenties she had studied acting at the Beverly Hills Playhouse and had fallen under the influence of Milton Katselas, the legendary acting teacher and Hubbard's former collaborator. They became lovers. Milton was spellbinding, but he was twenty-seven years older than Deborah, and their relationship was an exhausting roller-coaster ride. They stayed together for six years. When Paul met her, Deborah and Milton had recently broken up. She was a successful actress with a recurring role in the long-running television series *Dallas*—as J. R. Ewing's loyal but always unattainable secretary.

Paul was still going through his epic divorce. Early in his relationship with Deborah, Paul admitted that he was having a spiritual crisis. He said he'd raced up to the top of the Bridge on faith, but he hadn't gotten what he expected. "I don't believe I'm a spiritual being. I actually am what you see," Paul told her. Deborah advised him to get more auditing. Personally, she was having breakthroughs that led her to discover past lives. Images floated through her mind, and she realized, "That's not here. I'm not in my body, I'm in another place." She might be confronting what the church calls a "contra-survival action"—"like the time I clobbered Paul or threw something at him." She would look for an "earlier similar" in her life. Suddenly she would see herself in England in the nineteenth century. "It was a fleeting glimpse at what I was doing then. Clobbering husbands." When she examined these kindred moments in her current existence and past ones, the emotional charge would dissipate. Paul would say, "Don't you think you're making this up?" At first, she thought he might be right. But then she wondered if that really mattered. She felt she was getting better, so who cared whether they were memories or fantasies? As an actor she went through an analogous process when working on a scene; she would grab hold of a feeling from who knows where. It felt real. It helped her get into the role. As long as the process worked, why quibble?

Deborah made sure Paul showed up at the annual gala and became involved in Scientology charitable organizations. Over the years, Haggis spent about $100,000 on courses and auditing and an equal amount on various Scientology initiatives. This figure doesn't include the money that Diane gave to the church while she was married to Paul. Haggis also gave $250,000 to the International Association of Scientologists, a fund set up to protect and promote the church. Deborah spent about $150,000 on coursework of her own. Paul and Deborah held a fund-raiser in their home that raised $200,000 for a new Scientology building in Nashville, and they contributed an additional $10,000 from their own pocket. The demands for money—"regging," it's called in Scientology, because the calls come from the Registrar's Office—never stopped. Paul gave them money just to keep them from calling.

7

The Future Is Ours

Now that he was firmly in control of the church, Miscavige sought to restore the image of Scientology. The 1980s had been a devastating period for the church's reputation, with Hubbard's disappearance and eventual death, the high-profile lawsuits, and the avalanche of embarrassing publicity. Miscavige hired Hill & Knowlton, the oldest and largest public relations firm in the world, to oversee a national campaign. The legendarily slick worldwide chairman of Hill & Knowlton, Robert Keith Gray, specialized in rehabilitating disgraced dictators, arms dealers, and governments with appalling human-rights records. As representatives of the government of Kuwait, Hill & Knowlton had been partly responsible for selling the Persian Gulf War to the American people. One of the company's tactics was to provide the testimony of a fifteen-year-old girl, "Nayirah," to a human-rights committee in the US House of Representatives in October 1990. Nayirah described herself as an ordinary Kuwaiti who had volunteered in a hospital. She tearfully told the House members of watching Iraqi soldiers storm into the prenatal unit. "They took the babies out of the incubators, took the incubators, and left the babies on the cold floor to die," she said. The incident could never be confirmed, and the girl turned out to be the daughter of the Kuwaiti ambassador to the United States and had never volunteered at the hospital. The propaganda operation was, at the time, the most expensive and sophisticated public relations campaign ever run in the United States by a foreign government.

Gray had also worked closely with the Reagan campaign. He regaled the Scientologists with his ability to take a "mindless actor" and turn him into the "Teflon President." Hill & Knowlton went to work for the church, putting out phony news stories, often in the form of video news releases made to look like actual reports rather than advertisements. The church began supporting high-profile causes, such as Ted Turner's Goodwill Games, thereby associating itself with other well-known corporate sponsors, such as Sony and Pepsi. There were full-page ads in newsmagazines touting the church's philosophy, and cable television ads promoting Scientology books and *Dianetics* seminars.

Then, in May 1991, came one of the greatest public relations catastrophes in the church's history. *Time* magazine published a scathing cover story titled "Scientology: The Thriving Cult of Greed and Power," by investigative reporter Richard Behar. The exposé revealed that just one of the religion's many entities, the Church of Spiritual Technology, had taken in half a billion dollars in 1987 alone. Hundreds of millions of dollars from the parent organization were buried in secret accounts in Lichtenstein, Switzerland, and Cyprus. Many of the personalities linked with the church were savaged in the article. Hubbard himself was described as "part storyteller, part flimflam man." The Feshbach brothers were the "terrors of the stock exchanges," who spread false information about companies in order to drive down their valuations. Behar quoted a former church executive as saying that John Travolta stayed in the church only because he was worried that details of his sex life would be made public if he left. The article asserted that Miscavige made frequent jokes about Travolta's "allegedly promiscuous homosexual behavior." When Behar queried Travolta's attorney for the star's comment, he was told that such questions were "bizarre." "Two weeks later, Travolta announced that he was getting married to actress Kelly Preston, a fellow Scientologist," Behar wrote.

"Those who criticize the church—journalists, doctors, lawyers, and even judges—often find themselves engulfed in litigation, stalked by private eyes, framed for fictional crimes, beaten up, or threatened by death," Behar noted. He accused the Justice Department of failing to back the IRS and the FBI in bringing a racketeering suit against the church because it was unwilling to spend the money required to take the organization on. He quoted Cynthia Kisser, head of the Cult

Awareness Network in Chicago: "Scientology is quite likely the most ruthless, the most classically terroristic, the most litigious and the most lucrative cult the country has ever seen."

After the *Time* article appeared, Miscavige was invited to appear on ABC's *Nightline*, a highly prestigious news show, to defend the image of the church. He had never been interviewed in his life. He rehearsed for months, as much as four hours per day, with Rathbun and Rinder. He would prod them to ask him questions, then complain that they didn't sound like Ted Koppel, the show's courtly but incisive host. Miscavige would ask himself the questions in what he thought was Koppel's voice, then respond with a hypothetical answer. He sorted through what seemed to his aides an endless number of wardrobe choices before settling on a blue suit with a purple tie and a handkerchief in his breast pocket. Finally, on Valentine's Day, 1992, he went to New York, where the show would be broadcast live.

The interview was preceded by a fifteen-minute report by Forrest Sawyer about Scientology's claims and controversies. "The church says it now has centers in over seventy countries, with more on the way," Sawyer said. Heber Jentzsch, the president of the Church of Scientology International, was featured, claiming a membership of eight million people. Sawyer also interviewed defectors, who talked about their families being ripped apart, or being bilked of tens of thousands of dollars. Richard Behar, the *Time* reporter, recounted how Scientology's private investigators had obtained his phone records. Vicki Aznaran, a former high official in the church, who was then suing the church, told Sawyer that Miscavige ordered attacks on those he considered troublemakers—"have them, their homes, broken into, have them beaten, have things stolen from them, slash their tires, break their car windows, whatever."

Koppel allowed Miscavige to respond to the Sawyer report. "Every single detractor on there is a part of a religious hate group called Cult Awareness Network and their sister group called American Family Foundation," Miscavige said. "It's the same as the KKK would be with blacks." He seemed completely at ease.

"You realize there's a little bit of a problem getting people to talk critically about Scientology because, quite frankly, they're scared," Koppel observed.

"Oh, no, no, no, no."

"I'm telling you, people are scared," Koppel insisted.

"Let's not give the American public the wrong impression," said Miscavige. "The person getting harassed is myself and the church."

Koppel then lobbed what seemed like an easy question for a man who had spent so much time preparing for this encounter. "See if you can explain to me why I would want to be a Scientologist."

"Because you care about yourself and life itself," Miscavige said eagerly. He gave the example of communication skills. "This is something that major breakthroughs exist in Scientology, being able to communicate in the world around you," he said. "There's an actual formula for communication which can be understood. You can drill on this formula."

"So far in life, I haven't had a whole lot of trouble communicating," Koppel drolly noted.

"What in your life do you feel is not right, that you would like to help?" Miscavige asked. It was a classic Scientology technique, to find a subject's "ruin," the thing that was blocking his access to happiness.

"I feel perfectly comfortable with my life," Koppel replied.

Miscavige switched tactics. "Let's look at it this way, then, what Scientology does. If you look out across the world today, you could say that if you take a person who's healthy, doing well, like yourself, you'd say that person is normal, not a crazy, not somebody who is psychotic, you look at a wall and they call it an elephant," he said, extemporizing. "And you can see people below that—crazy people, criminals—that I think society in general will look at and say, 'That breed of person hasn't something quite right because they're not up to this level of personality.' . . . What we are trying to do in Scientology is take somebody from this higher level and move them up to greater ability."

"What about the folks 'down there'?"

"We don't ignore them. My point is this: Scientology is there to make the able more able."

"Another way of saying that is: you're interested in folks who've got money."

Miscavige objected, claiming that the money in the church goes to good causes. "We are the largest social reform group in the world," he said, adding that if a person stays in Scientology long enough, he'll have plenty of money. Then he referenced Sawyer's report again. "The one girl there that was complaining about it, a girl named Vicki Aznaran, which by the way, this is a girl who was kicked out for trying to bring criminals into the church, something she didn't mention."

"You say a 'girl.' I think we're talking about a grown woman, right?"

"A grown woman, excuse me," Miscavige said. "She violated the mores and codes of the group."

"Either you have made an accurate charge against someone or—what a number of . . . the pieces written about Scientology suggest is that when you have a critic before you, you destroy those people."

"That's easy to say—"

"You smear them."

"That's easy for the person to say, but she's the one on that program smearing me."

As for Richard Behar, the *Time* reporter, Miscavige remarked, "The man was on record on two occasions attempting to get Scientologists kidnapped. That is an illegal act."

The hour had ended, but Miscavige had just made another unsupported allegation. Koppel decided to extend the show "a few minutes," but it went on another half hour without any commercial breaks. He asked Miscavige to explain what he meant about Behar. "Some people had called him up and he was telling them to kidnap Scientologists out," Miscavige said.

"Now, kidnapping, as you well know, is a federal crime," Koppel observed. "So, why didn't you bring charges against him?"

"He didn't succeed," Miscavige said. "Ted, Ted, you're missing the point."

"There is such a thing as attempted rape, attempted murder, attempted kidnapping. It's also a crime."

"I think you're really missing the issue, Ted, because my point is this: That man represents himself as an objective reporter. Here he is on record a full three years before he wrote this article, stating that he felt Scientologists should be kidnapped to change their religion.

"Second of all," Miscavige continued, "let's look at this article, and let's not fool ourselves. It wasn't an objective piece. It was done at the behest of Eli Lilly," the pharmaceutical manufacturer. "They were upset because of the damage we had caused to their killer drug Prozac."

"I'm sure you have evidence of that," Koppel said. "You have affidavits?"

"Let me tell you what else I have—"

"You have affidavits?"

"From them? Of course not. You think they'd admit it?" Miscavige said. "We put in a call to Eli Lilly. Their response was, 'We can neither confirm nor deny.' "*

In Sawyer's report there was a brief clip of Hubbard telling his followers, "I was up in the Van Allen Belt. This is factual. And I don't know why they're scared of the Van Allen Belt, because it's simply hot. You'd be surprised how warm space is." Koppel observed, "When I hear about a man talking about having been taken out to the Van Allen space radiation belt or space ships that were essentially the same thing as the DC-8, I've got to tell you, I mean, if we're talking about this man's credibility, that certainly raises some questions in my mind."

Miscavige said that Hubbard's quote had been taken out of context.

"Take a minute, if you would, and see if you can put it into context for us so that it does not sound ridiculous," Koppel said.

"Okay," said Miscavige. "I want you to take the Catholic Church and take right now and explain to me, to make sense that the Virgin Mary was a virgin, scientifically impossible, unless we're talking about something . . ." He trailed off, then said, "Okay, I'll be like you, I'll be the cynic. If we're talking about artificial insemination, how could that be? If you're talking about going to Heaven, except we have a space shuttle going out there, we have the Apollo going out there, you do that. I'm not here—" He was obviously confused and uncomfortable.

"You were a Catholic as a child, right?" Koppel asked helpfully.

"Yeah."

"So you know full well that those issues are questions of faith."

Miscavige wouldn't accept the life raft that Koppel offered him. Scientology is sold as an entirely rational approach to understanding and mastering existence. "No, no," Miscavige replied. "Talk about the Van Allen Belt or whatever, that forms no part of current Scientology, none whatsoever."

"But what did he mean when he was talking about it?"

"Quite frankly, this tape here, he's talking about the origins of the universe, and I think you're going to find that in any, any, any religion, and I think you can make the same mockery of it. I think it's offensive."

---

*Behar says that a private investigator, posing as a distraught parent, called him and begged for help with a child who had gone into Scientology. Behar had referred the caller to the Cult Awareness Network. He says he never advised kidnapping. The private investigator taped the conversation, and Behar's attorneys subpoenaed the tape for his defense in the lawsuit brought by the church.

"I'm not mocking it, I'm asking you a question," Koppel replied. "You turn it around and ask me about Catholicism. I say we're talking about areas of faith."

"Well, it's not even a matter of faith," Miscavige insisted, "because Scientology is about you, yourself, and what you do. You're bringing up something that isn't part of current Scientology, that isn't something that Scientologists study, that is part of some tape taken from, I have no idea, and asking me about it and asking me to put it in context, that I can't do." Later, Miscavige told Koppel that he had never heard the Hubbard tape before. (It was a part of a lecture Hubbard gave in 1963, in which he talked about the between-lives period, when thetans are transported to Venus to have their memories erased.)

After the show, Miscavige returned to the greenroom, where Rinder, Rathbun, and Norman Starkey, another executive, were waiting. "How'd I do?" he asked.

"Gee, sir, you kicked ass," one of the men said.

"It was a home run," Rathbun assured him.

"Really?" Miscavige asked doubtfully. "Jesus Christ, I was just there and I don't know. The guy was pissing me off so much."

Koppel won an Emmy for that show. Miscavige took credit for it, saying, "I got Ted the Emmy." He even had a replica of an Emmy made and placed in the Officers Lounge at Gold Base. But he never went on television again.

THE *TIME* STORY WAS a turning point in the church's history. The embarrassment for Scientology celebrities undercut the church's strategy of making the religion appear to be a spiritual refuge for the show-business elite. One of the chief appeals of the religion to prospective recruits was the perceived network that Scientology provided its members, especially in Hollywood, awarding them an advantage in a ruthlessly competitive industry. With the *Time* article, affiliation with the church became an embarrassing liability.

Tom Cruise was one of the stars who appeared to be backing away from Scientology.* He stopped moving up the Bridge. He and Nicole adopted two children, Isabella and Connor, and began spending more

---

*Cruise, through his attorney, denies that he ever retreated from his commitment to Scientology.

time in Sydney, Kidman's hometown, where she could be close to her family. He hired a powerful publicist, Pat Kingsley, who was able to enforce rigid control over the content of the interviews the star granted. Although his affiliation with Scientology was generally known, there was no more fuel for the media mill. He seemed to be putting as much distance between himself and the church as possible.

The church began to plot its counterattack. The Cult Awareness Network, besieged by more than fifty lawsuits brought by Scientologists, went bankrupt in 1996. An individual Scientologist purchased its name and assets at auction. Soon after that, the reorganized Cult Awareness Network sent out a brochure lauding the Church of Scientology for its efforts to "increase happiness and improve conditions for oneself and others." The church also began a $3 million campaign against *Time*, placing full-page ads every day in *USA Today* for twelve weeks, charging that the magazine had "supported" Adolf Hitler, for instance, by naming him the 1938 "Man of the Year" because of his dominance in European affairs. A lengthy supplement was placed in *USA Today* titled "The Story That *Time* Couldn't Tell: Who Really Controls the News at *Time*—and Why," in which the church claimed that *Time* was actually under the sway of the pharmaceutical industry—specifically, Eli Lilly and Company, the maker of Prozac. The church had charged that Prozac caused people to commit mass murder and suicide. The *Time* article was the drug company's revenge, the church alleged.*

Rathbun directed the ferocious legal assault on *Time* and oversaw the team of private detectives probing into Behar's private life. The church, employing what was reported to be an annual litigation budget of $20 million and a team of more than a hundred lawyers to handle the suits already in the courts, filed a $416 million libel action against Time Warner, the parent company of the magazine, and Behar. Because the church is regarded under American law as a "public figure," Scientology's lawyers had to prove not only that the magazine's allegations were wrong but also that Behar acted with "actual malice"—a legal term meaning that he knowingly published information he knew to be false, or that he recklessly disregarded the facts, because he intended to damage the church. Although there was no convincing evidence proving that the facts were wrong or that the reporter was biased, the case

---

*A spokesperson for *Time* categorically denied this charge.

went all the way to the US Supreme Court, which sustained the district court's initial ruling against the church. In the process, it cost *Time* more money in defense costs than any other case in its history.

Rathbun's strategy followed Hubbard's dictate that the purpose of a lawsuit is "to harass and discourage rather than win." Hubbard also wrote: "If attacked on some vulnerable point by anyone or anything or any organization, always find or manufacture enough threat against them to cause them to sue for peace. . . . Don't ever defend. Always attack." He added: "NEVER agree to an investigation of Scientology. ONLY agree to an investigation of the attackers." He advised Scientologists: "Start feeding lurid, blood, sex, crime, actual evidence on the attackers to the press. . . . Make it rough, rough on attackers all the way. . . . There has never yet been an attacker who was not reeking with crime. All we had to do was look for it and murder would come out." These were maxims that Rathbun took as his guidelines.

The *Time* article capsized Miscavige's attempts to break free of the negative associations so many people had with Scientology. But there was an even larger battle under way, one in which the church's very existence was at stake: its fight with the IRS to regain its tax-exempt status as a bona fide religion, which it had lost in 1967.

The government's stance was that the Church of Scientology was in fact a commercial enterprise, with "virtually incomprehensible financial procedures" and a "scripturally based hostility to taxation." The IRS had ruled that the church was largely operated to benefit its founder. Miscavige inherited some of that liability when he took over after Hubbard's death. A tax exemption would not only put the imprimatur of the American government on the church as a certified religion, rather than a corrupt, profit-making concern, but it would also provide a substantial amount of immunity from civil suits and the persistent federal criminal investigations. A decision against the tax exemption, on the other hand, would destroy the entire enterprise, because Hubbard had decided in 1973 that the church should not pay its back taxes. Twenty years later, the church was $1 billion in arrears, with only $125 million in reserves. The founder had placed Scientology's head on the executioner's block.

The war between the church and the IRS had already gone on for more than two decades, with both sides waging a campaign of intimidation and espionage. Miscavige accused the Criminal Investigation Division of the IRS of engaging in surveillance of church leaders, wiretaps, and illegal opening of the church's mail. Now the church upped the ante by besieging the IRS with 200 lawsuits on the part of the church and more than 2,300 suits on behalf of individual parishioners in every jurisdiction in the country, overwhelming government lawyers, running up fantastic expenses, and causing an immense amount of havoc inside the IRS. Miscavige boasted that the entire legal budget of the federal agency was exhausted: "They didn't even have money to attend the annual American Bar Association conference of lawyers—which they were supposed to speak at!" The church ran ads against the agency, using the images of beloved celebrities (who were not Scientologists) such as John Wayne and Willie Nelson, who had been audited by the IRS. "All of America Loved Lucy," one ad said, over an iconic photo of Lucille Ball, "except the IRS." A ten-thousand-dollar reward was offered to potential whistle-blowers to expose IRS abuses. Private investigators dug into the private lives of IRS officials, going so far as to attend seminars and pose as IRS workers, to see who had a drinking problem or might be cheating on a spouse. Stories based on these investigations were promoted by a phony news bureau the church established, and also published in the church's *Freedom* magazine, which Scientologists passed out for free on the steps of the IRS headquarters in Washington. The hatred on both sides for the other was intense. It seemed bizarre that a rather small organization could overmatch the US government, but the harassment campaign was having an effect. Some government workers were getting anonymous calls in the middle of the night, or finding that their pets had disappeared. Whether or not these events were part of the Scientology onslaught, they added to the paranoia many in the agency were feeling.

Both the church and the IRS faced the challenge of addressing the question of what, exactly, constituted a religion in the eyes of the American government. On the church's side was a body of scholars who had arisen in defense of what were called "new religious movements," such as the Hare Krishnas, the Unification Church, and of course the Church of Scientology. The term was employed to replace the word "cult," because these academics found no reliable way of distinguishing a cult from a religion. They believe that new religious movements are persecuted and ridiculed simply because they are recent and seem exotic. Often, such experts are paid to testify in court on behalf of these organizations. In the courtroom setting, the casual distinctions that many people often make about cults and brainwashing have proven to be difficult to sustain, as the experts pose telling comparisons with the history of mainstream religions, whose practices and rituals have long since been folded into a broad cultural acceptance.

The Church of Scientology had decided to enlist such experts following the FBI raids in 1977, which exposed Operation Snow White and created a major crisis in the church. There was a deliberate campaign to provide religious cloaking for the church's activities. A Scientology cross was created. Scientology ministers now appeared wearing Roman collars. And religious scholars were courted; they were given tours and allowed to interview carefully coached church members.

Frank K. Flinn, a former Franciscan friar and a graduate of Harvard Divinity School, has testified repeatedly on behalf of Scientology—notably, in 1984, when the Church of Scientology, along with Mary Sue Hubbard, sued Gerald Armstrong, the former archivist for the church. Flinn defined religion as a system of beliefs of a spiritual nature. There must be norms for behavior—positive commands and negative prohibitions or taboos—as well as rites and ceremonies, such as initiations, sacraments, prayers, and services for weddings and funerals. By these means, the believers are united into an identifiable community that seeks to live in harmony with what they perceive as the ultimate meaning of life. Flinn argued that Scientology amply fulfilled these requirements, even if it differed in its expression of them from traditional denominations.

Like Catholicism, Flinn explained, Scientology is a hierarchical religion. He compared L. Ron Hubbard to the founders of Catholic religious orders, including his own, started by Saint Francis of Assisi, whose followers adopted a vow of poverty. Financial disparities within a church are not unusual. Within the hierarchy of Catholicism, for instance, bishops often enjoy a mansion, limousines, servants, and housekeepers; the papacy itself maintains thousands of people on its staff, including the Swiss Guards who protect the pope, and an entire order of nuns dedicated to being housekeepers for the papal apartments.

The Catholic Church also maintains houses of rehabilitation (like the RPF) for errant priests hoping to reform themselves. Flinn saw the RPF as being entirely voluntary and even tame compared to what he experienced as a friar in the Franciscan Order. He willingly submitted to the religious practice of flagellation on Fridays, whipping his legs and back in emulation of the suffering of Jesus before his crucifixion. Flinn also spent several hours a day doing manual labor. As a member of a mendicant order, he owned no material possessions at all, not even the robe he wore. Low wages and humble work were essential to his spiritual commitment.

There is a place for a Supreme Being in Scientology—in Hubbard's Eight Dynamics, it's at the top—but the God idea plays a diminished role compared to many religions. On the other hand, some religions worship objects—stones or icons or mandalas—rather than a deity. Scientologists don't pray; but then, neither do Buddhists. The idea of salvation, so central to Christianity, is not so different from Hubbard's assertion that the fundamental law of the universe is the urge to survive. Flinn compared the Scientology distinction between pre-clear and Clear to Buddhist notions of entanglement and enlightenment, or Christian doctrines of sin and grace. The Scientology creed that humans are "thetans" simply means we are beings with immortal souls, which no Christian would argue with.

One of Flinn's most interesting and contested points had to do with hagiography, by which he meant attributing extraordinary powers—such as clairvoyance, visions of God or angels, or the ability to perform miracles—to the charismatic founders of a religion. He pointed to the virgin birth of Jesus, the ability of the Buddha to "transmigrate" his soul into the heavens, or Moses bringing manna to the people of Israel. Such legends are useful in that they bolster the faith of a community, Flinn said. The glaring discrepancies in Hubbard's biography should be seen in the light of the fact that any religion tends to make its founder into something more than human.

Flinn was asked to testify about a policy Hubbard had written in 1965 titled "Fair Game Law," in which he laid down the rules for dealing with Suppressive Persons. That category includes non-Scientologists who are hostile to the church, apostates, and defectors, as well as their spouses, family members, and close friends. "A truly Suppressive Person or Group has no rights of any kind," Hubbard wrote. Such enemies, he said, may be "tricked, lied to or destroyed." In 1965, he wrote another policy letter ambiguously stating, "The practice of declaring people FAIR GAME will cease. FAIR GAME may not appear on any Ethics Order. It causes bad public relations. [The new ruling] does not cancel any policy on the treatment or handling of an SP." The supposed revocation of Fair Game took place before Operation Snow White, the harassment of Paulette Cooper and other journalists, the persecution of defectors, and many other actions undertaken by church insiders that were done in the spirit, if not the name, of the original policy.

"Almost all religious movements in their very early phase tend to be harsh," Flinn reminded the court. He contended that they tend to evolve and become more lenient over time. As for disconnection, he declared that it was "functionally equivalent to other types of religious exclusions," such as shunning of nonbelievers among Mennonites and the Amish. In the Book of Leviticus, for instance, which is part of the Torah and the Old Testament of the Christian Bible, idolaters and those who have strayed from the faith were to be stoned to death. That practice has disappeared; instead, Orthodox Jews will sit Shiva for the nonbeliever, treating him as if he is already dead. "So this kind of phenomenon is not peculiar to Scientology," Flinn concluded. The implication underlying Flinn's testimony was that Scientology is a new religion that is reinventing old religious norms; whatever abuses it may be committing are errors of youthful exuberance, and in any case they are pale imitators of the practices once employed by the mainstream religions that judges and jurors were likely to be members of.

In the 1990s, Flinn had interviewed several Scientologists who were doing RPF in Los Angeles. Their quarters didn't look any worse than his cell in the monastery, where he slept on a straw bed on a board. He asked if they were free to go. They told him they were, but they wanted to stay and do penance.

Flinn admits to having been a cutup when he was in the order, and he felt out of place. "I was an Irishman in a sea of Germans." He would be sent out to dig the potato field as punishment for his misbehavior. However, when he finally decided to leave his order, instead of being incarcerated or given a freeloader tab, he was given a dispensation releasing him from his vows. He never felt the need to escape. He took off his robe, put on civilian clothes, and walked away. His spiritual adviser gave him five hundred dollars to help him out. He was never punished or fined, or made to disconnect from anyone.

IN TRUTH, the IRS was ill equipped to make a case in court that Scientology—or any other creed—was not a religion. Moreover, the commissioner of the IRS, Fred T. Goldberg, Jr., had to balance the longing on the part of some of his executives to destroy the church against the need to keep his resources, both human and financial, from being sucked into the black hole that Scientology had created.

One afternoon in Washington, in October 1991, Miscavige and Rathbun were having lunch at the Bombay Club, a swank Indian restaurant near the White House. Miscavige was fed up with the stalemate, which looked as if it could go on forever, in an endless stream of billable hours to the church's attorneys. At the lunch, Miscavige announced to Gerald Feffer, one of their lawyers, "Marty and I are just going to bypass you entirely. We're going to see Fred."

Feffer laughed at the thought that Miscavige would talk directly to the commissioner.

"I'm not joking," Miscavige said. "Marty, do you want to go?"

The two men hailed a cab after lunch and went to 1111 Constitution Avenue, the IRS headquarters, and announced to the security officer that they wanted to see the commissioner.

"Is he expecting you?"

"No, but if you phone him on the intercom and tell him we are from the Church of Scientology, I'm sure he'd love to see us."

Within a few moments, several of the commissioner's aides came down to the lobby. Miscavige told them that he wanted to bury the hatchet. He said he knew how much hatred there was on each side, going back for decades, and that an intervention from the top was necessary. An hour later there was a call in their hotel room saying the commissioner would see them the following week.

In that first meeting with Goldberg, in a drab government conference room at a giant table, Miscavige, Rathbun, and Heber Jentzsch were facing about a dozen upper-level government bureaucrats, including the commissioner. The level of distrust between the negotiating parties was extreme, made even greater for the IRS representatives who knew that Scientologists had stolen documents and wiretapped meetings in that very building. Both sides had an incentive to bring the hostilities to an end, however. Miscavige and Rathbun made their carefully rehearsed presentation. Miscavige recited a litany of examples in which he felt the IRS had singled out Scientology for unfair treatment. "Am I lying?" he would turn and ask Rathbun theatrically. Rathbun had a briefcase stuffed with documents obtained from the 2,300 Freedom of Information Act lawsuits the church had filed, or the countless public records that the church had combed through. Among the many internal memos the Scientologists had gathered was one they called the Final Solution document. It was the minutes of a meeting in 1974 of several top IRS executives who were trying to define "religion" in a manner that excluded Scientology but not other faiths.

Miscavige made it clear that the barrage of lawsuits lodged against the IRS would come to an immediate halt if the church got what it wanted, which was an unqualified exemption for all of its activities. When Miscavige finished his presentation, Goldberg called for a break, but he signaled to Rathbun to hang back. Goldberg asked him privately if the government settled, would Scientology also turn off the personal attacks in *Freedom* magazine?

"Like a faucet," Rathbun told him.

Goldberg appointed his deputy commissioner, John Burke, who had no history with the conflict, to oversee a lengthy review of Scientology's finances and practices. That process went on for two years. During that time, Rathbun and Miscavige commuted to Washington nearly every week, toting banker's boxes stuffed with responses to the government's queries. Two hundred Scientologists in Los Angeles and New York were mobilized to go through the books of the church's tangled bureaucracy. The odds against success were high; the courts had repeatedly sided with the IRS's assertion that the Church of Scientology was a commercial enterprise. Miscavige and Rathbun were very much aware that the future of Scientology, if there was one, awaited the result of the IRS probe. Either the panel would rule against them, in which case the church's tax liability for the previous two decades would destroy it, or they would fall under the gracious protection of the freedom of religion clause of the First Amendment, in which case the Church of Scientology, and all its practices, would be sheltered by the US Constitution.

Overshadowing this debate was an incident that renewed the public concern about the dangerousness of totalistic movements. In February 1993, agents for the US Bureau of Alcohol, Tobacco, and Firearms tried to execute a search warrant on a religious commune a few miles east of Waco, Texas, that was run by a Christian apocalyptic group calling themselves the Branch Davidians. The leader, David Koresh, was stockpiling weapons, practicing polygamy, committing statutory rape, and was said to be physically abusing children, although that last charge was never proved. Following a shoot-out that caused the deaths of four government agents and six Branch Davidians, the FBI began a siege lasting nearly two months and culminating in a catastrophic blaze—broadcast all over the world—that consumed the entire compound. Seventy-five members of the sect died in the final assault, including twenty-five children. The Waco siege threatened to create a backlash against all new religious movements. On the other hand, the government's handling of the siege, and the disastrous finale, provoked an international uproar. The hazards of unorthodox belief were clearly displayed, as were the limitations of police forces to understand and deal with fanatical movements.

On October 8, more than a thousand Scientologists stood and cheered in the Los Angeles Sports Arena as Miscavige announced, "The war is over!" The IRS had settled with the church. Although the terms were secret, they were later leaked to the *Wall Street Journal*. Instead of the $1 billion bill for back taxes and penalties that the church owed, Scientology agreed to pay just $12.5 million to resolve outstanding disputes; the church also agreed to stop the cascade of lawsuits against the agency. In return, the IRS dropped its investigations. "The magnitude of this is greater than you can imagine," Miscavige said that night at the Sports Arena. He held up a thick folder of the letters of exemption for every one of the church's 150 American entities. The victory over the IRS was total, he explained. It gave Scientology financial advantages that were unusual, perhaps unique, among religions in the United States. For instance, schools using Hubbard educational methods received tax exemption. Eighty percent of individual auditing on the part of members was now a tax-deductible expense. Two Scientology publishing houses that were solely dedicated to turning out Hubbard's books, including his commercial fiction, also gained the tax exemption. The church even gained the power to extend its tax exemption to any of its future branches—"They will no longer need to apply to the IRS," Miscavige marveled. From now on, the church could make its own decisions about which of its activities were exempt.

"And what about all those battles and wars still being fought overseas?" Miscavige continued. "Well, there's good news on that front, too." In the past, he observed, foreign governments would say, "You are an American religion. If the IRS doesn't recognize you, why should we?" As a part of the settlement, Miscavige revealed, the agency agreed to send notices to every country in the world, explaining what Scientology was. "It is very complete and very accurate," Miscavige said of the government brochure. "How do I know? We wrote it!"

Miscavige summed up the mood in the Sports Arena: "The future is ours."

A MONTH AFTER the church's historic triumph over the IRS in 1993, Rathbun blew. He had come to see Miscavige in a different light during the two years they labored over the tax case. The last six months of the tax case had been particularly arduous. During that period, he slept only about four hours a night. The former athlete was a physical wreck. "I'm only doing this for LRH," he told himself, as he and Miscavige ate dinners together night after night in Washington and trudged back to the Four Seasons in Georgetown. "I'm not going to be this guy's bitch for the rest of my life."

No doubt the stress affected Miscavige as well. On the night of his big victory speech in the Sports Arena, Miscavige showed up for a run-through, but the stage manager, Stefan Castle, was still fiddling with the cues for a complicated laser and pyrotechnic display. According to Castle, Miscavige stormed out into the arena and began to strangle him. Miscavige let him go before any real harm was done, but it was an alarming signal. Amy Scobee, head of the Celebrity Centre at the time, also noted that Miscavige's personality began to shift immediately after the IRS decision, becoming more aggressive and hostile. At the party at the Celebrity Centre following his speech, Miscavige rudely shoved her aside as he entered. "You just want to get rid of me," she remembers him saying.

As far as Rathbun was concerned, it didn't help that Miscavige scarcely acknowledged him in the speech that night. Immediately after the event, reporters from *The New York Times* and the *Los Angeles Times* were calling Rathbun to ask about Miscavige's salary, which had been disclosed in the IRS documents. Miscavige and his wife together were making more than $100,000 a year—not an extraordinary figure by the standards of world religious leaders, but quite a contrast to the $30 a week most of the Sea Org members were earning. Miscavige was outraged by the impertinence of the reporters, and Rathbun felt that he was taking it out on him. This was all coming at a time when he had been postponing a final visit to see his father, who was dying of cancer.

The *St. Petersburg Times* published an editorial demanding that Congress investigate the tax-exemption decision. Rathbun was sent to

Florida to turn around the *Times* editorial board, who were not at all persuaded by his arguments. Miscavige was furious that Rathbun failed to handle the situation. One evening, Shelly Miscavige called everyone in Rathbun's office together, and in front of his subordinates she stripped the captain's bars off his uniform.

The next day, Rathbun took four gold Krugerrands that he had stored in a safe, got on his motorcycle, and drove to Yuma, Arizona. He called his father in Los Angeles from a bar, but a church official answered. He was waiting there with Rathbun's wife, Anne, who begged him to come back. Rathbun felt guilty and conflicted. Drinking steadily, he somehow made it to San Antonio, although he was in frequent communication with church leaders. He finally agreed to call Miscavige, who apologized for his treatment. "You know the kind of pressure I was under. Please just see me," the church leader said, adding that he could be in San Antonio in a matter of hours. "No, I want to see the Alamo," Rathbun told him. They agreed to meet for dinner at the Marriott in New Orleans two days later.

That evening, Miscavige showed a chastened, vulnerable side of himself that Rathbun had never seen before. According to Rathbun, Miscavige promised to "cease acting like a madman." He praised Rathbun for his part in gaining the IRS exemption. "Because you did this," he declared, "you're Kha-Khan." It was a title that Hubbard had come up with in one of his policy letters for a highly productive staff member, but in the culture it was understood that such a person would be forgiven for misdeeds in future lifetimes. Hubbard had awarded it to Yvonne Gillham after she died. Rathbun knew that Miscavige was manipulating him, but he was touched nonetheless. As a further reward, Miscavige offered Rathbun the opportunity to go to the Scientology ship, the *Freewinds*, and cruise the Caribbean for two years doing nothing but studying and training to be an auditor. Rathbun could finally obtain OT III. It was an offer he couldn't resist.

That was a rewarding time for Rathbun. But as soon as he got off the ship after his time away, Miscavige called him into his office and said, "I finally know who my SP is. The two years you were gone was the only unenturbulated time in my life." He ordered him to Clearwater, his rank broken, as a trainee. That didn't last, either. A number of tabloid sensations arose surrounding Scientology celebrities—Lisa Marie Presley was divorcing Michael Jackson, Kirstie Alley was divorcing actor Parker Stevenson—and Miscavige again turned to Rathbun to cool the press down.

Then, on December 5, 1995, a Scientologist named Lisa McPherson died following a mental breakdown. She had rear-ended a boat that was being towed in downtown Clearwater, Florida, near the church's spiritual headquarters. When paramedics arrived, she stripped off her clothes and wandered naked down the street. She said she needed help and was taken to a nearby hospital. Soon afterward, a delegation of ten Scientologists arrived at the hospital and persuaded McPherson to check out, against doctors' advice. McPherson spent the next seventeen days under guard in room 174 of the Fort Harrison Hotel.

For Scientologists, McPherson's mental breakdown presented a confounding dilemma. McPherson had been declared Clear just three months before, after ten years of courses and auditing and substantial contributions to the church. The process had been like "a gopher being pulled through a garden hose," she later said, but it had been worth it. "I am so full of life I am overwhelmed at the joy of it all!" she wrote. "WOW!"

Clears are supposed to be invulnerable to mental frailty. People on the base knew that McPherson had been acting strangely before her breakdown. Marty Rathbun, who was at Flag Base during this time, remembers seeing McPherson screaming in the hallways of the Fort Harrison Hotel, because she had just been declared Clear. "*Aaaaaah! Yahoo!*" she cried. She looked insane. How did she get to be Clear when she was obviously irrational? And who was responsible for deciding that she had achieved that state? According to Rathbun and several other former church officials who were present at the time, the case supervisor who pronounced Lisa McPherson Clear was David Miscavige. He had gone to Flag in the summer of 1995 to take over the auditing delivered at the base. He would also supervise the treatment of McPherson that followed.*

When McPherson entered room 174, she was a lovely, shapely young woman. She underwent an Introspection Rundown, the same procedure that Hubbard had developed on the *Apollo* two decades earlier to treat psychotic behavior. It involved placing McPherson in

---

*According to a church spokesperson, "Mr. Miscavige was not involved in any aspect of Ms. McPherson's spiritual progress in Scientology."

solitary confinement and providing her with water, food, and vitamin supplements. All communication had to be in writing. Instead of calming down, McPherson stopped eating. She screamed, she clawed her attendants, she spoke in gibberish, she fouled herself, she banged her head against the wall. Staff members strapped her down and tried to feed her with a turkey baster.

On December 5, McPherson slipped into a coma. When church members decided to take her to the hospital that night, they bypassed the Morton Plant Hospital, just down the street, where McPherson had originally been seen, and drove her forty-five minutes away, passing four other hospitals, to the Columbia New Port Richey Hospital, where there was a doctor affiliated with the church. The woman they finally wheeled into the emergency room was skeletally thin and covered with scratches, bruises, and dark brown lesions. She was also dead. She had suffered a pulmonary embolism on the way to the hospital. In the eyes of the world press, Scientology had murdered Lisa McPherson. She was one of nine Scientologists who had died under mysterious circumstances at the Clearwater facility.

The night after McPherson died, Rathbun got word from church officials to wait for a call at a pay phone at a nearby Holiday Inn. "Why aren't you all over this mess?" Miscavige demanded, when Rathbun answered the call. "The police are poking around. Do something."

Rathbun discovered that church officials in Clearwater had already lied in two sworn statements to the police, claiming that McPherson hadn't been subjected to an Introspection Rundown. The church's official response, under Rathbun's direction, was to continue to lie, stating that McPherson had been at the church's Fort Harrison Hotel only for "rest and relaxation" and there was nothing unusual about her stay. In the meantime, Rathbun went through the logs that McPherson's attendants had kept. As many as twenty people had been rotating in and out of McPherson's room; some of them were scratched and bruised from trying to subdue her; that was hardly the isolation and absolute silence and calm that the Introspection Rundown called for. Rathbun noted that, among other entries in the logs, one of the caretakers admitted that the situation was out of control and that McPherson needed to see a doctor. In the presence of a Scientology lawyer, Rathbun handed several of the most incriminating logs to a church executive, and said, "Lose 'em."

The McPherson case loomed over the church for five years, with an ongoing police investigation, protests in front of Scientology facilities, lawsuits on the part of the family, and endless unwanted press. Embarrassing details emerged, including the fact that McPherson had spent $176,700 on Scientology services in her last five years, but she had died with only $11 in her savings account. Rathbun and Mike Rinder, the church's spokesman, were responsible for managing the situation, but Miscavige supervised every detail. The level of tension was nearly unbearable.

Rinder had the particularly unrewarding task of defending the church to the public. He was articulate and seemingly unflappable, and he had a talent for disarming hostile interviewers. He had been a Scientologist since he was five years old, in South Australia, when the religion was banned. He had sailed with Hubbard aboard the *Apollo*. Few had a deeper experience of the religion than he and no one was more publicly identified with it. But even Rinder could not quell the furor that arose from the McPherson affair.

Perhaps because of Rinder's lifelong service to the church, Miscavige saw him as a rival; or perhaps the leader's frustration with the continual bad press made his spokesperson a particular object of his wrath. At any rate, Marty Rathbun got a call from Shelly Miscavige around Christmas in 1997, the first year of the protests over Lisa McPherson's death. Rathbun was back at Gold Base. Shelly said that Dave wanted him to report to his quarters right away. Rathbun rushed down the hill to Miscavige's bungalow, where Shelly was waiting just outside the screen door. A moment later, Mike Rinder, who had also been summoned, came racing around the corner of the house. According to both men, the screen door suddenly flew open and Miscavige came out, wearing a terry-cloth bathrobe. According to Rathbun and Rinder, Miscavige hit Rinder in the face and stomach, then grabbed him around the neck and slammed him into a tree. Rinder fell into the ivy, where Miscavige continued kicking him several times.* Rathbun just stood there, stunned and puzzled about why he had been ordered to watch this display. Afterward, he decided that he was there to back up Miscavige in case Rinder had the nerve to resist. He was the "silent enforcer."

Rathbun's management of the defense in the McPherson case

---

*The church denies that Miscavige has abused any members of the church, saying that the abuse claims have been propagated by a "group of vociferous anti-Scientologists."

was one of his most successful accomplishments for the church. The medical examiner in the case, Joan Wood, had vehemently denied the church's assertion that Lisa McPherson's illness and death were sudden. Her health had obviously deteriorated over a long period. She had been without liquids for at least five days, the medical examiner told a reporter, saying, "This is the most severe case of dehydration I've ever seen." She ruled that the cause of death was undetermined, and the State of Florida filed criminal charges against the church. If the church were to be convicted of a felony, it could lead to the loss of its tax exemption and then its probable extinction.

Miscavige and his team brought to bear Scientology's two greatest assets, money and celebrity. The church was building up a strong defense in its case by hiring some of the most prestigious medical examiners and forensic scientists in the country—experts who questioned Joan Wood's conclusion that the likely cause of death was a blood clot caused by dehydration. One of the local lawyers retained by the church arranged a personal meeting between Miscavige and Wood's attorney, Jeffrey Goodis. Miscavige and Rathbun made a number of presentations to Goodis, trying to persuade him that his client was in legal jeopardy because of her ruling in the McPherson case. Wood was known as an unflappable witness and a formidable opponent to defense attorneys; her testimony would be crucial if the case went to trial. Rathbun says that Miscavige repeatedly warned Goodis that the church was going to discredit his client and sue her "into the Stone Age." Four months before the McPherson case was set to go to trial, Joan Wood changed her ruling to say that McPherson's death was "accidental." The State's case collapsed, charges against the church were dropped, and Wood avoided a lawsuit. Wood retired and became a recluse. She told the *St. Petersburg Times* that she suffered panic attacks and insomnia. (She died of a stroke in 2011.)

The civil case against the church on the part of McPherson's family continued, however, along with the negative publicity. Tom De Vocht, who was head of the Flag Land Base in Clearwater, says he arranged a meeting with Mary Repper, an influential political consultant who had led the campaigns of many of the state and local officials in the area, including the state attorney who had filed the criminal charges against the church. Repper had the reputation of being anti-Scientology, but she agreed to have lunch with Rinder, Rathbun, and Miscavige at the Fort Harrison Hotel. It turned out that she was a fan of the soap-opera star Michelle Stafford, who was a Scientologist. Repper was invited to Los Angeles to meet her at a Celebrity Centre gala. When she returned, Repper began hosting a series of dinners and lunches for local officials to meet other Scientology celebrities. Tom Cruise dropped by Repper's house on several occasions to enjoy her famous coconut cake and schmooze with local officials including the mayor of Tampa and influential lawyers and judges. He showed clips of his movies and testified about how Scientology had changed his life. Fox News host Greta van Susteren provided sunset cruises on her yacht. Repper held a brunch for Michelle Stafford; the guests were mainly women who were fans of *The Young and the Restless,* including the secretaries of local judges. Meantime, the church threw black-tie galas in the ballroom of the Fort Harrison Hotel, where Edgar Winter, Chick Corea, or Isaac Hayes would perform. The Pinellas County sheriff attended these events, along with the mayors of Clearwater and Tampa, as well as a number of lawyers and judges who had been targeted by the church as community leaders. Rathbun says that when Miscavige learned that Jeffrey Goodis and his wife were big fans of John Travolta, they were invited to a gala at the Fort Harrison Hotel, and Travolta was asked to thank them for their help. Rathbun says the star was told, "This guy is really going to bat for us."

The church poured money into local charities. According to Rathbun and Rinder, the idea was to change the climate of public opinion and thereby influence the attitude of the courts toward the church. Rathbun says there was a parallel campaign to discredit Lisa McPherson's family as golddiggers who were exploiting their daughter's death.

In a recent deposition, Rathbun estimated that the entire campaign to shut down the prosecution of the church cost over $20 to $30 million. (The civil suit brought by the family settled for an undisclosed sum in 2004.)

SCIENTOLOGY WAS UNDER ATTACK elsewhere in the world as well. Germany, acutely sensitive to the danger of extremist movements, viewed Scientology with particular alarm. In Hamburg, in 1992, the state parliament created a commission to investigate "destructive groups," a category that included the Church of Satan, Transcendental Meditation, and the Unification Church, but was mainly aimed at Scientology. Scientologists were barred from holding government jobs and forbidden to join Germany's main political party, the Christian

Democratic Union, because they weren't considered Christians. The youth wing of the party organized boycotts of Cruise's first *Mission: Impossible* and Travolta's movie *Phenomenon*. The city of Stuttgart canceled a concert by Chick Corea when it was discovered that he was a Scientologist. Seventy percent of Germans favored the idea of banning the organization altogether.

The 1990s saw the rise of apocalyptic movements in many different countries. As the millennium drew near, the theme of science fiction and UFOs became especially pronounced and deadly. In October 1994, police in Switzerland, investigating a fire in a farmhouse, discovered a hidden room with eighteen corpses wearing ceremonial garments, arranged like spokes in a wheel. Other bodies were found elsewhere on the farm. Their heads were covered with plastic bags; some had been shot or beaten. The next day, three chalets burned in another Swiss village. Investigators found more than two dozen bodies in the ruins. They had been poisoned. Some of the dead had been lured to the scene and murdered, but most were followers of Joseph Di Mambro, a French jeweler, who had created a new religion, the Order of the Solar Temple. Di Mambro's chief lieutenant, a charismatic Belgian obstetrician named Luc Journet, preached that after death the members would be picked up by a spaceship and reunited on the star Sirius. Like Hubbard, Journet had been influenced by Aleister Crowley and the Ordo Templi Orientis. A year after these macabre incidents, the burned corpses of sixteen other members of the group were found in Grenoble, France; then, in 1997, five more members of the order burned themselves to death in Quebec, making a total of seventy-four deaths. In contrast to the Branch Davidians or the followers of Jim Jones, who were predominantly lower class, the members of the Solar Temple were affluent, well-educated members of the communities they lived in, with families and regular jobs, and yet they had given themselves over to a mystical science-fiction fantasy that turned them into killers, suicides, or helpless victims.

In March 1995, adherents of a Japanese movement called Aum Shinrikyo ("Supreme Truth") attacked five subway trains in Tokyo with sarin gas. Twelve commuters died; thousands more might have if the gas had been more highly refined. It was later discovered that this was just one of at least fourteen attacks the group staged in order to set off a chain of events intended to result in an apocalyptic world war. The leader of the group, Shoko Asahara, a blind yoga instructor, combined the tenets of Buddhism with notions drawn from Isaac Asimov's *Foundation Trilogy*, which depicts a secretive group of scientists who are preparing to take over the world. Many of Asahara's followers were indeed scientists and engineers from top Japanese universities who were enchanted by this scheme. They purchased military hardware in the former Soviet Union and sought to acquire nuclear warheads. When that failed, they bought a sheep farm in Western Australia that happened to be atop a rich vein of uranium. They cultivated chemical and biological weapons, such as anthrax, Ebola virus, cyanide, and VX gas. They had used such agents in previous attacks, but failed to create the kind of mass slaughter they hoped would bring on civil war and nuclear Armageddon. Still, Aum exposed the narrow boundary between religious cultism and terror, which would soon become more obvious with the rise of al-Qaeda. A spokesperson for the Church of Scientology in New Zealand explained that the source of Aum Shinri-kyo's crimes was the practice of psychiatry in Japan.

Just as the debate in Germany was coming to a climax, in March 1997, thirty-nine members of a group calling itself Heaven's Gate committed suicide in a San Diego mansion. They apparently had hoped to time their deaths in order to ascend to a spacecraft that they believed was following Comet Hale-Bopp. Marshall Applewhite, their leader, a former choirmaster, represented himself as a reincarnated Jesus who was receiving guidance from the television show *Star Trek*.

Although Scientology has persecuted its critics and defectors, it has never engaged in mass murder or suicides; however, the public anxiety surrounding these sensational events added to the rancor and fear that welled up in Germany. Could Scientology also turn violent? There were elements mixed into these various groups that resembled some features of Scientology—magical beliefs and science fiction being the most obvious. Past lives were a common theme. Like Aum Shinrikyo, Scientology has ties to Buddhist notions of enlightenment and Hindu beliefs in karma and reincarnation. Structurally, Aum Shinrikyo was the most similar to Scientology, having both a public membership and a cloistered clergy, like the Sea Org, called renunciates, who carried out directives that the larger organization knew little or nothing about. When the attacks on the subway took place, Aum's membership in Japan was estimated to be about 10,000, with an additional 30,000 in Russia, and some scattered pockets worldwide, with resources close to $1 billion—figures that compare with some estimates of Scientology today. What separated these groups from Scientology was their orientation toward apocalypse and their yearning for the end-time. That has never been a feature of Scientology. Clearly, however, the lure of totalistic religious movements defies easy categorization. Such groups can arise anywhere and spread like viruses, and it is impossible to know which ones will turn lethal, or why.

Both the German government and the Scientologists viewed their struggle through the prism of Germany's Nazi past. Ursula Caberta, the head of the Hamburg anti-Scientology task force, compared Hubbard's *Introduction to Scientology Ethics* to Adolf Hitler's *Mein Kampf*: "Hitler was thinking that the Aryans were going to rule the world, the *untermenschen*. The philosophy of L. Ron Hubbard is the same." In response to such statements, in January 1997 a group of Hollywood celebrities, agents, lawyers, and movie executives published a full-page open letter to Chancellor Helmut Kohl in the *International Herald Tribune*. "Hitler made religious intolerance official government policy," the letter stated. "In the 1930s it was the Jews. Today it is the Scientologists." The letter compared the boycotts of Cruise, Travolta, and Corea to Nazi book-burnings. The letter was written and paid for by Bertram Fields, then the most powerful lawyer in Hollywood, whose clients included Travolta and Cruise. None of the thirty-four signatories of the document were Scientologists, but many were Jews. Most of them—such as Oliver Stone, Dustin Hoffman, and Goldie Hawn—had worked with the two stars or were friends or clients of Fields.

Entertainment Tonight sent the actress Anne Archer, a well-known Scientologist, to Germany on a "fact-finding mission." She later testified before the US Congress, as did other Scientology celebrities—Travolta, Corea, and Isaac Hayes—about the suppression of religious freedom in Germany. "Individuals and businesses throughout Germany are routinely required to sign a declaration, referred to as a 'sect filter,' swearing that they are not Scientologists," Travolta told Congress. "Failure to sign means that companies will not hire them, trade unions will not admit them, they will not be permitted to join social groups, banks will not open accounts for them, and they are even excluded from sports clubs, solely because of their religion."

In April, John Travolta met with President Bill Clinton at a conference on volunteerism in Philadelphia. It was a freighted moment for the president, since Travolta was portraying a character based on him in the forthcoming movie *Primary Colors*. "He said he wanted to help me out with the situation in Germany," Travolta later said. "He had a roommate years ago who was a Scientologist and had really liked him, and respected his views on it. He said he felt we were given an unfair hand in that country, and that he wanted to fix it." Clinton set up a meeting for Travolta and Cruise with Sandy Berger, his national security advisor, who was given the additional assignment of being the administration's "Scientology point person."

None of this had any effect on Travolta's character in the film, as the movie had already been shot, nor on Germany's policy toward the church, which refused to recognize Scientology as a religion or allow members to join political parties. However, the US State Department began pressuring the German government on behalf of Scientology. The Germans were puzzled that their American counterparts seemed not to know or care about the church's RPF camps, which the Germans called penal colonies, and the reported practices of confinement, forced confessions, and punishing physical labor, which they said amounted to brainwashing. There was a belief within the German cabinet that the church's real goal was to infiltrate the government and create a Scientology superstate. "This is not a church or a religious organization," the labor minister, Norbert Blum, told *Maclean's* magazine. "Scientology is a machine for manipulating human beings."

8

Bohemian Rhapsody

Paul Haggis and Deborah Rennard married in 1997, soon after
Paul's divorce from Diane became final. Paul was still seeking
joint custody of his three daughters. Without consulting him,
Diane had taken Lauren and Katy out of the Delphi Academy, apparently intending to enroll them in public school. Paul and Diane were
ordered by the court to undergo psychiatric evaluation, a procedure
that Scientology abhors. In December 1998, the court surprised everyone by awarding Paul full custody of his daughters. According to
court records, the ruling followed the discovery that the girls were not
enrolled in school at all.

The girls were stunned. They had watched the hostilities through
Diane's eyes. No one had prepared them for the possibility that they
might be taken from her—until then, it had been the three girls and
their mother against the world. The girls thought the decision was
unbalanced and unfairly influenced by the fact that their father had
more money. Alissa vowed she would never speak to him again.

Haggis was also caught short by the court's decision. In addition
to the year-old son, James, he had with Deborah, he suddenly had two
teenage daughters on his hands as well. (Alissa was twenty-one at the
time, and lived on her own.) The girls felt uprooted and they missed
the emotional support of their mother. They didn't resent Deborah;
actually, they appreciated her advocacy and the way she balanced out
Paul. Still, it was a difficult adjustment for everyone.

Paul put the girls in a private school, but that lasted only six months. They weren't entirely comfortable talking to people who weren't Scientologists, and basic things like multiple-choice tests were unfamiliar. They demanded to be sent to a boarding institution on an isolated hilltop near Sheridan, Oregon, called the Delphian School—or the "mother school," as it was known to Scientologists.

Alissa had gone there when she was fourteen years old. It had been a mixed experience for her. She had brought a copy of *The Autobiography of Malcolm X* and books of eighteenth-century poetry, a CD of great speeches by Lincoln and Martin Luther King, and a pack of tarot cards. Although she loved the school, she never felt she fit in with the other kids. They wanted to talk about boys and pop culture, and she was more interested in philosophy and religion. But Delphian was just what Lauren needed. She got intensive tutoring to help her overcome her educational deficits; however, she also began to come up against some of the constraints of her church.

While she was at Delphian, Lauren decided to write a paper about religious intolerance. In particular, she felt that Scientology was under attack and she couldn't understand why. When she went online to see what the opposition was saying, a fellow student turned her in to Ethics. Lauren was told that Scientologists shouldn't look at negative stories about their religion. She was supposed to be saving the planet, so why was she wasting her time reading lies? Because of her isolation, and the censorship imposed on her education, when Lauren finally graduated from high school, at the age of twenty, she had never heard anyone speak ill of Scientology, nor did she question the ban on research about her religion. She thought, "I guess I'm not supposed to do these things. I will stay away." Like her father, she learned it was easier not to look.

Alissa had a different issue. She didn't really date in high school, and by the time she got to junior college it began to dawn on her that she was gay. She actually wasn't sure what that meant. She had two uncles who were gay, but for the longest time she didn't know what a lesbian was. Then her sister Katy, who is five years younger, and had grown up in the Internet-savvy culture, came out to her parents. Paul told Katy that there was no way that he would ever love her less. That made it easier for Alissa to talk about what she was discovering about herself. The vow never to speak to her father again began to lose its hold on her.

All the girls had grown up hearing prejudiced remarks from people in the church who saw homosexuality as an "aberration" that under-mined the survival of the species; gays themselves were seen as sinister perverts. These attitudes were informed by Hubbard's writings on the subject. But it wasn't just Scientology, Alissa realized; the entire society was biased against homosexuals. In her early twenties, Alissa finally found the courage to come out to her father. "Oh, yeah, I already knew that," he told her. He said he wondered why she had ever dated boys in the first place.

"You *knew*?" she said. "I didn't know! How did you know? Why didn't you tell me? You could have clued me in. It would have made it easier for me."

That was so typical of her father. He was maddening in that way, completely accepting but disengaged, as if it really didn't matter one way or the other.

To signify her newfound identity, Alissa got a tattoo of her favorite Latin poem, the opening line of Carmen 5 by Catullus: "*Vivamus mea Lesbia, atque amemus*" (Let us live, my Lesbia, and let us love). It snaked all the way down her left arm.

EVER SINCE the *Time* exposé, the church had been frantically trying to recover Tom Cruise. Both Cruise and Nicole Kidman were attain-ing ever greater success; Cruise became the first actor to star in five consecutive films to gross more than $100 million in the United States, including *Jerry Maguire* and the first *Mission: Impossible*; Kidman was also gaining international renown with her roles in *Batman For-ever* and *To Die For*. They gave the impression that they were putting Scientology behind them.

In 1996, Marty Rathbun had gone to Los Angeles to audit Cruise, but that one session went nowhere. According to Rathbun, Miscavige blamed Nicole Kidman, and viewed her as a gold digger who was fak-ing Scientology. He says that Miscavige was hopeful that if they por-trayed Nicole Kidman as a Suppressive Person, Cruise could be peeled away from her.

It was two years before Cruise agreed to go through another bout of auditing. This time, strict secrecy was imposed. Worried about scar-ing off the tentative star, Rathbun arranged the sessions so that even top officials in the church were unaware that Cruise was receiving ser-vices. For five days in October 1998, Cruise drove into a private parking lot in the back of the historic Guaranty Building on Hollywood Boulevard, with the yellow Scientology sign atop it that looms over the fabled district. Charlie Chaplin and Rudolph Valentino used to have their offices here. Now the lobby is a shrine to the life and works of L. Ron Hubbard. A giant bust of the founder greets the occasional visitor. Embedded in the sidewalk in front of the building are the stars of bygone celebrities on the Hollywood Walk of Fame—Otto Kruger, Tony Martin, Ann Rutherford, Richard Carlson, Jetta Goudal, Paul Winchell—who had their own moments of great renown and are now largely forgotten.

Cruise went in a back door that led to a basement hallway. There was an elevator at the end of the hallway that went directly to the "secret" eleventh floor, where both Miscavige and Rathbun maintained offices. The World Series was under way—New York versus San Diego—and Cruise wore his Yankees hat. "He was not in good shape, spiritually or mentally," Rathbun observed. "He was personally very enturbulated."

After that episode of auditing, Cruise went quiet again. He and Kidman were in England filming *Eyes Wide Shut* for Stanley Kubrick. In any case, Rathbun and Miscavige had their hands full, fending off the lawsuits and reporters swirling around the McPherson case. Rathbun said that, in January 2001, he got a call from Cruise asking for help. Cruise said that he and Kidman were finished.

Cruise never offered a public explanation for the divorce, and Kidman herself was clearly surprised by his decision. She later revealed that she had suffered a miscarriage two months after Cruise moved out, and she had asked the doctors to preserve samples of the fetus's DNA to prove that Cruise was the father. She pleaded with him to undergo marriage counseling at the church. Cruise refused, publicly declaring, "Nic knows exactly why we are getting a divorce."

This was a decisive moment in Cruise's relationship with Scientology. Rathbun provided the star with more than two hundred hours of auditing over the next couple of years. From July through Thanksgiving, 2001, Rathbun was with Cruise at the Celebrity Centre frequently, doing auditing rundowns and the PTS/SP (Potential Trouble Source/Suppressive Persons) course. He paired Cruise with another actor, Jason Beghe, to do training drills; for instance, Beghe would think of a hypothetical date, which Cruise had to figure out, using the E-Meter, an exercise Cruise found really frustrating.

A young man named Tommy Davis began acting as Rathbun's assistant. He brought sandwiches and helped out with Cruise's children, making sure they were receiving church services. Despite his youth, Davis was already a unique figure in the church: He was a second-generation Scientologist, a Sea Org member, and the scion of the Hollywood elite. His mother was Anne Archer, a talented and popular actress who had starred in a number of movies, including *Patriot Games* and *Fatal Attraction*, for which she was nominated for an Academy Award. She had been a deeply committed Scientologist since she began studying with Milton Katselas at the Beverly Hills Playhouse in her twenties. She had always been proud to associate herself with Scientology in public, speaking at innumerable events on behalf of the church. Her son Tommy embodied the aspiration of the church to establish itself in the Hollywood community; indeed, he was living proof that it had done so. He had known Cruise since he was eighteen years old, so it was natural that he soon became the church's liaison with the star, reporting directly to Shelly Miscavige. He had a relationship with Cruise similar to the one that Spanky Taylor once enjoyed with John Travolta. Rathbun assigned Davis to sit with Cruise in the parking lot of Home Depot in Hollywood while the star was doing his Tone Scale drills—guessing the emotional state of random people coming out of the store.

Cruise then took a break to promote his movie *Vanilla Sky*. The following February through April 2002, Cruise and Rathbun were once again working together full-time, mostly at Gold Base. Cruise was preparing for his role in *The Last Samurai*, directed by Ed Zwick, and between sessions with Rathbun he would go into the courtyard to practice his swordplay.

Cruise had begun dating the Spanish actress Penélope Cruz, and in the fall of 2001 Rathbun began auditing her as well. At the same time, he was still acting as Nicole Kidman's Ethics Officer in the church, even though she and Cruise were engaged in a bitter divorce proceeding. One of the issues was whether the children would be educated in schools using the Hubbard method, which Kidman opposed. That was another battle she lost. Although Tom and Nicole split custody of their children, both Isabella and Connor soon chose to live exclusively with their father. Rathbun says this was because the Scientology staff, especially Tommy Davis, quietly worked to turn the children against Kidman. "Tommy told them over and over again their mother was a sociopath and after a while they believed him," he recalled. "They had daily sessions with Tommy. I was there. I saw it."

According to several former Sea Org members, Rathbun's auditing sessions with Cruise were videotaped. Tom De Vocht, a former church official, said Miscavige would watch them and then regale his inner circle, over his nightly whiskey, with stories of Cruise's confessions, dwelling especially on his sex life.*

Rathbun was opposed to the endless courtship of Cruise. In his opinion, there was no need for it once Cruise was securely back on the Bridge. Rathbun told Miscavige, "I think I'm done with this guy." Miscavige responded, "He'll be done when he calls me." The leader was galled by the fact that Cruise had never contacted him when he came back for counseling. Rathbun continually urged Cruise to call "COB," as Miscavige is known in the church—Chairman of the Board. At one point Cruise asked for Miscavige's number, but then failed to call. His tentativeness was worrisome.

Whatever restraint Cruise felt about Miscavige eventually fell away, however, and Miscavige was once again folded into the star's inner circle. There were movie nights in Cruise's mansion. Miscavige flew with Cruise in the Warner Brothers jet to a test screening of *The Last Samurai* in Arizona. The two men became closer than ever. Cruise later said of Miscavige, "I have never met a more competent, a more intelligent, a more compassionate being outside of what I have experienced from LRH. And I've met the leaders of leaders. I've met them all."

Cruise's renewed dedication to Scientology permanently changed the relationship between the church and the Hollywood celebrity community. Cruise poured millions of dollars into the church—$3 million in 2004 alone. He was not simply a figurehead; he was an activist with an international following. He could take the church into places it had never been before. Whenever Cruise traveled abroad to promote his movies, he used the opportunity to lobby foreign leaders and American ambassadors to promote Scientology. Davis usually accompanied him on these diplomatic and lobbying missions. Cruise repeatedly consulted with former President Clinton, lobbying him to get Prime Minister Tony Blair's help in getting the Church of Scientology declared a tax-deductible charitable organization in the United Kingdom. Rath-

*The church denies that Cruise was videotaped, or that Miscavige watched such tapes, or used such information to manipulate anyone. Noriyuki Matsumaru, who worked in the RTC with Miscavige, confirms De Vocht's account.

bun was present for one telephone call in which Clinton advised Cruise he would be better served by contacting Blair's wife, Cherie, rather than the prime minister, because she was a lawyer and "would understand the details." Later, Cruise went to London, where he met with a couple of Blair's representatives, although nothing came of those efforts. In 2003, he met with Deputy Secretary of State Richard Armitage and Vice President Dick Cheney's chief of staff, Scooter Libby, to express the church's concerns over its treatment in Germany. Cruise had access to practically anyone in the world.

That same year, Cruise and Davis lobbied Rod Paige, the secretary of education during the first term of President George W. Bush, to endorse Hubbard's study tech educational methods. Paige had been impressed. For months, Cruise kept in contact with Paige's office, urging that Scientology techniques be folded into the president's No Child Left Behind program. One day Cruise flew his little red-and-white-striped Pitts Special biplane, designed for aerobatics, to Hemet, along with his Scientologist chief of staff, Michael Doven. Miscavige and Rathbun picked them up and drove them to Gold Base. Rathbun was in the backseat and recalls Cruise boasting to COB about his talks with the secretary.

"Bush may be an idiot," Miscavige observed, "but I wouldn't mind his being our Constantine."

Cruise agreed. "If fucking Arnold can be governor, I could be president."

Miscavige responded, "Well, absolutely, Tom."*

IN 2001, Haggis was fired from *Family Law*, the show he had created. His career, which for so long seemed to be a limitless staircase toward fame and fortune, now took a plunge. He began working at home.

Within a week, he started writing a movie script called *Million Dollar Baby*, based on a series of short stories by F. X. Toole. He spent a year working on it, drawing upon some of his own painful memories. He identified with the character of a sour old boxing coach, Frankie Dunn. Like Haggis, Frankie is estranged from his daughter. His letters

---

*Cruise, through his lawyer, denies this exchange and says he has no political ambition.

to her are returned. He turns to religion, going to Mass every day and seeking a forgiveness that he doesn't really believe in. Into the coach's dismal life comes another young woman, Maggie Fitzgerald, an aspiring boxer from a white trash background. All of the loss and longing he feels for his daughter is apparent in his mentoring of this gritty young fighter, who has more faith in him than he has in himself. But Maggie is paralyzed when her neck is broken in a fight. In a climactic moment, she begs Frankie to pull the plug and let her die. Haggis faced a similar choice in real life with his best friend, who was brain-dead from a staph infection. "They don't die easily," he recalled. "Even in a coma, he kicked and moaned for twelve hours."

Haggis dreamed of directing the movie himself. But as much as studios admired the writing, the story was so dark nobody wanted to get near it. Haggis began borrowing money to stay afloat. He turned down another TV series because he realized that his heart hadn't been in television for years.

One of his abandoned TV projects still haunted him. The idea sprang from an unsettling incident a decade before, when he and Diane were driving home from the premiere of *Silence of the Lambs*. Paul was wearing a tuxedo and driving a Porsche convertible. He stopped at a Blockbuster Video store on Wilshire Boulevard to rent some obscure Dutch film. When they got back into the car, two young black men with guns suddenly rushed up to them. The robbers ordered them out of the car and told them to walk toward a dark parking lot. That seemed like a really bad idea. Haggis pretended not to hear them. He put Diane in front of him and headed down Wilshire instead.

"Stop!"

Paul and Diane froze. They heard footsteps, and one of the thieves snatched the video out of Diane's hand. Then the Porsche roared off. That was the last Haggis ever saw of it.

Ten years later, Haggis awakened in the middle of the night and began chewing over this frightening episode once again. He often thought about it. The entire experience had lasted less than a minute, but it had colored his stance toward life in complicated ways. Where did these kids come from? They were living in the same city as he, but a universe of race and class separated them. He could imagine who he was in their eyes, just some rich white guy with much more than his share of what life had to offer. In a way, Haggis was on their side.

But it could have turned out so much worse; guns always make things dangerously unpredictable. He was shaken by that thought. The unexpected coda of snatching the rented videotape was intriguing. Haggis had managed a wisecrack to the cops at the time. "I think you'll discover that these men have been here quite often, looking for that video, and it was never in."

Specifically, what he thought about in the middle of the night was what those kids said to each other as they sped out of the Blockbuster parking lot onto Wilshire in his pearlescent Cabriolet. Could he find himself in them? Haggis got out of bed and began writing. By mid-morning he had a lengthy outline. It was about the manifold ways that people interact with each other—how the experience of having someone honk at you in traffic and shoot you the finger can affect your mood, so that you take it out on someone else at the first opportunity; or how, alternatively, someone lets you into a long line of traffic, and your day brightens. He saw life in America as a volatile collision of cultures—of immigrants who fail to read the codes that underlie our system, of races that resent and mistrust each other, of people coexisting in different social strata who look at each other with uncomprehending fear and hatred.

He had shopped the proposal around to different television producers, but they unanimously passed on it. Now, as he was struggling financially and artistically, Deborah suggested he consider writing the script as a movie. "You'll win an Academy Award," she told him.

Haggis contacted his friend Robert Moresco, who had been a writer on Haggis's series *EZ Streets*. He told Moresco, "I don't think anybody's going to make this, but it's a great story." The two men began working in Haggis's home office, next to the laundry room. They wrote a first draft in two weeks. Haggis decided to call it *Crash*.

The title refers to a fender bender that sets off a chain of events, revealing the contradictory elements of the characters and the city they inhabit. In the dizzying seconds after the collision an LAPD detective suddenly realizes what's missing in his life. "It's the sense of touch," he says in the movie's opening lines. "In LA no one touches you. . . . We're always behind metal and glass. Think we miss that touch so much, we crash into each other just to feel something."

Haggis insists on turning his heroes into villains and vice versa, such as the racist white cop who molests a tony, upper-class black woman in one scene, then saves her life in another. Haggis felt that by exploring such complexities he was teasing out the dark and light threads of his own personality.

For the next year and a half, he struggled to get the movie green-lit. He was still a first-time movie director, and that posed an obstacle. Moreover, the script called for an ensemble cast with no single starring role—always an obstacle in Hollywood. Haggis finally interested a producer, Bob Yari, who agreed to make the movie for $10 million if Haggis could assemble a star-studded cast.

Don Cheadle was the first to sign on, both as an actor and a producer, and his name added credibility to the project. Matt Dillon and Tony Danza came aboard. Heath Ledger and John Cusack agreed to work for scale, as everyone did. Still, the project dragged on. Finally, Haggis was told the movie was a go. He then sent the script to John Travolta and Kelly Preston, who he thought would be perfect as the district attorney and his wife.

"That's great, because now we really need them," one of the producers, Cathy Schulman, told him the next day. Heath Ledger had dropped out and Cusack was not far behind. Once again, the movie would need more big-name stars to get the financing. Haggis immediately sent a note to Preston, telling her he was withdrawing his offer.

Priscilla Presley, John Travolta, and Kelly Preston at the Church of Scientology Celebrity Centre's thirty-seventh-anniversary gala, Hollywood, August 2006

254 | GOING CLEAR

As a matter of pride, he felt it was wrong to use his friends in such a way—especially other Scientologists. Preston was miffed, since he had failed to explain his decision.

But without two more signature names the movie was back in limbo. Haggis was about to lose Cheadle as well, because he was scheduled to make *Hotel Rwanda.* Yari finally told Haggis to shut the production down.

The following Monday, when Schulman came into the production office, she found Haggis there, alone.

"What are you doing?" she asked.

"I'm prepping the movie."

Yari agreed to keep the office open for one more week, and then another, as each Monday Schulman would find Haggis at work preparing for a movie that now had no budget at all. Gradually, other people began working with him, for no pay.

"If you get Sandy Bullock, you got a green light," Schulman told him.

Haggis got Sandra Bullock for the role of the district attorney's wife, a brittle, racist socialite, a role far from the plucky gamines she had played in the past. In the movie, she's the one who gets carjacked at gunpoint. But the producers wanted one more name: Brendan Fraser. Haggis thought he was much too young for the part, as did Fraser, but he agreed to do it. The movie was finally green-lit, just four weeks before the shooting started. Only now, the ten million dollars had shrunk to six and a half.

For Haggis, everything was riding on this film. He mortgaged his house three times; he also used it as a set, in order to save on his location budget. He canceled many of the exterior scenes and borrowed the set of the television show *Monk* to film interiors. He was eating carelessly and smoking constantly. He lost weight. He desperately needed more time.

When he finished shooting a scene in Chinatown, Cathy Schulman caught up with him to ask about the next day's shoot. "You look like you're clutching your chest," she observed.

Haggis admitted that he was having some pains.

"Sharp pains?" Schulman urged him to see a doctor. He didn't want to hear that. He went home.

He woke the next morning in agony. He called his doctor, who told him it was probably stress, but agreed to see him just to set his mind at ease. By now, Paul was short of breath, so Deborah drove him to the doctor's office. The doctor did a few tests and said yes, it was stress and muscle fatigue. "But we'll do an electrocardiogram just in case."

A few moments later the doctor returned. His face was snow white. "Don't stand up!" he said in a professionally measured voice. "You've had a heart attack!"

That night in the hospital, Haggis suffered another cardiac failure. He received three stents in the arteries to his heart in an emergency operation. He was able to watch the entire procedure on the monitor. It was really like an out-of-body experience, watching his own fragile heart being repaired. The movie he was making didn't seem so important anymore.

That changed as soon as the operation was over.

Schulman arrived with some more bad news. "I talked to your doctor," she told Haggis. "He's not going to allow you to go back to work for another four or five months. I've got to hire another director."

"Fine," Haggis responded. He said he'd talk it over with his doctor.

The doctor confirmed the decision. "Paul, it's not just your heart attack," he told him. "You've had an operation. It'll put too much stress on your heart."

"I totally understand," Haggis replied. "Let me ask you how much stress you think I would be experiencing if I were just sitting at home while another director is finishing *my fucking film*!"

Production was shut down for a week and a half until Haggis returned, with a nurse at his side who checked his vital signs every quarter hour. Sandra Bullock brought him green tea and refused to let him drink coffee. Every time Haggis tried to stand up, she told him to sit down. She had a kind of implacable maternal authority. He finished the film in his chair with a cup of tea in his hands.

Clint Eastwood had been asked to read *Million Dollar Baby* for the role of Frankie Dunn, the boxing coach. He loved the script, but said he would only do the role if he could direct as well. Although Haggis hated to surrender the opportunity to direct, he knew it would be a bigger picture if Eastwood were behind it. Hilary Swank was cast as Maggie Fitzgerald, a part that would bring her an Academy Award. Morgan Freeman also would win in a supporting role, and Eastwood for directing—all that in addition to winning the Oscar for Best Picture. Haggis would be nominated for Best Screenplay. But that was still on the horizon.

While he was still editing *Crash*, Haggis began writing another movie for Eastwood, *Flags of Our Fathers*. They went to visit the producer of that project, Steven Spielberg, on the set of *War of the Worlds*, which he was shooting with Tom Cruise. Spielberg had called Haggis to talk over an idea for another script.

Haggis had met Cruise on a couple of occasions, once at a fundraiser and again at the Celebrity Centre. As the most popular and sought-after leading man in Hollywood, Cruise was given perks that few other stars could match. He had asked Tommy Davis, now his full-time Scientology handler, to set up a tent on the set of *War of the Worlds* in order to distribute church materials to the crew and provide Scientology assists. The precedent alarmed many in Hollywood, and Spielberg was widely criticized for letting it happen.

"It's really remarkable to me," Spielberg observed, as he and Haggis walked to his trailer. "I've met all these Scientologists, and they seem like the nicest people."

"Yeah, we keep all the evil ones in the closet," Haggis replied.*

A couple of days later, Tommy Davis called Haggis at home and told him someone from senior management needed to see him urgently. Haggis had no idea what was going on. He assumed that the church was going to pressure him to take some more auditing or another course, as had happened so often in the past. Davis met him at the Celebrity Centre and escorted him to a room where Greg Wilhere was waiting. Wilhere, a handsome former college football player, was a senior executive in the church assigned to be Cruise's personal auditor. (He accompanied the star even to the shooting of *Days of Thunder*, where a character in the movie was named after him.) Wilhere was livid because Haggis had upset Tom Cruise by subverting years of work on Cruise's part to recruit Spielberg into the church.

"It was a joke," Haggis protested. He said he had no idea how that could have undermined Cruise's efforts to draw the most powerful man in Hollywood into Scientology. Wilhere said that Steven was having a problem with one of his seven children, and Tom was working to "steer him in the right direction." All that was ruined, Wilhere said, because Spielberg now believed there were evil Scientologists who were locked in a closet.

Haggis felt like he was trapped in a farce. It all seemed wildly ridic-

*Spielberg's publicist says that the director doesn't recall the conversation.

BOHEMIAN RHAPSODY | 257

ulous, but he was the only one who thought so. Still, he'd be crazy to antagonize Tom Cruise and Steven Spielberg. He offered to explain to Spielberg that he had been kidding, there were no evil Scientologists, and if there were, they wouldn't be kept in a closet. He couldn't believe that Spielberg would actually think he had been serious.

Wilhere was unappeased. He said Cruise was apoplectic. He directed Haggis to write the star a letter of apology—this minute. Haggis dutifully wrote out a note on the paper handed to him, but Wilhere said it wasn't sufficient. Haggis wrote a more contrite note. Wilhere said he would pass it along. But Haggis never got a response from Cruise.*

Haggis came away from that meeting with a new appreciation of the significance of Tom Cruise to Scientology. He had heard that Cruise had often been enlisted to try to recruit famous people. They included James Packer, the richest man in Australia; David Beckham, the British soccer star, and his wife, Victoria, the former Spice Girl; and Cruise's good friends, the actors Will and Jada Pinkett Smith, who later funded a school that used Hubbard educational techniques. But there was no one else like Spielberg. Had Cruise been successful in his efforts, it would have been a transformative moment in the history of the church, especially in its relation to Hollywood. It would have given reality to the mythology of Scientology's influence in the entertainment industry. Who could guess how many recruits would flood into the church because of Spielberg's imprimatur? Or how much money would pour into Scientology's coffers by moguls and agents and aspiring movie stars seeking to gain favor? The ambition behind such a play on the part of the church was breathtaking. And Haggis had stepped into the middle of it with an innocent jest.

Cruise turned his attention to the other Scientologists in the industry. Many had gone quiet following the scandals in the church or had never openly admitted their affiliation with the church. Cruise called a meeting of other Scientology celebrities and urged them to become more outspoken about their religion. The popular singer Beck, who had grown up in the church, subsequently began speaking openly about his faith. Erika Christensen, a rising young actress who was also a second-generation Scientologist, called Cruise her spiritual mentor.

Inspired by a new sense of activism, a group of Scientology actors

*Tom Cruise's lawyer says that the actor doesn't remember the incident or his being upset with Haggis.

turned against Milton Katselas, the gray eminence of the Beverly Hills Playhouse. No one had been more instrumental in forging the bond between Scientology and Hollywood. Katselas had been a longtime friend of Hubbard's and still kept a photograph of him on his desk. The two men were similar in many ways, but especially in their transformative effect on those who studied under them. Humorous, compassionate, and charismatic, but also vain and demanding, Katselas was not above bullying his students to make a point; however, many of them felt that he had taken them to a higher level of artistry than they had ever thought they could achieve. When Katselas addressed an acting student, it wasn't just about technique; his lessons were full of savvy observations about life and behavior.

One of those students, Allen Barton, was a classical pianist as well as a promising actor. When Katselas heard him play, he found him a teacher and paid for his piano lessons. Barton eventually arranged a recital on a Sunday evening. Katselas showed up at the theater at eight that morning, just as the piano was being delivered. He noticed that the stage was scratched, there were piled-up boxes spilling out of the wings, and a large spiral staircase—a prop from an old production—was left on the stage, because it was simply too big to move. Barton explained that he was going to cover up as much as possible with black drapes. Katselas called his office and within an hour ten people arrived. He sent Barton off to relax and prepare himself for the performance. When Barton returned that afternoon, the staircase was gone, the boxes had disappeared, the stage had been sanded and painted, and four trees surrounded the piano. Even the pots the trees were planted in had been painted to match the backdrop. The overall effect was stunning. "Have a good show," Katselas said, and walked away. Overwhelmed, Barton ran after him. "How can I ever thank you?" he asked. As he drove off, Katselas said, "Learn to expect it of yourself."

Such stories became a part of the Katselas legend. He was an OT V and a very public Scientologist, but he had stopped moving up the Bridge, in part because he refused to travel to Flag, where the upper-level courses were offered. Moreover, he had gotten into Ethics trouble because of his behavior with some of his female students. Jenna Elfman was a leader of the revolt against Katselas. She had been one of his prize students, winning a Golden Globe Award in 1999 for her free-spirited performance in the sitcom *Dharma & Greg*. Allen Barton, who had become a teacher at the Playhouse, wrote Elfman a letter in June 2004, begging her to relent. He called the movement against Katselas "Scientological McCarthyism," harking back to the blacklisting of Hollywood celebrities in the 1950s because of their supposed Communist sympathies. "As Scientologists, are we now a group that blacklists, that casts aside friendships and alliances on the basis of how fast someone is moving up the Bridge?" he wrote. "If we as a group are going to take on the billions of wogs out in the world, how can we disconnect from each other?" Elfman never responded.

After Cruise rallied the Scientology celebrities, a group of students demanded that Katselas make the Playhouse a "WISE" business. The acronym stands for World Institute of Scientology Enterprises. Katselas refused, even though he lost a hundred students in a mass Scientology walkout. Many of them went to another school, the Acting Center, which was founded in 2006, based in part on Scientology techniques. Katselas died of heart failure in 2008, and the Beverly Hills Playhouse is no longer connected with the church. The long line of protégés that Katselas left behind cemented the association between the church and the Hollywood acting community, but in the end he was ostracized by the very people whose careers he had nurtured.

Tom Cruise was now considered the unofficial Ethics Officer of Hollywood. He was the embodiment of Hubbard's vision of a church with temples dedicated to celebrity rather than God. Cruise's intensity and commitment, along with his spectacular ambition, matched Miscavige's own. It was as if Miscavige had rubbed a magic lantern and Cruise had appeared, a genie who could open any door. He was one of the few people that Miscavige saw as a peer. Miscavige even wondered if there was some way to appoint Cruise the church's Inspector General for Ethics—Rathbun's job. "He'd say that Tom Cruise was the only person in Scientology, other than himself, that he would trust to run the church," one former Sea Org member recalled. Rathbun observed: "Miscavige convinced Cruise that he and Tom were two of only a handful of truly 'big beings' on the planet. He instructed Cruise that LRH was relying upon them to unite with the few others of their ilk on earth to make it onto 'Target Two'—some unspecified galactic locale where they would meet up with Hubbard in the afterlife."

HAGGIS HAD ALSO BEEN folded into the celebrity recruitment apparatus. He had put his money and his reputation in the hands of the
church. He, too, was serving Scientology. But he rarely spoke about
his affiliation to his employees or associates. Even his close friends
were surprised to learn that he was in the church. "He didn't have
that sort of straight-on, unambiguous, unambivalent view that so
many Scientologists project into the world," Marshall Herskovitz
observed.

For years, Herskovitz and several of Haggis's closest non-
Scientology friends participated in an irregular Friday get-together
called Boys' Night. They met at an Italian restaurant on Montana Avenue in Santa Monica. The actor Josh Brolin usually attended, along
with director Oliver Stone, producer Stephen Nathan, and a peace
activist and former priest named Blase Bonpane, among others. One
night an attractive *New York Times* reporter came to write about the
event, and the men decided that she made them all a lot more appealing than they were on other occasions. After that, they voted to invite
one woman to join them whenever they met. Usually, it's a beautiful
actress. Julie Delpy and Charlize Theron have both been accorded this
honor. Madeleine Stowe recalled it as the funniest evening she had
ever had, although she had the sense to bring her husband along. She
remembered Haggis sitting back, wisecracking, smoking a cigarette,
watching it all happen.

Although Brolin, Nathan, and Stone are three of Haggis's closest
male friends, they never talked to him about Scientology. And yet each
of the three had an experience in the church, which the others weren't
aware of. Steve Nathan had been hooked up to an E-Meter in the late
1960s by some British Scientologists who were looking for recruits, but
he hadn't been impressed. Oliver Stone didn't even know Haggis was
in Scientology. But for that matter, few knew that Stone had also spent
a month in the church. He was a young man just back from Vietnam,
full of trouble and questions. He signed up at the church's New York
center in the old Hotel Martinique. "It was like going to college and
reading Dale Carnegie, something you do to find yourself." The difference was that in Scientology there were nice parties and beautiful
girls. Scientology didn't answer his questions; but on the other hand,
he noted, "I got laid."

Brolin had known Haggis for many years. They had worked
together in television, and Brolin had helped with Haggis's charities.

Brolin and his wife, actress Diane Lane, shared a house in Italy during the summers with Paul and Deborah. One evening, lubricated with grappa, Brolin began recounting a story of a friend who had "infiltrated" Scientology. He wondered why Paul and Deborah were listening stony-faced. When he finished the tale, Deborah finally said, "You know, we're Scientologists."

"What?" Brolin exclaimed. "When the fuck did that happen?"

"A long time ago," Deborah said.

"I am so sorry, I had no idea!" Brolin said.

After that, Brolin went with Deborah to a couple of gatherings to hear about Scientology's opposition to psychotropic drugs. Although Brolin had never talked about it, he had gone to the Celebrity Centre himself, "in a moment of real desperation," and received spiritual counseling. He quickly decided Scientology wasn't for him. But he still wondered what the religion did for celebrities like Tom Cruise and John Travolta: "Each has a good head on his shoulders, they make great business decisions, they seem to have wonderful families. Is that because they were helped by Scientology?"

Brolin once witnessed Travolta giving a Scientology assist at a dinner party in Los Angeles. Marlon Brando arrived with a cut on his leg. He had been injured while helping a stranded motorist on the Pacific Coast Highway pull his car out of a mudslide, and he was in pain. Travolta offered to help, saying that he had just reached a new level in Scientology, which gave him enhanced abilities. Brando said, "Well, John, if you have powers, then absolutely." Travolta touched Brando's leg and they each closed their eyes. Brolin watched, thinking it was bizarre and surprisingly physical. After ten minutes, Brando opened his eyes and said, "That really helped. I actually feel different!"

IN 2003, Cruise continued working with Rathbun on his upper levels. While he was at Gold Base, instead of staying in the cottage he had formerly shared with Nicole Kidman, Cruise moved into the guesthouse of L. Ron Hubbard's residence, Bonnie View. One Sunday night, following a late-night meal in Hubbard's baronial dining room, Cruise got food poisoning. The culprit was thought to be an appetizer of fried shrimp in an egg roll. The cook was summarily sent to Happy Valley.

Rathbun accompanied Cruise to Flag Base in Clearwater where he could perform the exercises required to attain OT VII. Because Miscavige depended on Rathbun to handle so many of the church's most sensitive problems, he had been lulled into feeling a kind of immunity from the leader's violent temper. In September, he returned to Gold Base and gave a report to Miscavige about Cruise's progress.

Miscavige asked where Cruise would be doing his semiannual checkups. "At Flag," Rathbun said. All OT VIIs do their checkups at Flag.

"Who's going to do it?"

Rathbun named an auditor in Clearwater that he thought highly of.

Miscavige turned to his wife and said, "Can you believe this SP?" He declared that unlike any other OT VII, Cruise would get his checkups at Gold Base.

When Cruise duly arrived at Gold for his semiannual check, he was preparing for his role as a contract killer in *Collateral*. Miscavige took him out to the gun range and showed him how to shoot a .45-caliber pistol. Meanwhile, Rathbun administered the star's six-month checkup.

Because of his insubordination, Rathbun had to go through a program of penitence. One of the steps was to write up a list of his offenses against the church, which Miscavige had sketched out for him. "I am writing this public announcement to inform executives and staff that I have come to my senses and I am no longer committing present time overts and have ceased all attacks and suppressions on Scientology," Rathbun admitted in September 2003, adopting the abject tone that characterizes many Scientology confessions. Speaking in full-blown Scientologese, he wrote, "The end result is unmocked org form, overworked and enturbulated executives and staff." This meant that he had not thought out his intentions clearly, causing the church and the people who worked for it to be in disarray. He had a particular apology to make to David Miscavige: "Each and every time on major situations, COB has had to intervene to clean up wars I had exacerbated. . . . The cumulative amount of COB's time I have cost in terms of dropping balls, creating situations internally and externally, is on the order of eight years."

Rathbun was shocked, not just by being declared an SP, but also by the changes at Gold Base in the year and a half he had been posted to Flag. All communications into and out of the base had been cut off. The leader had several of his top executives confined to the Watchdog Committee headquarters—a pair of double-wide trailers that had been married together. By the end of the year, the number who were living there under guard had grown to about forty or fifty people. It was now called the Hole. Except for one long conference table, there was no furniture—no chairs or beds, just an expanse of outdoor carpet—so the executives had to eat standing up and sleep on the floor, which was swarming with ants. In the morning, they were marched outside for group showers with a hose, then back to the Hole. Their meals were brought to them—a slop of reheated leftovers. When temperatures in the desert location mounted to more than a hundred degrees, Miscavige turned off the electricity, letting the executives roast inside the locked quarters.

The leader ordered them to stay until they finally had rearranged the "Org Board"—the church's organizational chart—to his satisfaction, which was never given. Photographs of Sea Org personnel were continually moved from one position to another on the chart, which meant that people were constantly being reassigned to different posts, whimsically, and no post was secure. About nine hundred positions needed to be filled at Int and Gold Bases, and the stack of personnel and ethics files was five feet high. This anarchic process had been going on more or less intensively for four years.

At odd, unpredictable hours, often in the middle of the night, Miscavige would show up in the Hole, accompanied by his wife, Shelly, and his Communicator, Laurisse Stuckenbrock, each of whom carried a tape recorder to take down whatever Miscavige had to say. The detainees could hear the drumbeat of the shoes as Miscavige's entourage marched toward the trailers. The leader demanded that the executives engage in what were termed "séances"—endless hours of confessions about their crimes and failures, in this and previous lives, as well as whatever dark thoughts—"counter-intentions"—they might be harboring against him. If someone was not forthcoming with such confessions, the group would harass that person until he produced a confession. Sometimes these were sexual fantasies. That would be written up in a report, which Miscavige would then read aloud to other church officials.

The entire base became paralyzed with anxiety about being thrown into the Hole. People were trying desperately to police their thoughts, but it was difficult to keep secrets when staff members were constantly being security-checked with E-Meters. Even confidences whispered to a spouse were regularly betrayed. After one of COB's lengthy rants, recordings of his statement would be sent to a steno pool, then transcripts were delivered to the executives in the Hole, who had to read them aloud to each other repeatedly.

Mike Rinder was in the Hole for two years, even though he continued to be the church's chief spokesperson. Bizarrely, he would sometimes be pulled out and ordered to conduct a press conference, or to put on a tuxedo and jet off to a Scientology gala; then he would be returned to confinement. He and other executives were made to race around the room on their hands and bare knees, day after day, tearing open scabs on their knees and leaving permanent scars. Miscavige once directed De Vocht to rough up Rinder, because "he's just an SP." De Vocht took Rinder outside and gave him a going-over. But De Vocht was also frightened of Miscavige. He took to sleeping with a broken broom handle. When another executive spoke up about the violence, he was beaten by two of Miscavige's assistants and made to mop the bathroom floor with his tongue.

The detainees developed a particular expression whenever Miscavige came in, which he took note of. He called them "Pie Faces." To illustrate what he meant, Miscavige drew a circle with two dots for eyes and a straight line for a mouth. He had T-shirts made up with the pie face on it. Rinder was "the Father of Pie Faces." People didn't know

Mike Rinder, former chief spokesperson for the church, in Florida, 2012

how to react. They didn't want to call attention to themselves, but they also didn't want to be a Pie Face.

In Scientology, there is a phrase that explains mob psychology: Contagion of Aberration, meaning that groups of people can stimulate each other to do things that are insane. According to former church executives, one day Miscavige arrived at the Hole and demanded that Marc Yager, the Commanding Officer of the Commodore's Messengers Org, and Guillaume Lesevre, the Executive Director of the Church of Scientology International, confess that they were homosexual lovers. He threatened that Tom Cruise would come to "punch you guys out" if the other Sea Org members in the Hole failed to get a confession from the two men. The captive executives took this threat seriously. When Miscavige left, a group of women executives who had been appointed as leaders of the detainees urged some of the bigger men in the Hole to "give some people some black eyes before Tom has to." Several men dutifully beat up Lesevre and Yager. Then one of the women reported to Miscavige that the men had confessed that they were gay lovers. When Debbie Cook, the former Captain of Flag Service Org and one of the most respected executives in the church, said that wasn't true, she was declared a traitor. She was made to stand in a garbage can for twelve hours, as the other detainees demanded that she confess her own "homosexual tendencies." The women in the room repeatedly slapped her and poured water over her head. A sign was hung around her neck, saying LESBO.

Rathbun was seen as being COB's chief enforcer. During meetings in the Hole or elsewhere on the base, he would stand to one side and glare at his colleagues while he says Miscavige berated and abused them. Although he was physically intimidating, Rathbun was suffering from a number of physical ailments, including a bad back, gallstones, calcium deposits in his neck, and painful varicose veins, which he believed came from having to stand at attention for hours on end. He, too, was prone to bursts of sudden violence. "Once on a phone call I saw him get so mad that he put his fist right through a computer screen," his former wife recalled. Miscavige would send him down to observe what was going on in the Hole and come back with reports. In January 2004, when Rinder was accused of withholding a confession from the group, Rathbun took him outside and beat him up. Rathbun says Miscavige wasn't satisfied. He called Rathbun into his massive office in the Religious Technology Center, a cold and imposing room with steel walls and eighteen-foot ceilings, and accused him of letting Rinder "get away with murder." Then, according to Rathbun, out of nowhere, Miscavige grabbed him by the throat and slammed his head against the steel wall.* Rathbun blacked out for a moment. He wasn't hurt, but the terms had changed.

A few days later, Rathbun found himself in the Hole, along with the entire International Management team and other executives. Miscavige said they were going to stay there until they got the Org Board done.

Scientologists are trained to believe that whatever happens to them is somehow their fault, so much of the discussion in the Hole centered on what they had done to deserve this fate. The possibility that the leader of the church might be irrational or even insane was so taboo that no one could even think it, much less voice it aloud. Most of the people in the Hole had a strong allegiance to the group—Scientology and the Sea Org—and they didn't want to let their comrades down. Many had been in the Sea Org their entire adult lives and portions of their childhood. Mike Rinder joined the Sea Org when he was eighteen. Amy Scobee was sixteen. Tom De Vocht was thirteen. They had already surrendered the possibility of ordinary family life. Sex outside of marriage was taboo, so many members married in their teens; but since 1986, children have been forbidden to Sea Org members. Former church executives say that abortions were common and forcefully encouraged. Claire Headley married Marc when she was seventeen; by the time she was twenty-one she had been pushed to have two abortions. She estimates that sixty to eighty percent of the women on Gold Base have had abortions. "It's a constant practice," she said.†

Worried about pillow talk, Miscavige instituted a policy of imposed divorces in 2004; people in the Religious Technology Center, the Commodore's Messenger Organization, and Golden Era Productions could not be married to members in other divisions. For many of those people in the Hole, everyone they knew or cared about was in the church. The cost of leaving—emotionally and spiritually, as well as financially—was forbidding. And they knew if they tried to run away, they'd likely be found and punished.

*As previously noted, the church denies all allegations of abuse by Miscavige.
†The church denies that anyone in the Sea Org has ever been pressured to have an abortion.

Those who attempted to leave the Sea Org through the formal process of "routing out" would be presented with a freeloader tab for all the coursework and counseling they had received over the years. Claire and Marc Headley, for instance, were billed more than $150,000 when they left and told they would have to pay if they ever wanted to see their family again. Those who accept this offer can spend years paying off their debt. Those who don't stand to lose any connection to their friends and family who remain in Scientology.

Many had long since turned their back on friends and family who were not in the church, and the prospect of facing them again brought up feelings of shame. The thought of leaving loved ones still in the church was even more fraught. All of these conflicting emotions were informed by the Scientology theory that life goes on and on, and that the mission of the church is to clear the planet, so in the scheme of things the misery one might be suffering now is temporary and negligible. There is a larger goal. One is always working for "the greatest good for the greatest number of dynamics," as Scientology ethics prescribed. And so the executives of the church who had given their lives to the Sea Org directed their confusion and their anger inward, or toward their helpless colleagues.

Rinder was an inevitable target. He was seen as being arrogant and above it all. Few people other than Rathbun really understood Rinder's job; unlike the others, the two men were often off the base, dealing with lawyers, the government, and the press. No doubt there was resentment at work as well. The next time the Sea Org executives turned on Rinder, Rathbun exploded. He caught his friend in a headlock and slammed him to the ground, then sat astride him, pounding his head into the floor and shouting at him, nose to nose. Rinder managed to whisper, "Marty, I don't want to play this game anymore."

Suddenly, Rathbun froze. Words had been spoken that broke the spell. But it was only a moment.

One evening about eight o'clock, Miscavige arrived, with his wife and his Communicator, Shelly and Laurisse, flanking him as usual with tape recorders in their hands. He ordered that the conference table be taken away and chairs be brought in for everyone in the Hole—about seventy people at the time, including many of the most senior people in the Sea Org. He asked if anyone knew what "musical chairs" meant. In Scientology, it refers to frequent changes of post. About five hundred people had been moved off their jobs in the last five years, creating anarchy in the management structure. But that wasn't the point he was trying to make. Finally, someone suggested that it was also a game. Miscavige had him explain the rules: Chairs are arranged in a circle and then, as the players march around them, one chair is removed. When the music stops, everybody grabs a seat. The one left standing is eliminated. Then the music starts again. Miscavige explained that in this game the last person to grab a chair would be the only one allowed to stay on the base; everyone else was to be "offloaded"—kicked out of the Sea Org—or sent away to the least desirable Scientology bases around the world. Those whose spouses were not in the Hole would be forced to divorce.

While *Queen's Greatest Hits* played on a boom box, the church executives marched around and around, then fought for a seat when the music stopped. As the number of chairs diminished, the game got more physical. The executives shoved and punched each other; clothes were torn; a chair was ripped apart. All this time, the biting lyrics of "Bohemian Rhapsody" floated over the saccharine melody:

Is this the real life?
Is this just a fantasy?
Caught in a landslide
No escape from reality.

Rathbun, with his bad back, was eliminated fairly quickly. Rinder, De Vocht, Marc Headley—one by one, they found themselves standing alone, behind low cubicle walls, watching the surviving contestants desperately fighting to remain in the Hole rather than be sent off to God knows where. There was a clock over the door marking the hours that passed as the music played on and on then suddenly stopped and the riot began again. As people fell out of the game, COB had airline tickets for distant locations printed up for them at the base's travel office. There were U-Haul trucks waiting outside to haul away their belongings. "Is it real to you now?" Miscavige teased. They were told that buses would be ready to leave at six in the morning. Many were in tears. "I don't see anybody weeping for me," Miscavige said. The utter powerlessness of everyone else in the room was made nakedly clear to them. The game continued until 4 a.m., when a woman named Lisa Schroer grabbed the final chair.

The next morning the whole event was forgotten. No one went anywhere.

In several legal declarations he has made over the years, Miscavige has protested, "I am the ecclesiastical leader of the *religion*, not the Church." The distinction is important when the church is dragged into lawsuits or threatened with criminal liability; Miscavige can point to a chart that assigns organizational responsibility to other departments, whereas the sole responsibility of the Religious Technology Center, which he heads, is to protect Scientology doctrine and literature. And yet, Miscavige freely consigned those other department heads to the Hole or sent them to RPF. During the period that the organizational chart was being constantly rearranged, the only reliable posting on the base was his, that of COB RTC; everyone else was constantly being uprooted and repotted in other temporary assignments. There is really only one person in charge of the Church of Scientology.

A few days after the musical chairs episode, Miscavige ordered everyone in the Hole to report to Golden Era Productions to stuff CDs into cases. At one point, he began sharply interrogating De Vocht, who was shaken and stuttered in response. According to De Vocht, Miscavige punched him in the face. He felt his head vibrate. He tried to turn away from the next blow, but Miscavige grabbed his neck and shoved him into the floor, pummeling and kicking him.* De Vocht had served Miscavige for years, and had even considered him a friend. He had dedicated his life to Scientology and had been in the Sea Org for nearly thirty years. He recalls thinking, "Now here I am, being beat up by the top dog in front of my peers."

After the attack, Miscavige continued his speech. De Vocht was so humiliated that he couldn't bring himself to look at his companions. Finally, he managed a glance at them. Pie faces.

Rathbun was there, and at that moment he made a decision. As the other executives were being led back to the Hole, he slipped away and got his motorcycle and hid in the bushes. When a car finally approached, he raced through the open gate into the outside world.

---

*The church denies that Miscavige has ever abused members of the church.

9

TC and COB

Great fame also imposes a kind of cloister on those who join its ranks. Tom Cruise had been a movie star since he was twenty-one, with two popular movies in the same year, *The Outsiders* and *Risky Business*. By age twenty-five, he was the biggest star in Hollywood, on his way to becoming one of the most famous movie legends in history. At the same age, Miscavige had become the de facto leader of Scientology. Each of these men assumed extraordinary responsibilities when their peers were barely beginning their careers. Their youth and position set them apart. So it was natural that two such powerful, isolated men would see themselves mirrored in each other.

A number of Sea Org members who observed Cruise when he came to Gold Base remarked that he seemed liberated to be in an environment where no one hassled him, or took his photograph, or asked for autographs. There are cottages built for the use of other well-known Scientologists, such as John Travolta, Kirstie Alley, Edgar Winter, and Priscilla Presley, so the base can sometimes feel like a secret celebrity spa. Once, Miscavige had the entire Gold Base crew line up at the gate and salute Cruise when he arrived. Cruise must have felt self-conscious about this display, because it happened only once. People on the base have been directed not to speak to Cruise at all, unless spoken to. In this way, Cruise tastes the life that Miscavige has lived for decades, one of seclusion and deference, concentrated on spiritual advancement.*

Similarly, after becoming associated with Cruise, the style of Miscavige's life began to reflect that of a fantastically wealthy and leisured movie star. He normally awakens at noon, with a cup of coffee and a Camel cigarette. The coffee is fresh-ground Starbucks, preferably a Guatemala or Arabian Mocha Java, made with distilled water, to which he adds raw sugar and half-and-half. Then he takes breakfast, the first of his five meals.

According to Miscavige's former chef, Sinar Parman, the church leader was eating "three squares and a snack at night," until the late nineties. One day, while on a Delta flight from LA to Clearwater, Miscavige walked to the cabin from his seat in first class and showed some photos from a muscle magazine to Parman and his steward, who traveled with him. He told them he wanted to "get ripped and have six-pack abs." After the flight, Miscavige changed physical trainers and began taking bodybuilding supplements. He also adopted a strict diet that requires each meal to be at least forty percent protein and to contain no more than four hundred calories. Soon, he was looking like the men in the muscle magazines.

To maintain his physique, Miscavige's chefs have to enter each portion size into a computer, including the cream in his morning coffee. Miscavige often starts with an omelet of one whole egg and five egg whites. Two and a half hours later, lunch is provided. Two choices would be prepared daily, for both him and his wife—four meals altogether. Miscavige prefers pizza, soup, and submarine sandwiches. Throughout the day cigarettes, bottled water, and protein bars are stationed wherever he might be working. Dinner is a five-course meal, and once again, dual entrées are prepared for him to choose from. Miscavige's favorite foods include wild mushroom risotto, linguine in white clam sauce, and pâté de foie gras. Fresh fruit and vegetables are purchased from local markets or shipped in from overseas. Several times a week, a truck from Santa Monica Seafood brings Atlantic salmon, or live lobster, flown in fresh from the East Coast or Canada. Corn-fed lamb arrives from New Zealand. When guests such as Tom Cruise come

*Cruise's attorney says that Sea Org members were not directed to salute him and that he has had many cordial exchanges with them.

to dinner, the kitchen goes into extravagant bursts of invention, with ingredients sometimes flown in from different continents. Two hours after dinner, the first evening snack arrives, with lighter offerings, such as Italian white bean soup or clam chowder. After midnight, there is a final late-night snack—a selection of nonfat cheeses, an apple crisp, or blueberry crepes, often garnished with edible flowers. Shelly usually preferred a fruit platter. She would drink only almond milk, which was made on-site from organic almonds. She insisted that all the food be consistent with the diet recommended for their blood type (both Shelly and David are type O). Two full-time chefs work all day preparing these meals, with several full-time stewards to serve them.

According to Claire Headley, who oversaw the finances for the Religious Technology Center between 2000 and 2004, the food costs for David and Shelly and their guests would range between $3,000 to as much as $20,000 per week. At the end of the evening, Miscavige retires to his den and drinks Macallan Scotch and plays backgammon with members of his entourage, or listens to music on his $150,000 stereo system (he loves Michael Jackson), or watches movies in his private screening room (his favorite films are *Scarface* and the *Godfather* trilogy). He usually turns in around three or four in the morning.

Miscavige enjoys shooting pool or playing video games in his lounge. He has a tanning bed, and a high-end gym that few people other than Cruise are permitted to use. Although he is short in stature, Miscavige exudes physical power. He favors tight-fitting T-shirts that show off his chiseled biceps. He collects guns, maintains at least six motorcycles, and has a number of automobiles, including an armor-plated GMC Safari van with bulletproof windows and satellite television, and a souped-up Saleen Mustang that Cruise gave him to match his own. His uniforms and business suits are fashioned by Richard Lim, a Los Angeles tailor whose clients include Cruise, Will Smith, and Martin Sheen. Miscavige's shoes are custom-made in London by John Lobb, bootmaker to the royal family. His wardrobe fills an entire room. Two full-time stewards are responsible for his cleaning and laundry. Cruise admired the housecleaning so much—even Miscavige's lightbulbs are polished once a month—that the church leader sent a Sea Org team to Cruise's Telluride retreat to train the star's staff.

Until 2007, when he traveled, Miscavige would often rent Cruise's Gulfstream jet, but he has since upgraded to a roomier Boeing business jet, at a cost of thirty to fifty thousand dollars per trip. He brings along his personal hairdresser and chiropractor. He loves underwater photography, and when he returns from his annual trip on the *Freewinds*, he has the photography staff put the photos into slides so they can be appreciated by the entire Gold Base staff.

The contrast with the other Sea Org members is stark. They eat in a mess hall, which features a meat-and-potatoes diet and a salad bar, except for occasional extended periods of rice and beans for those who are being punished. The average cost per meal as of 2005 (according to Marc Headley, who participated in the financial planning each week) was about seventy-five cents a head—significantly less than what is spent per inmate in the California prison system. When members join the Sea Org, they are issued two sets of pants, two shirts, and a pair of shoes, which is their lifetime clothing allotment; anything else, they purchase themselves. Although the nominal pay for Sea Org members is fifty dollars a week, many are fined for various infractions, so it's not unusual to be paid as little as thirteen or fourteen dollars. Married couples at Gold Base share a two-bedroom apartment with two other couples, meaning that one pair sleeps on the couch. In any case, few get more than five or six hours of sleep a night. There are lavish exercise facilities at the base—an Olympic pool, a golf course, basketball courts—but they are rarely used. Few are permitted to have access to computers. Every personal phone call is listened to; every letter is inspected. Bank records are opened and records kept of how much money people have. Cultural touchstones common to most Americans are often lost on Sea Org members at Gold Base. They may not know the name of the president of the United States or be able to tell the difference between the Republican and Democratic parties. It's not as if there is no access to outside information; there is a big-screen television in the dining hall, and people can listen to the radio or subscribe to newspapers and magazines; however, news from the outside world begins to lose its relevance when people are outside of the wider society for extended periods of time. Many Sea Org members have not left the base for a decade.

On April 30 of each year, Scientology staff from around the world are pressed to contribute to Miscavige's birthday present. One year, as birthday assessments were being passed around, few could contribute because they hadn't been paid for months. Finally, staffers got their back pay so that they could make their donations. Janela Webster, who worked directly under Miscavige for fifteen years, received $325, out of which she paid $150 for Miscavige's gift. Such presents include tailored suits and leather jackets, high-end cameras, diving equipment, Italian shoes, and a handmade titanium bicycle. One year Flag Service Org in Clearwater gave him a Vyrus 985 C3 4V, a motorcycle with a retail price of $70,000.* Another division presented him with a BMW.

Miscavige keeps a number of dogs, including five beagles. He had blue vests made up for each of them, with four stripes on the shoulder epaulets, indicating the rank of Sea Org Captain. He insists that people salute the dogs as they parade by. The dogs have a mini-treadmill where they work out. A full-time staff member feeds, walks, and trains the dogs, takes them to the veterinarian, and enters one of them, Jelly, into contests, where he has attained championship status. Another of Miscavige's favorites, a Dalmatian–pit bull mix named Buster, went on a rampage one day and killed ten peacocks on the property, then proudly laid them out for all to see. Buster has also attacked various members of the staff, sending one elderly woman to the emergency room and earning Buster his own Ethics folder. Miscavige eventually had the dog taken away to another Sea Org base, even though he believed that Buster had a nose for "out ethics" behavior. The relieved staff members joked that Buster had been sent to Dog RPF.

From an early age, Miscavige had taken control of his family. His father, Ron Senior, joined the Sea Org following a charge of attempted rape lodged against him in 1985. Former church members say that significant church resources were used to contain the scandal, and that David forced his father to join the Sea Org. Because David's mother, Loretta, refused to sign up for that, she and Ron agreed to divorce. She continued in Scientology, rising to the summit as an OT VIII. She worked as an accountant for the law firm of Greta Van Susteren, the television commentator, and her husband, John Coale, both Scientologists, who maintain a mansion on Clearwater Beach. Loretta was a heavy smoker who suffered from emphysema and obesity—scarcely the image of an Operating Thetan—but her self-deprecating, sometimes goofy sense of humor made her popular among the staff and upper-level Scientologists—"the court jester of the Scientology country club," as Rathbun called her. Loretta's regal position as the leader's

---

*According to Tommy Davis, "From their perspective, it was the least they could do to express their affection."

mother allowed her to give rein to gossipy stories about Dave's child-hood, which she told in a thick Philly accent. Miscavige complained that his mother was trying to destroy him. He ordered Rathbun to run a security check on her, using the E-Meter. When Loretta realized what he was up to, she burst out laughing.

Miscavige sent his personal trainer to help his mother get in shape, and he had church members monitoring her diet, but her chronic health problems overtook her. "She was sick for a long time," her granddaugh-ter, Jenna Miscavige Hill, recalled. "She was not happy with the turn the church took." Sometimes Loretta would burst into tears. "I would try to help her the only way I knew how," Hill said. "She was an amaz-ing grandma." (Loretta Miscavige died in 2005.)

THE LEVEL OF ABUSE at the Gold Base was increasing year by year as—unpoliced by outside forces—other senior executives began emu-lating their leader. Rinder, De Vocht, and Rathbun all admit to strik-ing other staff members. Even some of the women became physically aggressive, slapping underlings when they didn't perform up to stan-dard. Debbie Cook, the former leader of Flag Base, says that although Miscavige never struck her, he ordered his Communicator to do so. Another time, she said, he told his Communicator to break Cook's finger. She bent Cook's finger but failed to actually break it.

Miscavige can be charming and kind, especially to Sea Org mem-bers who need emotional or medical assistance. He has a glittering smile and a commanding voice. And yet former Scientologists who were close to him recall that his constant profanity and bursts of unpro-voked violence kept everyone off balance. Jefferson Hawkins, a former Sea Org executive who had worked with Paul Haggis on the rejected Dianetics campaign, says he was beaten by Miscavige on five occasions, the first time in 2002. He had just written an infomercial for the church. Miscavige summoned him to a meeting, where about forty members were seated on one side of a long conference table; Miscavige routinely sits by himself on the other side. He began a tirade about the shortcom-ings of the infomercial. When Hawkins started to respond, Miscavige cut him short. "The only thing I want to hear from you is your crimes," Miscavige said, meaning that Hawkins was to confess his subversive intentions. Then, without warning, Miscavige jumped on the table and launched himself at Hawkins, knocking him against a cubicle wall and battering him in the face. The two men fell to the floor, and their legs became entangled. "Let go of my legs!" Miscavige shouted.

Miscavige extricated himself and left the room, leaving Hawkins on the floor, shocked, bruised, disheveled, humiliated, and staring at the forty people who did nothing to support him. "Get up! Get up!" they told him. "Don't make him wrong."

Even if he had had access to a phone, Hawkins wouldn't have called the police. If a Sea Org member were to seek outside help, he would be punished, either by being declared a Suppressive Person or by being sent off to do manual labor for months or years. Far more important, Hawkins believed, was the fact that his spiritual immortality was on the line. Scientology had made him aware of his eternal nature as he moved from life to life, erasing his fear of mortality. Without that, he would be doomed to dying over and over again, "in ignorance and darkness," he said, "never knowing my true nature as a spirit." Miscavige, he concluded, "holds the power of eternal life and death over you."

The church provided an affidavit of a former Sea Org member, Yael Lustgarten, who stated that she was present at the meeting and that the attack by Miscavige never happened. She claims that Hawkins made a mess of his presentation—"He smelled of body odor, he was unshaven, his voice tone was very low and he could hardly be heard"—and he was merely instructed to shape up. On the other hand, Amy Scobee said she witnessed the attack—it was her cubicle the two men fell into—and after the altercation, she recalled, "I gathered all the buttons from Jeff's shirt and the change from his pockets and gave them back to him."

Tommy Davis later testified that he had conducted an investigation of the charges of abuse at the base. He said that all of the abuse had been committed by Rinder, Rathbun, and De Vocht—none by Miscavige.

TOM DE VOCHT GREW UP in a little central Florida town called Fort Meade. When he was ten years old, in 1974, his cousin, Dicky Thompson, a keyboardist in the Steve Miller Band, came to visit, riding a Harley-Davidson motorcycle. That year the band had a number one song, "The Joker," and Thompson rode into town with a glow of fame around him. "He had a weird stare," De Vocht remembered. "He invited my sister to meet Steve Miller and John Travolta." Within a year, most of De Vocht's family had joined the Church of Scientology. In July 1977, thirteen-year-old Tom De Vocht signed the billion-year contract for the Sea Org.

De Vocht became one of Miscavige's allies and moved up the bureaucratic ladder quickly. In 1986, he was appointed the Commanding Officer of the Commodore's Messengers Org at Flag. In 2001, Miscavige called him, complaining, "Tom, I can't get my building done." The new headquarters for the Religious Technology Center at Gold Base, Building 50, was years behind schedule and well over budget. Miscavige directed De Vocht to come to Gold Base and oversee the construction. The first day he got there, De Vocht realized that "this building is going to be the end of me."

Forty-seven million dollars—more than a thousand dollars per square foot—had previously been spent on the new center. The building had already been completed a couple of times, using the highest-grade materials—cold rolled steel, and anigre, a beautiful but extremely hard, pinkish African wood—only to have components ripped out because they didn't meet Miscavige's standards. Miscavige's desk, also made of steel, was so heavy that De Vocht worried whether the structure would support it. He discovered that there were no actual architectural drawings for the building; there were only renderings of what it should look like. The stucco exterior walls were already cracked because the whole edifice was at a 1.25-inch tilt. The walls weren't actually connected to the floors. Even a minor earthquake (Gold Base was just west of the San Andreas Fault) might cause the whole building to collapse. De Vocht recommended that the building be torn down and rebuilt from scratch, but Miscavige rejected that idea.

The expense of essentially rebuilding a poorly constructed building from the inside was immense. When De Vocht had almost finished construction, having spent an additional $60 million, Miscavige still had a list of complaints. He was also critical of the landscaping. Gold Base is in a desert, but Miscavige demanded that the building appear to be set in a forest.

One morning, De Vocht says, Miscavige and his wife were inspecting the large vault in the legal department of Building 50, when the leader stopped in his tracks and began rubbing his head. He turned pale. "Where did we put the gold bullion?" he asked his wife. For a full minute, Miscavige kept rubbing his head and asking about the gold, but then he snapped out of it and went on as if nothing had happened.

De Vocht recalls that forty-five minutes later, Shelly Miscavige called him and asked him, "What are we going to do? He's losing it." She told him that Dave had gone "Type 3"—psychotic—because of all the Suppressive Persons at the base.*

While De Vocht was working on Building 50, he was forced to attend a séance with five hundred other Sea Org members on Gold Base. People were called out by name and asked, "What crimes have you committed against David Miscavige?" One after another, people approached the microphone and confessed to ways in which they were suppressing the dissemination of Scientology or thinking taboo thoughts. De Vocht was disgusted by the orgy of self-abasement. One night, he simply took over the meeting and brought some semblance of order to it. That night, Shelly Miscavige asked him to be the Commanding Officer of the Commodore's Messengers Org, which essentially put him in charge of the entire base. "It's out of control," she pleaded, saying that her husband counted on him and had no one else to turn to.

In 2004, De Vocht finished reconstructing the 45,000-square-foot Building 50, which wound up costing $70 million. "You're the biggest spender in the history of Scientology," Miscavige told him. "You should be shot."

EVEN THOUGH MEMBERSHIP in the church has been declining for years, according to polls and census figures, money continues to pour into Scientology coffers in fantastic sums. Donors are accorded higher status depending on the size of their gifts to the International Association of Scientologists—Patron Maximus for a $25 million pledge, for instance. Nancy Cartwright, the voice of Bart Simpson, became a Patron Laureate for her $10 million gift to the association in 2007. The IAS now holds more than $1 billion, mostly in offshore accounts, according to former executives of the church. Scientology coursework alone can be very pricey—as much as $400,000 to reach the level of OT VIII. That doesn't count the books and materials or the latest-model E-Meter, which is priced at $4,650. Then there is the auditing, which ranges in price from $5,000 to $8,000 for a twelve-hour "intensive,"

*According to Tommy Davis, "These incidents are pure fantasy by Tom De Vocht."

depending on the location and the level of the auditor. Services sold in Clearwater alone amount to $100 million a year.

Despite the frequent cost overruns on construction, Scientology undertook a worldwide building campaign, kicked off by Miscavige's decision to use the occasion of 9/11 to issue a call for a massive expansion of the church. "Bluntly, we are the only people of Earth who can reverse the decline," he announced. "The way to do better is to get big."

In some cases, the building projects have become significant moneymakers for the church. Across the street from Scientology's Fort Harrison Hotel in Clearwater is the Super Power Building, intended to be a training facility to enhance the perceptions of upper-level thetans. The fund-raising kicked off with a $1 million gift from the Feshbach brothers. Despite years-long construction delays and fines imposed by the City of Clearwater, the 380,000-square-foot Super Power Building has proven to be a bonanza for the church, which has taken in at least $145 million in donations to complete the project—$120 million more than it was projected to cost when first proposed, in 1993. The church explains that the plan has been enlarged from its original goals, which has created delays and additional expenses. Tom De Vocht, who worked on the construction for years, said that the building remained unfinished for so long because no one knew what super power was.

Under Miscavige's leadership, the church has aggressively launched a program called Ideal Orgs, which aim to replicate the grandeur of Hubbard's Saint Hill Manor. A number of the Ideal Orgs have been shuttered—including Boston and New Haven—because the local Scientology communities were unable to support them. Other notable churches and missions are now boarded up or unloaded—including one in Santa Monica that Paul and Deborah Haggis raised money to establish.

THE INTENSITY OF the pressure on Sea Org members to raise money for the church—while working for next to nothing—can be understood in part through the account of Daniel Montalvo. His parents joined the Sea Org when he was five, and the very next year he signed his own billion-year contract. He says that he began working full-time in the organization when he was eleven and recalls that, along with other Sea Org members, including children, his days stretched from eight in the morning until eleven thirty at night. Part of his work was shoveling up asbestos that had been removed during the renovation of the Fort Harrison Hotel. He says no protective gear was provided, not even a mask. He rarely saw his parents. While he was at Flag Base in 2005, when he was fourteen, he guarded the door while Tom Cruise was in session. The sight of children working at a Sea Org facility would not have been unusual. They were separated from their parents and out of school. According to Florida child labor laws, minors who are fourteen and fifteen years old are prohibited from working during school hours, and may work only up to fifteen hours a week. Daniel said that he was allowed schooling only one day a week, on Saturday.

When Daniel was fifteen, he was assigned to work on the renovation of Scientology's publications building in Los Angeles, operating scissors lifts and other heavy equipment. According to California child labor laws, fifteen-year-old children are allowed to work only three hours per day outside of school, except on weekends—no more than eighteen hours per week total. Sixteen is the minimum age for children to work in any manufacturing establishment using power-driven hoisting apparatus, such as the scissors lift. Daniel graduated to work at the church's auditing complex nearby, called the American Saint Hill Organization; then from six in the evening until three in the morning he volunteered at Bridge Publications. He was paid thirty-six dollars a week.

Daniel's work at Bridge Publications was sufficiently impressive that he was posted full-time in the manufacturing division there the following year. The church had issued a new edition of Hubbard's books and lectures called *The Basics*, which was being aggressively marketed to Scientologists. One of Daniel's jobs was to cut the "thumb notches" that mark the glossary and the appendix in these handsomely made books, like the notches one would find in an unabridged dictionary. A machine with a guillotine steel blade slices through the pages to produce the half-moon indentation. California law specifically forbids the operation of the machine by anyone under the age of eighteen. Daniel noted about twenty other minors working at the plant, all of them sleep deprived and working around heavy equipment. One night Daniel chopped off his right index finger on the notching machine. A security officer picked up his finger and put it in a plastic bag with ice, then took Daniel to the children's hospital in Hollywood. He was instructed to tell the admitting nurse that he had injured himself in a skateboarding accident. The doctors were unable to reattach his finger.

After that, Daniel was sent to the sales division of Bridge Publications. Sales had been declining since *The Basics* had first been published in 2007. *The Basics* included eighteen books and a number of Hubbard lectures on CD; the complete package cost $6,500. Sea Orgs all over the world had call centers set up to sell them. In Los Angeles, there were hourly quotas to be met, and those who failed suffered various punishments, such as having water dumped on their head or being made to do push-ups or run up and down the stairs. There were security guards on every floor. A salesperson had to get a slip verifying that he had made his quota before he was permitted to go to bed.

Often it was simply impossible to make the quota legitimately, so people ran unauthorized credit cards. Members of the Sea Org sales force would break into the church's financial records and pull up the credit card information of public members. Members who had money on account at the church for future courses would see it drained to pay for books they didn't order. Parishioners who balked at making contributions or buying unwanted materials were told they were in violation of church ethics, and their progress in Scientology was blocked or threatened.

Members who pledge more than they can afford can find themselves in a compromised situation. One Scientologist who was a bank teller says he was told to comply with a robbery in order to pay off his debt to the church; the robbers took four thousand dollars. In 2009, Nancy Cartwright's fiancé, Stephen E. Brackett, a contractor, had taken a substantial construction advance to renovate a restaurant. The company that insured the project later sued Cartwright, claiming that she and Brackett had diverted the money to the Church of Scientology. Brackett, an OT V, had been featured in a church ad for the Super Power Building, identified as a "key contributor." "Mankind needs your help," Brackett was quoted as saying in the ad. He later took his life by jumping off a bridge on Pacific Coast Highway near Big Sur.*

The biggest financial scandal involving church members was a Ponzi scheme operated by Reed Slatkin; he was one of the co-founders, with Paul Haggis's friend Sky Dayton, of EarthLink. Slatkin's massive

---

*The case against Cartwright was settled out of court.

fraud involved more than half a billion dollars in investments; much of the initial "profit" was returned to Scientology investors, such as Daniel and Myrna Jacobs, who earned nearly $3 million on a $760,500 "investment." According to Marty Rathbun, Slatkin's Scientology investors included Anne Archer and Fox News commentator Greta Van Susteren. Later investors were not so lucky. Slatkin was convicted of defrauding $240 million; it is still not known how much of that money went directly to the church, although the court found that about $50 million was funneled to the church indirectly by investors with massive gains. In 2006, groups affiliated with the Church of Scientology, including the Celebrity Centre, agreed to pay back $3.5 million.

IN JULY 2004 Miscavige hosted Tom Cruise's forty-second birthday party aboard the Scientology cruise ship *Freewinds*. The Golden Era Musicians, including Miscavige's father on trumpet, played songs from Cruise's movies as film clips flickered on the giant overhead screens installed especially for the occasion. Cruise himself danced and sang "Old Time Rock and Roll," reprising a famous scene in *Risky Business*, the movie that firmly established him as a star.

Occasionally, the *Freewinds* is used to confine those Sea Org members that the church considers most at risk for flight. Among the crew on the ship during Cruise's birthday party was Valeska Paris, a twenty-six-year-old Swiss woman. Paris had grown up in Scientology and joined the Sea Org when she was fourteen. Three years later, her stepfather, a self-made millionaire, committed suicide, leaving a diary in which he blamed the church for fleecing his fortune. When Valeska's mother denounced the church on French television, Valeska was isolated at the Clearwater base in order to keep her away from her mother. The next year, at the age of eighteen, she was sent to the *Freewinds*. She was told she would be on the ship for two weeks. She was held there against her will for twelve years. Shortly before Cruise arrived, Paris developed a cold sore, which caused Miscavige to consign her to a condition of Treason, so she wasn't allowed to go to the birthday party, but she later did wind up serving Cruise and his girlfriend at the time, the Spanish actress Penélope Cruz.

In October, Miscavige acknowledged Cruise's place in Scientology by awarding him the Freedom Medal of Valor. Miscavige called Cruise "the most dedicated Scientologist I know" before an audience of Sea Org members who had spent much of their lives working for the church for a little more than seven dollars a day. Then he hung the diamond-encrusted platinum medallion around the star's neck.

"I think you know that I am there for you," Cruise said to the thrilled audience. "And I do care, so very, very, very much." He turned to an imposing portrait of Hubbard, standing beside a globe. "To LRH!" he said, with a crisp salute.

Lana Mitchell, the cook who had been accused of feeding Cruise the poisoned shrimp a few months before, had gotten out of Happy Valley, but she watched the ceremony while in RPF, along with some two hundred of her detained colleagues. About fifty of them were Sea Org executives who had been purged by Miscavige. They were being held in the Los Angeles complex on L. Ron Hubbard Way, in the massive blue former hospital where Spanky Taylor and so many others had been confined. Some had been in the organization for more than twenty years and had worked directly for Hubbard. They were completely cut off from the outside world—no television, radio, or even any music. As many as forty people were crammed into each of the former hospital rooms, with only one bathroom to share. Often there was not enough food to go around. Some of those confined had severe medical conditions, including Uwe Stuckenbrock, the former international security chief, who suffered from multiple sclerosis and had deteriorated to the point of being unable to speak. One of the jobs Mitchell was assigned on RPF was welding, but she had never done it before, and she burned her eyes because she wasn't wearing the protective glasses correctly. She got no medical attention at all.

Every effort was made to keep RPF'ers out of view. Windows were curtained so no one could see in or out. They traveled through tunnels and over rooftops when they needed to move about within the complex. There were no days off, although they were allowed to call their families on Christmas. Their sole diversion was watching the big Scientology galas on television. After all, the elaborate sets for these events were constructed by the RPF'ers in Los Angeles or at Flag Base in Clearwater. To view the big Cruise event, they were all taken to the mess hall.

One of the penitents was Mark McKinstry, who had been National Sales Manager at Bridge Publications when the movie version of *Battlefield Earth*, starring John Travolta, came out in 2000. Hubbard's tale is about an alien race of "Psychlos," who have turned people into slaves—until a hero arises to liberate humanity. Travolta had worked for years to get the movie made, and wound up paying a significant portion out of his own pocket. It was at the peak of his career. "I told my manager, 'If we can't do the things now that we want to do, what good is the power?' " he remarked at the time. Miscavige had been deeply involved in the filming from the beginning. He would watch dailies of the film in Clearwater while he was overseeing the handling of the Lisa McPherson case. His critiques would then be typed up and sent to the Scientology representative who was always at Travolta's side. When the movie was completed, Miscavige called Travolta to congratulate him, saying that LRH would be proud. He predicted it was going to be a blockbuster.

McKinstry had been working for a year promoting the movie edition of the book. He traveled across the country with Travolta to push the book in bookstores, malls, and Walmarts. About 750,000 copies were sold. Like many others who have spent time with Travolta, McKinstry came to like him immensely. The actor was devoting a substantial amount of his own time and energy to making the book a success. But when the movie came out, it was a critical and box-office catastrophe. Even at the premiere, Sea Org members had to be bused in to Mann's Chinese Theatre on Hollywood Boulevard to fill the empty seats for as many as three shows a day. For some of them, it was the first movie they had seen in years. " 'Battlefield Earth' may well turn out to be the worst movie of this century," the *New York Times* critic observed, in what proved to be a typical review. There were false accusations that the film contained subliminal messages promoting Scientology. Travolta's career went into a lengthy dark period. Cruise later complained to Miscavige, saying that the movie was terrible for the church's public image.* Miscavige responded that it would never have been made if he'd had anything to do with it.

McKinstry was dismayed when he went to a screening of the movie and watched people walking out or booing. His wife could see that he was upset and asked what was wrong. "Why didn't anyone watch this movie before it was released?" he said. She reported to the church what he had said, and he was ordered to RPF.

---

*Cruise's attorney notes, "Mr. Cruise has never expressed anything but support and respect for the work on *Battlefield Earth*."

SHORTLY BEFORE HE RECEIVED Scientology's top award, Cruise ended his three-year relationship with Penélope Cruz. Shelly Miscavige had been supervising her auditing and helping her through the Purification Rundown. But, like Nicole, Penélope was suspect in the eyes of the church's leader. She was an independent-minded person and continued to meditate and identify herself as a Buddhist.

Cruise traveled with a Scientology delegation to open a magnificent new church in Madrid, where he read his speech to the crowd in halting Spanish. Before the opening, however, he was sitting with his sister Lee Anne, who had become his publicist. Mike Rinder, who was in the room, remembers that Cruise heatedly complained to his sister that no one had been able to find him a new girlfriend. Miscavige walked in, Rinder says, and Cruise made the same complaint to him.*

Miscavige took the hint. "I want you to look for the prettiest women in the church," Tom De Vocht remembers Miscavige saying. "Get their names and phone numbers." Miscavige then assigned Greg Wilhere and Tommy Davis to audition all the young actresses who were in Scientology—about a hundred, according to Marc Headley, who observed some of the videos. Shelly Miscavige, the leader's wife, oversaw the project personally. Wilhere and Davis immediately went to work. The women weren't told why they were being interviewed, but they were asked about their opinions of Cruise and where they were on the Bridge. Wilhere, who was actually in the Hole at the time, was taken out of confinement, given a BlackBerry and five thousand dollars to buy civilian clothes at a Saks Fifth Avenue outlet, then sent to New York and Los Angeles to videotape the interviews. Rinder noticed that when Cruise arrived at the Freedom Medal of Valor ceremony a month later, he was accompanied by a raven-haired young actress and model, Yolanda Pecoraro. She was born into Scientology and had completed a number of courses at the Celebrity Centre and on the *Freewinds*, but she was only nineteen years old. Cruise was forty-two at the time.

The Scientology search team came up with another aspiring actress, Nazanin Boniadi, twenty-five years old, who had been born in Iran

---

*Cruise's attorney says Cruise did not complain about not having a girlfriend at the opening of the church in Madrid.

and raised in London. Naz was well educated and beautiful in the way that Cruise was inclined to respond to—dark and slender, with large eyes and a flashing smile. She had studied pre-med at the University of California at Irvine before deciding to try her luck as an actress. More important for the purposes of the match, however, was the fact that Boniadi was an OT V. Her mother was also a Scientologist.

In early November 2004, Naz was informed that she had been selected for a special program that was critical to the future of the church, but it was so secret she wouldn't be allowed to tell anyone, even her mother. Naz was moved immediately into the Celebrity Centre, where she spent a month going through security checks and special auditing programs. She hoped the project had something to do with human rights, which was her special interest, but all she was told was that her participation would end bigotry against Scientology.

At one point during the intensive auditing and security checks, Wilhere informed her that she would have to break up with her longtime boyfriend in order for the project to proceed. She refused. She couldn't understand why her boyfriend posed any kind of problem; indeed, she had personally introduced him to Scientology. Wilhere persisted, asking what it would take for her to break off the romance. Flustered, she responded that she would break up if she knew he had been cheating on her. According to Naz's friends, the very next day, Wilhere brought in her boyfriend's confidential auditing files and showed her several instances of his infidelities, which had been circled in red. Naz felt betrayed, but also guilty, because Wilhere blamed her for failing to know and report her boyfriend's ethical lapses herself; after all, she had audited him on several occasions. Obviously, she had missed his "withhold." She confronted her boyfriend and he confessed. That was the end of their relationship.*

Another time, Naz was asked what her "ideal scene for 2-D"—in other words, her dream date—would be. It was eating sushi and going ice-skating. But she wondered why that was important.

One of her assignments was to study a bulletin of Hubbard's titled "The Responsibilities of Leaders." It is Hubbard's deconstruc-

*The church has stated, "Scientology ministers maintain and practice a code of conduct known as the Auditor's Code. The Auditor's Code provides standards to ensure that priest-penitent communications remain strictly confidential. All such information is kept *strictly confidential* by a Scientology minister and the Church."

tion of the lives of the nineteenth-century South American military leader Simón Bolívar and his ferociously protective mistress, a socialite named Manuela Sáenz. Bolívar, Hubbard writes, "was a military commander without peer in history. Why he would fail and die an exile to be later deified is thus of great interest. What mistakes did he make?" Sáenz, his consort, "was a brilliant, beautiful and able woman. She was loyal, devoted, quite comparable to Bolivar, far above the cut of average humanoids. Why then did she live a vilified outcast, receive such violent social rejection and die of poverty and remain unknown to history? What mistakes did she make?"

Hubbard's analysis was that Bolívar knew how to do only one thing brilliantly—to lead men in battle—and therefore he tended to resort to military solutions when diplomacy or politics would better serve. "He was too good at this one thing," Hubbard observes. "So he never looked to any other skill and he never even dreamed there was any other way." Bolívar failed to use his immense authority to reward his friends and punish his enemies; thus his friends deserted him and his enemies grew stronger. Craving glory and the love of his people, Bolívar disdained the bloody intrigues that might have kept him in power. "He never began to recognize a suppressive and never considered anyone needed killing except on a battlefield," Hubbard coldly sums up. "His addiction to the most unstable drug in history—fame—killed Bolivar."

Manuela Sáenz might have saved him. She had qualities that he lacked, but she, too, made mistakes. For all her cleverness, she never contrived to make Bolívar marry her, which would have given her the standing that she badly needed. "She was utterly devoted, completely brilliant and utterly incapable of bringing off an action of any final kind," Hubbard notes. "She violated the power formula in not realizing that she had power." She should have taken on the portfolio of Bolívar's secret police chief (as Mary Sue did for Hubbard). "She was not ruthless enough to make up for his lack of ruthlessness and not provident enough to make up for his lack of providence," Hubbard writes. "She was an actress for the theater alone."

In Hubbard's view, the moral of Bolívar and Sáenz's tragedy is that those with power must use it. Someone close to power, like Manuela, has to dedicate herself to enlarging the strength of her partner. "Real powers are developed by tight conspiracies of this kind," Hubbard writes. If Manuela had been willing to support Bolívar completely,

Hubbard concludes, she would have been a truly historic figure, rather than being "unknown even in the archives of her country as the heroine she was."

Nazanin Boniadi was obviously being groomed for leadership. Why else would she be reading about Bolívar and Sáenz? But what lesson was she supposed to draw? She was puzzled by the demands the church was placing on her, which had little to do with human rights. Along with the security checks and the coursework, Naz was told to have her braces taken off and was given very expensive beauty treatments. Wilhere informed her that the "director" of the special project had decided that her hair had too much red in it, so a stylist to the stars came to the Celebrity Centre to darken and highlight her hair. Then came the shopping spree. Wilhere took Naz to Rodeo Drive and spent twenty thousand dollars for her new wardrobe.

Finally, Naz and Wilhere flew to New York, first class. She guessed that the mission would finally be revealed to her. They stopped at the New York Org, ostensibly on routine business, but there they happened to run into Tom Cruise. Tommy Davis was with him. Although it all seemed like a happy coincidence, Naz was a little flustered. Not only was Cruise the biggest star in the world, he had also just been accorded the highest honor in Scientology. She said to him, "Very well done, sir." (Later she was corrected for saying that, because you don't commend your senior.)

Cruise was charming. He said that he and Davis were headed over to the Empire State Building and then to Nobu for some sushi—why didn't they join them? Afterward, they all went skating at Rockefeller Center, which was closed to the public while they were on the rink. It was beginning to seem a little too perfect. She spent that first night with Cruise in the Trump Tower, where he had taken an entire floor for his entourage.

Cruise invited Naz to hang out on the set of *War of the Worlds*, which was shooting in Athens, New York, the next morning. At the end of the day, Davis accompanied her back to the city. In the limo, he handed Naz a non-disclosure agreement. There was no lawyer present, and she wasn't given a copy of what she signed. He informed her that the "mission" was now off the table. This—the relationship with Cruise—was far more important. Davis warned that if she did anything to upset Cruise he would personally destroy her.

Naz wasn't resistant. She wanted to help the world, and she had faith that Scientology could do that. Cruise was dazzling. Scientology was deeply important to both of them. It was obviously meant to be, so why question it?

According to several knowledgeable sources, within a few weeks Naz moved into Cruise's house. Davis and Jessica Feshbach were constantly tutoring her in how to behave toward the star. One evening, she and Cruise had dinner with several Scientologists, including Tommy Davis and Cruise's niece, Lauren Haigney, who was in the Sea Org and was posted to Gold Base. She had been Katy Haggis's best friend all through their childhood. They were at the Delphian School together. At the dinner, Lauren talked about her friendship with Katy, and how she had decided to break off their relationship when Katy said she was a lesbian. Naz was shocked, not just by the comment but by the fact that everyone agreed with her decision.*

In December, Cruise took Naz to his vacation house in Telluride, where they were joined by David and Shelly Miscavige. While they were at Cruise's retreat, David and Shelly watched a screener of *Million Dollar Baby*. Afterward, Miscavige said it had been difficult to sit through. He complained about what a poor example of a Scientologist Haggis was, and said that he needed to get back on the Bridge and stop making such awful, low-tone films. Cruise agreed. "He needs to get his ethics in," he remarked.

Naz was having an awful menstrual period, and she wanted to beg off the festive dinner they had planned, but she knew she was obliged to play the hostess. Still, she felt miserable and her mind was foggy. A couple of times, Miscavige addressed comments to her, and she couldn't quite understand what he said. Miscavige speaks in a rapid-fire Philly brogue, and Naz had to ask him to repeat himself more than once. The next day, both Davis and Cruise dressed her down for disrespecting the church leader—specifically, for "insulting his TR 1." In Scientology lingo, that refers to the basic Training Routine about communicating with another person. Naz had embarrassed Miscavige because he wasn't able to get his message across. Davis said that her conduct was inexcusable. If she was in pain, she should have taken a Tylenol.

*Cruise's attorney says that this conversation never took place. According to Tommy Davis: "Katy did not lose her friend because she admitted she was gay, she lost her friend because Katy lied to her about being gay."

With his characteristic intensity, Cruise himself later explained the seriousness of the situation: "You don't get it. It goes like this." He raised his hand over his head. "First, there's LRH." He moved his hand down a few inches. "Then, there is COB." Bringing his hand down to his own eye level, he said, "Then there's me."

Two weeks later, Jessica Feshbach told Naz to pack her things. Cruise was too busy to say good-bye. Naz's last glimpse was of him working out in his home gym.

Davis later explained to her that Cruise had simply changed his mind about the relationship, deciding that he needed someone with more power. But the star was willing to make amends by paying for a package that would allow her to attain OT VII. Continuing up the Bridge would help her deal with her grief and loss, Davis assured her.

In February 2005, Naz went to Clearwater to take the courses. At first, she was treated like a VIP, but soon one of her friends noticed dramatic changes in her—she was weeping all the time. Naz confided that she had just gone through a wrenching breakup with Tom Cruise. The shocked friend immediately reported her to Ethics. Naz was assigned a condition of Treason and ordered to do reparations for the damages she had done to the group by revealing her relationship with Cruise. She was made to dig ditches and scrub public toilets with a toothbrush. Finally, in June, she worked her way back into good standing with the church, but she was ordered to stay away from the Celebrity Centre. Davis advised her to go live in some far corner of the world and never utter another word about Tom Cruise.*

The search for a new mate for the star now went beyond Scientologists. Cruise briefly courted the Colombian actress Sofía Vergara, whom he met at a pre-Oscar party hosted by Will and Jada Pinkett Smith, but that relationship dissolved when Vergara refused to become a Scientologist. The religion was a crucial factor, both for Cruise and for the church. Cruise was particularly interested in Jennifer Garner. Other actresses were invited to the Celebrity Centre to audition for what they believed was a role in the *Mission: Impossible* series. The names included Kate Bosworth, Jessica Alba, Lindsay Lohan, Scarlett Johansson—and Katie Holmes.

---

*Several sources independently told me of Boniadi's experiences with Tom Cruise. All their recollections were consistent. Cruise's attorney says that no Scientology executives set him up with girlfriends, and that no female Scientologist that Cruise dated moved into his home.

Holmes was an ingenue with almond-shaped brown eyes, who described herself as a twenty-six-year-old virgin. She had been a top student at an all-girls Catholic high school in Toledo, Ohio, but like Tommy Davis, she had dropped out of Columbia University after a single semester. Soon she was starring on the teenage soap opera *Dawson's Creek* and had a modest film career in coquettish roles. Church researchers discovered an interview she had given to *Seventeen* in October 2004. "I think every young girl dreams about [her wedding]," Holmes told the magazine. "I used to think I was going to marry Tom Cruise." She had developed a crush on the actor when he appeared in *Risky Business*. At the time, she was four years old.

Katie and Tom met in April 2005. "I was in love from the moment that I shook his hand for the first time," she later told talk-show host Jay Leno. Cruise is famous for his ardent courtship—flowers, jewelry, and imaginative dates. He took Katie on a nighttime helicopter ride over Los Angeles, with take-out sushi. Within a little more than two weeks, she had moved into Cruise's Beverly Hills mansion, fired her manager and agent and replaced them with his representatives, and had begun to be accompanied by Jessica Feshbach, who was explained in press interviews as being her "best friend."

In May, Cruise appeared on *The Oprah Winfrey Show*. The audience, nearly all women, were in a near-hysterical state of anticipation even before Cruise came out on the stage, so his behavior has to be seen against a backdrop of a highly titillated screaming mass, to which he responded like a surfer catching a massive wave. He pumped his fist in the air and knelt on the floor. "Something's happened to you!" Winfrey exclaimed.

"I'm in love!" he explained.

"We've never seen you behave like this before!"

"I know!" Cruise said, jumping backward onto her couch. Then he grabbed Winfrey's hands and began wrestling with her. "You're gone!" she kept saying. "You're gone!" It was a scene of complete delirium.

Cruise's spectacular and highly public romance was overshadowing the promotion for *War of the Worlds*, the movie he had just made with Spielberg, which would be released the following month. A few weeks after the Winfrey show, Cruise did an interview with *Today* show host Matt Lauer as Holmes sat nearby. The questions were friendly, and Cruise seemed happy and relaxed until Lauer mentioned that Holmes had agreed to take up Scientology. "At this stage in your life, could you be with someone who doesn't have an interest?" Lauer asked.

"You know, Scientology is something that you don't understand," Cruise responded. "It's like, you could be a Christian and be a Scientologist, okay."

"So, it doesn't replace religion," Lauer offered.

"It is a religion, because it's dealing with the spirit. You as a spiritual being."

Lauer then asked about a comment that Cruise had recently made about actress Brooke Shields, who had written that antidepressants had helped her get through her postpartum depression. "I've never agreed with psychiatry—ever!" Cruise said. He was dressed in black, his muscular arms on display; he had a stubble beard and his hair was draped in bangs across his forehead. He radiated an athletic intensity and a barely contained fury. "As far as the Brooke Shields thing, look, you've got to understand, I really care about Brooke Shields. I think, here's a wonderful and talented woman. And I want to see her do well. And I know that psychiatry is a pseudo-science."

"But, Tom, if she said that this particular thing helped her feel better, whether it was the antidepressants or going to a counselor or psychiatrist, isn't that enough?"

"Matt, you have to understand this," Cruise said, glowering. "Here we are today, where I talk out against drugs and psychiatric abuses of electric-shocking people—okay, against their will—of drugging children with them not knowing the effect of these drugs. Do you know what Adderall is? Do you know Ritalin? Do you know now that Ritalin is a street drug? Do you understand that?"

"The difference is—"

"No, no, Matt."

"This wasn't against her will, though."

"Matt, Matt, Matt, Matt."

"But this wasn't against her will."

"Matt, I'm asking you a question."

"I understand there's abuse of all these things."

"No, you see, here's the problem," Cruise said. "You don't know the history of psychiatry. I do."

Lauer was taken aback by Cruise's aggressiveness, but he pressed on. "Do you examine the possibility that these things do work for some people? That yes, there are abuses, and yes, maybe they've gone too far in some areas. Maybe there are too many kids on Ritalin. Maybe electric shock—"

"Too many kids on Ritalin?" Cruise said, shaking his head. "Matt."

"Aren't there examples where it works?"

"Matt, Matt, Matt, you don't even—you're glib. You don't even know what Ritalin is." He said there were ways that Shields could solve her depression—he mentioned diet and exercise—other than drugs. "And there are ways of doing it without that, so that we don't end up in a brave new world. The thing that I'm saying about Brooke is that there's misinformation, okay. And she doesn't understand the history of psychiatry. She doesn't understand in the same way that you don't understand it, Matt."

SCIENTOLOGY'S HISTORY OF psychiatry holds it responsible for many of the ills that have affected humanity—war, racism, ethnic cleansing, terrorism—all in the pursuit of social control and profit. The church has opened an exhibit, "Psychiatry: An Industry of Death," on Sunset Boulevard in Hollywood. It describes the often grisly and benighted practices that have characterized the evolution of the profession, including madhouses, lobotomies, electroshock therapy, and the proliferation of psychiatric drugs to treat spurious diagnoses. Scientology views this history as a long march by psychiatrists to manipulate human behavior and institute world government.

Although it's not included in the exhibit, Hubbard's chronology of psychiatry actually begins "five billion years ago" with the development of a particular technique that was developed "in the Maw Confederation of the Sixty-third Galaxy":

Take a sheet of glass and put it in front of the preclear—clear, very clear glass—which is supercooled, preferably about a −100 centigrade. You got that? Supercooled, you know? And then put the preclear right in front of this supercooled sheet of glass and suddenly shove his face into the glass. . . .

Takes about twenty seconds, then, to accomplish a total brainwash of a case.

Now, if you wish to play God, as the whole-track psychiatrist did at that time, all you have to say at this time is, of course, "Go to Earth and be president," or something like that, you know? And a thetan, being properly brainwashed now, will take off, and that's that.

Hubbard also blamed psychiatrists, allied with the tyrant Xenu, for carrying out genocide in the Galactic Confederacy seventy-five million years ago. There are obvious parallels in this legend with the Nazi regime, which used doctors, including psychiatrists, to carry out the extermination of the mentally ill, along with homosexuals, Gypsies, and Jews; and also by the Soviet government, which employed psychiatrists to diagnose political dissidents and lock them away. Hubbard lived through these shameful events, and they no doubt colored his imagination.

After Hubbard's death, Miscavige continued the campaign. In 1995, he told the International Association of Scientologists that the church's goals for the new millennium were to "place Scientology at the absolute center of society" and to "eliminate psychiatry in all its forms." The Citizens Commission on Human Rights, a lobby group created by the Church of Scientology that runs the psychiatry museum, maintains that no mental diseases have ever been proven to exist. In this view, psychiatrists have been responsible for the Holocaust, apartheid, and even 9/11. The commission is not above bending the truth to make its point. The president of CCHR, Dave Figueroa, asserts that Osama bin Laden's chief deputy, Ayman al-Zawahiri, was a psychiatrist who took control of bin Laden's "thought patterns." "Whatever type of drugs that Zawahiri used to make that change in bin Laden, we don't know," Figueroa explained. "We know there was a real change in that guy's attitude." This view is reiterated in the terrorism portion of the museum. (In fact, Zawahiri is a general surgeon, not a psychiatrist.)*

*Also in the exhibit is a photograph of Imad Eddin Barakat Yarkas, known as Abu Dadah, who is described as a psychiatrist and the mastermind of the Madrid train bombings in 2004. Yarkas, an al-Qaeda fund-raiser, was a used-car salesman who had little or nothing to do with the Madrid bombings. In a list of 218 international known Islamist militants, the only one who ever studied psychology was Ali Mohammed, an Egyptian operative who helped plan the American Embassy bombings in 1998. "Psychologists are conspicuous by their absence," Steffen Hertog, a lecturer in comparative politics at the London School of Economics, wrote me in a private communication. "The pattern is similar for other types of extremist groups: Among 215 leading German Nazis with known higher education, there are only 2 psychologists, compared to 71 lawyers." In another Citizens Commission on Human Rights report, titled "Chaos and Terror: Manufactured by Psychiatry" (www.cchrstl.org/documents/terror.pdf), the supposed mastermind of the Madrid bombings is now said to be "Moroccan psy-

CCHR's main effort has been an international campaign against the use of psychiatric drugs, especially for children. The surgeon general of the United States issued a report in 2001 claiming that more than twenty percent of children ages nine to seventeen had a diagnosable mental or addictive disorder, and that four million American children suffered from major mental illness. There is obviously an immense market for medications to treat such disorders. About ten percent of Americans over the age of six are on antidepressants, and antipsychotic drugs are the top-selling category of drugs in the country. They have become a plague on the schoolgrounds of America, with indiscriminate prescriptions creating a new culture of drug dependency—one that the pharmaceutical industry and the medical profession bear some responsibility for.

Haggis has been a substantial supporter of the CCHR. As a boy, he says, he spent most of his days staring out the window, daydreaming—a candidate for an attention deficit disorder diagnosis. "I identified with the oddballs and the misfits," he said. "Those who conform have very little chance of making a difference in life." He was sure that if his parents had medicated him, he might never have become a writer. He hosted fund-raisers for CCHR in his home. "I simply believe that psychiatric drugs are over-prescribed, especially to children," he said. "I think that is a crime."

Scientologists have been seeking ways of criminalizing psychiatric remedies. In the same period that Cruise was chastising Brooke Shields for taking antidepressants, Kirstie Alley and Kelly Preston were testifying before state lawmakers in Florida, who passed a bill, written in part by Scientologists, that would hold schoolteachers criminally liable for suggesting to parents that their children might be suffering from a mental health condition, such as attention deficit disorder. Governor Jeb Bush vetoed the bill. Governor Jon Huntsman did the same in Utah. Similar bills have been pushed by the CCHR in other states. In her Florida testimony, Kirstie Alley held up photographs of children who had committed suicide after taking psychotropic drugs. "None of these children were psychotic before they took these drugs," she asserted, sobbing so hard she could barely speak. "None of these children were suicidal before they took these drugs."

---

chiatrist Abu Hafizah." No such person exists on the list of known Islamist terrorists, nor is anyone by that name attached to the Madrid bombings.

Some drug makers have covered up studies that indicate an increased danger of suicidal or violent thoughts caused by psychotropic medicines. Eli Lilly, for instance, suppressed data showing that patients who were taking the popular drug Prozac—the only antidepressant certified as safe for children—were twelve times more likely to attempt suicide than patients taking similar medications. Antidepressants have been implicated in a number of schoolyard shootings, such as the 1999 Columbine High School massacre, where two students killed twelve of their classmates and a teacher. One of the killers was taking Luvox at the time. Adderall—one of the drugs cited by Cruise—is an amphetamine often prescribed for attention-deficit/hyperactivity disorder; it sometimes causes increased aggression in children and adolescents. Ritalin, the most common drug prescribed for ADHD, is similar to cocaine in its potential for addiction. According to *The Primary Care Companion to the Journal of Clinical Psychiatry*, a person using Ritalin, Adderall, or other cocaine-like drugs "can experience nervousness, restlessness, agitation, suspiciousness, paranoia, hallucinations and delusions, impaired cognitive functions, delirium, violence, suicide, and homicide."

But people who are taking antidepressants, antipsychotics, and mood-stabilizing drugs are already at a higher risk for suicide or violent behavior. One of the dangers of prescribing an antidepressant is that it may give the patient the stimulus he or she needs to act on suicidal impulses that are already present. Sudden withdrawal from antidepressants can prompt suicidal thoughts as well. Several studies have found that the risk of suicide was just as great for those who don't receive antidepressants as for those who do; over time, however, patients taking antidepressants are less likely to kill themselves. Such medications now come with warnings about increased suicidal behavior. And yet, one study noted the steady decline of overall suicide rates in the United States since fluoxetine (Prozac) was introduced in the American market. The authors estimated that the drug was responsible for saving 33,600 lives between 1988 and 2002.

There are numerous examples of Scientologists who have considered or actually committed suicide, or engaged in violence, who might have been helped if they had taken psychotropic medicines. In Buffalo, New York, on March 13, 2003 (L. Ron Hubbard's birthday), twenty-eight-year-old Jeremy Perkins stabbed his mother seventy-seven times.

He was a schizophrenic with a history of violence and hallucinations, who had rejected psychiatric treatment because he was a Scientologist. Hana Eltringham, who had been Hubbard's chief deputy, believes that Scientology itself caused her own shattered mental state. For years after attaining OT III, Eltringham had frequent thoughts of suicide. The unremitting migraines and voices in her head made her despair. Several times, she came close to jumping off the top floor of the church's headquarters in Clearwater, but restrained herself because she was worried that it would bring disgrace upon the church and Hubbard's teachings. It was only when she left the church and began taking Prozac that her headaches and her suicidal thoughts went away. "It has changed my life," she claimed. Her friend Mary Florence Barnett, Shelly Miscavige's mother, had similar symptoms—constant headaches and suicidal thoughts. She confided to Eltringham that she wanted to kill herself in order to stop the suppressive body thetans from taking over her mind. Barnett eventually went outside the official church to receive Scientology counseling, a heretical practice known in Scientology as squirreling. (The church denies that Barnett became involved with dissident Scientologists, but if she had, that would have placed David and Shelly Miscavige in a compromised position with the church. They would have been Potential Trouble Sources if they failed to disconnect from her.) On September 8, 1985, Barnett's body was found. She had been shot three times in the chest and once through the temple with a rifle. Both of her wrists were slashed. She left two suicide notes. The Los Angeles County Medical Examiner ruled her death a suicide.

In 2007, Kyle Brennan, twenty years old, who was not a Scientologist, went to stay with his father, a member of the church, in Clearwater. Brennan was taking Lexapro, an antidepressant heavily promoted by its manufacturer, Forest Laboratories. He was also under the care of a psychiatrist. According to court records, Brennan's father, Thomas, was ordered to "handle" his son. Thomas Brennan's auditor was Denise Miscavige Gentile, David Miscavige's twin sister. She spoke on the phone to Kyle's mother, who was not a Scientologist, and urged her to enroll her son in Narconon, the church's drug-treatment program. His mother refused, pointing out that the program costs approximately $25,000; moreover, Kyle was not a drug addict. She sued, charging that church officials had ordered Thomas Brennan to lock his son's Lexapro in the trunk of his car. Days after that, Kyle shot himself to death with a .357 Magnum that his father kept in his bedside table. (The suit was dismissed for lack of evidence.)

The long history of humanity's inadequate attempts to deal with depression, and the manifold ways in which insanity expresses itself, have never yielded a clear path. Tragedies such as the suicide of Kyle Brennan demonstrate the danger of dogmatic interpretations of psychiatry, such as those offered by Tom Cruise and other Scientology celebrities on the subject. The American Psychiatric Association felt so threatened by Cruise's statements on the *Today* show that the president of the organization issued a statement affirming that mental illnesses are real medical conditions. "It is irresponsible for Mr. Cruise to use his movie publicity tour to promote his own ideological views and deter people with mental illness from getting the care they need," said Steven S. Sharfstein, the president of the APA. But at the 2005 annual meeting of the International Association of Scientologists, Mike Rinder, who had been let out of the Hole for the occasion, credited Cruise with persuading the Food and Drug Administration to post suicide warnings on the labels of two psychiatric drugs within days of his interview with Lauer.

"If someone wants to get off drugs, I can help them," Cruise told the German magazine *Der Spiegel*, in April 2005. "I myself have helped hundreds of people get off drugs."

HAGGIS HAD SENT a rough cut of his movie *Crash* to the Toronto Film Festival, an important venue for independent films that are looking for distribution. In September 2004, the movie met its first audience at the Elgin Theatre, an elegant old vaudeville house downtown, not far from the spot where Paul sold tickets at the soft-porn theater his professor used to run.

As he watched the movie, Haggis was appalled. Everything that was wrong was glaringly apparent on the huge screen. He sat glumly waiting for it to end, calculating what could be salvaged. So when the audience rose to its feet at the end, cheering, Haggis couldn't believe what was happening. Lion's Gate Films bought *Crash* for $3.5 million and scheduled it for release the following spring.

Crash opened quietly in April 2005. There were no billboards or bus signs, which were already touting the arrival of *War of the Worlds* in June. The reviews for *Crash* were passionate but polarized. Roger Ebert gave it four stars, calling it "a movie of intense fascination." A. O. Scott, who reviewed it for *The New York Times*, was less infatuated. It was a "frustrating movie," he wrote, "full of heart and devoid of life; crudely manipulative when it tries hardest to be subtle; and profoundly complacent in spite of its intention to unsettle and disturb." There was no actual premiere, just a screening at the Academy Theater on Wilshire Boulevard, and no grand party afterward. Haggis and his family went out to dinner.

Despite the conflicting reviews and limited distribution, a groundswell was building for the movie, driven entirely by audiences who were caught up in a national conversation over race and class that the movie prompted. It would go on to earn nearly $100 million in international sales. *Million Dollar Baby* had just won the Academy Award for Best Picture that February. Haggis was writing a James Bond movie, *Casino Royale*, in addition to the Eastwood picture *Flags of Our Fathers*. He was flying.

Tom Cruise's career was headed in the opposite direction. Haggis had seen him at the *Vanity Fair* Oscar party. Cruise and Tommy Davis arrived on Ducati motorcycles, wearing black jackets, and were let in the back door of Morton's Steakhouse in Beverly Hills. They said hello to Haggis, but nothing more. Polls showed that Cruise was still ranked as the most powerful actor in Hollywood, and even the most powerful celebrity in the world, but he was also ranked number one as the celebrity that people would least like to have as their best friend.

When Cruise returned to Gold Base, Miscavige showed off his Harley-Davidson V-rod motorcycle, which had been custom-painted a candy-apple red over a brushed nickel surface. Miscavige's brother-in-law, John Brousseau, known for his elegant craftsmanship, had done the work. In addition to overseeing the renovation of the *Freewinds*, Brousseau had installed bars on the doors of the Hole shortly after Rathbun escaped.

According to Brousseau, "Cruise was drooling" over the motorcycle. "God, could you paint my bike like that?" he asked. Brousseau looked at Miscavige, who nodded. Cruise brought in two motorcycles to be painted, a Triumph Rocket III and a Honda Rune. Spielberg had given him the Honda after the filming of *War of the Worlds*; it had already been custom-painted by the set designer. Brousseau had to take

Tom Cruise and David Miscavige at the Church of
Scientology opening in central Madrid, 2004

each motorcycle apart completely and nickel-plate all the parts before
painting them.* Cruise drove the newly painted Rune, with Katie on
the back, to the fans' screening of his movie at Grauman's Chinese
Theatre in June.

After that, Brousseau was regularly assigned to work on special projects for Cruise. Shelly Miscavige had drafted Brousseau and
seven other Sea Org members, along with many of Cruise's employees
at Odin Productions, to work for more than two weeks rehabilitat-

---

*The church denies Brousseau's account. Cruise's attorney denies that his client ever
saw Miscavige's motorcycle and claims,"We have photographic evidence showing the
actual painter doing the job. It's not Mr. Brousseau." However, the attorney did not
provide the photos. Brousseau did provide photos of the work he says he did on each of
Cruise's vehicles he claimed to have worked on.

ing Cruise's leased nine-bedroom mansion on Alpine Drive in Beverly Hills—painting, fixing the roof, doing cabinet work, stretching the carpet, rewiring, pressure-washing the tennis court, weeding and planting, repairing the irrigation system, and even reorganizing the clothes in the closets. In the last week, Brousseau says, he had at least a hundred contractors under his direction in order to get the house ready for Cruise.

Brousseau and a Sea Org executive, Steve Marlowe, also oversaw the renovations on a Blue Bird bus, like Hubbard's, that Cruise had purchased. Later, Cruise bought another bus, which he called *The Silver Screen*. Brousseau spent three months commuting to the Marathon Coach factory in Coburg, Oregon, to oversee the retrofitting of the forty-foot vehicle into an elaborate motor home. Brousseau estimates that the redesign cost about $1.5 million, but that doesn't include his labor or that of Sea Org members in the Golden Era prop department, who manufactured the furniture, countertops, and cabinetry. In 2006, Brousseau also customized a limousine for the star, using the body of a Ford Excursion that he says Cruise acquired using the Scientology fleet discount. Katie was pregnant and wanted a new vehicle with a baby seat. Miscavige had wanted to impress the couple by renovating the Excursion at a local custom shop, but the job was poorly done. Miscavige purchased another Excursion for Cruise to replace the one that had been botched. Meanwhile, Brousseau spent the next six months personally rebuilding the original Excursion. He ripped the vehicle down to its frame and installed handmade reclining seats and wood paneling fashioned from a burl of a eucalyptus tree that had been toppled in a storm. He spent about two thousand hours on the project. The materials were paid for by Cruise's production company, but according to Brousseau, his labor, and that of about ten other Sea Org members, was not compensated. "It was a half-million-dollar beauty all done by me, with other folks from Scientology," Brousseau said.

Brousseau had even carved a matching Montblanc pen out of the burl, its own hidden storage case in the vehicle. When Cruise showed it to Katie, she was dazzled. She turned to Brousseau and asked, "Oh, J.B., did you make that?"

"Don't thank me," Brousseau quickly responded. "I'm just the hammer. This—," he said, pointing to Miscavige, "is the hand that wields me."

Cruise, who became a pilot while filming *Top Gun*, keeps a hangar at an airport in Burbank for his airplane collection. Sea Org members completely renovated the hangar, installing a luxurious office that had been fabricated at Golden Era Productions. Brousseau says that the furniture—a dry bar, table and chairs, desks, et cetera—was milled at an RPF base in Los Angeles. Brousseau took dozens of photographs documenting his handiwork on the star's behalf.

No member of the Sea Org has spent more time in Cruise's service than Tommy Davis, who was viewed within the church as the star's special handler and personal assistant. Although Davis maintains that he provided similar services for other celebrities, his assignment to Cruise was his primary duty between 2000 and 2004. However, he asserted, "None of the Church staff involved were coerced in any way to assist Mr. Cruise. Church staff, and indeed Church members, hold Mr. Cruise in very high regard and are honored to assist him."

IN JUNE 2006, Shelly Miscavige disappeared.

She had spent her whole life conveying orders and gathering intelligence for a powerful, erratic, domineering church leader, first for Hubbard and then for her husband. She and Miscavige were always respectful toward each other in public, if not openly affectionate. As he gained power within the church, she began to see the two of them as reincarnations of Simón Bolívar and Manuela Sáenz, and the lesson she drew from that previous existence was that she needed to be fiercely protective of her mate, and to keep him from making the kinds of mistakes that his character was destined to commit. In the eyes of some Sea Org members, Shelly was brittle and imperious, but Rathbun noted that she sometimes objected when Miscavige's physical assaults threatened to get out of hand. No one else did.

That spring, Shelly returned from a *Freewinds* voyage before her husband did, and in his absence she decided to arrange the Org Board herself. There were no settled posts, executives were still churning in the Hole, and the management structure was a mess. Taking matters into her own hands, Shelly made a number of appointments.

Soon after her husband came back, Shelly's mood visibly changed. Her brother-in-law, John Brousseau, observed that she looked cowed: "The bulldog was gone." Shortly before she disappeared, she asked Mike Rinder if Dave still had his wedding ring on. Then she vanished. Although a missing-person report has been filed, the Los Angeles Police

Department will not comment on her whereabouts. She was escorted to her father's funeral in August 2007. That's the last time she was seen in public. Former Sea Org members say she is being guarded at a church facility in Running Springs, California, near Lake Arrowhead, one of the several repositories for Hubbard's writings. It gets cold there in the winter. Miscavige sent Shelly a sweater and a pair of gloves for Christmas.

In November 2006, Tom Cruise and Katie Holmes married in a fifteenth-century castle outside of Rome. Among the celebrities attending were Jennifer Lopez and Marc Anthony, Will and Jada Pinkett Smith, Jenna Elfman, and even Brooke Shields. Once again, David Miscavige served as the best man.

Part III

THE PRISON OF BELIEF

10

The Investigation

Proposition 8, the California initiative to ban marriage between same-sex couples, appeared on the ballot in 2008. Paul Haggis was deeply involved in fighting the initiative, marching in demonstrations and contributing financially. His advocacy placed a strain on his relationship with Scientology. For several years, he had been concerned about the bigotry he found inside the church, especially when it was directed at his two gay daughters. Katy, in particular, had expressed her discomfort with the way she was treated at the Celebrity Centre, where she had been taking some courses. She had decided to go to another Scientology mission where she wouldn't feel so judged.

One evening, Paul and Deborah went to a small fund-raising dinner at John Travolta and Kelly Preston's house. Deborah and Kelly were on the parents' committee to raise funds for a new Delphi school in Santa Monica. Several other couples were there, all of them Operating Thetans. One of the guests referred to the waiter as a faggot.

It is difficult to imagine such open bigotry in Hollywood, a liberal stronghold, but especially in the home of John Travolta, who has dodged rumors of his sexual orientation since he first became a star. Despite the onslaught of publicity and sexual harassment suits that have been lodged against the star over the years, many Scientologists, including Haggis, believed that Travolta was not gay. Haggis had been impressed by his apparently loving relationship with his wife and children; but it is also common to assume that homosexuality is handled at the OT III level, where the body thetans that cause such problems can be audited away. The other diners may have been so convinced of Travolta's sexual orientation that they felt free to display their prejudice. In any case, Travolta reprimanded his guest, saying that such remarks were not tolerated in their home.

Haggis was flooded with admiration for the firm but graceful way that the star had handled the situation. After the other guests had departed, Haggis and Travolta had a conversation in his small study. They talked about the bigotry they had observed in the church. Haggis confided that Katy had been made to feel unwanted at the Celebrity Centre. Travolta said that Hubbard's writings had been misinterpreted, and he later provided some references that Katy could use to defend herself.

When Hubbard wrote *Dianetics*, in 1950, he reflected the prevailing social prejudices, including the psychiatric community, which considered homosexuality a mental illness. (It was not removed from the American Psychiatric Association's *Diagnostic and Statistical Manual of Mental Disorders* until 1973.) "The sexual pervert"—by which Hubbard meant the homosexual—"is actually quite ill physically," he writes. The following year, he published the Tone Scale in *Science of Survival*. Near the bottom, at 1.1 on the scale, is the Covertly Hostile personality. People in this state engage in casual sex, sadism—and homosexual activity. Hubbard describes this as "the most dangerous and wicked level. . . . Here is the person who smiles when he inserts a knife blade between your vertebrae." "This is the level of the pervert, the hypocrite, the turncoat. This is the level of the subversive. . . . A 1.1 is the most dangerously insane person in society and is likely to cause the most damage. . . . Such people should be taken from the society as rapidly as possible and uniformly institutionalized." Another way of dealing with them, he writes, is "to dispose of them quietly and without sorrow." He went on: "The sudden and abrupt deletion of all individuals occupying the lower bands of the Tone Scale from the social order would result in an almost instant rise in the cultural tone and would interrupt the dwindling spiral into which any society may have entered."

Hubbard occasionally moderated his stance, although he never entirely repudiated or discarded his prejudice. In 1952, he said, "Homosexuality is about as serious as sneezes." In 1965, he refers in an executive letter to a "squirrel" who, he says, "was sacked for homosexuality and theft." Another disaffected Scientologist, Hubbard notes in the same letter, "is a set-up for an arrest as a homosexual." Two years later, when social attitudes toward gays were slowly changing, he declared, "It has never been any part of my plans to regulate or attempt to regulate the private lives of individuals." However, because everything Hubbard wrote is sacrosanct in the church, these early views are indelibly fixed in the minds of many Scientologists. Long after the founder's death it was still generally believed that auditing would "sort out" homosexuality. Gays in the church were frequently pressed to buy courses or take additional auditing in order to handle their condition.

The ambivalence in the church over the question of sexual orientation is evident in its treatment of Travolta. Over the years, the church has acted to protect his reputation. Marty Rathbun has said there were many allegations that he helped "to make go away." He sometimes worked in concert with Travolta's attorneys, attempting to keep stories out of the press. In 2003, a gay artist, Michael Pattinson, sued the church, Travolta, and more than twenty other individuals, claiming that the star had been held up as an example of how Scientology can cure homosexuality. Pattinson said that he spent twenty-five years in the church, and half a million dollars, trying to change his sexual orientation, without success. (That case was voluntarily withdrawn following an avalanche of countersuits. Both Pattinson and his attorney say they were driven into bankruptcy.)

Haggis identified with homosexuals because they were a minority. They were the underdogs. They were also two of his daughters. The backers of Proposition 8 were using scare tactics to drive their campaign, claiming that homosexuals were going to take over the schools and teach people to be gay. Lauren Haggis actually heard people saying that. Then someone pointed her to a website that listed the proposition's backers. The Church of Scientology of San Diego was on the list. "I was just floored," she said. "And so I sent an e-mail to my sisters and my dad saying, um, what's going on?"

Haggis began peppering Tommy Davis with e-mails, demanding that the church support efforts to reverse the marriage ban. "I am going to an anti Prop 8 rally in a couple of hours," he wrote on November 11, 2008, a week after the initiative passed with 52 percent of the state's voters. "When can we expect the public statement?" Davis responded with a proposed letter that would go to the San Diego media, saying that the church had been "erroneously listed among the supporters of

Proposition 8." " 'Erroneous' doesn't cut it," Haggis fired back. "The church may have had the luxury of not taking a position on this issue before, but after taking a position, even erroneously, it can no longer stand neutral." He demanded that the church openly declare itself in favor of gay rights. "Anything less won't do."

Davis stopped responding. When Haggis prodded him again, Davis admitted that the correction to the San Diego media was never actually sent. "To be honest I was dismayed when our emails (which I thought were communications between us) were being cc'd to your daughters," he wrote. Davis was frustrated because, as he explained to Haggis, the church avoids taking political stances.* Davis insisted that it wasn't the "church" in San Diego that adopted a position against Prop 8. "It was *one guy* who somehow got it in his head it would be a neat idea and put Church of Scientology San Diego on the list," Davis insisted. "When I found out, I had it removed from the list."

As far as Davis was concerned, that should have been the end of the matter. Any further actions on the part of the church would only call attention to a mistaken position on an issue that the church wanted to go away. "Paul, I've received no press inquiries," he said. "If I were to make a statement on this it would actually bring *more* attention to the subject than if we leave it be."

But Haggis refused to let the matter drop. "This is not a PR issue, it is a moral issue," he wrote in February 2009. "Standing neutral is not an option."

In the final note of this exchange, Haggis conceded, "You were right: nothing happened—it didn't flap—at least not very much. But I feel we shamed ourselves."

Since Haggis's children had been copied on the correspondence with Davis, it helped clarify Lauren's stance with the church. At first, Davis's responses gave her hope, but then she realized, "They're just trying to minimize it as much as possible." After that, "I was totally done with the church."

The experience also helped her to see her father in a different light. "It's like night and day from when I first moved in with him," she said. "I didn't know that my dad loved me."

*Four years before, the church had actively campaigned against Proposition 63, the Mental Health Services Act, which raised taxes to provide for increased care for the mentally ill; the proposition passed.

BECAUSE HAGGIS STOPPED COMPLAINING, Davis felt that the issue had been laid to rest. But, far from putting the matter behind him, Haggis began an investigation into the church. His inquiry, much of it conducted online, echoed the actions of the lead character he was writing for Russell Crowe in *The Next Three Days*, who goes on the Internet to research a way to break his wife out of jail.

What is so striking about Haggis's investigation is that few prominent figures attached to the Church of Scientology have actually looked into the charges that have surrounded their institution for many years. The church discourages such examination, telling its members that negative articles are "entheta" and will only cause spiritual upset. In 1996, the church sent CDs to members to help them build their own websites, which would then link them to the Scientology site; included in the software was a filter that would block any sites containing material that vilified the church or revealed esoteric doctrines. Keywords that triggered the censorship were Xenu, OT III, and the names of prominent Scientology critics.

Although Haggis never used such a filter, one already existed in his mind. During his thirty-four years in the church he had purposely avoided asking too many questions or reading materials that he knew would disparage his faith. But now, frustrated by his exchange with Davis, he began "poking around." He came upon an interview on You-Tube with Tommy Davis that had been broadcast by CNN in May 2008. "The worldwide interest in Scientology has never been higher," Davis boasts on the show. "Scientology has grown more in the last five years than the last five decades combined." The anchor, John Roberts, asks Davis about the church's policy of disconnection, in which followers are urged to separate themselves from friends or family members who might be critical of the organization. "This is a perfect example of how the Internet turns things and twists things," Davis responds. "There's no such thing as disconnection as you're characterizing it. And certainly, we have to understand—"

"Well, what is disconnection?" Roberts tries to interject.

"Scientology is a new religion," Davis continues, talking over the host. "The majority of Scientologists in the world, they're first generation. So their family members aren't going to be Scientologists. . . . So, certainly, someone who is a Scientologist is going to respect their family members' beliefs—"

"Well, what is disconnection?" Roberts asks again.

"And we consider family to be a building block of any society, so anything that's characterized as disconnection, or this kind of thing, it's just not true. There isn't any such policy."

Haggis knew this was a lie. His wife, Deborah, had disconnected from her parents twice. When she was in her twenties and acting in *Dallas*, her mother and stepfather broke away from the church. They were close friends of Hana Eltringham, who had stood up for them at their wedding, so when they had doubts about their faith, they went to see her. Eltringham was then counseling people who were considering getting out of Scientology or other new religions. She helped Scientologists confront the contradictions that were implicit in their faith, such as Hubbard speaking of events that had taken place trillions or quadrillions of years in the past, although scientists estimate the age of the universe to be less than 14 billion years, or the fact that it has never been shown that anyone has ever obtained any enhanced OT abilities. Eltringham also talked about the abuses she observed and experienced. "Hana told us how Sea Org members were treated," Mary Benjamin, Deborah's mother, recalled, "how they were kept in a basement in Los Angeles and fed rice and beans if they didn't keep their stats up. How, in the desert, in terrible heat, they would march in a circle for hours."

Like many active members of the church, the Benjamins kept money on account—in their case, $2,500—for future courses they intended to take. Deborah's mother insisted on getting the money back. Deborah knew what a big deal that was for the church. She didn't speak to her parents for more than three years, automatically assuming that they must have been declared Suppressive Persons. But when her sister was about to get married, Deborah wrote to the International Justice Chief, the Scientology official in charge of such matters, who said that she was allowed to see her parents as long as they didn't say anything against Scientology. The Benjamins readily agreed.

A decade later, however, Deborah went to Clearwater, intending to take some upper-level courses, and learned that the previous ruling no longer applied. If she wanted to do more training, she would have to confront her parents' mistakes. The church recommended that she take the Potential Trouble Source/Suppressive Persons course.

Many Scientologists have taken the same course. Deborah's friend

Kelly Preston had taken it as well. "I was PTS, but I didn't realize it, and so I was told, 'You need to be on PTS/SP,' " Preston later recalled in her interview for *Celebrity* magazine. She discovered that her life was full of Suppressive Persons. "Being an artist and having a lot of theta, you really attract those type of people," Preston said. ("Theta" is a Scientology term for life force.) "I ended up having to handle or disconnect from quite a few different people."

It took Deborah a year to complete the course, but it didn't change her parents' status. She petitioned officials at the Celebrity Centre in Los Angeles for help. They put her on another program that took two more years to finish. Still, nothing changed. If she failed to "handle" her parents—by persuading them to make amends to the church—she would have to disconnect not only from them but also from everyone who spoke to them, including her siblings. She realized, "It was that, or else I had to give up being a Scientologist." The fact that Paul refused to disconnect from her parents posed yet another conflict.

According to the church, Deborah's parents had been part of a class-action lawsuit against Scientology by disaffected members in 1987, which was dismissed the following year.* The church required them to denounce the anti-Scientology group and offer a "token" restitution. That meant performing community service and following a rehabilitation course, called A to E, for penitents seeking to get back into the church's good graces; it includes repaying debts, taking additional courses, and making public declarations of error. Deborah told her parents that if they wanted to remain in contact with her they had to follow the church's procedures. Her parents, worried that they would also be cut off from their grandson, agreed to perform community service. For three months they delivered food in a Meals on Wheels program in Los Angeles. But the church wasn't satisfied. Deborah was told that if she maintained contact with her parents she would be labeled a Potential Trouble Source—a designation that would alienate her from the entire Scientology community and render her ineligible for further training. A senior official counseled her to agree to disconnect from her parents and have them formally branded SPs. "Until then, they won't turn around and recognize their responsibilities," he said.

"Okay, fine," Deborah responded. "Go ahead and declare them. Maybe it'll get better."

*Mary Benjamin says they were never parties to the suit.

The official then granted Deborah permission to begin upper-level coursework in Clearwater.

In August 2006, a formal notice on yellow parchment, called a "goldenrod," was posted at the Celebrity Centre declaring Deborah's parents Suppressive Persons, explaining that they had withdrawn the money they had placed on deposit for future coursework and that they had associated with "squirrels"—that is, they received unauthorized Scientology counseling. A month later, Mary Benjamin sent her daughter a letter. "We tried to do what you asked, Deborah. We worked the whole months of July & Aug. on A-E." They gave the church back the $2,500 for the courses that they never intended to take. After all that, she continued, a church adjudicator had told them to hand out three hundred copies of L. Ron Hubbard's booklet "The Way to Happiness" to libraries and to document each exchange with photographs. Her parents had had enough. "If this can't be resolved, we will have to say Good-Bye to you & James will lose his Grand-Parents," her mother wrote. "This is ridiculous."

In April 2007, Deborah received a letter from the lawyer who represented her parents, threatening a lawsuit for the right to visit their grandson. Deborah had to hire an attorney. Eventually, the church relented. Deborah was summoned to the Celebrity Centre and shown a statement rescinding the decision, although she wasn't allowed to have a copy of it.

WHILE HE WAS RESEARCHING on the Internet, Haggis came upon a series of articles that had run in the *St. Petersburg Times** beginning in June 2009, titled "The Truth Rundown." The paper has maintained a special focus on Scientology, since the church maintains such a commanding presence in Clearwater, which is adjacent to St. Petersburg. Although the paper and the church have frequently been at odds, the only interview that David Miscavige has ever given to a newspaper resulted in a rather flattering profile in the *Times* in 1998. (Since then, Miscavige has not spoken to the press at all.)

In the series, Haggis learned for the first time that several of the top managers of the church had quietly defected—including Marty Rathbun. For several years, the word in the Scientology community was

*Now called the *Tampa Bay Times*.

that Rathbun had died of cancer. Mike Rinder, the chief spokesperson, and Tom De Vocht, the former landlord of all the church properties in Clearwater, were also speaking out about the abuses that were taking place inside the top tier of management—mainly at the hands of the church leader. Amy Scobee, who had overseen the Celebrity Centre in Los Angeles, pointed out that the reason no one outside of the executive circles knew of the abuse, even other Scientologists like Haggis, was that people were terrified of Miscavige—and not just physically. Their greatest fear was expulsion. "You don't have any money. You don't have job experience. You don't have anything. And he could put you on the streets and ruin you."

Tommy Davis had produced nine senior church executives who told the *Times* that the abuse had never taken place. Dan Sherman, the church's official Hubbard biographer and Miscavige's speechwriter, recounted a scene in which he observed Miscavige talking to an injured sparrow. "It was immensely tender," Sherman told the reporters.

Much of the abuse being alleged had taken place at Gold Base. Haggis had visited the place only once, in the early 1980s, when its existence was still a closely held secret. That was when he was preparing to direct the Scientology commercial that was ultimately rejected. At first glance, it seemed like a spa, beautiful and restful; but he had been put off by the uniforms, the security, and the militarized feel of the place.

"At the top of the church, people were whacking folks about like Laurel and Hardy," Haggis said. He was embarrassed to admit that he had never even asked himself where Rathbun and Rinder had gone. He decided to call Rathbun, who was now living on Galveston Bay in South Texas. Although the two men had never met, they were well known to each other. After being one of the most powerful figures in Scientology, Rathbun was scraping together a living by freelancing stories to local newspapers and selling beer at a ballpark. He figured that South Texas was about as far from Los Angeles and Clearwater as he could hope to get. Haggis was floored when he learned that Rathbun had had to escape. He was also surprised to learn that other friends, such as Jim Logan, the man who brought him into the church so long ago on the street corner in Ontario, had also fled or been declared Suppressive Persons. One of Haggis's closest friends in the church hierarchy, Bill Dendiu, told Haggis that he had escaped from Gold Base by driving a car—actually, an Alfa Romeo convertible that Haggis had sold him—through the fence. He still had scars on his forehead to show for that.

"What kind of organization are we involved in where people just disappear?" Haggis wondered.

He also came across a number of anti-Scientology websites, including Exscientologykids.com, which was created by Jenna Miscavige Hill, the leader's niece, who joined the Sea Org when she was twelve. For her and many others, formal education had stopped when they entered the organization, leaving them ill prepared for life outside the church. Jenna says that for much of her early life, she was kept in a camp with other Sea Org children and little adult supervision. They rarely saw their parents. "We ran ourselves completely," she recalled.

For several years, Haggis had been working with a charity he established to set up schools in Haiti. These stories reminded him of the child slaves he had encountered in that country. "They were ten, twelve years old, signing billion-year contracts—and their parents go along with this!" he said of the Sea Org children. "And they work morning, noon and night. . . . Scrubbing pots, manual labor—that so deeply touched me. My God, it horrified me!"

AFTER TOM CRUISE'S BEHAVIOR on *Oprah* and the *Today* show, Sumner Redstone, the chairman of Viacom, which owns Paramount Studios, chose not to renew Cruise's deal. "He turned off all women," Redstone explained. "He was embarrassing the studio. And he was costing us a lot of money." Cruise and his longtime producing partner, Paula Wagner, worked out a deal with MGM to resurrect the struggling United Artists studio. Soon after that, Wagner approached Haggis, offering him a very generous deal. He wrote one script for them, a big-budget children's movie, but the studio was so financially pressed that it couldn't afford to produce it.

In January 2008, just as it seemed that the derision that was directed at Cruise was about to die down, a video was posted on the Internet. It was a taped interview with the star that preceded his acceptance of the Freedom Medal of Valor four years earlier. Wearing a black turtleneck, with the theme music from *Mission: Impossible* playing in the background, Cruise spoke to Scientologists in language they understood. "Being a Scientologist, you can look at someone and know absolutely that you can help them," Cruise said. "So for me it really is KSW, and it's something that I don't mince words with that—with anything!—but that policy with me has really gone—*phist!*" He made a vigorous gesture. "Boy! There's a time I went through when I said, you know what, when I read it I just went *pooh!* That's it! That's exactly it!"

The video was placed on YouTube and viewed by millions who had no idea what he was talking about. Cruise's urgency came off as the ravings of a wild-eyed fanatic, but to Scientologists it was a sermon they had heard many times. "KSW" refers to a policy letter that Hubbard wrote in 1965 titled "Keeping Scientology Working." In the letter Hubbard reprimanded his followers for straying from the narrow path he had laid out for them. "When somebody enrols [*sic*], consider he or she has joined up for the duration of the universe—never permit an 'open-minded' approach," Hubbard writes. "If they're aboard, they're here on the same terms as the rest of us—win or die in the attempt." Hubbard concludes: "The whole agonized future of this planet, every Man, Woman and Child on it, and your own destiny for the next endless trillions of years depend on what you do here and now with and in Scientology."

The church instantly began taking down the video from the Internet, threatening lawsuits because of copyright violations. A loose coalition of Internet hackers who called themselves Anonymous seized on the issue. "We were a bunch of kids who didn't care about anything," Gregg Housh, a computer-repair technician in Boston who acts as an unofficial spokesperson for the group, recalled. Until then, they had never protested anything, but they considered the Internet their turf and were offended that the church would attempt to control what they watched. In truth, they knew little about Scientology, but the more they learned, the more aroused they became.

"We shall proceed to expel you from the Internet and systematically dismantle the Church of Scientology in its present form," Anonymous declared in a creepy video of its own. "We are anonymous. We are legion. We do not forgive. We do not forget. Expect us." Some members of the Anonymous coalition waged denial-of-service attacks on church computers, shutting down their websites for an extended period. On February 10, 2008, Anonymous organized protests in front of Scientology churches and missions in a hundred cities across the world. Many of the demonstrators were wearing what has now become the signature of the Anonymous movement—the Guy Fawkes mask, taken from the film *V for Vendetta*.

At the center of the controversy was the beleaguered Tom Cruise. An unflattering, unauthorized biography by the British writer Andrew Morton was published days after the YouTube video of Cruise appeared, creating a new round of headlines—"Cruise Out of Control," "Explosive Claims on Cruise Baby," "German Historian Likens Cruise Speech to Goebbels"—that were intensely personal and insulting. Questions of his religion, his sexual orientation, his relationship with his wife, even the paternity of his daughter were laid out like a banquet for public consumption. Several top executives at United Artists, including Cruise's partner, Paula Wagner, decided to leave.

Haggis was in his office in Santa Monica when he got a call from Cruise. He hadn't heard a word from him since writing the apology for his wisecrack to Spielberg. Haggis still had his deal at United Artists, which Cruise was running. Now the star had a favor to ask. He wanted to gather a group of top Scientologists in Hollywood—Kirstie Alley, Anne Archer, and Haggis—to go on *Oprah* or *Larry King Live* to denounce the attacks on Cruise as religious persecution. Haggis told Cruise that was a terrible idea. He said that Cruise should stop trying to be a mouthpiece for the church and go back to doing what he does best—being a movie star. People love him for that, not for having the answers to all of life's problems. He also advised the star to have a sense of humor about himself—something that is often lacking in Scientology. Instead of constantly going on the attack, he might simply say, "Yeah, I get that it sounds crazy, but it works for me."*

Cruise didn't want to hear what Haggis had to say at the time, but soon after this conversation, he took a wildly comic turn in the Ben Stiller film *Tropic Thunder,* playing a profane studio executive who reminded a number of Hollywood insiders of Sumner Redstone. He also went back on the *Today* show for another interview with Matt Lauer. This time, he was chastened and introspective. "I came across as arrogant," he admitted, when reflecting on their previous interview three years earlier. "That's not who I am. That's not the person I am. . . . I'm here to entertain people. That's who I am and what I want

---

*Cruise's attorney, Bertram Fields, denies this took place: "Mr. Cruise has never asked Mr. Haggis or anyone else to denounce media attacks on Mr. Cruise on the *Larry King* show or anywhere else or to do anything like that."

to do." Outside the windows of the studio, a crowd of people in the plaza of Rockefeller Center waved and blew kisses.

HAGGIS WAS CASTING *The Next Three Days* in the summer of 2009, and he asked Jason Beghe to read for the part of a detective. Beghe's best-known film role was as the love interest for Demi Moore in *G.I. Jane*. In the late nineties, when Haggis had worked with the gravel-voiced actor on a CBS series, *Family Law*, Beghe had been an occasional front man for Scientology. He had come to the church, like so many others, through the Beverly Hills Playhouse. In old promotional materials for the church, Beghe is quoted as saying that Scientology is "a rocket ride to spiritual freedom." He says that Miscavige once called him "the poster boy for Scientology."

"I just want you to know I'm no longer in Scientology," Beghe told

Paul Haggis on the set of *The Next Three Days,* in a Pittsburgh, Pennsylvania, train yard

Haggis when he called. "Actually, I'm one of its most outspoken critics. The church would be very unhappy if you hire me."

"Nobody tells me who I cast," Haggis responded, but he decided to look at the lengthy video Beghe had posted on the Internet, in which he denounces the church as "destructive and a rip-off." Haggis thought the actor had gone over the edge, but he asked if they could talk.

The two men met at Patrick's Roadhouse, a pleasantly shabby coffee shop on the Pacific Coast Highway. Beghe was calmer than he had been in the video, which he now called "a snapshot of me having been out only three months." He could see that Haggis was troubled. Even though Beghe had renounced the church, he continued to use Scientology when dealing with former members. In his several meetings with Haggis, he employed techniques based on Hubbard's Ethics Conditions. These range from Confusion at the bottom and ascend through Treason, Enemy, Doubt, Liability, Emergency, and so on, up to Power. Each of the conditions has a specific set of steps to follow in order to advance to a higher state. Assuming that Haggis was in the condition of Doubt, Beghe knew that the proper formula required him to provide information.

He told Haggis that in the late nineties he began having emotional problems. The church prescribed more auditing and coursework. In retrospect, Beghe felt that it had done no good. "I was paying money for them to fuck me up," he said, estimating that he had spent as much as $600,000 in the process, and nearly $1 million in his thirteen-year Scientology career. When he finally decided to leave the church, he told Tommy Davis that the church was in a condition of Liability to him. Ordinarily, when a Scientologist does something wrong, especially something that might damage the image of the organization, he has to make amends, often in the form of a substantial contribution. But now the situation was reversed, Beghe maintained. He proposed that the church buy some property and lease it to him at a negligible rate. "You guys don't have any policies to make up the damage, so I'm doing this for your own good—and for mine," he explained to Davis and others. "Because I don't have a policy of taking it in the ass."*

While talking to Haggis, Beghe was reluctant to use the word "brainwashing"—"whatever the fuck that is"—but he did say that somehow his mind had been taken over. "You have all these thoughts,

---

*The church characterizes this as an attempt at extortion.

all these ways of looking at things, that are L. Ron Hubbard's," he explained. "You think you're becoming more you, but within that is an implanted thing, which is You the Scientologist."

Haggis was disturbed by Beghe's account of what had happened after he left the church. He claimed that none of his Scientology friends would talk to him, his son had been kicked out of school, he was being followed by private investigators and threatened with lawsuits. Perhaps because Haggis had never been as much of a true believer as some members, he didn't nurse the same sense of betrayal. "I didn't feel that some worm had buried itself in my ear, and if you plucked it out you would find L. Ron Hubbard and his thought," he said. But he did feel that he had been cautioned.

"TOMMY," HAGGIS'S LETTER of August 19, 2009, abruptly begins. "As you know, for ten months now I have been writing to ask you to make a public statement denouncing the actions of the Church of Scientology of San Diego. Their public sponsorship of Proposition 8, which succeeded in taking away the civil rights of gay and lesbian citizens of California—rights that were granted them by the Supreme Court of our state—is a stain on the integrity of our organization and a stain on us personally. Our public association with that hate-filled legislation shames us."

The tone of the letter is both aggrieved and outraged, mixing Haggis's personal experiences with the results of his one-man investigation into the church. He mentions how Katy Haggis's friends had turned against her when she came out to them as a lesbian. Katy had told him that another friend of hers had applied to be the assistant for Jenna and Bodhi Elfman, the Scientology acting couple. Lauren Haigney, Tom Cruise's niece in the Sea Org, had been assigned to vet the applicants. Katy says that Lauren wrote up a report saying that Katy's friend was known to hang out with lesbians. The friend did not get the job, Katy said.*

Haggis also recounted the scene at John Travolta and Kelly Preston's house, when another Scientologist made the slur about the gay

*The church forwarded a letter to me from Katy Haggis's friend in which she denies losing a job because of their friendship and asserting that the church is welcoming to everyone, regardless of their sexual orientation. The friend, whose parents are both employed by the church, did not respond to a request to talk further.

waiter. "I admire John and Kelly for many reasons; one of them is the way they handled that," Haggis stated. "You and I both know there has been a hidden anti-gay sentiment in the church for a long time. I have been shocked on too many occasions to hear Scientologists make derogatory remarks about gay people, and then quote LRH in their defense." He said that the church's decision not to denounce the bigots who supported Proposition 8 was cowardly. "Silence is consent, Tommy. I refuse to consent."

He referenced Davis's interview on CNN. "I saw you deny the church's policy of disconnection. You said straight-out there was no such policy, that it did not exist," he wrote. "I was shocked. We all know this policy exists. I didn't have to search for verification. I didn't have to look any further than my own home." He reminded Davis of Deborah's experience with her parents. "Although it caused her terrible personal pain, my wife broke off all contact with them. . . . That's not ancient history, Tommy. It was a year ago." He added: "To see you lie so easily, I am afraid to ask myself: what else are you lying about?"

Then, he said, he had read the series of articles in the *St. Petersburg Times*. "They left me dumbstruck and horrified. These were not the claims made by 'outsiders' looking to dig up dirt against us. These accusations were made by top international executives who had devoted most of their lives to the church. Say what you will about them now, these were staunch defenders of the church, including Mike Rinder, the church's official spokesman for 20 years!

"Tommy, if only a fraction of these accusations are true, we are talking about serious, indefensible human and civil rights violations."

He continued:

And when I pictured you assuring me that it is all lies, that this is nothing but an unfounded and vicious attack by a group of disgruntled employees, I am afraid that I saw the same face that looked in the camera and denied the policy of disconnection. I heard the same voice that professed outrage at our support of Proposition 8, who promised to correct it, and did nothing.

I was left feeling outraged, and frankly, more than a little stupid.

Haggis was especially disturbed by the way the church's *Freedom* magazine had responded to the newspaper's revelations. It included a lengthy annotated transcript of conversations that had taken place prior to the publication of the series between the *Times* reporters, Joe Childs and Thomas C. Tobin, and representatives of the church, including Tommy Davis and Jessica Feshbach, the two international spokespersons for the church. In the *Freedom* account, the names of the defectors were never actually stated, perhaps to shield Scientologists from the shock of seeing familiar figures such as Marty Rathbun and Amy Scobee publicly denouncing the organization and its leader. Rathbun was called "Kingpin" and Amy Scobee "The Adulteress." At one point in the conversation, Davis had told reporters that Scobee had been expelled from the church because she had had an affair. The reporters responded that she had denied any sexual contact outside her marriage. "That's a lie," Davis told them. Feshbach, who carried a stack of documents, then said, "She has a written admission [of] each one of her instances of extramarital indiscretions. . . . I believe there were five."

When Haggis read this, he immediately assumed that the church had gotten its information from auditing sessions.* He was inflamed. "A priest would go to jail before revealing secrets from the confessional, no matter what the cost to himself or his church," he wrote. "You took Amy Scobee's most intimate admissions about her sexual life and passed them on to the press and then smeared them all over the pages of your newsletter! . . . This is the woman who joined the Sea Org at 16! She ran the entire celebrity center network, and was a loyal senior executive of the church for what, 20 years?" He added that he was aware that the church might do the same to him. "Well, luckily, I have never held myself up to be anyone's role model."

Haggis concluded:

The great majority of Scientologists I know are good people who are genuinely interested in improving conditions on this planet and helping others. I have to believe that if they knew what I now know, they too would be horrified. But I know how easy it was for me to defend our organization and dismiss our critics, without ever truly looking at what was being said; I did it for thirty-five years. . . . I am

---

*Tommy Davis gave me an affidavit, signed by Scobee, in which she admits to having liaisons. Scobee told me there were only two incidents, both of which involved a kiss and nothing more. She says she did not write the affidavit; she says she only signed it in the hope of leaving the church on good terms so that she could stay in touch with relatives. The church maintains that it does not use confidential information derived from auditing sessions.

324 | GOING CLEAR

only ashamed that I waited this many months to act. I hereby resign my membership in the Church of Scientology.

AT THE TIME Haggis was doing his investigation, the FBI was also looking into Scientology. In December 2009, Tricia Whitehill, a special agent from the Los Angeles office, flew to Florida to interview former members of the church at the bureau's office in downtown Clearwater, which happens to be directly across the street from Scientology's spiritual headquarters. Tom De Vocht, who spoke to Whitehill then, got the impression that the investigation had been going on for quite a while. He says that Whitehill confided that she hadn't told the local agents what the investigation was about, in case the office had been infiltrated. Amy Scobee also spoke to Whitehill for two full days, mainly about the abuse she had witnessed.

Whitehill and Valerie Venegas, the lead agent on the case, also interviewed former Sea Org members in California. One was Gary Morehead, who had developed the blow drill. He explained how his security team would use emotional and psychological pressure to bring escapees back; but failing that, physical force has been used.*

Whitehill and Venegas worked on a special task force devoted to human trafficking. The laws regarding trafficking were built largely around forced prostitution, but they also pertain to slave labor. Under federal law, slavery is defined, in part, by the use of coercion, torture, starvation, imprisonment, threats, and psychological abuse. The California Penal Code lists several indicators that someone may be a victim of human trafficking: signs of trauma or fatigue; being afraid or unable to talk because of censorship or security measures that prevent communication with others; working in one place without the freedom to move about; owing a debt to one's employer; and not having control over identification documents. Those conditions resemble the accounts of many former Sea Org members who lived at Gold Base. If proven, those allegations would still be difficult to prosecute given the religious status of Scientology.

Marc Headley escaped from Gold Base in 2005; he says this was after being beaten by Miscavige.† His defection was especially painful

---

*The church denies that blow drills exist.

†According to Tommy Davis, "Mr. Miscavige has never physically assaulted Marc Headley or anyone else."

for the church, because Marc says he was the first person Tom Cruise audited. In Scientology, the auditor bears a significant responsibility for the progress of his subject. "If you audit somebody and that person leaves the organization, there's only one person whose fault that is—the auditor," Headley explained. Later that year, Marc's wife, Claire, also escaped. In 2009, they sued the church, claiming that the working conditions at Gold Base violated labor and human-trafficking laws. The church responded that the Headleys were ministers who had voluntarily submitted to the rigors of their calling, and that the First Amendment protected Scientology's religious practices. The court agreed with this argument and dismissed the Headleys' complaints, awarding the church forty thousand dollars in litigation costs.

In April 2010, John Brousseau also fled. He, too, represented a dangerous liability to the church. He had been a Sea Org member for decades; he had worked personally for Hubbard; and he knew Miscavige intimately. But what was of most concern to the church was the fact that he had worked on or overseen numerous special projects for Tom Cruise. None of these unique and costly gifts come anywhere close to the millions of dollars that the star has donated to the church over the years, but they do call into question the private benefit afforded a single individual by a tax-exempt religious organization.

Brousseau knew the lengths to which the church would go in order to find him and bring him back. He drove to Carson City, Nevada, and bought a netbook computer at a Walmart, along with an air card, then set up an encrypted e-mail account. He sent a note to Rathbun, saying, "I just left and I'm freaked out, and I've got nowhere to go." Rathbun invited him to South Texas. Expecting that the church would have hired private detectives to stake out key intersections on the interstate highways, Brousseau stuck to county roads. It took him three days to make it to Texas. He was driving a black Ford Excursion, much like the one that he had fashioned into a limousine for Cruise.

Brousseau and Rathbun met at a Chili's restaurant near Corpus Christi. They decided to hide Brousseau's truck at a friend's house. Rathbun then checked Brousseau into a Best Western motel under a different name. Despite the precautions, two days later, at five thirty in the morning, when Brousseau went out on the balcony to smoke, he heard a door open nearby and footsteps walking toward him. It was Tommy Davis and three other church members.

"Hey, J.B.," Davis said. "You got yourself in some shit."

Brousseau turned and walked away.

"Where are you going?" Davis demanded.

Brousseau said he was going to get some coffee. Davis and the Scientology delegation followed behind him. The Circle K across the street wasn't open yet, so Brousseau went into the motel lobby. He told the receptionist, "Call the police. These guys are stalking me."

She laughed in disbelief.

"We've got a room here, too," Davis said.

Brousseau said he needed to go to the bathroom. As soon as he got back to his room he bolted the door and called Rathbun. "Marty, they came for me," he said.

After calling 911, Rathbun jumped in his truck to go to the motel, but four cars filled with Scientologists blocked his way. He says they were led by Michael Doven, Cruise's former personal assistant.

Brousseau waited in his room until the police officers arrived. Davis and the others left empty-handed.*

Brousseau talked to Whitehill and Venegas at the FBI. He was under the impression that the federal agents were considering a raid on Gold Base. Brousseau says he was shown high-resolution photos of the base taken from a drone aircraft. He says he was told that they had even gathered the tail numbers on Tom Cruise's aircraft, in case Miscavige tried to escape. Brousseau and others claim to have discouraged the idea, saying that such a raid would turn Miscavige into a martyr; and, in any case, no one would testify against him. Rinder told the agents it would be a waste of time, because everyone would tell them their lives are all "seashells and butterflies." The investigation was reportedly dropped.†

AFTER SENDING COPIES of his resignation letter to his closest friends in Scientology, Haggis wasn't surprised when he came home from work

*Davis later said that he had never followed a Sea Org member who had blown and had only gone to see Brousseau because he was "a very good friend of mine" (Deposition of Thomas Davis, *Marc Headley vs. Church of Scientology International*, and *Claire Headley vs. Church of Scientology International*, US District Court, Central District of California, July 2, 2010).
†Valerie Venegas told one of her sources that higher-up officials had spiked it; later, she blamed me, because I had uncovered the probe and had called to verify it with the agents (Tony Ortega, "FBI Investigation of Scientology: Already Over before We Even Heard of It," *Village Voice Blogs*, Mar. 19, 2012).

a few days later to find nine or ten of them standing in his front yard. "I can't imagine why you're here," he joked, but he invited them to sit on the back porch and talk. Anne Archer and her husband, Terry Jastrow, an Emmy-winning producer for ABC Sports, were there. Mark Isham, a composer who worked with Haggis for years, came with his wife, Donna. Sky Dayton, the founder of EarthLink and Boingo Wireless, joined them, along with several other friends and a representative of the church that Haggis didn't know. His friends could have served as an advertisement for Scientology—they were wealthy high achievers with solid marriages who exuded a sense of spiritual well-being.

Scientologists are trained to believe in their persuasive powers and the need to keep a positive frame of mind. But the mood on Haggis's porch was downbeat and his friends' questions were full of reproach.

"Do you have any idea that this might damage a lot of wonderful Scientologists?" Jastrow asked. "It's such a betrayal of our group."

Haggis responded that he didn't mean to be critical of Scientology. "I love Scientology," he said. Everyone knew about Haggis's financial support of the church and the occasions when he had spoken out in its defense. He reminded his friends that he had been with them at the Portland Crusade, when he had been drafted to write speeches.

Archer had a particular reason to feel aggrieved: Haggis's letter had called her son a liar. She could understand the pain and anger Haggis felt over the treatment of his own gay daughters, but she didn't think that was relevant. In her opinion, homosexuality is not the church's issue. She had personally introduced gay friends to Scientology.

Isham was especially frustrated. He felt that they weren't breaking through to Haggis. Of all the friends present, Isham was the closest to Haggis. They had a common artistic sensibility that made it easy to work together. Isham had won an Emmy for the theme music he composed for Haggis's 1996 television series, *EZ Streets*. He had scored *Crash* and Haggis's last movie, *The Valley of Elah*. Soon he was supposed to start work on *The Next Three Days*. Now both their friendship and their professional relationship were at risk.

Isham had been analyzing the discussion from a Scientological perspective. In his view, Haggis's emotional state on the Tone Scale at that moment was a 1.1, Covertly Hostile. By adopting a tone just above it—Anger—he hoped to blast Haggis out of the psychic place where he seemed to be lodged. Isham made what he calls an intellectual decision to be angry.

"Paul, I'm pissed off," he told Haggis. "There are better ways to do this. If you have a complaint, there's a complaint line." Anyone who genuinely wanted to change Scientology should stay within the organization, Isham argued, not quit. All of his friends believed that if he wanted to change Scientology, he should do it from within. They wanted him to recant and return to the fold or else withdraw his letter and walk away without making a fuss.

Haggis listened patiently. A fundamental tenet of Scientology is that differing points of view must be fully heard and acknowledged. But when his friends finished, they were still red-faced and angry. Haggis suggested that as good Scientologists, they should at least examine the evidence. He referred them to the *St. Petersburg Times* articles that had so shaken him, and to certain websites written by former members. He explained that his quarrel was with the management and the culture of the church, not with Scientology itself. By copying them on his resignation letter, he had hoped that they would be as horrified as he by the practices that were going on in the name of Scientology. Instead, he realized, they were mainly appalled by his actions in calling the management of the church to account.

Haggis's friends came away from the meeting with mixed feelings— "no clearer than when we went in," Archer felt. What wasn't said in this meeting was that this would be the last time any of them would ever speak to Haggis. Isham did consider Haggis's plea to look at the websites or the articles in the *St. Petersburg Times*, but he decided "it was like reading *Mein Kampf* if you wanted to know something about the Jewish religion."

After that first meeting with friends on his back porch, Haggis had several lengthy encounters with Tommy Davis and other representatives of the church. They showed up at his office in Santa Monica—a low-slung brick building on Broadway, covered in graffiti, like a gang headquarters. The officials brought thick files to discredit people they heard or assumed he had been talking to. This was August 2009; shooting for *The Next Three Days* in Pittsburgh was going to start within days, and the office desperately needed Haggis's attention. His producing partner, Michael Nozik, who is not a Scientologist, was frustrated. Haggis was spending hours, day after day, dealing with Scientology delegations. He resorted to getting members of his staff to walk him out to his car because he knew that Scientology executives would be waiting for him, and he wanted to give the impression he was too busy to speak—which he was. But then he would give up and let them into the office for another lengthy confrontation.

During one of these meetings, Davis showed Haggis a policy letter that Hubbard had written, listing the acts for which one could be declared a Suppressive Person. Haggis had stepped over the line on four of them.

"Tommy, you are absolutely right, I did all those things," Haggis responded. "If you want to call me that, that's what I am."

"We can still put this genie back in the bottle," Tommy assured him, but it would mean that Haggis would withdraw the letter and then resign quietly.

Although Haggis listened, he didn't change his mind. It seemed to him that the Scientology officials became more "livid and irrational" the longer they talked. For instance, Davis and the other church officials insisted that Miscavige had not beaten his employees; his accusers, they said, had committed the violence. "Whoa, whoa, whoa," Haggis responded, "okay, let's say that's true, Miscavige never touched anyone. I'm sorry, but if someone in my organization were going around beating people, I'd know about it! You think I'd put up with it? And I'm not that good a person." Haggis noted that if the rumors about Miscavige's violent temper were true, it just proved that even the greatest leaders are fallible. "Look at Martin Luther King, Jr.," he said, referring to one of his heroes. "If you look at his personal life, it's been said he has a few problems in that area."

"How dare you compare Dave Miscavige with Martin Luther King!" one of the officials shouted.

Haggis was aghast. "They thought that comparing Miscavige to Martin Luther King was debasing his character," he said. "If they were trying to convince me that Scientology was not a cult, they did a very poor job of it."*

Copies of Haggis's e-mail resignation letter were forwarded to various members of the church, although few outside of church circles knew about it. By October, the letter had found its way to Marty Rathbun. He had become an informal spokesperson for Scientology defectors who, like him, believed that the church had broken away from Hubbard's original teachings. He called Haggis, who was shooting in Pittsburgh, and asked if he could publish the letter on his blog. "You're

---

*Tommy Davis says that Martin Luther King, Jr.'s name never came up.

a journalist, you don't need my permission," Haggis said, although he did ask him to excise the portion of the letter that dealt with his dinner with John Travolta and Kelly Preston and the part about his daughter Katy's homosexuality.

Haggis didn't think about the consequences of his decision. He thought it would show up on a couple of websites. He was a writer, not a movie star. But Rathbun got fifty-five thousand hits on his blog that afternoon.

The next morning, the story was in newspapers around the world. Haggis got a call from Tommy Davis. "Paul, what the hell!"

11

Tommy

When I first contacted Davis in April 2010, asking for his cooperation on a profile I was writing about Haggis for *The New Yorker*, he expressed a reluctance to talk, saying that he had already spent a month responding to similar queries. "It made little difference," he said. "The last thing I'm interested in is dredging all this up again." He kept putting me off, saying that he was too busy to get together, although he promised that we would meet when he was more available. "I want our time to be undistracted," he explained in an e-mail. "We should plan on spending at least a full day together as there is a lot I would want to show you." We finally arranged to meet on Memorial Day weekend.

I flew to Los Angeles and spent much of that weekend waiting for him to call. On Sunday at three o'clock, Davis appeared at my hotel, with Jessica Feshbach. We sat at a table on the patio. Davis has his mother's sleepy eyes. His thick black hair was combed forward, with a lock falling boyishly onto his forehead. He wore a wheat-colored suit with a blue shirt that opened onto a chest that seemed, among the sun-worshippers at the pool, strikingly pallid. Feshbach, a slender, attractive woman, anxiously twirled her hair.

Davis now told me that he was "not willing to participate in, or contribute to, an article about Scientology through the lens of Paul Haggis." I had come to Los Angeles specifically to talk to him, at a time he had chosen. I wondered aloud if he had been told not to talk to me. He said no.

"Maybe Paul shouldn't have posted the letter on the Internet," Feshbach interjected. "There are all sorts of shoulda woulda coulda." She said that she had just spoken to Mark Isham, the composer, whom I had interviewed. "He talked to you about what are supposed to be our confidential scriptures." That I would ask about the church's secret doctrines was offensive, she said. "It's a two-way street happening," she concluded.*

"Everything I have to say about Paul, I've already said," Davis declared. He agreed to respond to fact-checking queries, however.

THE GARDEN BEHIND Anne Archer and Terry Jastrow's home in the Brentwood neighborhood of Los Angeles is a peaceful retreat, filled with olive trees and hummingbirds. A fountain gurgles beside the swimming pool. Jastrow was recounting his first meeting with Archer, in Milton Katselas's class. His friend David Ladd, son of the Hollywood legend Alan Ladd, had invited him to visit. "I saw this girl sitting next to Milton," Jastrow recalled. "I said, 'Who's that?' "

Archer smiled. There was a cool wind blowing in from the Pacific, and she drew a shawl around her. "We were friends for about a year and a half before we had our first date," she said. They were married in 1978.

"Our relationship really works," Jastrow said. "We attribute that essentially a hundred percent to applying Scientology."

The two spoke of the techniques that had helped them, such as never being critical of the other and never interrupting.

Scientology "isn't a 'creed,' " Archer said. "These are basic natural laws of life." She described L. Ron Hubbard as "an engineer, not a faith healer," who had codified human emotional states, in order to guide

*In my meeting with Isham, he had asserted that Scientology is not a "faith-based religion." Leaving aside the question of what religion is without faith, I pointed out that in Scientology's upper levels, there was a cosmology that would have to be accepted on faith. Isham responded that he wasn't going to discuss the details of OT III, nor had I asked him to. "You understand the only reason it's confidential is because in the wrong hands it can hurt people," he told me, evidently referring to Hubbard's warning that those who are not spiritually prepared to receive the information would die, of pneumonia.

the adept to higher levels of existence—"to help a guy rise up the Tone Scale and feel a zest and a love for life."

Jastrow had been an acolyte in an Episcopal church when he was studying at the University of Houston, but doubts overwhelmed him. "I walked out in the middle of communion," he said. "I was an atheist for ten years. That was the condition I was in when I started at the Beverly Hills Playhouse." He had never heard of Scientology at the time.

Archer said that the controversy that continually surrounds the church hadn't touched her. "It's not that I'm not aware of it." She added that Scientology is growing despite the public criticism. "It's in a hundred and sixty-five countries."

"Translated into fifty languages!" Jastrow interjected. "It's the fastest-growing religion." In his opinion, "Scientologists do more good things for more people in more places around the world than any other organization ever." He added, "When you study historical perspective of new faiths, they've all been—"

"Attacked," said Archer. "Look at what happened to the—"

"The Christians!" Jastrow said simultaneously. "Think of the Mormons and the Christian Scientists."

They talked about the church's focus on celebrities. "Hubbard recognized that if you really want to inspire a culture to have peace and greatness and harmony among men, you need to respect and help the artist to prosper and flourish," Archer said. "And if he's particularly well known he needs a place where he can be comfortable. So, Celebrity Centres provide that." She blamed the press for concentrating too much on Scientology celebrities. Journalists, she said, "don't write about the hundreds of thousands of other Scientologists."

"Millions!"

"*Millions* of other Scientologists. They only write about four friggin' people!"

Jastrow suggested that Scientology's critics often had a vested interest. He pointed to psychiatrists, psychologists, doctors, drug makers, pharmacies—"all those people who make a living and profit and pay their mortgages and pay their college educations and buy their cars, et cetera, et cetera, based on people not being well."

"Who advertise in the newspapers and on television, more than any other advertisers," Archer added.

"But this is a collateral issue, darling, in terms of what I'm talking about," Jastrow continued. "For the first time in America's experience with war, there are more mental illnesses from Iraq and Afghanistan than physical illnesses," he said, citing a recent article in *USA Today*. "So mental illnesses become a big business." Drugs merely mask mental distress, he said, whereas "Scientology will solve the source of the problem." The medical and pharmaceutical industries are "prime funders and sponsors of the media," he said, and therefore might exert "influence on people telling the whole and true story about Scientology just because of the profit motive." He said that only Scientology could help mankind right itself. "What else is there that we can hang our hopes on?"

"That's improving civilization," Archer added.

"Is there some other religion on the horizon that's going to help mankind?" Jastrow asked. "Just tell me where. If not Scientology, where?"

ANNE ARCHER BEGAN STUDYING with Katselas in 1974, two years after her son Tommy Davis was born. She was the exceptionally beautiful daughter of two successful actors. Her father, John Archer, was best known during the 1930s and 1940s as the voice introducing the radio drama *The Shadow*. ("Who knows what evil lurks in the hearts of men? The Shadow knows," he said at the beginning of the program.) He went on to appear in more than fifty films. Her mother, Marjorie Lord, played Danny Thomas's wife on the popular television show *Make Room for Daddy*. With such a bloodline, it might be expected that Archer would be aiming toward stardom, but when she entered the Beverly Hills Playhouse she was coming off a television series (*Bob & Carol & Ted & Alice*) that she didn't respect and that had been canceled after a single season. She was a young mother in a dissolving marriage and an actor with diminishing career prospects.

Katselas had a transformative effect. Like so many others, Archer was magnetized by this ebullient Greek, with his magnificent beard and his badgering, teasing, encouraging, and infuriating personality. He was one of the most inspiring people Archer had ever met. Where had he acquired such wisdom? Some of the other students told her that Katselas was a Scientologist, so she decided to try it out. She began going two or three times a week to the Celebrity Centre to take the Life Repair Program. "I remember walking out of the building and walking down the street toward my car, and I felt like my feet were not touching the ground. I said to myself, 'My God, this is the happiest I've ever been in my entire life. I've finally found something that works!' " She added, "Life didn't seem so hard anymore. I was back in the driver's seat."

When Tommy was old enough, Archer would bring him to the Playhouse while she was taking lessons. He would wander around the theater, venturing into the light booth and watching his mother learning her craft. Jastrow recalled being struck by Tommy's poise even as a five-year-old child. "I am a really good dad, and he taught me how," Jastrow said. He gave the example of a visit from his own parents, who had flown out from Midland, Texas, to meet Terry's new family. After Jastrow had driven them back to the airport, Tommy said, "I notice that your dad was pretty strict with you." Jastrow agreed that his father had been very stern when he was growing up. Then Tommy continued, "I was noticing that you're pretty strict with me." Jastrow pointed to that as a defining moment in their relationship. "I realized I wanted to be his friend first," he said. "He was the senior being in that relationship."

Anne and Terry soon found their way into Scientology, but Tommy was initially raised in his mother's original faith, Christian Science. His father, William Davis, is a wealthy financier and real-estate developer who was once reported to be among the largest owners of agricultural property in California. He was also a well-known fund-raiser for Ronald Reagan and George H. W. Bush, and personally contributed an estimated $350,000 a year to Republican causes. Although Tommy grew up in an environment of money and celebrity, he impressed people with his modesty. He longed to do something to help humanity. Scientology seemed to offer a direction.

Paul Haggis met Tommy at the Celebrity Centre in 1989, when he was seventeen years old—"a sweet and bright boy." Their meeting came at a critical moment in Tommy's life. He had just broken up with his girlfriend. Archer had taken him to the Celebrity Centre for counseling, where he took a course called Personal Values and Integrity.

Tommy's presence immediately caused a stir inside the church. The president of the Celebrity Centre, Karen Hollander, fixed on the idea that Tommy should be her personal assistant. He was young, very rich, and handsome enough to be a movie star himself. He had grown up mixing with famous people. It would be a perfect fit. Whenever celebrities came in, there would be Anne Archer's son. But that required coaxing Tommy to join the Sea Org. Hollander called in the younger members of her staff to woo him. "You can either go to college and get a wog education, or you can join Sea Org and be doing the best service you could ever do for mankind—and for yourself," John Peeler, Hollander's secretary at the time, would tell him.

Although Anne and Terry say they wanted Tommy to get a college education, they knew of the efforts to recruit him and didn't stand in the way. That fall, Tommy entered Columbia University, but lasted only a single semester. Over Christmas break, he went back into Hollander's office, and when he came out, he excitedly told Peeler he had just signed the billion-year contract.

His job for Hollander was to attend to the celebrities who lounged around the president's office. Lisa Marie Presley was often there, as were Kirstie Alley, and writer-director Floyd Mutrux. John Travolta would drop by occasionally. Also in this crowd was a clique of young actors who had grown up in the church, including Giovanni Ribisi and his sister Marissa, Jenna Elfman, and Juliette Lewis. Davis would arrange for them all to go to movies together. He was charming, attractive, he had a great sense of humor, and eventually, David Miscavige began to notice. "Miscavige liked the fact that he was young and looked trendy and wore Brioni or Armani suits," Mike Rinder observed. "He had a cute BMW. It was an image that Miscavige liked."

Davis moved into Sea Org berthing in a dodgy neighborhood on Wilcox Street in West Hollywood. It was quite a step down from the luxurious life he had enjoyed until then. He was quickly introduced to some of the inner secrets of the organization. In about 1994, he was involved in an embarrassing cover-up when a well-known spokesperson for the church was captured in a video having sex with several other men. Amy Scobee says that church executives were frantic that their spokesperson would be exposed as being gay. Scobee and Karen Hollander set a briefcase with the spokesperson's auditing files in the backseat of the car that Hollander was borrowing at the time— actually, Tommy Davis's BMW—intending to take the files to Gold Base the next day for senior managers to review. Because the car was in a highly secure parking lot, they thought nothing of it. Davis returned late that night, however. He found his car and decided to take it back to the Sea Org dormitory. When he parked the car on Wilcox Street, he happened to notice the briefcase, so he locked it in the trunk and went to bed.

The next day, Scobee got a call from a sheepish Davis. He said that someone had broken into his car and stolen the briefcase out of the trunk. "When we told Tommy what was in the briefcase, he freaked," Scobee recalled. "He went around for a week, searching through Dumpsters." Finally, someone approached Davis about the reward he had offered and led him to the thief, a homeless man who was trying to sell the briefcase; the contents, which were still in it, meant nothing to him. Davis gave the man twenty dollars.* Davis was disappointed because the search forced him to miss the ceremony where John Travolta was awarded a Scientology medal.

Davis went through a period of doubt and actually considered dropping out of the Sea Org, according to Scobee, but then he recommitted and became so enthusiastic that he had the Sea Org logo—a laurel wreath with twenty-six leaves representing the stars in the Galactic Confederacy—tattooed on his arm. When Miscavige found out, he berated Davis, saying that he had violated the church's copyright.

Davis began working with Marty Rathbun during his intensive auditing of Cruise. When Rathbun was thrown in the Hole, Davis became something more than a gofer for the star. He provided a line to Cruise at a time when the actor's relationship with the church was not yet solidified, and his constant presence beside the superstar boosted the image of Scientology as a hip, insider network. Although Cruise is ten years older, the two men physically resemble each other, with long faces and strong jaws, a likeness that is enhanced by similar spiky haircuts. Their relationship evolved into a friendship, but one that reflected the immense power imbalance between them, as well as Davis's position as a deputy of the church in the service of its most precious asset. Until his association with Cruise, Davis had been called Tom, but he became Tommy to distinguish him from the star. In other ways, he became more like him—his clothes, his hair, his intensity.

At the age of nineteen, Davis married a dreamy Belgian woman, Nadine van Hootegem, who was also in the Sea Org. "I made the decision to forward the aims of Scientology," she told the ABC News program 20/20 in 1998. "I actually compare it a little bit like Mother Teresa." She added, "It's a fun activity to set men free." According to Mike Rinder, Nadine Davis became intensely involved in Tom Cruise's

*The church denies that this ever happened. Davis admits that the briefcase was lost but claims that there were no sex-related videos inside.

entourage. "Somehow dealing with Katie Holmes, she did something wrong," Rinder says. "She became a non-person." He says that Tommy was forced to divorce her.*

Soon after Cruise's troubles in 2005, Tommy Davis was sent to Clearwater to participate in the Estates Project Force. Normally, the EPF functions as a kind of boot camp for new Sea Org members. Donna Shannon was a veterinarian who had risen to OT VII before signing her billion-year contract. She was surprised to find that about half the people undergoing training were veteran Sea Org members who were being disciplined, including Davis. He seemed like a nice guy, so she was puzzled that he was subjected to the worst hazing. "He complained about being out scrubbing the Dumpster with a tooth-brush till late at night," she recalled, "then he'd be up at six to do our laundry." Sometimes Davis would be paraded in front of the other Sea Org members as his Ethics Officer shouted, "This guy is not a big shot! He's lying to you!" Only later did Shannon learn that Davis was Anne Archer's son. (As it happens, Archer was also at the Clearwater base, taking advanced courses. A teenage Sea Org member—Daniel Montalvo, the same one who guarded Cruise during his auditing sessions—was assigned to keep her in the dark and make sure that she never encountered her son.)

Shannon and Davis worked together, maintaining the grounds. "I was supposedly supervising him," Shannon said. "I was told to make him work really hard." That didn't seem to be a problem for Davis. At one point, Shannon said, he borrowed about a hundred dollars from her because he didn't have money for food.

One day, Shannon and Davis were taking the bus to a work project. Shannon asked why he was in the EPF.

"I got busted," Davis told her. "I fucked up on Tom Cruise's lines"—meaning that he had botched a project Cruise was involved in.

"So what are your plans now?" she asked.

"I just want to do my stuff and get back on post," Davis replied.

Shannon said that suddenly "it was like a veil went over his eyes, and he goes, 'I already said too much.' "

Several months later, Davis paid her back the money.†

*Davis says he and his wife divorced because of irreconcilable differences, and that "it had nothing to do with the organization."
†Davis says that he does not recall meeting Shannon, has never scrubbed a Dumpster, and has no need to borrow money.

Tommy Davis

When Davis finished the EPF, he replaced Rinder as chief spokesperson for the church, because Rinder was confined to the Hole. One of his first assignments was to deal with John Sweeney, an aggressive reporter for the BBC, who was doing a story on Scientology and had been working with Rinder until then. Davis made the mistake of admitting to Sweeney that he reported to Miscavige every day, spoiling the illusion of the leader as being unavailable and above the fray. Miscavige pulled Rinder out of the Hole and ordered him to help Davis deal with the BBC, although he added, "You're Tommy Davis's servant."

Sweeney immediately sensed that Rinder had been demoted. Rinder was "gaunt, hollow-eyed, strange with a hint of niceness." Tommy was now "the top dog, gleaming teeth, snappily suited, charming but creepily so." When Sweeney refused to accede to the church's restrictions (mainly that he agree not to use the word "cult" in his report) and began independently reporting on the accusations of defectors, he was shadowed by private investigators. A Scientology film crew showed up to document the making of the BBC documentary. Cameras were pointed at cameras. Davis appeared unannounced at Sweeney's hotel and even traveled across the country to disrupt his interviews with Scientology dissidents. Sweeney had covered wars in Afghanistan, Bosnia, and Chechnya, but he had never had such emotional and psychological pressure placed upon him. During these confrontations, Rinder trailed behind Davis, staring blankly into space as Davis goaded the reporter, inches from his face. When Sweeney suggested that Scientology is a "sadistic cult," Davis, wearing sunglasses, checked with his cameraman to see that the camcorder was running, then said, "Now listen to me for a second. You have no right to say what is and what isn't a religion. The Constitution of the United States of America guarantees one's right to practice and believe freely in this country. And the definition of religion is very clear. And it's not defined by John Sweeney. For you to repeatedly refer to my faith in those terms is so derogatory and so offensive and so bigoted. And the reason you kept repeating it is 'cause you wanted a reaction like you're getting right now. Well, buddy, you got it! Right here, right now, I'm angry! Real angry!"

Davis turned and walked away, trailed by Sweeney, who protested, "It's your turn to listen to me! I'm a British subject. . . . "

Another confrontation took place at the "Psychiatry: An Industry of Death" exhibit in Hollywood. Davis once again moved in, nose to nose with Sweeney. "You're accusing members of my religion of brainwashing!" He was referring to an earlier interview Sweeney had conducted with another Scientologist.

"No, Tommy," Sweeney responded, his voice rising, "you were not there—"

"Brainwashing is a crime," Davis said.

"Listen to me! You were not there! At the beginning! Of the interview!" Sweeney shouted in an oddly slow cadence. "You did not hear! Or record! The interview!"

"Do you understand that brainwashing is a crime?" Davis said, unfazed by Sweeney's enraged screams.

Davis's composure and his spirited defense of his church made quite a contrast with the sputtering and eventually deeply chagrined reporter, who apologized to BBC viewers on the air.

In March 2007, John Travolta's new movie, *Wild Hogs*, a comedy about two middle-aged men who decide to become bikers, was scheduled to open in Britain. Concerned that Sweeney would confront Travolta during the publicity for the film, Rinder and Davis planned to travel together to London, but on the day of departure, Davis failed to show up. Someone went to his room, but he was nowhere to be found. Rinder had to travel to London alone. He learned from Miscavige's communicator that Davis had blown. Sweeney immediately sensed that something was up and kept pestering Rinder about where Davis was. Rinder told him Davis had the flu.

As part of the film promotion, Travolta arrived at the red-carpet London premiere on a motorcycle. Sweeney was standing in the crowd in Leicester Square, well away from the star, crying out, "Are you a member of a sinister, brainwashing cult?" Travolta's fans shouted Sweeney down.

Later, Sweeney asked Rinder if it was true that Miscavige had beaten him, claiming to have an eyewitness.

"Who's the witness?" Rinder asked.

"He wishes to remain confidential because he says he is scared."

"John, that is typical of what you do," Rinder said.

"He says that David Miscavige knocked you to the ground."

"Absolute rubbish, rubbish, rubbish, not true, rubbish."

Rinder threatened to sue if Sweeney aired such allegations. When the BBC program ran, there was no mention of physical abuse. Rinder felt that he had spared the church considerable embarrassment. But, far from being grateful, Miscavige told him that Sweeney's piece should never have run at all. He ordered Rinder to report to an RPF facility in England. Rinder decided he'd had enough. He blew.

Davis called the church and returned voluntarily from Las Vegas, where he had been hiding.* He was sent to Clearwater, where he was security-checked by Jessica Feshbach. The aim of the check is to gain a confession using an E-Meter. It can function as a powerful form of thought control.

Davis and Feshbach subsequently married.

ON A RAINY MORNING in late September 2010, I finally got my meeting with Tommy Davis. The profile of Paul Haggis I had been preparing was nearing publication. Davis and Feshbach, along with four attorneys representing the church, traveled to Manhattan to meet with me; my editor, Daniel Zalewski, and David Remnick, the editor of *The New Yorker*; the two lead fact-checkers on the story, Jennifer Stahl and Tim Farrington, as well as the head of the magazine's fact-checking department, Peter Canby; and our lawyer, Lynn Ober-

*Davis denies that he blew or was in Las Vegas. Noriyuki Matsumaru, who was a finance officer in the Religious Technology Center at the time, told me he was in charge of handling Davis's punishment when he returned.

lander. Leading the Scientology legal delegation was Anthony Michael Glassman, a former assistant US attorney who now has a boutique law firm in Beverly Hills, specializing in representing movie stars. On his website, he boasts of a $10 million judgment against *The New York Times*. The stakes were obvious to everyone.

The Scientology delegation brought with them forty-eight three-ring binders of supporting material, stretching nearly seven linear feet, to respond to the 971 questions the checkers had posed. It was an impressive display. The binders were labeled according to categories, such as "Disappearance of L. Ron Hubbard," "Tom Cruise," "Gold Base," and "Haggis's Involvement in Scientology." Davis emphasized that the church had gone to extraordinary lengths to prepare for this meeting. "Frankly, the only thing I can think that compares would be the presentation that we made in the early 1990s to the IRS."

We sat around a large blond conference table with the kaleidoscopic lights of Times Square garishly whirling in the background. I particularly recall the Dunkin' Donuts sign over Davis's shoulder as he began his presentation. First, he ruled out any discussion of the church's confidential scripture. He compared it to "shoving an image of the Prophet Mohammed in the face of a Muslim" or "insisting that a Jew eat pork." He then attacked the credibility of some of the sources for the piece, whom he called "bitter apostates." "They are unreliable," he said. "They make up stories." He produced a paper by Bryan Wilson, who was an eminent Oxford sociologist and prominent defender of new religious movements (he died in 2004). Wilson argues that testimony from disaffected members should be treated skeptically, noting, "The apostate is generally in need of self-justification. He seeks to reconstruct his own past to excuse his former affiliations and to blame those who were formerly his closest associates. . . . He is likely to be suggestible and ready to enlarge or embellish his grievances to satisfy that species of journalist whose interest is more in sensational copy than in an objective statement of the truth." Davis had highlighted the last part for my benefit.

As an example, Davis singled out Gerald Armstrong, the former Scientology archivist, who received an $800,000 settlement in a fraud suit against the church in 1986. Davis charged that Armstrong had forged many of the documents that he later disseminated in order to discredit the church's founder, although he produced no evidence to substantiate that allegation. He passed around a photograph of Armstrong, which, he said, showed Armstrong "sitting naked" with a giant globe in his lap. "This was a photo that was in a newspaper article he did where he said that all people should give up money," Davis said. "He's not a very sane person."*

Davis also displayed photographs of what he said were bruises sustained by Mike Rinder's former wife in 2010, after Rinder physically assaulted her in a Florida parking lot.† Davis then showed a mug shot of Marty Rathbun in a jailhouse jumpsuit, after being detained in New Orleans in July 2010 for public drunkenness. "Getting arrested for being drunk on the intersection of Bourbon and Toulouse?" Davis cracked. "That's like getting arrested for being a leper in a leper colony." Other defectors, such as Claire and Marc Headley, were "the most despicable people in the world." Jefferson Hawkins was "an inveterate liar."

If these people were so reprehensible, I asked, how had they all arrived at such elevated positions in the church?

"They weren't like that when they were in those positions," Davis replied.

The defectors we were discussing had not only risen to positions of responsibility within the church; they had also ascended Scientology's ladder of spiritual accomplishment. I suggested that Scientology didn't seem to be effective if people at the highest levels of spiritual attainment were actually liars, adulterers, wife beaters, drunks, and embezzlers.

"This is a religion," Davis responded movingly. "It aspires to greatness, hope, humanity, spiritual freedom. To be greater than we are. To rise above our craven, humanoid instincts." Scientology doesn't pretend to be perfect, he said, and it shouldn't be judged on the misconduct of a few apostates. "I haven't done things like that," Davis said. "I haven't suborned perjury, destroyed evidence, lied—contrary to what Paul Haggis says." He spoke of his frustration with Haggis after his resignation: "If he was so troubled and shaken on the fundamentals of Scientology . . . then why the hell did he stick around for

*Armstrong told me that he was actually wearing running shorts in the photo, which were obscured by the globe. His settlement with the church prohibited him from talking about Scientology, a prohibition he has ignored, and the church has won two breach-of-contract suits against him, including a $500,000 judgment in 2004, which Armstrong didn't pay. He gave away most of his money and continues to speak openly about the church.

†Rinder denies committing violence against his wife. A sheriff's report supports this.

thirty-five years?" He continued: "Did he stay a closet Scientologist for some career-advancement purpose?" Davis shook his head in disgust. "I think he's the most hypocritical person in the world." He said he felt that he'd done all he could in dealing with Haggis over the issue of Proposition 8. He added that the individual who had made the mistake of listing the San Diego church as a supporter of the initiative—he didn't divulge his name—had been "disciplined" for it. I asked what that meant. "He was sat down by a staff member of the local organization," Davis explained. "He got sorted out."

Davis thought I was making too much out of the issue of Suppressive Persons in the piece. "Do you know how many people, grand total, there are in the world who have been declared Suppressive?" he asked rhetorically. "A couple of thousand over the years. At most." He said that in fact many had been restored to good standing. "Yet again, you're falling into the trap of defining our religion by the people who've left."

Hubbard had said that only two and a half percent of the human population were suppressive, but one of the problems I faced in writing about Scientology, especially its early days, is that the preponderance of people who had been close to Hubbard had either quietly left the church or been declared Suppressive. Some, like Pat Broeker, had gone underground. Many others, like David Mayo, had signed non-disclosure agreements. Those who remained in the church were off-limits to me.*

We discussed the allegations of abuse lodged by many former members against Miscavige. "The only people who will corroborate are their fellow apostates," Davis said. "They're a pack of sanctimonious liars." He produced affidavits from other Scientologists refuting their accusations. He noted that in the tales about Miscavige, the violence always seemed to come out of nowhere. "One would think that if such a thing occurred, which it most certainly did not, there'd have to be a reason," Davis said.

I had wondered about these outbursts as well. When Rinder and Rathbun were in the church, they claimed that allegations of abuse were baseless. Then, after Rinder defected, he said that Miscavige had beaten him fifty times. Rathbun had told the *St. Petersburg Times* in 1998 that in the twenty years he had worked closely with Miscavige,

---

*At this point Paul Haggis had not been declared Suppressive. He later was.

he had never seen him hit anyone. "That's not his temperament," he had said. "He's got enough personal horsepower that he doesn't need to resort to things like that." Later, he acknowledged to the *Times*, "That's the biggest lie I ever told you." He has also confessed that in 1997 he ordered incriminating documents destroyed in the case of Lisa McPherson, the Scientologist who died of an embolism while under church care. If these men were capable of lying to protect the church, might they not also be capable of lying to destroy it?

However, twelve former Sea Org members told me that Miscavige had assaulted them; twenty-one have told me or testified in court that they have witnessed one or more assaults on other church staff members by their leader.* Marc Headley, one of those who say Miscavige beat them on several occasions, said he knows thirty others who were attacked by the church leader. Rinder says he witnessed fourteen other executives who were assaulted, some on multiple occasions, such as the elderly church president, Heber Jentzsch, who has been in the Hole since 2006. Some people were slapped, others punched or kicked or choked. Lana Mitchell, who worked in Miscavige's office, saw him hit his brother, Ronnie, in the stomach, during a meeting. Mariette Lindstrom, who also worked in Miscavige's office, witnessed as many as twenty attacks. "You get very hardened," she admitted. She saw Miscavige banging the heads of two of his senior executives, Marc Yager and Guillaume Lesevre, together repeatedly, until blood came from Lesevre's ear. Tom De Vocht says he witnessed Miscavige striking other members of the staff about a hundred times. Others who never saw such violence spoke of their constant fear of the leader's wrath.

The attacks often came out of the blue, "like the snap of a finger," as John Peeler described it. Bruce Hines, who was a senior auditor in 1994, told me that before he was struck, "I heard his voice in the hallway, deep and distinctive, 'Where is that motherfucker?' He looked in

---

*The list of those who told me they had been physically assaulted by David Miscavige: Mike Rinder, Gale Irwin, Marty Rathbun, Jefferson Hawkins, Tom De Vocht, Mark Fisher, Bruce Hines, Bill Dendiu, Guy White, Marc Headley, Ulf Olofsson, and Stefan Castle. Those who said they had witnessed such abuse: Marty Rathbun, Janela Webster, Tom De Vocht, Marc Headley, Eric Knutson, Amy Scobee, Dan Koon, Steve Hall, Claire Headley, Mariette Lindstein, John Peeler, Andre Tabayoyan, Vicki Aznaran, Jesse Prince, Mark Fisher, Bill Dendiu, Mike Rinder, David Lingerfelter, Denise (Larry) Brennan, Debbie Cook, and Lana Mitchell. One witness refused to have his name printed. Other witnesses have been reported in the press.

my office. 'There he is!' Without another word he came up and hit me with an open hand. I didn't fall down. It was at that point I was put in RPF. I was incarcerated six years."

Davis admitted that the musical chairs episode occurred, even though the church denies the existence of the Hole, where it took place. He explained that Miscavige had been away from Gold Base for some time, and when he returned, he found that many jobs had been reassigned without his permission. The game was intended to demonstrate how disruptive such wholesale changes could be on an organization. "All the rest of it is a bunch of embellishment and noise and hoo-haw," Davis told me. "Chairs being ripped apart, and people being threatened that they're going to be sent to far-flung places in the world, plane tickets being purchased, and they're going to force their spouses—and on and on and on. I mean, it's just nuts!"

The Scientology delegation objected to the negative tenor of *The New Yorker* queries about the church's leader, including such small details as whether or not he had a tanning bed. "I mean, this is *The New Yorker*. It sounds like the *National Enquirer*," Davis complained. He wouldn't say what Miscavige's salary was (the church is not required to publicly disclose that information), but he derided the idea that the church leader enjoyed a luxurious lifestyle. Miscavige, he contended, doesn't live on the ostentatious scale of many other religious leaders. "There's no big rings. There's no fancy silk robes," he said. "There's no mansion. There's no none of that. None, none, none. Zero, zilcho, not." As for the extravagant birthday presents given to the church leader, Davis said that it was tradition for Sea Org members to give each other gifts for their birthdays. It was "just obnoxious" for me to single out Miscavige.

"It's not true that he's gotten for his birthday a motorcycle, fine suits, and leather jackets?" I asked.

"I gave him a leather jacket once," Davis conceded.

"So it is true?" I asked. "A motorcycle, fine suits?"

"I never heard that," he responded. "And as far as fine suits, I've got some fine suits. The church bought those." In fact, he was wearing a beautiful custom-made suit, with actual buttonholes on the cuffs. He explained that for IRS purposes it was considered a uniform. When Sea Org members mix with the public, he explained, they dress appropriately. "It's called Uniform K."

Davis declined to let me speak to Miscavige; nor would he or the other members of the group agree to talk about their own experiences with the church leader.

I asked about the leader's missing wife, Shelly Miscavige. John Brousseau and Claire Headley believe that she was taken to Running Springs, near Big Bear, California, one of several sites where Hubbard's works are stored in underground vaults. "She'll be out of sight, out of mind until the day she dies," Brousseau had predicted, "like Mary Sue Hubbard."

In the meeting, Tommy Davis told me, "I definitely know where she is," but he wouldn't disclose the location.

Davis brought up Jack Parsons's black magic society, which he asserted Hubbard had infiltrated. "He was sent in there by Robert Heinlein, who was running off-book intelligence operations for naval intelligence at the time." Davis said that the church had been looking for additional documentation to support its claim. "A biography that just came out three weeks ago on Bob Heinlein actually confirmed it at a level that we'd never been able to before, because of something his biographer had found."

The book Davis was referring to is the first volume of an authorized Heinlein biography, by William H. Patterson, Jr. There is no mention there of Heinlein sending Hubbard to break up the Parsons ring. I wrote Patterson, asking if his research supported the church's assertion. He responded that Scientologists had been the source of the claim in the first place, and that they provided him with a set of documents that supposedly backed it up. Patterson said that the material did not support the factual assertions the church was making. "I was unable to make any direct connection of the facts of Heinlein's life at the time to that narrative or any of its supporting documents," Patterson wrote. (The book reveals that Heinlein's second wife, Leslyn, had an affair with Hubbard. Interestingly, given Hubbard's condemnation of homosexuality, the wife charged that Heinlein had as well.)

"Even those allegations from Sara Northrup," Davis continued, mentioning the woman who had been Parsons's girlfriend before running off with Hubbard. "He was never married to Sara Northrup. She filed for divorce in an effort to try and create a false record that she had been married to him." He said that she had been under a cloud of suspicion, even when she lived with Parsons. "It always had been considered that she had been sent in there by the Russians," he said. "I can never pronounce her name. Her actual true name is a Russian name." Davis was referencing a charge that Hubbard once made when he was portraying his wife as a Communist spy named Sara Komkova-damanov. "That was one of the reasons L. Ron Hubbard never had a relationship with her," Davis continued. "He never had a child with her. He wasn't married to her. But he did save her life and pull her out of that whole black magic ring." Davis described Sara as "a couple beers short of a six-pack, to use a phrase." He included in the binders a letter from her, dated June 11, 1951, a few days before their divorce proceedings:

> I, Sara Northrup Hubbard, do hereby state that the things I have said about L. Ron Hubbard in the courts and the public prints have been grossly exaggerated or are entirely false.
>
> I have not at any time believed otherwise than that L. Ron Hubbard was a fine and brilliant man.

She went on to say, "In the future I wish to lead a quiet and orderly existence with my little girl far away from the enturbulating influences which have ruined my marriage." (Sara did live a quiet and orderly existence until her death, of breast cancer, in 1997. She explained why she made the tapes, in her last months of life. "I'm not interested in revenge," she said. "I'm interested in the truth.")

The meeting with the Scientology delegation lasted all day. Sandwiches were brought in. Davis and I discussed an assertion that Marty Rathbun had made to me about the OT III creation story. While Hubbard was in exile, Rathbun said, he wrote a memo suggesting an experiment in which ascending Scientologists might skip the OT III level—a memo Rathbun says that Miscavige had ordered destroyed. "Of every allegation that's in here," Davis said, waving the binder containing fact-checking queries, "this one would perhaps be, hands down, the absolutely, without question, most libelous." He explained that the cornerstone of the faith was the writings of the founder. "Mr. Hubbard's material must be and is applied precisely as written," Davis said. "It's never altered. It's never changed. And there probably is no more heretical or more horrific transgression that you could have in the Scientology religion than to alter the technology."

But hadn't certain derogatory references to homosexuality found in some editions of Hubbard's books been changed after his death?

Davis agreed that was so, but he maintained that "the current editions are one-hundred-percent, absolutely fully verified as being according to what Mr. Hubbard wrote." Davis said they were checked against Hubbard's original dictation.

"The extent to which the references to homosexuality have changed are because of mistaken dictation?" I asked.

"No, because of the insertion, I guess, of somebody who was a bigot," Davis replied. "The point is, it wasn't Mr. Hubbard."

"Somebody put the material in those—"

"I can only imagine," Davis said, cutting me off.

"Who would have done it?"

"I have no idea."

"Hmm."

"I don't think it really matters," Davis said. "The point is that neither Mr. Hubbard nor the church has any opinion on the subject of anyone's sexual orientation. . . ."

"Someone inserted words that were not his into literature that was propagated under his name, and that's been corrected now?" I asked, trying to be clear.

"Yeah, I can only assume that's what happened," Davis said. "And by the way," he added, referring to Quentin Hubbard, "his son's not gay."

During his presentation, Davis showed an impressively produced video that portrayed Scientology's worldwide efforts for literary programs and drug education, the translation of Hubbard's work into dozens of languages, and the deluxe production facilities at Gold Base. "The real question is who would produce the kind of material we produce and do the kinds of things we do, set up the kind of organizational structure that we set up?" Davis asked. "Or what kind of man, like L. Ron Hubbard, would spend an entire lifetime researching, putting together the kind of material, suffer all the trials and tribulations and go through all the things he went through in his life . . . or even with the things that we, as individuals, have to go through, as part of the new religion? Work seven days a week, three hundred sixty-five days a year, fourteen-, fifteen-, eighteen-hour days sometimes, out of sheer total complete dedication to our faith. And do it all, for what? As some sort of sham? Just to pull the wool over everyone's eyes?" He concluded, "It's ridiculous. Nobody works that hard to cheat people. Nobody gets that little sleep to screw over their fellow man."

We came to the section in the queries dealing with Hubbard's war record. His voice filling with emotion, Davis said that if it was true that Hubbard had not been injured, then "the injuries that he handled by the use of Dianetics procedures were never handled, because they were injuries that never existed; therefore, Dianetics is based on a lie; therefore, Scientology is based on a lie." He concluded: "The fact of the matter is that Mr. Hubbard was a war hero."

I believe everyone on *The New Yorker* side of the table was taken aback by this daring equation, one that seemed not only fair but testable. As proof of his claim that Hubbard had been injured, Davis provided a letter from the US Naval Hospital in Oakland, dated December 1, 1945. It states that Hubbard had been hospitalized that year for a duodenal ulcer, but was pronounced "fit for duty." Davis had highlighted a passage in the letter: "Eyesight very poor, beginning with conjunctivitis actinic in 1942. Lame in right hip from service connected injury. Infection in bone. Not misconduct, all service connected." Davis added later that according to Robert Heinlein, Hubbard's ankles had suffered a "drumhead-type injury"; this can result, Davis explained, "when a ship is torpedoed or bombed."

Despite subsequent requests to produce additional records, this was the only document Davis provided to prove that the founder of Scientology was not lying about his war injuries. And yet, Hubbard's medical records show that only five days after receiving the doctor's note, Hubbard applied for a pension based on his conjunctivitis, an ulcer, a sprained knee, malaria, and arthritis in his right hip and shoulder. His vision was little changed from what it had been before the war. This was the same period during which Hubbard claimed to have been blinded and made a hopeless cripple.

Davis acknowledged that some of Hubbard's medical records did not corroborate the founder's version of events. The church itself, Davis confided, had been troubled by the contradiction between Hubbard's story and the official medical records. But he said there were other records that *did* confirm Hubbard's version of events, based on various documents the church had assembled. I asked where the documents had come from. "From St. Louis," Davis explained, "from the archives of navy and military service. And also, the church got it from various avenues of research. Just meeting people, getting records from people."

The man who examined the records and reconciled the dilemma, he said, was "Mr. X." Davis explained, "Anyone who saw *JFK* remembers a scene on the Mall where Kevin Costner's character goes and meets a man named Mr. X, who's played by Donald Sutherland." In the film, Mr. X is an embittered intelligence agent who explains that the Kennedy assassination was actually a coup staged by the military-industrial complex. In real life, Davis said, Mr. X was Colonel Leroy Fletcher Prouty, who had worked in the Office of Special Operations at the Pentagon. (Oliver Stone, who directed *JFK*, says that Mr. X was a composite character, based in part on Prouty.) In the 1980s, Prouty worked as a consultant for Scientology and was a frequent contributor to *Freedom* magazine. "We finally got so frustrated with this point of conflicting medical records that we took all of Mr. Hubbard's records to Fletcher Prouty," Davis continued. Prouty told the church representatives that because Hubbard had an "intelligence background," his records were subjected to a process known as "sheep-dipping." Davis explained that this was military parlance for "what gets done to a set of records for an intelligence officer. And, essentially, they create two sets." (Prouty died in 2001.)

The sun was setting and the Dunkin' Donuts sign glowed brighter. As the meeting was finally coming to an end, Davis made a plea for understanding. "We're an organization that's new and tough and different and has been through a hell of a lot, and has had its ups and downs," he said. "And the fact of the matter is nobody will take the time and do the story right."

Davis had staked much of his argument on the veracity of Hubbard's military records. The fact-checkers had already filed a Freedom of Information Act request for all such material with the National Archives in St. Louis, where military records are kept. Such requests can drag on well past deadline, and we were running short on time. An editorial assistant, Yvette Siegert, flew to St. Louis to speed things along.

Meantime, Davis sent me a copy of a document that he said clearly confirmed Hubbard's heroism: a "Notice of Separation from the US Naval Service," dated December 6, 1945. The document specifies medals won by Hubbard, including a Purple Heart with a Palm, implying that he was wounded in action twice. But John E. Bircher, the spokesman for the Military Order of the Purple Heart, wrote me that the Navy uses gold and silver stars, "NOT a palm," to indicate multiple wounds. Davis included a photograph of the actual medals Hubbard supposedly won, but two of them weren't even created until after Hubbard left active service.

There was a fire in the St. Louis archives in 1973, which destroyed a number of documents, but Yvette returned with more than nine hundred pages of what the archivists insisted were Hubbard's complete military records. Nowhere in the file is there mention of Hubbard's being wounded in battle or breaking his feet. X-rays taken of Hubbard's right shoulder and hip showed calcium deposits, but there was no evidence of any bone or joint disease in his ankles.

There is a Notice of Separation in the official records, but it is not the one Davis sent me. The differences in the two documents are telling. The St. Louis document indicates that Hubbard earned four medals for service, but they reflect no distinction or valor. The church document indicates, falsely, that Hubbard completed four years of college, obtaining a degree in civil engineering. The official document correctly notes two years of college and no degree.

The official Notice of Separation was signed by Lieutenant (jg) J. C. Rhodes, who also signed Hubbard's detachment paperwork. On the church document, the commanding officer who signed off on Hubbard's separation was "Howard D. Thompson, Lt. Cmdr." The file contains a letter, from 2000, to another researcher, who had written for more information about Thompson. An analyst with the National Archives responded that the records of commissioned naval officers at that time had been reviewed and "there was no Howard D. Thompson listed."

The church, after being informed of these discrepancies, asserted, "Our expert on military records has advised us that, in his considered opinion, there is *nothing* in the Thompson notice that would lead him to question its validity." Eric Voelz and William Seibert, two longtime archivists at the St. Louis facility, examined the church's document and pronounced it a forgery.*

Eric Voelz additionally told *The New Yorker*, "The United States has never handed out Purple Hearts with a palm." He said that ditto marks, which are found on the document provided by the church, do not typically appear on forms of this kind. The font was also suspect,

---

*The reader can compare the two Notices of Separation by going to *The New Yorker*'s posting on DocumentCloud: http://documents.newyorker.com/2011/02/notice-of-separation-l-ron-hubbard/. Gerald Armstrong testified that he had seen a document, "either a fitness report or something similar around the time of the end of the war," that bore the signature of "a Commander Thompson," which he believed that Hubbard had actually forged (*Church of Scientology California vs. Gerald Armstrong*, May 15, 1984).

since it was not consistent with the size or style of the times. Voelz had never heard of the "Marine Medal," and he took issue with the "Br. & Dtch. Vict. Meds." found on the church document, saying that medals awarded by foreign countries are not listed on a Notice of Separation, and that they were unlikely to have been awarded to an American in any case.

A few months after this meeting, Davis and Feshbach stopped representing Scientology, even though they continued to be listed as the top spokespeople on the church website. Rumor from former members is that Davis blew but was recovered and once again subjected to sec-checking. Then Feshbach became seriously ill. According to the church, they are on a leave of absence from the Sea Org for medical reasons. They are now living in Texas. When I last spoke to Davis, he said, "I think you should know my allegiances haven't changed—at all." He added: "I don't have to answer your questions anymore."

Epilogue

If Scientology is based on a lie, as Tommy Davis's formulation at the *New Yorker* meeting suggests, what does it say about the many people who believe in its doctrine or—like Davis and Feshbach—publicly defend and promote the organization and its practices?

Of course, no religion can prove that it is "true." There are myths and miracles at the core of every great belief system that, if held up to the harsh light of a scholar or an investigative reporter, could easily be passed off as lies. Did Mohammed really ride into Heaven on the back of his legendary transport, the steed Buraq? Did Jesus' disciples actually encounter their crucified leader after his burial? Were these miracles or visions or lies? Would the religions survive without them?

There is no question that a belief system can have positive, transformative effects on people's lives. Many current and former Scientologists have attested to the value of their training and the insight they derived from their study of the religion. They have the right to believe whatever they choose. But it is a different matter to use the protections afforded a religion by the First Amendment to falsify history, to propagate forgeries, and to cover up human-rights abuses.

Hubbard once wrote that "the old religion"—by which he meant Christianity—was based on "a very painful lie," which was the idea of Heaven. "Yes, I've been to Heaven. And so have you," he writes. "It was complete with gates, angels and plaster saints—and electronic implantation equipment." Heaven, he says, was built as an implant station

43 trillion years ago. "So there was a Heaven after all—which is why you are on this planet and were condemned never to be free again—until Scientology." He went on: "What does this do to any religious nature of Scientology? It strengthens it. New religions always overthrow the false gods of the old, they do something to better man. We can improve man. We can show the old gods false. And we can open up the universe as a happier place in which a spirit may dwell."

One might compare Scientology with the Church of Latter Day Saints, a new religion of the previous century. The founder of the movement, Joseph Smith, claimed to have received a pair of golden plates from the angel Moroni in upstate New York in 1827, along with a pair of magical "seeing stones," which allowed him to read the contents. Three years later, he published *The Book of Mormon*, founding a movement that would provoke the worst outbreak of religious persecution in American history. Mormons were chased all across the country because of their practice of polygamy and their presumed heresy. Smith himself was murdered by a mob in Carthage, Illinois. His beleaguered followers sought to escape the United States and establish a religious theocracy in the territory of Utah, which they called Zion. Mormons were so despised that there was a bill in Congress to exterminate them. And yet Mormonism would evolve and go on to become one of the fastest-growing denominations in the twentieth, and now the twenty-first, centuries. Members of the faith now openly run for president of the United States. In much of the world, this religion, which was once tormented because of its perceived anti-American values, is now thought of as being the most American of religions; indeed, that's how many Mormons think of it as well. It is a measure not only of the religion's success but also of the ability of a faith to adapt and change.

And yet Joseph Smith was plainly a liar. In answer to the charge of polygamy, he claimed he had only one wife, when he had already accumulated a harem. A strange but revealing episode occurred in 1835, when Smith purchased several Egyptian mummies from an itinerant merchant selling such curiosities. Inside the mummy cases were scrolls of papyrus, reduced to fragments, which Smith declared were the actual writings of the Old Testament patriarchs Abraham and Joseph. Smith produced what he called a translation of the papyri, titled *The Book of Abraham*. It still forms a portion of Mormon doctrine. In America at the time, Egyptian was still thought to be indecipherable, but the Rosetta Stone had already been discovered, and Jean-François

Champollion had successfully rendered the hieroglyphic language into French. In 1966, the Joseph Smith papyri were discovered in the collection of the Metropolitan Museum of Art. It was soon shown that the passages that Smith "translated" were common funerary documents with no reference to Abraham or Joseph whatsoever. This fraud has been known for decades, but it has made little difference in the growth of the religion or the devotion of its adherents. Belief in the irrational is one definition of faith, but it is also true that clinging to absurd or disputed doctrines binds a community of faith together and defines a barrier to the outside world.

The evolution of Scientology into a religion also resembles the progression of Christian Science, the faith Tommy Davis was born into. Like Hubbard, Mary Baker Eddy, the founder of Christian Science, experimented with alternative ways of healing. Like Hubbard, she claimed to have been an invalid who cured herself; she, too, wrote a book based on her experience, *Science and Health with Key to the Scriptures*, which became the basis for the founding of the Church of Christ, Scientist, in 1879. Far more than is the case with Scientology, Christian Science stands against mainstream medical practices, even though both organizations lay claim to being more "scientific" than religious. Many religions, including Christian Science, Jehovah's Witnesses, even Christianity—have known scorn and persecution. Some, like the Shakers and the Millerites, died out, but others, including Mormons and Pentecostals, have elbowed their way into the crowded religious landscape of American society.

The practice of disconnection, or shunning, is not unique to Scientology, nor is the longing for religious sanctuary. America itself was founded by true believers who separated themselves from their non-Puritan kinfolk by placing an ocean between them. New religious leaders continually appear, giving expression to unmet spiritual needs. There is a constant churning of spiritual movements and denominations all over the world, one that advances with freedom of expression. One must look at L. Ron Hubbard and the odyssey of his movement against this historical backdrop and the natural human yearning for transcendence and submission.

In the late 1970s, I lived for several months in an Amish and Mennonite community in central Pennsylvania, researching my first book.*

City Children, Country Summer (Scribner's, 1979).

Their movement had been nearly annihilated in Europe, but in the 1720s they began taking refuge in William Penn's colony, the "holy experiment" of Pennsylvania. Amish life has remained essentially unchanged since then, a kind of museum of eighteenth-century farm life. The adherents live sequestered lives, out of the drift of popular culture, on a kind of religious atoll. I was moved by the beauty and simplicity of their lives. The Amish see the Earth as God's garden, and their duty is to tend it. The environment they surround themselves with is filled with a sense of peace and a purposeful orderliness. Individuality is sanded down to the point that one's opinions are as similar to another's as the approved shape of a bonnet or the regulation beard. Because fashion and novelty are outlawed, one feels comfortably encased in a timeless, unchanging vacuum. The enforced conformity dims the noise of diversity and the anxiety of uncertainty; one feels closer to eternity. One is also aware of the electrified fence of orthodoxy that surrounds and protects this Edenic paradise, and the expulsion that awaits those who doubt or question. Still, there is a kind of quiet majesty in the Amish culture—not because of their rejection of modernity, but because of their principled non-violence and their adherence to a way of living that tempers their fanaticism. The Amish suffer none of the social opprobrium that Scientologists must endure; indeed, they are generally treated like beloved endangered animals, coddled by their neighbors and smiled upon by society. And yet they are highly schismatic, willing to break off all relations with their dearest relatives on what would seem to an outsider to be an inane point of doctrine or even the question of whether one can allow eaves on a house or pictures on a wall.

As adorable as the Amish appear to strangers, such isolated and intellectually deprived religious communities can become self-destructive, especially when they revolve around the whims of a single tyrannical leader. David Koresh created such a community in the Branch Davidian compound that he established near Waco and aptly called Ranch Apocalypse. In 1993, I was asked to write about the siege that was then under way. I decided not to, because there were more reporters on the scene than Branch Davidians; however, I had been unsettled by the sight of the twenty-one children that Koresh sent out of the compound shortly before the fatal inferno. Those children left behind their parents and the only life they had known. They were ripped out of the community of faith, placed in government vans, and ushered through a curtain of federal agents and reporters onto the stage of an alien world and who knows what future. I thought there must be other children who had experienced similar traumas; what had become of them?

There is a strangely contorted mound in a cemetery in Oakland, California, close by the naval hospital where Hubbard spent his last months in uniform. Under an undistinguished headstone rest four hundred bodies out of the more than nine hundred followers of Jim Jones who perished in Jonestown in 1978. The caskets had been stacked on top of each other on the side of a bulldozed hillside, then the earth was filled in, grass was planted, and the tragedy of Jonestown was buried in the national memory as one more inexplicable religious calamity. The members of the Peoples Temple, as Jones called his movement, had been drawn to his Pentecostal healing services, his social activism, and his racial egalitarianism. Charisma and madness were inextricably woven into the fabric of his personality, along with an insatiable sexual appetite that accompanied Jones's terror of abandonment. In his search for a secure religious community, Jones had repeatedly uprooted his congregation. Finally, in May 1977, the entire movement disappeared, virtually overnight. Without warning, leaving jobs and homes and family members who were not a part of the Peoples Temple, they were spirited away to a jungle encampment in Guyana, South America, which Jones billed as a socialist paradise. There he began to school them in suicide.

I learned that not everyone had died in Jonestown. Among the survivors were Jones's three sons: Stephan, Tim, and Jim Junior. They had been away from the camp playing basketball against the Guyanese national team in the capital city of Georgetown. These haunted young men had never before told their stories. One of the privileges of being a journalist is to be trusted to hear such memories in all their emotional complexity. One night I went to dinner with Tim Jones and his wife, Lorna. Tim was physically powerful, able to press a hundred pounds with either arm, but he couldn't fly on an airplane because of his panic attacks. He wanted his wife to come along because he had never given her a full account, and he wanted to be in a public place so he wouldn't cry. It was Tim who had to return to Jonestown to identify the bodies of everyone he knew, including his parents, his siblings, and his own wife and children, his whole world. He was convinced that, if he had been there, he could have prevented the suicides. He told this story, bawling, pounding the table, as the waiter steered away and the other diners stared at their plates. Never have I felt so keenly the danger of new religious movements and the damage that is done to people who are lured into such groups, not out of weakness in character but through their desire to do good and live meaningful lives.

SCIENTOLOGY WANTS TO BE understood as a scientific approach to spiritual enlightenment. It has, really, no grounding in science at all. It would be better understood as a philosophy of human nature; seen in that light, Hubbard's thought could be compared with that of other moral philosophers, such as Immanuel Kant and Søren Kierkegaard, although no one has ever approached the sweep of Hubbard's work. His often ingenious and minutely observed categories of behavior have been shadowed by the bogus elements of his personality and the absurdity that is interwoven with his bouts of brilliance, making it difficult for non-Scientologists to know what to make of it. Serious academic study of his writing has also been constrained by the vindictive reputation of the church.

The field of psychotherapy is Scientology's more respectable cousin, although it cannot honestly claim to be a science, either. Freud's legacy is that of a free and open inquiry into the motivations of behavior. He also created postulates—such as the ego, the superego, and the id—that might not endure strict scientific testing, but do offer an approach to understanding the inner workings of the personality. Hubbard's concept of the reactive and analytical minds attempts to do something similar. Jung's exploration of archetypes, based on his psychological explorations, anticipates the evolution of Dianetics into Scientology—in other words, the drift from therapy to spiritualism.

There is no point in questioning Scientology's standing as a religion; in the United States, the only opinion that really counts is that of the IRS; moreover, people do *believe* in the principles of Scientology and live within a community of faith—what else is required to accept it as such? The stories that invite ridicule or disbelief, such as Xenu and the Galactic Confederacy, may be fanciful—or pure "space opera," to use Hubbard's term—but every religion features bizarre and uncanny elements. Just consider some of the obvious sources of Hubbard's unique concoction—Buddhism, Hinduism, magic, General Semantics, and shamanism—that also provide esoteric categories to explain the ineffable mysteries of life and consciousness. One can find parallels in many faiths with the occult beliefs and practices of Scientology. The concept of expelling body thetans, for instance, is akin to casting out demons in the Christian tradition. But like every new religion, Scientology is handicapped by the frailties of its founder and the absence of venerable traditions that enshrine it in the culture.

To an outsider who has struggled to understand the deep appeal of Scientology to its adherents, despite the flaws and contradictions of the religion that many of them reluctantly admit, perhaps the missing element is art. Older faiths have a body of literature, music, ceremony, and iconography that infuses the doctrinal aspects of the religion with mystery and importance. The sensual experience of being in a great cathedral or mosque may have nothing to do with "belief," but it does draw people to the religion and rewards them emotionally. Scientology has built many impressive churches, but they are not redolent palaces of art. The aesthetic element in Scientology is Hubbard's arresting voice as a writer. His authoritative but folksy tone and his impressionistic grasp of human nature have cast a spell over millions of readers. More important, however, is the nature of his project: the self-portrait of the inside of his mind. It is perhaps impossible to reduce his mentality to a psychiatric diagnosis, in part because his own rendering of it is so complex, intricate, and comprehensive that one can only stand back and appreciate the qualities that drove him, hour after hour, year after year, to try to get it all on the page—his insight, his daring, his narcissism, his defiance, his relentlessness, his imagination—these are the traits of an artist. It is one reason that Hubbard identified with the creative community and many of them with him.

Scientology orients itself toward celebrity, and by doing so, the church awards famousness a spiritual value. People who seek fame—especially in the entertainment industry—naturally gravitate to Hollywood, where Scientology is waiting for them, validating their ambition and promising recruits a way in. The church has pursued a marketing strategy that relies heavily on endorsements by celebrities, who actively promote the religion. They speak of the positive role that Scientology has played in their lives. When David Miscavige awarded Tom Cruise the Freedom Medal of Valor in 2004, he praised his effectiveness as a spokesperson, saying, "Across ninety nations, five thousand people hear his word of Scientology every hour." It is difficult to know how such a figure was derived, but according to Miscavige, "Every minute of every hour someone reaches for LRH technology, simply because they know Tom Cruise is a Scientologist." Probably no other member of the church derives as much material benefit from his religion as Cruise does, and consequently none bears a greater moral responsibility for the indignities inflicted on members of the Sea Org, sometimes directly because of his membership. Excepting Paul Haggis, no prominent Hollywood Scientologist has spoken out publicly against the widespread allegations of physical abuse, involuntary confinement, and forced servitude within the church's clergy, although many such figures have quietly walked away.

Since leaving Scientology, Haggis has been in therapy, which he has found helpful. He's learned how much he blames others for his problems, especially those closest to him. "I really wish I had found a good therapist when I was twenty-one," he said. In Scientology, he always felt a subtle pressure to impress his auditor and then write up a glowing success story. Now, he said, "I'm not fooling myself that I'm a better man than I am."

The same month that Haggis's resignation from the church had become public, United Artists, Tom Cruise's studio, terminated Haggis's development deal. I asked if the break had anything to do with his resignation. Haggis thought for a moment, then said, "You don't do something that obvious—it'd be a bad PR move." He added, "They'd run out of money, so we all knew we were being kicked out."

Recently, he and Deborah decided to divorce. They have moved to the same neighborhood in New York, so that they can share custody of their son. Deborah has also left the church. Both say that the decision to end their marriage has nothing to do with their renunciation of Scientology.

On November 9, 2010, *The Next Three Days* premiered at the Ziegfeld Theatre, in Manhattan. Movie stars lined the red carpet as photographers fired away. Jason Beghe was there, and he told me that he had taken in Daniel Montalvo, the young man who lost his finger in the church book-publishing plant. Montalvo had recently blown from the Sea Org. He was nineteen years old. "He's never seen television," the actor marveled. "He doesn't even know who Robert Redford is." Nazanin Boniadi, who has a small part in the movie, was also there; Haggis had given her the role after learning what had happened to her after the church had engineered her match with Tom Cruise.

"Naz's story was one of those that made me realize I had been lied to for a long time, that I had to leave and do so loudly," Haggis later confided.

After the screening, everyone drifted over to the Oak Room of the Plaza Hotel. Haggis was in a corner receiving accolades from his friends when I found him. I asked if he felt that he had finally left Scientology. "I feel much more myself, but there's a sadness," he admitted. "If you identify yourself with something for so long, and suddenly you think of yourself as not that thing, it leaves a bit of space." He went on, "It's not really the sense of a loss of community. Those people who walked away from me were never really my friends." He understood how they felt about him, and why. "In Scientology, in the Ethics Conditions, as you go down from Normal through Doubt, you get to Enemy, and finally, near the bottom, there is Treason. What I did was a treasonous act."

The film did poorly at the box office. It had the misfortune of opening to mixed reviews on the same night that the last installment of the *Harry Potter* series premiered. Haggis had to close his office. It looked like another bleak period in his career, but he followed it by writing a screenplay for a video game, *Modern Warfare 3*, which would go on to set a sales record, earning $1 billion in the first sixteen days after its release.

I once asked Haggis about the future of his relationship with Scientology. "These people have long memories," he told me. "My bet is that, within two years, you're going to read something about me in a scandal that looks like it has nothing to do with the church." He thought for a moment, then said, "I was in a cult for thirty-four years. Everyone else could see it. I don't know why I couldn't."

MARTY RATHBUN DIVIDES the people who leave Scientology into three camps. There are those who reject the teachings of L. Ron Hubbard entirely, such as Paul Haggis; and those who still believe entirely, but think that the church under David Miscavige has taken Scientology away from the original, true teachings of the founder. There is a third category, which he has been struggling to define, that includes those people who are willing neither to swallow all the dogma nor to throw away the insights they gained from their experience. Hubbard's life and teachings are still the guideposts of their lives. "It wouldn't stick if there wasn't a tremendous amount of good it did for them," Rathbun says. He's been studying the history of other religions for parallels, and he quotes an old Zen proverb: "When the master points at the Moon, many people never see it at all, they only look at the master."

Rathbun has been counseling Scientologists who leave the church, and because of that he's been subject to continual monitoring and harassment from the church. His computers have been hacked and phone records have been stolen. A group of "Squirrel Busters" moved into his little community of Ingleside on the Bay, near Corpus Christi, in order to spy on him and drive him away through constant harassment. They wore video cameras on their hats and patrolled the neighborhood in a golf cart or occasionally a paddleboat. This lasted for 199 days. That tactic didn't work, because his neighbors rallied to his support. Many other defectors have been harassed and followed by private investigators.

On a sweltering Fourth of July weekend, 2011, a group of about a hundred "independent" Scientologists gathered at a lake cabin in East Texas. Rathbun and Mike Rinder had organized it. A few courageous swimmers were leaping off the dock, but rumors of alligators kept most people on the shore. A brief, powerful storm rolled through, driving everyone to shelter.

One of the attendees was Stephen Pfauth, known as Sarge, a Vietnam veteran who had gotten into Scientology in 1975. He is a slender man with haunted eyes. "It was one of those sudden things that happened," he explained. "I was looking for something, especially spiritually." He had run across an advertisement on the back of a magazine for Hubbard's book *Fundamentals of Thought*. Soon after reading it, he flew to Washington, DC, and took a three-day workshop called Life Repair Auditing. "I was blown away." He immediately quit his job. "I sold my house and bought the Bridge." Soon, a church official began cultivating him, saying, "LRH needs your help." Pfauth joined the Sea Org that November.

He became head of Hubbard's security detail, and was with the founder on his Creston ranch in his final days, with Pat and Annie Broeker. In early 1985, Hubbard became extremely ill and spent a week in a hospital. Pfauth was told it was for pancreatitis. "I didn't find out about the strokes until later," he said. After that, Hubbard stayed mostly in his Blue Bird bus, except when he came out to do his own laundry. Pfauth might be shoveling out the stables and they'd talk.

Marty Rathbun with an E-Meter at his home in Ingleside on the Bay, Texas, 2011

Six weeks before the leader died, Pfauth hesitantly related, Hubbard called him into the bus. He was sitting in his little breakfast nook. "He told me he was dropping his body. He named a specific star he was going to circle. That rehabs a being. He told me he'd failed, he's leaving," Pfauth said. "He said he's not coming back here to Earth. He didn't know where he'd wind up."

"How'd you react?" I asked.

"I got good and pissy-ass drunk," Pfauth said. "Annie found me at five in the morning in my old truck, Kris Kringle, and I had beer cans all around me. I did not take it well."

I mentioned the legend in Scientology that Hubbard will return.

"That's bull crap," Pfauth said. "He wanted to drop the body and leave. And he told me basically that he'd failed. All the work and everything, he'd failed."

I had heard a story that Pfauth had built some kind of electroshock mechanism for Hubbard in the last month of his life. I didn't know what to make of it, given Hubbard's horror of electroshock therapy. Pfauth's eyes searched the ceiling as if he were looking for divine help. He explained that Hubbard was having trouble getting rid of a body thetan. "He wanted me to build a machine that would up the voltage and basically blow the thetan away. You can't kill a thetan but just get him out of there. And also kill the body."

"So it was a suicide machine?"

"Basically."

Pfauth was staggered by Hubbard's request, but the challenge interested him. "I figured that building a Tesla coil was the best way to go." The Tesla coil is a transformer that increases the voltage without upping the current. Pfauth powered it with a 12-volt automobile battery, and then hooked the entire apparatus to an E-Meter. "So, if you're on the cans, you can flip a button and it does its thing," Pfauth explained. "I didn't want to kill him, just to scare him."

"Did he try it?"

"He blew up my E-Meter. Annie brought it back to me, all burnt up."

This was just before Christmas, 1985. Hubbard died a few weeks later of an unrelated stroke.

The believers are still waiting for his return.

Acknowledgments and
a Note on Sources

Compared with other religions I have written about, the published literature on Scientology is impoverished and clouded by bogus assertions. Some crucial details one would want to know about the church have been withheld—for instance, the number of people who are members of the International Association of Scientologists, which would be the best guide to knowing the true dimensions of the church's membership. The church promised to provide an organizational chart, but never did so; in any case, it would have been more notional than actual in terms of the flow of authority and responsibility, since many of the church's executive hierarchy have been quarantined for years in the Hole at the direction of the only individual who controls the institution.

L. Ron Hubbard's extensive—indeed, record-breaking—published works form the core of the documentary material that this book draws upon. Hubbard expressed himself variously in books, articles, bulletins, letters, lectures, and journals; one cannot understand the man or the organization he created without examining his work in each of these media. The church has published a useful compendium of Hubbard's thought in *What Is Scientology?* Although the church employs a full-time Hubbard biographer and has commissioned several comprehensive works in the past, there is still no authorized account of Hubbard's life. One of the previous Hubbard biographers, Omar Garrison, did write a full-scale account of Hubbard's life, which was suppressed. The church has published a series of *Ron* magazines, which have been compiled as a highly selective encyclopedia. For years, the church has been mopping up other documents—journals, letters, photographs—and withholding them from public view, which makes it difficult for independent researchers to fill in blanks in the historical record.

There are several important repositories of information that I have used in this book, however: the Manuscript Division of the Library of Congress; the Heinlein Prize Trust and the UC Santa Cruz Archives; the Kenneth Spencer Research Library of the University of Kansas; and the National Personnel Records Center in St. Louis, Missouri. The Stephen A. Kent Collection on Alternative Religions, University of Alberta, Edmonton, Alberta, Canada, houses an important collection of Scientology material, and Professor Kent graciously allowed my assistant, Lauren Wolf, to work in his archive. In addition to being an endless source of memories on the history of the church, Karen de la Carriere made her extensive photographic archive available. Many thanks to these valuable resources for their cooperation.

There are three major unauthorized biographies of L. Ron Hubbard: Russell Miller's excellent *Bare-Faced Messiah* (1987) was the first in-depth look at the man. Scientology unsuccessfully sued Miller, a British journalist, who says that while researching his book he was spied upon, his phone was tapped, and efforts were made to frame him for a murder he did not commit. Soon thereafter, Bent Corydon's *L. Ron Hubbard: Messiah or Madman?* (1987) appeared, followed by Jon Atack's *A Piece of Blue Sky* (1990). The church attempts to discredit both of these authors because they are former Scientologists who the church says were expelled from the organization. It is notable that no comprehensive biography of Hubbard has been attempted since the church's campaign against these books.

The scarcity of academic work on the church and its leaders testifies to the caution with which scholars regard the subject, as well as the reluctance of the organization to divulge information about its members, beliefs, and inner workings to qualified social scientists. In 1976, Roy Wallis published *The Road to Total Freedom: A Sociological Analysis of Scientology*, the first significant academic study of the church. While he was researching his book, Wallis was spied upon, and forged letters were sent to his colleagues and employers implicating him in a homosexual relationship. *Renunciation and Reformulation: A Study of Conversion in an American Sect*, an insightful book by Harriet Whitehead, an anthropologist, appeared in 1987. Since then, contributions from the academy have been meager. At this point,

I should also acknowledge the work of Hugh Urban, at Ohio State University, David S. Touretzky at Carnegie Mellon University, and Stephen Kent, at the University of Alberta. Each of these scholars has produced important contributions to the understanding of Scientology, despite the obstacles and threats posed by the church.

Court documents contain a valuable record of the history and culture of the church and its founder; this is especially true of the landmark 1991 suit *Church of Scientology California vs. Gerald Armstrong*. David Miscavige has been shy about giving interviews, but he has provided testimony and declarations in several lawsuits, most extensively in 1990, in *Bent Corydon v. Church of Scientology*.

A handful of courageous journalists have provided much of the essential information available about the culture of Scientology. Paulette Cooper opened the door with her 1971 exposé, *The Scandal of Scientology*. I have outlined in this book some of the harassment that she endured. Joel Sappell and Robert W. Welkos of the *Los Angeles Times* did a remarkable six-part series in 1990. Richard Leiby has been writing about Scientology since the early 1980s, first for the *Clearwater Sun* and subsequently for the *Washington Post*. Richard Behar covered the subject in *Barron's* and most notably in his 1991 exposé for *Time*, "The Thriving Cult of Greed and Power." Janet Reitman had unparalleled access to the church for her 2006 *Rolling Stone* article, "Inside Scientology," which became a book of the same title in 2011. Chris Owen, an independent researcher, has written extensively about the church online, and has revealed much of the information available about Hubbard's wartime experiences. Tom Smith has conducted a number of knowledgeable interviews on his radio show, *The Edge*, broadcast by Hillsborough Community College in Tampa, Florida. Joe Childs and Thomas C. Tobin of the *Tampa Bay Times* (formerly the *St. Petersburg Times*) have written groundbreaking stories, especially about the abuse inside the church hierarchy. Tony Ortega has been writing about Scientology since 1995, for the *Phoenix New Times*, and he continued as a valuable resource in the pages and the blog of the *Village Voice* until his recent resignation. Several of these journalists have been harassed, investigated, sued, or threatened in various ways. I am the beneficiary of their skill and persistence.

In the last decade, defectors from the Sea Org have provided a rich trove of personal accounts. These have taken the form of memoirs and blog postings, and they have accumulated into an immense indictment of the inner workings of the church. Among the memoirs I should single out are Marc Headley's *Blown for Good: Behind the Iron Curtain of Scientology* (2009); Nancy Many's *My Billion Year Contract* (2009); Amy Scobee's *Abuse at the Top* (2010); and Jefferson Hawkins's *Counterfeit Dreams* (2010). Kate Bornstein's *A Queer and Pleasant Danger* (2012) provides an especially interesting account of the *Apollo* days.

Websites devoted to challenging the church have proliferated, beginning with alt.religion.scientology in 1991. Some of the most active are Andreas Heldal-Lund's Operation Clambake at xenu.net; Steve Hall's scientology-cult.com; Arnaldo Lerma's lermanet.com, and the Ex Scientology Message Board, which is an online community for former members of the church, founded by "Emma" and now run by "Mick Wenlock and Ethercat." Exscientologykids.org, started by Jenna Miscavige Hill, David Miscavige's niece, among others, played an important role in Paul Haggis's decision to leave the church. Although many of the postings on these websites are anonymous, they provide rich texture to a subculture that few outsiders can appreciate.

One blog has become a rallying point for "independent" Scientologists who have renounced the official church: Marty Rathbun's *Moving on Up a Little Higher*, which began in 2009. It has been the source of many telling personal stories, as well as documents leaked by church insiders. Rathbun and his wife, Monique Carle, have suffered constant harassment, along with surveillance by private investigators, because of his open challenge to Miscavige's authority.

In researching this book, I conducted hundreds of interviews, the preponderance of them on the record. I have always been sparing in relying on anonymous sources, but writing about Scientology poses a challenge for a reporter. A number of my sources were fearful of retribution by the church—in particular, legal harassment and the loss of contact with family members. Many key individuals have signed confidentiality agreements that enforce their silence. I owe all my sources a great debt of gratitude for their willingness to speak to me despite the risk to their own well-being.

Paul Haggis plays a unique role in this book. He never intended to talk publicly about his experience in the church. That he opened up to me, knowing the church's reputation for retribution, is a measure of his courage and his forthrightness.

This book is dedicated to my colleagues at *The New Yorker*, and so my list of debts includes the many people there who assisted me in writing the profile of Paul Haggis ("The Apostate," Feb. 14 and 21, 2011) that became the starting point for my research into Scientology. I had talked previously with David Remnick, the editor of the magazine, about an article on the Church of Scientology. David appreciated the legal hazards, but I don't think either of us realized the amount of time and resources the piece would ultimately require. His commitment was all the more meaningful coming during a period when the magazine was under the same financial stress that other print media were experiencing. My editor at *The New Yorker*, Daniel Zalewski, has shepherded me through many articles, and his steadiness and advocacy are always deeply appreciated. Daniel's assistant at the time, Yvette Siegert, cheerfully flew to St. Louis as our deadline approached to fetch L. Ron Hubbard's military records from the archives there. Lynn Oberlander, the magazine's lawyer, was a stalwart ally, undaunted by the legal team arrayed by the church and by certain celebrities who were mentioned in the article. Ann Goldstein, the magazine's copy chief, did her usual careful and respectful job. Nick Traverse and Kelly Bare labored to put the thousands of pages of documents on the Cloud—a highly experimental procedure at this old-school magazine—so that we could all have access to the same material simultaneously. I want to pay particular tribute to the *New Yorker* fact-checking department, headed by Peter Canby. Jennifer Stahl was the lead checker, spending six months full-time on the piece; her scrupulousness was inspiring, and she commanded the respect of everyone who dealt with her. Tim Farrington also worked intensely on the article. Eventually, a good portion of the department pitched in, including Nandi Rodrigo, Mike Spies, Katia Bachko, and even Peter himself. To be supported by such truly professional colleagues means so much.

Although the Church of Scientology was not a willing partner in the effort to write this book, I want to thank the spokespeople I worked with—Tommy Davis, Jessica Feshbach, and Karin Pouw—for responding to what must have seemed an endless stream of queries from me and the fact-checkers. I have no doubt that they will quarrel with the results, but the book is more accurate because of their participation, however reluctant that might have been. Initially, Davis permitted me to speak with several active members of the church, but the door closed on that opportunity. I was never allowed to talk to David Miscavige or any of the upper-tier executives I requested. (As I would learn, many of them were sequestered and not available in any case.) A reporter can only talk to people who are willing to talk to him; whatever complaints the church may have about my reporting, many limitations can be attributed to its decision to restrict my interactions with people who might have provided more favorable testimony.

Robert Jay Lifton did me the honor of reading this book in manuscript and providing his insights, especially on the issue of thought reform. R. Scott Appleby helped me place Scientology in the context of other world religions. My friend Stephen Harrigan also commented on an early draft, as he has done on many occasions. A writer depends on such willing friends.

My editor at Knopf, Ann Close, has been through five books with me—a marvelous relationship that has now spanned a quarter of a century. For this book, the Knopf team labored under a stressful deadline, and I would like to acknowledge the extraordinary efforts of Anke Steinecke, legal counsel; Katherine Hourigan, the managing editor; Paul Bogaards, the director of publicity; Kim Thornton, the publicist for this book; Kevin Bourke, the production editor; Claire Bradley Ong, the production manager; and Cassandra Pappas, the designer. I also thank my agent, Andrew Wylie, for his sage counsel.

When I began writing the book, I hired two young and talented fact-checkers, Axel Gerdau and Lauren Wolf. They were both interested in long-form journalism, and I thought I might be able to teach them something about that; so, one evening a week, I held a class for them, in which the text was the unwritten book we were working on. Axel and Lauren were immediately plunged into the recondite world of Scientology, but they adroitly managed to negotiate the language and the thinking. After Axel went on to other pursuits, Lauren remained as my research assistant. The book has gained immeasurably from her curiosity and doggedness, as well as her natural human sympathy—qualities that will certainly ensure her future career and reward those who have the good fortune to enjoy her company.

As usual, I owe special thanks to my wife, Roberta, who has once again set aside many anxieties to support my work.

Notes

INTRODUCTION

ix **8 million members:** Interview with Tommy Davis, the former chief spokesperson for the Church of Scientology International. He explains the difficulty in getting exact numbers: "There's no process of conversion, there is no baptism." Becoming a Scientologist is a simple decision: "Either you are or you aren't."

ix **welcomes 4.4 million:** "What Is Scientology?" YouTube video, posted by Church of Scientology, January 2, 2012, www.youtube.com/watch?v=Vcb_4L8T8gg.

ix **about 30,000 members:** Interview with Mike Rinder. Rinder is the former head of Scientology's Office of Special Affairs and functioned as the church's chief spokesperson from 1991 through 2007.

ix **$1 billion in liquid assets:** Interview with Mark "Marty" Rathbun. Rathbun is the former Inspector General for Ethics for the church. Tony Ortega, "Scientology in Turmoil: Debbie Cook's E-mail, Annotated," *Runnin' Scared* (blog), *The Village Voice*, Jan. 6, 2012. According to the distinguished religious historian R. Scott Appleby at the University of Notre Dame, even the Roman Catholic Church is unlikely to have $1 billion in cash on hand. R. Scott Appleby, personal communication.

ix **12 million square feet of property:** Church of Scientology International, "Scientology: Unparalleled Growth Since 2004," www.scientologynews.org/stats .html.

ix **The most recent addition:** Kevin Roderick, "Scientology Reveals Plans for Sunset Boulevard Studio," *LA Observed*, July 12, 2012.

x **apartment buildings, hotels:** Pinellas County Property Appraiser, 2012 tax roll.

xi **5,000, 6,000, or 10,000 members:** Church of Scientology International, *What Is Scientology?*, p. 324; interview with Tommy Davis; personal communication from Karin Pouw.

xi **between 3,000 and 5,000:** Claire Headley and Mike Rinder, personal communication. Rinder, who offers the higher number, places about 2,000 Sea Org members at Flag, 1,500 in LA, 500 at Gold Base and Int Base, 200 in the UK, 300 in Denmark, 150 in Australia, 200 on the *Freewinds*, and the rest scattered around Africa, Italy, Canada, and Mexico.

I. THE CONVERT

3 **"You have a mind":** Interview with Jim Logan.

4 **"What is true":** According to Haggis, the passage came from the Hubbard Qual-

ified Scientologist course. It was later published in Hubbard's book *The Way to Happiness*. Hubbard, *The Way to Happiness*, p. 48.

4 "find the ruin": Peter F. Gillham, *Tell It Like It Is: A Course in Scientology Dissemination* (Los Angeles: Red Baron Publishing, 1972), p. 37.

4 "Once the person": Hubbard, "Dissemination Drill," Hubbard Communications Office Policy Letter, Oct. 23, 1965.

6 "Speed City": Interview with Herman Goodden.

8 "You walked in one day": Hubbard, "Clearing Congress Lectures," Shoreham Hotel, Washington, DC, July 4, 1958.

9 "A civilization without insanity": *What Is Scientology?*, p. xiii.

9 "Scientology works 100 percent": Ibid., p. 215.

10 Most of them were white: Harriet Whitehead, "Reasonably Fantastic: Some Perspectives on Scientology, Science Fiction, and Occultism," in Zaretsky and Leone, *Religious Movements in Contemporary America*, p. 549.

11 "After drugs": Interview with Jim Dincalci.

11 superhuman powers: Interview with Skip Press.

12 The device measures: Hubbard, *Electropsychometric Auditing Operators Manual*, 1952.

13 "It gives Man his": *What Is Scientology?*, p. 175.

13 "Our most spectacular feat": James Phelan, "Have You Ever Been a Boo-Hoo?," *Saturday Evening Post*, March 21, 1964, pp. 81–85.

13 The E-Meter is presumed: Response of the Church of Scientology to queries.

13 "The needle just idles": Hubbard, *E Meter Essentials 1961—Clearing Series*, vol. 1, p. 18.

15 "Be three feet back": Hubbard, *Philadelphia Doctorate Course Transcripts*.

15 Free of the limitations: Ibid.

15 The ultimate goal: Whitehead, *Renunciation and Reformulation*, p. 176.

15 The goal of Scientology: Vosper, *The Mind Benders*, p. 31.

15 Among other qualities: Hubbard, *Dianetics*, pp. 170–73.

15 "The dianetic *clear* is": Ibid., p. xv.

16 "Operating Thetan": *What Is Scientology?*, p. 167.

16 "neither Buddha nor Jesus": *Ability*, unsigned, undated (probably 1958), issue 81, reprint of an editorial from *Certainty*, vol. 5, no. 10.

16 "Note several large": WikiLeaks, "Church of Scientology Collected Operating Thetan Documents," March 24, 2008, wikileaks.org/wiki/Church_of _Scientology_collected_Operating_Thetan_documents; Revised Declaration of Hana Whitfield, *Church of Scientology vs. Steven Fishman and Uwe Geertz*, US District Court, Central District of California, April 4, 1994.

16 "Laughter comes from the rear": WikiLeaks, "Church of Scientology Collected Operating Thetan Documents," March 24, 2008, wikileaks.org/wiki/Church _of_Scientology_collected_Operating_Thetan_documents.

16 "The material involved": Hubbard, "Ron's Journal '67," taped lecture.

18 "parlor tricks": Interview with Jefferson Hawkins.

18 "OT Phenomena": *Advance!*, no. 33, p. 8.

18 "A theta being is": Hubbard, *Scientology: A History of Man*, pp. 71–72.

18 "How do you answer": Hubbard, "State of OT," lecture, May 23, 1963.

18 "Telephone rings, it springs": Hubbard, "An OT's Basic Problem," adapted from a lecture of Dec. 2, 1952, quoted in *Advance!*, no. 38, p. 14.

2. SOURCE

21 two bordellos: www.helenahistory.org/family_theatre_reeves.htm.

21 Lafayette Waterbury: Miller, *Bare-Faced Messiah*, pp. 8–15.

21 "I was riding broncs": Hubbard, handwritten memo dated "10 Mar 74."

21 **"devouring shelves of classics":** *The Humanitarian: Education*, The *Ron* magazines, 1996, p. 9.
21 **Hubbard's family was Methodist:** Karin Pouw, personal communication.
21 **"Many members of my":** Hubbard, "Case Analysis: Rock Hunting" question and answer period, Aug. 4, 1958.
21 **"I learned long ago":** The Old Tom Madfeathers story is related by Hubbard's official biographer, Dan Sherman, at the L. Ron Hubbard Centennial Celebration, March 13, 2011; Hubbard's quote was a voice-over. A spokesperson for the Blackfoot Nation says that blood-brotherhood is not a part of their tradition.
21 **"Snake" Thompson:** Thompson's existence has been called into question. Russell Miller says, "He cannot be identified from US Navy records, nor can his relationships with Freud be established" (*Bare-Faced Messiah*, p. 25). Since Miller's book, however, there have been a number of new Snake Thompson discoveries, which add substance to this extraordinary man. Among other enterprises, he helped found the Zoological Society of San Diego, served as the vice president of the Washington Psychoanalytic Association, and was director of the Siamese Cat Society. Thompson's activities as a spy are chronicled in an eccentric memoir by Rhoda Low Seoane, *Uttermost East and the Longest War* (New York: Vantage Press, 1968).
   The Church of Scientology provided a passenger manifest for the transport ship, USS *Grant*, in November 1923, which lists Commander J. C. Thompson, along with the Hubbard family.
21 **"a very careless man":** Hubbard, "The Story of Dianetics and Scientology," lecture, Oct. 18, 1958.
22 **"I was just a kid":** Hubbard, "Dianetics: The Modern Miracle," lecture, Feb. 6, 1952.
23 **"Man has two fundamental":** Commander J. C. Thompson, "Psychoanalytic Literature," *United States Naval Medical Bulletin* 19, no. 3 (Sept. 1923): 281–85.
23 **"I never knew what to believe":** "Barbara Kaye," quoted in Miller, *Bare-Faced Messiah*, pp. 168–69.
23 **"He braved typhoons":** *Adventurer/Explorer: Daring Deeds and Unknown Realms*, The *Ron* magazines, 1996, p. 6.
23 **"for weeks on end":** *What Is Scientology?*, p. 31.
23 **" 'Why?' Why so much":** Ibid., p. 32.
24 **"The very nature of the Chinaman":** Details of Hubbard's trip to China are to be found in the testimony of Gerald Armstrong in *Church of Scientology, California vs. Armstrong*, 1984, and in his handwritten journals of the period, which were provided as exhibits in the trial. Some points were confirmed by the Church of Scientology responses to queries. A redacted account from Hubbard's diary is in *Letters and Journals: Early Years of Adventure*, The *Ron* magazines, 1997, pp. 46–50.
   The church maintains that there were other travels during this period, saying that Hubbard roamed through Asia for fourteen months, without his parents, returning to China and stopping in India and Singapore, among other places. There is no evidence of those trips in his journals, although he makes references to such experiences in later lectures.
   The church provided a 1929 news article from the *Helena (MT) Independent*, to substantiate Hubbard's extensive travel claims, but the article speaks only of a "trip to the orient last summer with his parents" on their way to Guam. Other records of Hubbard's Asian travels, Tommy Davis told me, had been destroyed because until the Second World War they were being held in Hiroshima.
24 **gliding license was #385:** *Adventurer/Explorer: Daring Deeds and Unknown Realms*, The *Ron* magazines, 1996, p. 53. Hubbard listed his age on the license as twenty-six, although he was nineteen at the time.

24 **"We carefully wrapped"**: Hubbard, "Tailwind Willies," republished in *Adventurer/Explorer: Daring Deeds and Unknown Realms*, The *Ron* magazines, 1996, pp. 44–50.

25 **"Restless young men"**: *Adventurer/Explorer: Daring Deeds and Unknown Realms*, The *Ron* magazines, 1996, p. 10.

25 **"collect whatever one collects"**: Miller, *Bare-Faced Messiah*, p. 52.

25 **That was almost the end**: "Seekers of Pirate Haunts Finally Go," *Baltimore Morning Sun*, June 25, 1932.

26 **It soon became evident**: James Free letter to Robert H. Burgess, June 21, 1986; James Stillman Free oral history, National Press Club, Mar. 25, 1992.

26 **seven or eight hundred dollars**: James Stillman Free oral history, National Press Club, Mar. 25, 1992.

26 **"I tied a hangman's noose"**: *Doris Hamlin* "Daily Record," 1932, in Library of Congress collection.

26 **"the worst and most unpleasant"**: "Doris Hamlin, Jinx Ship, Reaches Port," *Baltimore Evening Sun*, Sept. 7, 1932.

26 **"glorious adventure"**: Miller, *Bare-Faced Messiah*, p. 56.

27 **To fill the usual**: Gruber, *The Pulp Jungle*, pp. 20–24.

28 **a hundred thousand words**: *What Is Scientology?*, p. 581. Hubbard's eldest son, L. Ron Hubbard, Jr., claimed that his father exaggerated his output. "Through the early fifties, he used to tell everybody that he had written seven million words of fiction. But, in fact, it probably never exceeded a million words." Testimony of L. Ron Hubbard, Jr., City of Clearwater Commission Hearings Re: The Church of Scientology. May 5, 1982. Of course, that's still an extraordinary output.

28 **a roll of butcher paper**: *Harlan Ellison: Dreams with Sharp Teeth*, DVD, directed by Erik Nelson, 1982.

28 **It was a physical act**: Russell Hays tape with Barbara Hays Duke, June 30, 1984.

28 **"First draft, last draft"**: Interview with anonymous former Sea Org member.

28 **Ron fashioned an incubator**: Miller, *Bare-Faced Messiah*, pp. 64–65.

28 **"the prettiest place"**: Hubbard letter to Russell Hays, Sept. 14, 1936.

28 **"vague offers"**: Ibid. Aug. 18, 1936.

28 **"I have discarded Hollywood"**: Ibid., Sept. 14, 1936.

28 **But in the spring**: Ibid., Mar. 7, 1936.

28 **He later claimed**: Miller, *Bare-Faced Messiah*, p. 69.

29 **"dumb Jew producers"**: Hubbard letter to Russell Hays, July 21, 1937.

29 **"Never write about"**: Ibid., Dec. 4, 1937, quoted in *Letters and Journals: Literary Correspondence*, The *Ron* magazines, 1997, pp. 55–58.

29 **"While under the influence"**: Hubbard letter, Jan. 1, 1938, quoted in *The Philosopher: The Rediscovery of the Human Soul*, The *Ron* magazines, 1996, p. 9.

29 **The nurse looked startled**: Forrest Ackerman interview, "Secret Lives—L. Ron Hubbard," Channel 4, UK, 1997; Arthur J. Cox, "Deus Ex Machina: A Study of A. E. van Vogt," *Science-Fiction Advertiser*, July 1952. Cox's account varies in that he reports Hubbard as saying that the incident took place "during an operation being performed upon him for certain injuries received in the service."

29 **"Don't let him know!"**: Church of Scientology International, "Port Orchard Washington, January 1, 1938," 2012, www.ronthephilosopher.org/phlspher/page08.htm.

30 **"Once upon a time"**: *The Philosopher: The Rediscovery of the Human Soul*, The *Ron* magazines, 1996, pp. 11–12.

30 **"I have high hopes"**: Miller, *Bare-Faced Messiah*, p. 81.

30 **Hubbard explained to his agent**: Ibid., p. 79. Gerald Armstrong testified that Hubbard "stated that seven people originally read it and a couple of them jumped out of windows and another two went insane." *Church of Scientology California vs. Gerald Armstrong.*

30 **The last time he showed Excalibur:** Forrest Ackerman interview, "Secret Lives—L. Ron Hubbard," Channel 4, UK, 1997.

31 **"worthless":** Hubbard letter to Russell Hays, Oct. 20, 1938. (Also quoted and mistakenly dated as Dec. 31, 1937, in *Letters and Journals: Literary Correspondence,* The *Ron* magazines, 1997, pp. 59–61.)

31 **"a tall, large man":** Asimov, *I. Asimov,* p. 72.

31 **"A deviant figure of":** Amis, *New Maps of Hell,* p. 84.

31 **Fanzines and sci-fi clubs:** I was aided in this insight by Steven Weinberg, who recalled for me the science-fiction club at Bronx High, which he attended in the 1940s; he and his classmate Sheldon Glashow, who was also in the club, went on to share the Nobel Prize in Physics in 1979.

31 **"Science fiction, particularly":** Hubbard, introduction to *Battlefield Earth,* p. xix.

31 **"I had, myself, somewhat":** Ibid., p. xvi.

32 **"In his late twenties":** L. Sprague de Camp, "El-Ron of the City of Brass," from "Literary Swordsmen and Sorcerers," *Fantastic,* August 1975.

32 **"Because of her coldness":** "The Admissions of L. Ron Hubbard," www.gerryarmstrong.org/50grand/writings/ars/ars-2000-03-11.html. The church disputes the authenticity of this document, claiming that it is a forgery.

33 **"I loved her and she me":** Ibid.

33 **Polly had discovered:** Russell Miller interview with Robert MacDonald Ford, "The *Bare-Faced Messiah* Interviews," Sept. 1, 1986, www.cs.cmu.edu/~dst/Library/Shelf/miller/interviews/robford.htm.

33 **"two-fold, one to win":** Miller, *Bare-Faced Messiah,* p. 89.

33 **While he was stranded:** Ibid., pp. 90–91.

33 **"Throughout all this":** Church of Scientology International, "1939–1944, Explorer and Master Mariner," 2005, www.hubbard.org/pg007.html.

34 **he failed the entrance examination:** Miller, *Bare-Faced Messiah,* pp. 45–46.

34 **"I do not have the time":** Hubbard request to US Marine Corps, July 18, 1931.

34 **"a well-known writer":** Warren G. Magnuson letter to "The President," April 8, 1941; L. Ron Hubbard military records, National Personnel Records Center.

34 **"one of the most brilliant men":** Miller, *Bare-Faced Messiah,* p. 93.

34 **Hubbard said that he:** Thomas Moulton testimony, *Church of Scientology California vs. Gerald Armstrong.* "I never saw the scars," Moulton admitted. For a comprehensive list of the contradictions in Hubbard's various war accounts, see Chris Owen, "Ron the 'War Hero,'" July 1999, www.spaink.net/cos/warher/battle.htm#doc-a.

35 **"first U.S. returned casualty":** Hubbard, "A Brief Biography of L. Ron Hubbard," brochure for the First Australian Congress of the Hubbard Association of Scientologists International, Nov. 7–8, 1959.

35 **By assuming unauthorized authority:** L. D. Causey to Commandant, Twelfth Naval District, Feb. 14, 1942.

35 **USS YP-422:** Chris Owen, "Ron the 'War Hero,'" July 1999, www.cs.cmu.edu/~dst/Cowen/warhero/battle.htm. Owen notes that this vessel is often referred to as the USS *Mist,* but that no such ship existed.

35 **"Upon entering the Boston":** *The Humanitarian: The Road to Self-Respect,* The *Ron* magazines, p. 12. 1996. Chris Owen, "Ron the 'War Hero,'" July 1999, www.cs.cmu.edu/~dst/Cowen/warhero/yp-422.htm.

35 **"with some seventy depth charge runs":** Chris Owen, "Ron the 'War Hero,'" July 1999, www.cs.cmu.edu/~dst/Cowen/warhero/battle.htm.

35 **"not temperamentally fitted":** Lieutenant (jg) F. A. Del Marinal cable, Sept. 25, 1942.

35 **He arrived wearing dark:** Thomas Moulton testimony, *Church of Scientology California vs. Gerald Armstrong.*

36 "a very loose person": "The Admissions of L. Ron Hubbard," www.gerryarm strong.org/50grand/writings/ars/ars-2000-03-11.html.

36 Hubbard was finally given: Chris Owen, "Ron the 'War Hero,' " July 1999, www .spaink.net/cos/warher/battle.htm#doc-a.

36 "These little sweethearts": "Ex-Portlander Hunts U-Boats," *Oregon Journal*, April 22, 1943.

37 bottom of his class: Chris Owen, "Ron the 'War Hero,' " July 1999, www.cs .cmu.edu/~dst/Cowen/warhero/battle.htm.

37 "It made noises like": Thomas Moulton testimony, *Church of Scientology California vs. Gerald Armstrong.*

37 "The target was moving": Hubbard, "An Account of the Action Off Cape Lookout," undated report.

38 with dawn breaking: Ibid.

38 "There was no submarine": Commander Frank Jack Fletcher to Commander in Chief, Pacific Fleet, June 6, 1943.

38 Japanese records after: Chris Owen, "Ron the 'War Hero,' " July 1999, www .spaink.net/cos/warher/battle.htm#doc-a.

39 "This on top of": "The Admissions of L. Ron Hubbard," www.gerryarmstrong .org/50grand/writings/ars/ars-2000-03-11.html.

39 He spent the next: Miller, *Bare-Faced Messiah*, p. 107.

39 "Once conversant with the": Hubbard request to School of Military Government, Sept. 9, 1944.

39 none proved useful: Patterson, *Robert A. Heinlein*, Vol. 1: *In Dialogue with His Century*, p. 350.

39 "Ron had had a busy war": Miller, *Bare-Faced Messiah*, p. 109.

40 Hubbard had an affair with Heinlein's wife: Patterson, *Robert A. Heinlein*, pp. 369-70.

40 "He almost forced me": "The Admissions of L. Ron Hubbard," www.gerryarm strong.org/50grand/writings/ars/ars-2000-03-11.html.

40 Vida Jameson . . . "Quiet, shy little greymouse": Samme Buck, personal correspondence; Frederik Pohl, "The Worlds of L. Ron Hubbard, Part 2," *The Way of the Future Blogs.*

40 "Blinded with injured optic": Hubbard, "My Philosophy," *The Philosopher: The Rediscovery of the Human Soul*, The *Ron* magazines, p. 85.

40 "I had no one": Ibid.

40 Doctors at Oak Knoll: Miller, *Bare-Faced Messiah*, p. 112.

41 nor do his military records: Hubbard said in 1950 that he was treated for "ulcers, conjunctivitis, deteriorating eyesight, bursitis and something wrong with my feet." Albert Q. Maisel, "Dianetics: Science or Hoax?" *Look*, Dec. 5, 1950.

41 "And I was watching this": Hubbard, "The Story of Dianetics and Scientology," lecture, Oct. 18, 1958.

41 "My wife left me": "The Admissions of L. Ron Hubbard," www.gerryarm strong.org/50grand/writings/ars/ars-2000-03-11.html.

41 Hubbard towed a house trailer: Alva Rogers, quoted in Carter, *Sex and Rockets*, p. 103.

41 "James Dean of the occult": Hugh B. Urban, "The Occult Roots of Scientology? L. Ron Hubbard, Aleister Crowley, and the Origins of a Controversial New Religion," *Novo Religio: The Journal of Alternative and Emergent Religions* (February 2012): 94.

41 He acquired a three-story: Kansa, *Wormwood Star*, p. 28.

41 twelve-car garage: Sara Elizabeth Hollister (formerly Sara Northrup Hubbard) tapes, Stephen A. Kent Collection on Alternative Religions.

41 The house had once belonged: Letter from Arthur Fleming to John Muir, Feb. 8, 1911; Pendle, *Strange Angel*, p. 208.

42 **"Must not believe in God"**: Russell Miller interview with Nieson Himmel, "The *Bare-Faced Messiah* Interviews," www.cs.cmu.edu/~dst/Library/Shelf/miller /interviews/himmel.htm.

42 **Among those passing**: Carter, *Sex and Rockets*, pp. 84–86; Pendle, *Strange Angel*, pp. 244–45.

42 **"women in diaphanous gowns"**: Carter, *Sex and Rockets*, p. 84.

42 **captured in a portrait**: Pendle, *Strange Angel*, p. 209.

42 **"The breakup of the home"**: Parsons, *Freedom Is a Two-Edged Sword*, p. 69.

42 **Sara Elizabeth "Betty" Northrup**: Pendle, *Strange Angel*, p. 255. Miller, *Bare-Faced Messiah*, p. 116.

42 **lost her virginity**: Pendle, *Strange Angel*, p. 203.

42 **"Her chief interest"**: Ibid.

43 **when she was fifteen**: Sara Elizabeth Hollister (formerly Sara Northrup Hubbard) tapes, Stephen A. Kent Collection on Alternative Religions.

43 **"He was not only a writer"**: Ibid.

43 **"He dominated the scene"**: Alva Rogers, quoted in Carter, *Sex and Rockets*, p. 103.

43 **"the most gorgeous"**: Miller, *Bare-Faced Messiah*, p. 117.

43 **"a gentleman, red hair"**: Ibid., p. 118.

44 **angry debate**: The Church of Scientology forced the authors of a 1952 Crowley biography, *The Great Beast*, to remove any suggestion that there was a connection between Scientology and black magic. *Church of Scientology of California and John Symonds, MacDonald & Co. (Publishers) Limited, Hazell Watson & Viney*. High Court of Justice, Queen's Bench Division, 1971. The church also provided me with its correspondence with the London *Sunday Times* in 1969 and 1970, in which the newspaper agreed to retract similar statements and not make such references in the future.

44 **envious of his talent**: Grant and Symonds, *The Confessions of Aleister Crowley*, p. 18.

44 **He may have served**: Spence, *Secret Agent 666*.

44 **"Do what thou wilt"**: Grant and Symonds, *The Confessions of Aleister Crowley*, p. 18.

44 **Nibs—Hubbard's estranged**: Allan Sonnenschein, "Inside the Church of Scientology: An Exclusive Interview with L. Ron Hubbard, Jr.," *Penthouse*, June 1983.

45 **"What a lot of people"**: Ibid. The church fiercely disputes any of the derogatory remarks made by Hubbard's son, especially in the *Penthouse* interview. In 1984, L. Ron Hubbard, Jr.—who had changed his name to Ronald DeWolf—stated, "The interview of me in the June 1983 issue of *Penthouse* is true and accurate, period." Transcript of Tape #1 of June 28, 1984—Ron DeWolf. www.lerma net.com/scientology-and-occult/tape-by-L-Ron-Hubbard-jr.htm. However, in 1987, DeWolf signed an affidavit recanting his statements against his father, saying they were "no more than wild flights of fantasy based on my own unlimited imagination." Affidavit of Ronald Edward DeWolf, May 20, 1987, Carson City, Nevada. But five years later, DeWolf testified that he had signed the recantation "in order to protect my wife and children" from threats made by the church. *City of Clearwater Commission Hearings Re: The Church of Scientology*. May 6, 1982, Morning Session.

45 **"spiritual progress did not depend"**: Grant and Symonds, *The Confessions of Aleister Crowley*, pp. 582–83.

45 **"The Abyss"**: Ibid., p. 929 n. 57.

45 **"my very good friend"**: Hubbard, "Conditions of Space/Time/Energy," *Philadelphia Doctorate Course Transcripts*, Dec. 5, 1952.

45 **"That's when Dad decided"**: City of Clearwater Commission Hearings Re: The Church of Scientology. May 6, 1982, Morning Session.

45 "a savage and beautiful woman": Hugh B. Urban, "The Occult Roots of Scientology? L. Ron Hubbard, Aleister Crowley, and the Origins of a Controversial New Religion," *Novo Religio: The Journal of Alternative and Emergent Religions* (February 2012): 98.

45 "invocation of wand": Carter, *Sex and Rockets*, pp. 122–23. Interview with Anthony Torchia.

46 "We observed a brownish": Miller, *Bare-Faced Messiah*, pp. 120–21.

46 "I don't know where I am": Kansa, *Wormwood Star*, p. 41.

46 Cameron's version is that: Ibid., p. 28.

46 "I have my elemental!": Miller, *Bare-Faced Messiah*, p. 121.

46 "Display thyself": Ibid., pp. 122–23.

46 "Instructions were received": Ibid., p. 124.

46 "Apparently Parsons or Hubbard": Ibid., p. 124.

47 aborted another pregnancy: Carter, *Sex and Rockets*, p. 151.

47 "Babalon is incarnate upon": Quoted in Pendle, *Strange Angel*, p. 266.

47 more than twenty thousand dollars: Ibid., p. 267.

47 "I cannot tolerate": Hubbard, Appeal to Administration of Veterans Affairs, July 4, 1946.

47 "I have know": S. E. Northrup letter to Veterans Administration, Los Angeles, July 1, 1946.

47 "Banishing Ritual": Miller, *Bare-Faced Messiah*: p. 127.

47 ship was too damaged: Sara Elizabeth Hollister (formerly Sara Northrup Hubbard) tapes, Stephen A. Kent Collection on Alternative Religions.

47 Parsons gained a judgment: Miller, *Bare-Faced Messiah*, p. 127.

48 "keep him at arm's": Robert Heinlein letter to John Arwine, May 10, 1946.

48 "a very sad case": Virginia Heinlein to Catherine and Sprague de Camp, Aug. 7, 1946.

48 "All right, I'll marry you": Sara Elizabeth Hollister (formerly Sara Northrup Hubbard) tapes, Stephen A. Kent Collection on Alternative Religions. Both the church and Hubbard himself denied that he was ever married to Northrup, although there is a marriage certificate on file in the Kent County Courthouse in Chestertown, Maryland, recording the marriage of Lafayette Hubbard and Sara Elizabeth Northrup on Aug. 10, 1946. Northrup also cites that date in her divorce pleading.

48 "I suppose Polly was": L. Sprague de Camp letter to Heinleins, Aug. 13, 1946.

48 In fact, Polly didn't learn: Miller, *Bare-Faced Messiah*, p. 189.

48 "Mr. Hubbard accomplished": Church of Scientology response to queries. Parsons lost his security clearance in 1948 because he was suspected of leaking state secrets to a foreign power. In 1952, while his wife was at the grocery store, he blew himself up in his garage, apparently accidentally. According to Anthony Torchia, a former member of the OTO, the order dissolved in the 1960s but re-formed in the 1970s and continues to this day. Moreover, the OTO does not consider itself "black" magic.

48 "No work since discharge": Veterans Administration Report of Physical Examination, Sept. 19, 1946.

49 "I got up and left": Sara Elizabeth Hollister (formerly Sara Northrup Hubbard) tapes, Stephen A. Kent Collection on Alternative Religions.

49 churning out plots: Ibid. Among the stories Sara Northrup claimed to have written were the Ole Doc Methuselah series in *Amazing Science Fiction*.

49 "I kept thinking": Ibid.

49 Nibs told her: Ibid.

49 Ron was arrested: Ibid.

50 I am utterly unable": Hubbard letter to Veterans Administration, Oct. 15, 1947.

50 "a manic depressive": Miller, *Bare-Faced Messiah*, p. 175.

50 "He said he always wanted": www.cs.cmu.edu/~dst/Library/Shelf/miller/interviews/barbkaye.htm.

50 "Paranoid personality": Jim Dincalci, personal communication.

50 "malignant narcissism": Stephen Wiseman, personal communication.

51 "a kind of self-therapy": *Church of Scientology, California, v. Gerald Armstrong.* Information that has become available since the Armstrong trial, such as the Heinlein and Hays letters, confirms much of the material in the Affirmations, adding to its credibility.

54 "the Empress": Atack, *A Piece of Blue Sky*, p. 100, says that Hubbard may also have called his Guardian Hathor, an Egyptian goddess usually depicted with cow horns. In the Affirmations, Hubbard explicitly names his Guardian Flavia Julia. He may have been referring to Flavia Julia Titi, daughter of the Roman Emperor Titus; or, perhaps more likely, to the Empress Flavia Julia Helena Augustus, also known as Saint Helen, mother of Constantine the Great, who is credited with finding the "True Cross." Jim Dincalci told me that L. Ron Hubbard, Jr., referred to his father's Guardian as the source of his automatic writing; also, that Aiwass, Crowley's Guardian, was in charge of this sector of the universe.

54 miniature kangaroos: Miller, *Bare-Faced Messiah*, p. 140.

54 hypnotize Sara's mother: Sara Elizabeth Hollister (formerly Sara Northrup Hubbard) tapes, Stephen A. Kent Collection on Alternative Religions.

55 "The organization is clearly schizophrenic": Judge Paul G. Breckenridge, *Church of Scientology, California, v. Gerald Armstrong.*

55 "I went right down": Hubbard, "The Story of Dianetics and Scientology," lecture, Oct. 18, 1958.

56 "I used to sit": Sue Lindsay, "Book Pulls Hubbard into Public," *Rocky Mountain News*, Feb. 20, 1983.

56 "I cannot imagine how": Hubbard letter to Veterans Administration, Jan. 27, 1948.

56 "Been amusing myself making": Hubbard letter to Russell Hays, July 15, 1948.

56 he floats the idea of a book: Ibid.

56 "I got to revolutionize": Ibid., Aug. 16, 1948.

56 "I was hiding behind": Hubbard, "The Story of Dianetics and Scientology," lecture, Oct. 18, 1958.

57 "I will soon, I hope": Hubbard letter to Robert Heinlein, Nov. 24, 1948.

57 a Guggenheim grant: Ibid., Sept. 25, 1948.

57 a loan of fifty dollars: Ibid., Feb. 17, 1949.

57 "Golly, I never was": Ibid., Mar. 3, 1949.

57 "getting case histories": Ibid.

57 "My hip and stomach": Ibid., Mar. 8, 1949.

57 It ain't *agin* religion": Ibid., Mar. 31, 1949.

58 "Dammit, the man's got": John Campbell letter to Robert Heinlein, July 26, 1949.

58 "deep hypnosis": Ibid.

58 "I was born": Ibid., Sept. 15, 1949.

59 lost twenty pounds: Ibid.

59 "The key to world sanity": Ibid.

59 "a little old shack": Hubbard letter to Robert Heinlein, Dec. 30, 1949.

59 Announcing a New Hubbard Edition: Undated correspondence from Hubbard to Robert and Virginia Heinlein.

60 "Ron is going at": Sara Hubbard letter to Robert and Virginia Heinlein, May 2, 1950.

60 "begun Jan. 12, '50": Hubbard letter to Robert and Virginia Heinlein, Mar. 28, 1950.

60 the Empress, had dictated: Atack, *A Piece of Blue Sky*, p. 101.

60 Sara read Korzybski: Sara Elizabeth Hollister (formerly Sara Northrup Hubbard) tapes, Stephen A. Kent Collection on Alternative Religions.

60 "Bob Heinlein sat down": Hubbard, "Study of the Particle," lecture, Oct. 29, 1953.

61 "This article is *not* a hoax": Quoted in Miller, *Bare-Faced Messiah*, p. 153.

61 "I know dianetics is": Ibid, pp. 152–53.

61 Nobel Peace Prize: Alfred Bester, "Part 6 of Alfred Bester and Frederik Pohl—The Conversation," recorded at The Tyneside, Newcastle upon Tyne, UK, June 26, 1978.

61 "fifty thousand years": *What Is Scientology?*, p. 106.

61 "with 18 million copies sold": Ibid.

61 "Cells are evidently sentient": Hubbard, *Dianetics*, p. 70.

62 "The operator then touches": Ibid., pp. 55–56.

62 "handled like a marionette": Ibid., p. xiii.

62 "many years of exact research": Ibid., p. xxv.

62 "She is rendered": Ibid., p. 60.

62 "This is not theory": Ibid., p. 75.

62 "exact science": Ibid., p. xviii.

62 "Dianetics deletes": Ibid., p. xiii

63 "You will find many": Ibid., p. xxv.

63 outnumbering those being treated: "Care of Mental Patients Remains Major Problem," *Associated Press*, Apr. 29, 1949. Reitman, *Inside Scientology*, p. 26.

64 "in less than twenty hours": Hubbard, *Dianetics*, p. ix.

64 "It was sweepingly": Hubbard, "The Story of Dianetics and Scientology," lecture, Oct. 10, 1958.

64 "This volume probably": Isidor Isaac Rabi, "Dianetics: The Modern Science of Mental Health, by L. Ron Hubbard (review), *Scientific American*, January 1951, pp. 57–58

64 "expressive of a spirit": Erich Fromm, " 'Dianetics'—For Seekers of Prefabricated Happiness," *The New York Herald Tribune Book Review*, September 3, 1950, p. 7.

64 "The art consists": S. I. Hayakawa, "From Science-fiction to Fiction-science," *Etc.* 8, no. 4 (Summer 1951).

65 "While listening to Hubbard": Winter, *A Doctor's Report on Dianetics*, p. 11.

65 "When I count": Hubbard, *Dianetics*, p. 201.

65 "He would hold hands": Sara Elizabeth Hollister (formerly Sara Northrup Hubbard) tapes, Stephen A. Kent Collection on Alternative Religions.

65 "He has on a long": Winter, *A Doctor's Report on Dianetics*, pp. 15–16.

66 "Everything goes back": Freud letter to Wilhelm Fliess, May 2, 1897.

66 "It seems to me": Ibid., p. 461.

66 "The extreme achievement on these lines": Freud, "The Paths to the Formations of Symptoms," Lecture 23 in *Introductory Lectures on Psycho-Analysis*, trans. Jas. Strachey, p. 460. Whitehead comments on this passage: "To generalize from the experience of Freud and his colleagues and from later experiments in hypnotic age-regression, the further one pushes the subject back into the past, the more apt one is to provoke confabulation." Whitehead, *Renunciation and Reformulation*, p. 80.

67 "had passed for 'normal' ": Hubbard, *Dianetics*, pp. 299–300.

67 "It is a scientific": Ibid., p. 132.

67 "Twenty or thirty abortion attempts": Ibid., p. 158.

67 "However many billions": Ibid., pp. 132–33.

68 "One I observed when":" L. Ron Hubbard, Jr., testimony. City of Clearwater Commission Hearings Re: The Church of Scientology, May 5, 1982.

68 "I was born at six": Allan Sonnenschein, "Inside the Church of Scientology: An Exclusive Interview with L. Ron Hubbard, Jr.," *Penthouse*, June 1983. The church's objections to Hubbard Jr.'s statements, based on his signed retraction, and his disavowal of the retraction, are noted above.

68 "but conceived despite all precautions": "The Admissions of L. Ron Hubbard," www.gerryarmstrong.org/50grand/writings/ars/ars-2000-03-11.html

68 Hubbard kicked her: Sara Elizabeth Hollister (formerly Sara Northrup Hubbard) tapes, Stephen A. Kent Collection on Alternative Religions.

68 Hubbard told one of his lovers: "Barbara Kaye," quoted in Miller, *Bare-Faced Messiah*, p. 168.

68 "Migraine headache": Church of Scientology International, letter from L. Ron Hubbard to the American Psychological Association, Apr. 13, 1949, www.ron thephilosopher.org/phlspher/page16.htm.

68 In a similar letter: *Letters and Journals: The Dianetics Letters*, The Ron magazines, pp. 14–15.

68 When scientists tested: Ibid., p. 74.

68 "The psychiatrist and his front groups": Hubbard, "Today's Terrorists," psych fraud.freedommag.org/page44.htm.

69 "had the power to torture": Hubbard, *Introduction to Scientology Ethics*, p. 264.

69 "the sole cause of decline": Hubbard, "Pain and Sex," HCO Bulletin, Aug. 26, 1982.

69 "The money was just": Corydon, *L. Ron Hubbard*, p. 307.

69 The people who were drawn: Wallis, *The Road to Total Freedom*, p. 56.

69 Through Dianetics, they hoped: Ibid., pp. 62–63.

69 "has complete recall": Hubbard, *Dianetics*, p. 171.

69 "World's First Clear": Miller, *Bare-Faced Messiah*, p. 165.

70 "there were never any clears": O'Brien, *Dianetics in Limbo*, p. xi.

70 "With or without an argument": Sara Elizabeth Hollister (formerly Sara Northrup Hubbard) tapes, Stephen A. Kent Collection on Alternative Religions.

70 "I do not want to be an American husband": *Sara Northrup Hubbard vs. L. Ron Hubbard*, Complaint for Divorce. Los Angeles, Apr. 23, 1951.

70 Sara and Miles were plotting: Miller, *Bare-Faced Messiah*, p. 176.

71 "He didn't want her": Sara Elizabeth Hollister (formerly Sara Northrup Hubbard) tapes, Stephen A. Kent Collection on Alternative Religions.

71 "dianetic baby": W. A. Sprague and Roland Wild, "Can We Doctor Our *Minds* at Home?" *Oakland Tribune*, Oct. 29, 1950.

71 "Don't sleep.": Corydon, *L. Ron Hubbard*, p. 306.

71 "We have Alexis": "Dianetics Chief's Conduct Lashed," *Los Angeles Times*, Apr. 25, 1951.

72 a young couple had just left: "Hiding of Baby Charged to Dianetics Author," *Los Angeles Times*, Apr. 11, 1951.

72 clean bill of health: Miller, *Bare-Faced Messiah*, p. 179.

72 "cut her into little pieces": Sara Elizabeth Hollister (formerly Sara Northrup Hubbard) tapes, Stephen A. Kent Collection on Alternative Religions.

72 "He believed that as long": Miller, *Bare-Faced Messiah*, p. 179.

72 "systematic torture": *Sara Northrup Hubbard vs. L. Ron Hubbard et al.* Superior Court, State of California, April 23, 1951.

73 "If I can help": Miller, *Bare-Faced Messiah*, p. 189.

73 a monkey in a cage: Ibid. Sara Elizabeth Hollister (formerly Sara Northrup Hubbard) tapes, Stephen A. Kent Collection on Alternative Religions.

73 Hubbard wrote all night: Russell Miller interview with Richard de Mille, "The *Bare-Faced Messiah* Interviews," July 25, 1986, www.cs.cmu.edu/~dst/Library /Shelf/miller/interviews/demille.htm.

73 **"People below the 2.0 level"**: Hubbard, *Science of Survival*, p. 28.
74 **"Sex," he wrote**: Ibid., pp. 114–15.
74 **"Here is the harlot"**: Ibid., p. 116.
74 **"we get general neglect"**: Ibid., p. 118.
74 **To Alexis Valerie Hubbard**: Ibid. The dedication was removed from subsequent editions.
75 **"as a classified scientist"**: "Dianetics Man Reports He's in Cuban Hospital," *Los Angeles Times*, May 2, 1951.
75 **"a Cadillac so damn long"**: Russell Hays tape with Barbara Hays Duke, June 30, 1984.
75 **"I am, basically, a scientist":**" Hubbard letter to the Attorney General, Department of Justice, May 14, 1951.
75 **"He told me that I was under the influence"**: Sara Elizabeth Hollister (formerly Sara Northrup Hubbard) tapes, Stephen A. Kent Collection on Alternative Religions.
77 **The foundation he had**: "Science Group in Bankruptcy," *Wichita Beacon*, February 25, 1952.
77 **"That didn't please him"**: Russell Hays tape with Barbara Hays Duke, June 30, 1984.
78 **"It sees all, knows all"**: Hubbard, *Electropsychometric Auditing Operator's Manual*, p. 57.

3. GOING OVERBOARD

79 **constructing the intricate bureaucracy**: When Hubbard was alive, he oversaw the church bureaucracy. Directly under him were the Executive Director International, who handled administration, and a Senior Case Supervisor International, who oversaw the tech. Hubbard appointed both officials. To one side of the EDI on the organizational chart was the Watchdog Committee, which consisted of executives in charge of each division of the international orgs. Under Miscavige, the EDI was essentially eliminated. Interview with Roy Selby.
79 **"sperm dreams"**: Hubbard, *Dianetics*, p. 294.
79 **"as early as shortly before"**: Hubbard, *Dianetics: The Evolution of a Science*, p. 93.
79 **"The subject of past deaths"**: Hubbard, *Science of Survival*, p. 61.
80 **"There is a different feel to"**: O'Brien, *Dianetics in Limbo*, p. 14.
80 **"I literally shuddered"**: Ibid., p. 20.
81 **about twenty percent of the population**: Hubbard, *Scientology: A New Slant on Life*, p. 192.
81 **"A Suppressive Person will"**: Hubbard, *Introduction to Scientology Ethics*, p. 171.
81 **"The artist in particular"**: Hubbard, *Scientology: A New Slant on Life*, p. 195.
81 **Imitators and competitors came**: Cf. Wallis, *The Road to Total Freedom*, pp. 80 ff.
82 **"I'd like to start a religion"**: Eshbach, *Over My Shoulder*, p. 125. Hubbard allegedly made this remark in 1948 or 1949. Arnie Lerma, a former Scientologist who maintains an anti-Scientology website, compiled a list of nine witnesses who said that they heard Hubbard make similar claims; www.lermanet.com/reference/hubbard-start-a-religion.htm. Hubbard's son, L. Ron Hubbard, Jr., said, "He told me and a lot of other people that the way to make a million was to start a religion." Allan Sonnenschein, "Inside the Church of Scientology: An Exclusive Interview with L. Ron Hubbard, Jr.," *Penthouse*, June 1983. Sara Northrup recalled that Hubbard "kept saying 'If you want to make any money

the only way to do it is to make a religion so the government wouldn't take it all.' So he thought he could make a religion out of Dianetics." Sara Elizabeth Hollister (formerly Sara Northrup Hubbard) tapes, Stephen A. Kent Collection on Alternative Religions.

82 "To keep a person on": Revised Declaration of Hana Whitfield, *Church of Scientology vs. Steven Fishman and Uwe Geertz,* US District Court, Central District of California, Apr. 4, 1994.

82 "Perhaps we could call": Hubbard letter to Helen O'Brien, "RE CLINIC, HAS," Apr. 10, 1953.

83 Hubbard incorporated three different churches: Wallis, *The Road to Total Freedom,* p. 128.

83 The Church of Scientology of California: Miller, *Bare-Faced Messiah,* pp. 220–21.

83 "many, many reasons": Jas. Phelan, "Have You Ever Been a Boo-Hoo?" *Saturday Evening Post,* Mar. 21, 1964.

84 "The goal of Dianetics": Hubbard, *Science of Survival,* p. xxxviii.

84 "injected entities": Hubbard, *Scientology: A History of Man,* p. 20.

84 "In the bivalve state":" Ibid., pp. 40–42.

85 "pragmatic, cold, cunning": Hal Holmes, personal communication.

85 She had flinty blue eyes: Ken Urquhart, "Friendly Recollections of Mary Sue Hubbard," marysuehubbard.com/ken.shtml.

85 Hubbard was prospering once again: Miller, *Bare-Faced Messiah,* pp. 226–27.

85 "so knock off the idolizing.": Interview with Philip Spickler.

86 "It should be taken daily": Hubbard, *All About Radiation,* p. 113.

86 much of their time unsupervised: Interview with anonymous former Sea Org member.

86 extensive household staff: Anderson, *Report of the Board of Inquiry into Scientology,* p. 42.

87 The headline in *Garden News:* Quoted in Miller, *Bare-Faced Messiah,* p. 235.

88 "mapping out the bank": Interview with anonymous former Sea Org member.

88 School was, as usual: Ibid.

89 "What is this 'Scientology'?": Ibid.

89 "little old English lady": Ken Urquhart, "My Friend, the Titan," *IVy* 60, Jan. 2003.

89 "Your friends": Ibid.

90 It was rumored that: Miller, *Bare-Faced Messiah,* pp. 215–16.

90 "My attention wandered": Ken Urquhart, "My Friend, the Titan," *Ivy* 60 (Jan. 2003).

90 "all mental and nervous disorders": Malko, *Scientology,* p. 76. Miriam Ottenberg, *The Evening Star,* January 1963.

90 The IRS began an audit: The IRS audit began in 1965. The Church of Scientology of California was informed by the IRS that it no longer was recognized as a tax-exempt religious organization in July 1967. That status remained in effect for twenty-six years.

91 "There are some features": *Report of the Board of Inquiry into Scientology,* p. 1.

91 "a man of restless energy": Ibid., p. 42.

91 "Some of his claims": Ibid., p. 43.

91 "an insensate hostility": Ibid., p. 47.

91 The report led to: Rev. Kenneth J. Whitman, President of the Church of Scientology of California and National Spokesman, undated "Press Statement" (although stamped "Top Secret"). Documents that the church obtained through Freedom of Information requests do show widespread cooperation among various international investigative agencies.

91   another "first Clear": Lamont, *Religion, Inc.*, p. 53. Hana Eltringham says it was in August 1966, but Hubbard and McMaster were already in Rhodesia by then. Affidavit of Hana Eltringham Whitfield, Mar. 8, 1994.

91   McMaster adopted a clerical: Lamont, *Religion, Inc.*, p. 57.

92   Scientology's first "pope": Ibid. Kenneth Urquhart remembers the post as being merely a "cardinal." Kenneth Urquhart, personal communication.

92   "He was very pronounced": Interview with Jim Dincalci.

92   "curb the growth": Wallis, *The Road to Total Freedom*, p. 195.

92   "I had been ill": "Further Information on L. Ron HUBBARD and Laurence L. HAUTZ," CIA dispatch, Aug. 22, 1966.

92   He resigned as Executive: Reitman, *Inside Scientology*, p. 80; and Malko, *Scientology*, p. 82.

92   Rhodes was homosexual: Rotberg, *The Founder*, p. 408.

92   Hubbard had a fantasy: Interview with Hana Eltringham Whitfield.

93   issuing passports: Hana Eltringham (Whitfield), interview, "Secret Lives— L. Ron Hubbard," Channel 4, UK, 1997.

93   However, the current prime minister: Miller, *Bare-Faced Messiah*, p. 258.

93   "He told me Ian Smith": Lamont, *Religion, Inc.*, p. 54.

93   "drinking lots of rum": Corydon, *L. Ron Hubbard*, p. 59. The church says an apostate fabricated this letter.

93   "Your Sugie": Interview with Dan Koon. Neville Chamberlin told me he saw Hubbard's "pharmaceutical cabinet," which was amply supplied with drugs, and he says he witnessed Hubbard injecting himself in the thigh on one occasion, but he doesn't know what substance Hubbard was using. "He used drugs almost as a shaman," Chamberlin speculates.

93   "I want to die": Virginia Downsborough, quoted in Miller, *Bare-Faced Messiah*, p. 266.

93   "All this recent career": Hubbard, "Ron's Journal '67." Taped lecture.

94   Blavatsky had prophesied: Interview with Hana Eltringham Whitfield. This was her impression, although there doesn't seem to be a reference to such a redheaded leader in Blavatsky. It seems to have been an impression that Whitfield carried with her when she first met Hubbard.

94   "There's a course starting": Interview with Hana Eltringham Whitfield.

95   "That is where the Fifth Invaders": Ibid.

96   "The rollers! The rollers!":.Ibid.

96   "Eyes tire easily": Veterans Administration, Report of Medical Examination for Disability Evaluation, July 27, 1951.

97   Hubbard had written: Hubbard, *Dianetics*, pp. 10–11.

97   a habit of squinting: Interview with Dr. Catherine Kennedy. Hana Eltringham, for instance, told me that although she never saw Hubbard wearing glasses, "I often saw him squint when he picked up a paper to read. . . . He did the same when he looked at people he was talking to."

97   "astigmatism, a distortion": Hubbard, Professional Auditor's Bulletin No. 111, "Eyesight and Glasses," compiled from ACC tape material, May 1, 1957.

97   "You're doing yourself": Tracy Ekstrand, personal communication.

97   All of Hubbard's senses: Interviews with Dan Koon, Tracy Ekstrand, Hana Eltringham Whitfield, and Sinar Parman.

98   Yvonne Gillham: Interviews with Hana Eltringham Whitfield and anonymous former Sea Org members.

99   There were three ships: According to Karin Pouw, there were ten ships in the Scientology fleet, but she includes recreational sailboats. There were two "station ships" in Long Beach and Los Angeles, the *Excalibur* and the *Bolivar*, but Hubbard was never on either of them. Mike Rinder, personal communication.

99   The smokestack: Hawkins, *Counterfeit Dreams*, p. 60.

99 **Hubbard spent most of his time:** Ken Urquhart, "What Was Ron Really Like?" address to 2012 Class VIII Reunion, Los Angeles, July 14–15, 2012.

99 **His restless leg:** Interviews with Daniel Holeman and anonymous former Sea Org member.

99 **"I think he was doing":** Interview with Jim Dincalci.

99 **Hubbard and Mary Sue would dine:** Interviews with Tracy Ekstrand, Bel Ferradj, and Jim Dincalci.

100 **Anyone who registered:** Monica Pignotti, "My Nine Lives in Scientology," 1989. www.cs.cmu.edu/~dst/Library/Shelf/pignotti/.

100 **"We Come Back":** Hubbard, *Mission into Time*, p. 27.

100 **"The end justifies the means":** Interview with Jim Dincalci. Actually, Machiavelli never made that statement, although it is frequently attributed to him. It is a mistranslation of a key passage from *The Prince*: "*e nelle azioni di tutti li uomini, e massime de' principi, dove non e iudizio da reclamare, si guarda al fine.*" "The much quoted fragment—si guarda al fine—can be translated as 'one must consider the outcome' but in context, it really refers to consequences of his acts for the stature of the prince, that is, to the blame or praise he earns and not to the relationship between means and ends generally." Philip Bobbitt, personal communication.

100 **a marshal to Joan of Arc:** Joel Sappel and Robert W. Welkos, "The Scientology Story," *Los Angeles Times*, June 24–26, 1990.

100 **Tamburlaine's wife:** Miller, *Bare-Faced Messiah*, p. 362.

100 **driving a race car:** Reitman, *Inside Scientology*, p. 103.

101 **"liaisons in the moonlight":** Interview with Hana Eltringham Whitfield.

101 **We had a lot of good-looking girls":** Hubbard, *Mission into Time*, p. 34.

101 **None was found:** Miller, *Bare-Faced Messiah*, p. 284.

101 **"Recall a time":** Interview with Hana Eltringham Whitfield.

103 **"If there's time":"** Ibid.

103 **"The girl would say":** Hubbard, *Mission into Time*, p. 34.

104 **"We did find the tunnel":** Ibid., p. 40.

104 **"The world we live in now":** Hubbard's lecture, "Assists," Class VIII, Tape 10, Oct. 3, 1968.

105 **"three-D, super colossal":** Hubbard's handwritten note, "Incident 2," part of the OT III materials, Oct. 28, 1968.

105 **"He is not likely":** Hubbard's lecture, "Assists," Class VIII, Tape 10, Oct. 3, 1968.

105 **"the planet of ill repute":** This story is drawn largely from Hubbard's lecture, "Assists," Ibid. It does not come from the actual OT III materials, which the Church of Scientology insists are secret and a trade secret, although they are easily available on the Internet. They do not differ substantively from the material Hubbard discussed in this lecture and wrote about elsewhere.

106 **"We won't go into that":** Interview with Hana Eltringham Whitfield.

106 **threw up violently:** Interview with anonymous former Sea Org member.

107 **"a fucking asshole":** Gerald Armstrong interview, "Secret Lives—L. Ron Hubbard," Channel 4, UK, 1997.

107 **"They held the power":** Interview with Hana Eltringham Whitfield.

107 **intimate but not overtly sexual:** Affidavit of Tonja Burden, Jan. 25, 1980.

107 **When the girls became:** Sue Lindsay, "Genius in a Yellow Straw Hat," *Rocky Mountain News*, Feb. 16, 1986.

107 **"putting ethics in":** Hubbard, *Introduction to Scientology Ethics*, p. 20.

107 **Good and evil actions:** Ibid., pp. 13–14.

108 **"the greatest good":** Ibid., p. 101.

108 **"You have to establish":** Hubbard's lecture, "Ethics and Case Supervision," Oct. 9, 1968.

108 **his cigarette smoking:** "With respect to our parishioners, smoking is a personal choice"; Karin Pouw, personal correspondence.

109 **It had begun with Gibraltar:** Miller, *Bare-Faced Messiah*, p. 275.

109 **England banned foreign Scientologists:** Ibid., p. 289.

109 **"She was like Cinderella":** Interview with "Catherine Harrington."

109 **Mary Sue used to have parties:** Interview with Candy Swanson.

110 **"gorgeous":** Interview with Belkacem Ferradj.

110 **"I hit the bulkhead":** Ibid.

110 **"Never question LRH":** Hana Eltringham Whitfield lecture, Hamburg Symposium, Mar. 26, 2010.

110 **even in rough seas:** "The degree of swell or wave has no bearing on whether they go overboard or not." Hubbard, Flag Order 1499, Oct. 21, 1968.

110 **John McMaster . . . was tossed:** Lamont, *Religion, Inc.*, pp. 53–54.

110 **He left the church:** The church says of McMaster: "He was in his day a 'squirrel' who sought to profit from his off-beat alterations of Mr. Hubbard's discoveries. . . . He died in 1990, an alcoholic, and virtually no one in Scientology today has heard of him." Karin Pouw, personal communication.

111 **"She screamed all the way":** Hana Eltringham Whitfield lecture, Hamburg Symposium, Mar. 26, 2010.

111 **"raw, bleeding noses":** Russell Miller interview with David Mayo, "The *Bare-Faced Messiah* Interviews," Aug. 28, 1986, www.cs.cmu.edu/~dst/Library/Shelf/bfm/interviews/mayo.htm.

111 **Children who committed minor:** Sharone Stainforth, theapolloseries.blogspot.com/2012/07/my-transcript-for-dublin-conference.html.

111 **Derek Greene:** Interview with Hana Eltringham Whitfield. Elsewhere, Whitfield has said the child was confined for four days and nights. Hana Eltringham Whitfield lecture, Hamburg Symposium, Mar. 26, 2010.

111 **Other young children were:** Russell Miller interview with David Mayo, "The *Bare-Faced Messiah* Interviews," Aug. 28, 1986, www.cs.cmu.edu/~dst/Library/Shelf/bfm/interviews/mayo.htm. Tonja Burden recalls "one boy held in there for 30 nights, crying and begging to be released." Affidavit of Tonja Burden, Jan. 25, 1980. Monica Pignotti also writes about the chain locker: Monica Pignotti, "My Nine Lives in Scientology," www.cs.cmu.edu/~dst/Library/Shelf/pignotti/. Sharone Stainforth recalls seeing a four- or five-year-old girl with her top half sticking out of a ship chain locker, and that she was filthy and red-faced from crying. Sharone Stainforth, theapolloseries.blogspot.com/2012/07/my-transcript-for-dublin-conference.html. According to another former Sea Org member, the little girl's name was Angela, "a cute little blond girl that LRH thought was an SP and assigned her to the chain locker. She was so small I believe she crawled out of the locker up the chain to the poop deck as I remember seeing her coming out of that hole. I don't remember what she did but it certainly made me swear to myself to never let that happen to me. I believe Lonnie Garrapie (not sure of the spelling), young boy from Canada, was assigned to the chain locker for stealing and throwing people's belongings, that he stole, over the side—he did that with Kenny Campelman's silver flute, David Ziff's jewelry, and other items. Divers were sent over the side to try and retrieve the items, as they were all of great value." Anonymous former Sea Org member, communication with Lauren Wolf.

112 **Hubbard ruled that they:** Interview with anonymous former Sea Org member.

112 **One little girl, a deaf:** Corydon, *L. Ron Hubbard*, pp. 29–30; Atack, *A Piece of Blue Sky*, p. 180.

112 **"did not have the confront":** Interview with Hana Eltringham Whitfield.

112 **"You would say to yourself":** infinitecomplacency.blogspot.com/2010/03/17-tracing-it-back-to-source_29.html.

112 **"hidden government"**: Hubbard, "Orders of the Day," Dec. 8, 1968.

113 **"useless or unfixable"**: "Catherine Harrington," personal communication.

114 **"I like how you Americans work!"**: Interview with "Catherine Harrington."

114 **"for your protection"**: Ibid.

114 **All were registered**: Robert Gillette, "Scientology Flagship Shrouded in Mystery," *Los Angeles Times*, Aug. 29, 1978, http://www.anti-scientologie.ch/Nan -McLean/Video-Transcript-for-Australia-Final.pdf.

114 **"the pride of the Panamanian fleet"**: "About the Apollo," undated press release.

114 **"the sanest space"**: Monica Pignotti, "My Nine Lives in Scientology," 1989. www.cs.cmu.edu/~dst/Library/Shelf/pignotti/.

115 **"secure Morocco"**: "Catherine Harrington," personal communication.

116 **Mary Sue was thrilled**: Interview with Jim Dincalci.

116 **A hundred people were killed**: Henry Ginger, "Hassan II: Never Sure He'll Be King at Nightfall," *New York Times*, Aug. 20, 1972. General Oufkir's daughter Malika placed the toll at "more than two hundred." Oufkir and Fitoussi, *Stolen Lives*, 81.

116 **create an elite guard**: Interview with Hana Eltringham Whitfield.

117 **"Stop firing!"**: Joseph R. Gregory, "Hassan II of Morocco Dies at 70; A Monarch Oriented to the West," *New York Times*, July 24, 1999.

117 **had committed "suicide"**: Oufkir and Fitoussi, *Stolen Lives*, p. 94.

117 **The shaken king turned his attention**: Garrison, *Playing Dirty*, pp. 79–80. Gillette, "Scientology Flagship Shrouded in Mystery," *Los Angeles Times*, Aug. 29, 1978.

117 **In December 1972**: Ali Amar, "Hassan II, Oufkir et l'eglise de scientology," *Le Journal Hebdomadaire*, Apr. 15, 2006, www.anti-scientologie.ch/Nan -McLean/Video-Transcript-for-Australia-Final.pdf.

117 **"A friend came to me"**: Interview with Paulette Cooper.

118 **"Your mother was with me"**: *Church of Scientology California v. Gerald Armstrong*.

118 **"street-walker"**: Letter from Sara Northrup Hubbard Hollister to Paulette Cooper, March 1972. This letter was posted on the Internet at https://whywe protest.net/community/threads/lrhs-wife-2-wrote-to-paulette-cooper.44174/, but Paulette Cooper verified its authenticity.

118 **"In July 1949 I was in Elizabeth"**: *Church of Scientology California v. Gerald Armstrong*.

118 **"Your good friend, J. Edgar Hoover"**: Letter from Sara Northrup Hubbard Hollister to Paulette Cooper, March 1972.

119 **"an insatiable lust"**: David Mayo interview with Russell Miller, "The *Bare-Faced Messiah* Interviews," Aug. 28, 1986, www.lermanet.com/barwell/david-mayo -interview.txt.

119 **"MAKE MONEY"**: Hubbard, HCO policy letter, "Income Flows and Pools," Issue I, Finance Series 11, Mar. 9, 1972.

119 **more than $300 million**: Robert Lindsey, "Scientology Chief Got Millions, Ex-Aides Say," *New York Times,* July 11, 1984. Reitman notes that by the 1970s Hubbard held accounts in Switzerland, Luxembourg, and Liechtenstein. Money was transferred from a Liberian shell corporation, the Religious Research Foundation, into his accounts. She quotes Laurel Sullivan: "It was fraud, an out-and-out ripping off of funds that were supposed to go to the church." *Inside Scientology*, p. 97.

119 **"Church's was bigger"**: Kima Douglas interview with Russell Miller, "The *Bare-Faced Messiah* Interviews," www.cs.cmu.edu/~dst/Library/Shelf/miller /interviews/kima.htm.

119 **"great chunks of cash"**: L. Ron Hubbard, Jr., testimony, "City of Clearwater Commission Hearings Re: The Church of Scientology," May 6, 1982.

120 **"Making money, I think":** Hana Eltringhim (Whitfield) interview, "Secret Lives—L. Ron Hubbard," Channel 4, UK, 1997.

120 **Hubbard had lost interest:** Interviews with Tracy Ekstrand, Jim Dincalci, and Hana Eltringham Whitfield.

120 **"I could hear him chortling":** Interview with Hana Eltringham Whitfield.

120 **When she learned:** Interview with anonymous former Sea Org member.

120 **"Maybe a hundred Sea Org":** Bornstein, *A Queer and Pleasant Danger*, p. 93.

120 **Hubbard observed that 1972:** Interview with Kate Bornstein.

121 **flown to New York:** Interview with Hana Eltringham Whitfield and anonymous Sea Org member.

121 **convicted in absentia:** Robert Gillette and Robert Rawitch, "Scientology: A Long Trail of Controversy," *Los Angeles Times*, Aug. 27, 1978.

121 **Hubbard flew to New York:** Jim Dincalci, personal communication.

121 **It was an odd interlude:** Interview with Jim Dincalci.

122 **"I'm PTS to nations":** Ibid.

122 **"free to frequent":** Hubbard, "Guardian Order, Secret, Snow White Program," Apr. 20, 1973.

122 **Under Mary Sue's direction:** Reitman, *Inside Scientology*, p. 115; Unsigned, "Mystery of the Vanished Ruler," *Time*, Jan. 31, 1983; Gordon Gregory, "Prosecutors: Scientologists Infiltrated Washington Post," *St. Petersburg Times*, Dec. 4, 1979; "Sentencing Memorandum," *United States of America v. Mary Sue Hubbard, et al.*, US District Court for the District of Columbia.

123 **In September 1973:** Interviews with Jim Dincalci and anonymous former Sea Org member.

124 **They strapped Hubbard's injured arm:** Interviews with Jim Dincalci and anonymous former Sea Org members. www.cs.cmu.edu/~dst/Library/Shelf/miller/interviews/kima.htm.

124 **"You're trying to kill me!":** Interview with Jim Dinealei.

124 **"If he is who":** Interview with Hana Eltringham Whitfield.

125 **"redemption":** Hubbard, Flag Order 3434B, "The Rehabilitation Project Force," Jan. 7, 1974, revised Aug. 21, 1976, re-revised May 30, 1977.

125 **When Eltringham came aboard:** Interview with Hana Eltringham Whitfield. Ken Urquhart, who was then Hubbard's "personal communicator," actually wrote the protocol for the RPF. Ken Urquhart, personal communication.

125 **"He was in total control":** Interview with Karen de la Carriere.

126 **Bruce Welch:** Interviews with Mike Rinder, Mike Goldstein, Karen de la Carriere, and Daniel Holeman.

126 **"Bring the Commodore":** Interview with Mike Rinder.

126 **"You're the devil":** Interview with Karen de la Carriere.

126 **"I have made a technical":** Hubbard, "The Technical Breakthrough of 1973! The Introspection Rundown," Hubbard Communications Office Bulletin, Jan. 23, 1974.

127 **"A madman was made sane":** Interview with Karen de la Carriere.

128 **"revolutionize music":** Interviews with Mike Goldstein and Neil Safarti.

128 **Quentin wanted to join:** Miller, *Bare-Faced Messiah*, p. 325.

128 **Quentin's great ambition:** Interviews with Candy Swanson, Hana Eltringham Whitfield, and Mike Goldstein; Hal Holmes, personal communication.

128 **Jim Dincalci, the medical:** Interview with Jim Dincalci.

129 **"You have to improve":** Interview with Hana Eltringham Whitfield.

129 **"Daddy doesn't love me":** Interview with anonymous former Sea Org member.

130 **sexually involved with a woman:** Monica Pignotti, "My 9 Lives in Scientology," www.cs.cmu.edu/~dst/Library/Shelf/pignotti/.

130 **180 IRS agents:** "Catherine Harrington," personal communication.

130   **The federal agents had:** *Church of Scientology of Hawaii v. The United States of America.*

130   **He sent a pizza:** "Catherine Harrington," personal communication.

130   **Hubbard was just five miles:** Garrison, *Playing Dirty*, pp. 83–84.

130   **He weighed 260 pounds:** Kima Douglas, "The *Bare-Faced Messiah* Interviews," Aug. 27, 1986, www.cs.cmu.edu/~dst/Library/Shelf/miller/interviews/kima.htm.

130   **teeth and fingers were darkly stained:** Interview with Mike Rinder and Jim Dincalci. The church maintains that Hubbard was not a chain-smoker and that he quit smoking in the later years of his life. Karin Pouw, personal correspondence.

130   **In Curaçao, he suffered:** Personal correspondence with anonymous former Sea Org member.

130   **"He's risking his life":** Interview with anonymous former Sea Org member.

130   **kicked out of Barbados:** Garrison, *Playing Dirty*, p. 86.

131   **When the mayor:** Ibid., p. 245. Nancy Many, personal correspondence.

131   **Several months passed:** Charles Stafford; Bette Orsini, "Scientology: An In-Depth Profile of a New Force in Clearwater," *St. Petersburg Times*, Jan. 9, 1980. "Religion: A Sci-Fi Faith," *Time*, Apr. 5, 1976. Gary Weber, "Apology to Mayor Gabe Cazares, Richard Leiby and the Citizens of Clearwater Florida by an ex-Scientology Guardian," www.lermanet.com/garyweber/apology.htm.

131   **his tailor leaked the news:** Tracy Ekstrand, personal communication.

131   **"There they are!":** Russell Miller interview with Kima Douglas, "The *Bare-Faced Messiah* Interviews," Aug. 27, 1986, www.cs.cmu.edu/~dst/Library/Shelf/miller/interviews/kima.htm. According to church spokesperson Karin Pouw, Hubbard left Florida "to pursue additional research."

132   **"He looked like Wild Bill":** Interview with Dan Koon.

132   **He kept a hopped-up:** Unsigned, "Mystery of the Vanished Ruler," *Time*, Jan. 31, 1983.

132   **"She looked like a witch":** Interview with Karen de la Carriere.

132   **"I think a lot of my father's stuff":** Dennis Erlich, "The End of the Quentin," www.lermanet.com/exit/quentincoroner.htm. Interview with Dennis Erlich.

132   **Tracy Ekstrand, who was:** Interview with Tracy Ekstrand.

132   **He left a confused note:** Interviews with anonymous former Sea Org member.

133   **Quentin had only just:** Interview with anonymous former Sea Org member.

133   **He was scarcely qualified:** Interview with anonymous former Sea Org member.

133   **Frantic, Mary Sue dispatched:** Interviews with anonymous former Sea Org members.

133   **"He was so happy":** Interview with Cindy Mallien.

133   **But only a few days:** Sharon Spigelmyer, "Scientology Student Death Probe," *Las Vegas Sun*, Nov. 25, 1976.

133   **"That little shit":** Interview with anonymous former Sea Org member and Hana Eltringham.

134   **semen in his rectum:** Interview with Kima Douglas in "The *Bare-Faced Messiah* Interviews," www.cs.cmu.edu/~dst/Library/Shelf/miller/interviews/kima.htm.

134   **Quentin had been on vacation:** Sharon Spigelmyer, "Scientology Student Death Probe," *Las Vegas Sun*, Nov. 25, 1976.

134   **Meantime, Mary Sue arranged:** Atack, *A Piece of Blue Sky*, p. 214.

134   **Hubbard himself was convinced:** Interview with anonymous former Sea Org member.

4. THE FAITH FACTORY

137   **"magnetically impregnated":** McWilliams, *Southern California*, p. 254.

137   **An organization called Mighty I AM:** Ibid., p. 263.

138 **Charlie Chaplin:** Epstein, *Sister Aimee*, p. 420.
138 **Milton Berle:** Berle with Frankel, *Milton Berle*, p. 129.
138 **nautical outfits:** McWilliams, *Southern California*, p. 260.
138 **"They all fell short":** Quinn, *The Original Sin*, p. 127.
138 **"any person important enough":** Hubbard, "Celebrity Defined," HCO Policy Letter, Nov. 6, 1980.
138 **"If you want one":** Unsigned editorial, *Ability* magazine, undated. According to the church, the magazine was published in March 1955. The church claims that William Burke Belknap, Jr., an early Dianeticist, whose byline is on the article following the "Project Celebrity" editorial, most likely wrote the article. Robert Vaughn Young, who was the chief spokesperson for the church but left the organization in 1989, wrote that Hubbard personally authored the "Project Celebrity" editorial. Young, "The Cult of Celebrities," Sept. 27, 1997, http://www.xenu.net /archive/celebrities/.
139 **"make celebrities even better known":** Hubbard, "Celebrity Centre: Major Target," HCO Policy Letter, Oct. 19, 1980.
139 **"The Master did his Sunday best":** Peggy Conway letter to Gloria Swanson, Sept. 25, 1956.
139 **"Without Scientology, I would":** *What Is Scientology?*, p. 235.
140 **"I AM A SCIENTOLOGIST":** John H. Richardson, "Catch a Rising Star," *Premiere*, Sept. 1993, p. 87.
140 **"increase your self-confidence":** *Variety*, Sept. 9, 1993, p. 7.
140 **"make it in the industry":** Ibid., Dec. 22, 1988, p. 22.
140 **Scientologists stood outside:** Interview with Tom McCafferty.
140 **Jerry Seinfeld:** "When It Comes to Comedy, He's 'All In,' " *Parade* magazine, www.parade.com/celebrity/articles/071017-jerry-seinfeld.html.
140 **Elvis Presley:** Interview with Spanky Taylor.
140 **Rock Hudson:** Interview with Spanky Taylor, and Gary Hart, personal communication. It is rumored that Hudson's auditor hit on a homosexual "withhold," that Hudson refused to acknowledge, and so he bolted. Interview with Skip Press. Hart says that as a result of the Hudson fiasco, Hubbard kicked the auditor off the staff and placed Yvonne Jentzsch in a condition of Danger.
140 **fifty thousand documents:** Reitman, *Inside Scientology*, p. 112.
140 **"Operation Freakout":** *US v. Jane Kember, Morris Budlong*, Sentencing Memorandum, pp. 23–25.
141 **One of the doors:** Interview with Jesse Prince. Also, Stephen A. Kent, "Brainwashing in Scientology's Rehabilitation Project Force (RPF)," Sept. 13, 2000, www.solitarytrees.net/pubs/skent/brain.htm.
141 **Altogether, about 120:** Interview with Jesse Prince.
142 **"Fuck you":** Ibid.
143 **"Behind ideological totalism":** Lifton, *Thought Reform and the Psychology of Totalism*, p. 436.
144 **"thought-terminating cliché":** Ibid., p. 429.
144 **"a common, ordinary,":** Hubbard, "Scientology Definitions I: OT and Clear Defined," lecture, Nov. 29, 1966.
145 **Johannesburg Confessional List:** Hubbard, "Johannesburg Confessional List," HCO Policy Letter, Apr. 7, 1961, revised Nov. 15, 1987.
145 **The result of the sec-check:** Monica Pignotti, "My Nine Lives in Scientology," www.cs.cmu.edu/~dst/Library/Shelf/pignotti/.
145 **"apparent converts":** Robert Jay Lifton, personal correspondence.
145 **"truth blurred":** Lifton, *Witness to an Extreme Century*, p. 44.
146 **the real intention:** Klein, *The Shock Doctrine*, p. 47.

146 After 9/11, documents emerging: Lifton, *Witness to an Extreme Century*, p. 380.

146 "You are a good mother": Klein, *The Shock Doctrine*, p. 39.

147 In 1955, he distributed: On Hubbard's authorship of the pamphlet, see Corydon, *L. Ron Hubbard*, pp. 108–9. Hubbard himself later claimed: "It was written by a man named Paul Fadkeller, and it was published in Berlin in 1947." Hubbard, "Operational Bulletin #8," Dec. 13, 1955.

147 "Brain-Washing": See Brian Ambry, "Revisiting the Textbook on Psychopolitics, Also Known As the Brainwashing Manual," www.freewebs.com/slyand talledgy/Brainwashing%20Manual%20Parallels.pdf.

147 "[t]he art and science: Anonymous [Hubbard?], "Brain-Washing: Synthesis of the Russian Textbook on Psychopolitics," 1955, p. 6.

147 The text specifies how: Ibid., pp. 25–26.

147 "A psychopolitician must work": Ibid., p. 3.

147 From the perspective of: See Dick Anthony, "Tactical Ambiguity and Brainwashing Formulations," in Zablocki and Robbins, *Misunderstanding Cults*, p. 282.

148 "tumultuous": interview with Jesse Prince.

148 Brainwashing theory: See Benjamin Zablocki's essay, "Scientific Theory of Brainwashing," in Zablocki and Robbins, *Misunderstanding Cults*, pp. 159–214.

149 "You just kinda get sprinkles": Lawrence Wollersheim Interviews Jesse Prince, www.lermanet.com/prince/.

149 Grateful Dead: Interview with Daniel Holeman.

150 "He glommed on to me": Interview with Joan Prather.

150 "It sounded really interesting": "Scientology Shines in the New TV Hit, 'Welcome Back, Kotter.' John Travolta." *Celebrity*, unnumbered, undated (1975).

150 "Before *Dianetics*, if people said": Quoted in John H. Richardson, "Catch a Rising Star," *Premiere*, Sept. 1993.

150 "I went outside my body": Andrews, *John Travolta: The Life*, p. 39.

150 "We want John Travolta": Interview with Sandy Kent Anderson.

151 "My career immediately took": *What Is Scientology?*, p. 233.

151 "any person who receives": Hubbard, *Introduction to Scientology Ethics*, p. 463.

151 "You always have the fear": Clarkson, *John Travolta: Back in Character*, p. 118.

151 He introduced a number: Reitman, *Inside Scientology*, p. 264.

151 largest FBI raid in history: Garrison, *Playing Dirty*, p. 129.

151 They brought battering rams: Timothy S. Robinson, "Scientology Raid Yielded Alleged Burglary Tools," *Washington Post*, July 14, 1977.

152 "When I got out of the limo": "Disco Fever: 'Saturday Night Fever' Premiere Party," Paramount Television, 1977, www.youtube.com/watch?v=kMCxsmOTm-k.

153 "If she wants to go": Interview with Spanky Taylor.

153 There were thirty infants: Sheila Huber, personal communication. Huber says that later six volunteer nannies were added to take care of the infants and toddlers. She can remember only one occasion when the children were taken outside: "They sat in a circle the size of their cribs under a tree. They were afraid, very afraid—of the sun, the grass, everything."

153 "You can't do that *now*!": Interview with Spanky Taylor.

154 Nearly two hundred people: Interviews with Jesse Prince, Spanky Taylor, and Sandy Kent Fuller.

154 "We would like you": Interview with Spanky Taylor.

154 "America's newest sex symbol.": Judson Klinger, "Playboy Interview: John Travolta," *Playboy*, Dec. 1978.

157 Edwards fetched some clothes: Lauren Wolf interview with Kate Edwards.

158 "Spanky!": Interview with Spanky Taylor.

159 they were kept away: Interview with Hana Eltringham Whitfield.

159 "Please help him": Interview with "Catherine Harrington."

160 "There are two sides": Judson Klinger, "Playboy Interview: John Travolta," *Playboy*, Dec. 1978.

160 expose his sexual identity: Richard Behar, "The Thriving Cult of Greed and Power," *Time*, May 6, 1991.

161 threatening to marry a man: Lawrence Wollersheim Interviews Jesse Prince, www.lermanet.com/prince/.

161 "My sessions are protected": Interview with William "Bill" Franks.

161 Dead Agent pack: Interview with Gary Weber. Also, Gary Weber, "Apology to Mayor Gabe Cazares, Richard Leiby and the Citizens of Clearwater Florida by an ex-Scientology Guardian," www.lermanet.com/garyweber/apology.htm.

161 He had stopped his coursework: Interview with Mark "Marty" Rathbun.

161 "Well done": Interview with Spanky Taylor.

161 "I'll call Spanky": Interview with Spanky Taylor.

5. DROPPING THE BODY

163 He wrote innumerable scripts: Kima Douglas, "The *Bare-Faced Messiah* Interviews," Aug. 27, 1986, www.cs.cmu.edu/~dst/Library/Shelf/miller/interviews/kima.htm.

163 "Revolt in the Stars": www.forum.exscn.net/showthread.php?23706-Milton-Katselas-and-scientology.

163 Milton Katselas: Interviews with Allen Barton and Art Cohan.

164 She shopped the script: Interview with "Catherine Harrington."

164 "over the rainbow": Interview with anonymous former Sea Org member.

164 bellowing orders: Russell Miller interview with David Mayo, "The *Bare-Faced Messiah* Interviews," Aug. 28, 1986, www.cs.cmu.edu/~dst/Library/Shelf/bfm/interviews/mayo.htm.

164 "Someone came in": Interview with anonymous former Sea Org member.

164 "He was shouting": Ibid.

164 One of the perpetrators: Interview with Sinar Parman.

165 severe bouts of asthma: Jason Nark, "From Here to Scientology: Worldwide Leader David Miscavige's Philly-Area Roots," *Philadelphia Daily News*, Jan. 3, 2012.

165 "I experienced a miracle": Declaration of David Miscavige, *Larry Wollersheim vs. the Church of Scientology California*.

165 "the Wonder Kid": Interview with Karen de la Carriere.

165 "wonderful and bright": Interview with Ervin Scott.

168 "Those fucking women!": Ibid.

168 "They told us that David": Interview with Karen de la Carriere. When queried about this incident, the Church of Scientology refused to respond.

168 "sickened by the declining": Deposition of David Miscavige, *Larry Wollersheim vs. David Miscavige and Church of Scientology California*, Oct. 30, 1999.

168 he dropped out of tenth grade: Deposition of David Miscavige, *Bent Corydon vs. Church of Scientology*, July 19, 1990.

169 David redeemed himself: Interview with Sinar Parman.

169 Mitt Romney would name: Jim Rutenberg, "Romney Favors Hubbard Novel," *The New York Times*, Apr. 30, 2007.

169 "Get me John Travolta": Interview with Bill Franks. Marty Rathbun believes that Miscavige didn't meet Travolta until the 1990s.

169 Hubbard slipped away: Sinar Parman, personal communication.

170 It had been customized: Interview with John Brousseau.

170 "Jack Farnsworth": Interviews with Steve "Sarge" Pfauth and Tory Christman;

Sue Lindsay, "Genius in a Yellow Straw Hat," *Rocky Mountain News*, Feb. 16, 1986.

170 **about $100,000:** Interview with Denise (Larry) Brennan.

170 **Fifty such treatments were prepared:** Church of Scientology response to queries.

171 **"What they wanted":** Interview with Paul Haggis.

171 **Miscavige refused this direct order:** Reitman, *Inside Scientology*, p. 136.

171 **Brousseau got a call:** John Brousseau and Gale Irwin, personal communication. Brousseau remembers that Marc Yager destroyed the phone with the tire iron, but Irwin remarks, "I have a vivid image of Miscavige smashing the phone."

172 **A year later, in 1984:** Reitman, *Inside Scientology*, pp. 136–37.

172 **David Mayo was sent:** Interview with Bent Corydon.

172 **She suffered from chronic:** Interview with anonymous former Sea Org member.

172 **"She was frail and thin":** Interview with Mark "Marty" Rathbun.

172 **If Mary Sue were sufficiently alienated:** Russell Miller interview with David Mayo, "The *Bare-Faced Messiah* Interviews," Aug. 28, 1986, www.cs.cmu .edu/~dst/Library/Shelf/bfm/interviews/mayo.htm.

173 **making sure that Hubbard's name:** Interview with anonymous former Sea Org member. Gerald Armstrong testified that the crew was instructed to destroy "anything which connected L. Ron Hubbard to the Gilman or La Quinta properties; anything which showed any connection to the Guardian's Office; anything which showed Hubbard's control of Scientology or Scientology finances; anything which showed any orders being written by Hubbard into the Scientology organizations." *Church of Scientology California, vs. Gerald Armstrong*, Superior Court of the State of California for the County of Los Angeles.

173 **In the spring of 1981:** Interviews with William "Bill" Franks and John Brousseau.

173 **about fifty at the time:** Thomas C. Tobin, "The Man behind Scientology," *St. Petersburg Times*, Oct. 25, 1998.

173 **Several thousand Guardians:** Declaration of David Miscavige, *Church of Scientology International vs. Steven Fishman and Uwe Geertz*. Klaus Buchele, who worked in the Guardian's Office, estimates there were 600 to 700 Guardians worldwide. Interview with Klaus Buchele.

173 **She had treated them:** Interview with Sandra Holeman Barnes.

173 **Indeed, they hadn't spoken:** Mary Sue Hubbard testimony, *Church of Scientology California, vs. Gerald Armstrong*, Superior Court of the State of California for the County of Los Angeles.

173 **Mary Sue cursed Miscavige:** Peter Small, "Crimes Outraged Church Trial Told," *Toronto Star*, May 29, 1992.

173 **"Little Napoleon":** Interview with anonymous former Sea Org member.

174 **a couple of murders:** Interview with William "Bill" Franks.

174 **"Hubbard wanted her out":** Ibid.

174 **"I don't believe":** Mary Sue Hubbard testimony, *Church of Scientology California, vs. Gerald Armstrong*, Superior Court of the State of California for the County of Los Angeles.

175 **"Scottish Highland Quietude Club":** Terry Colvin, "Scientology at Gilman: Hubbard Said at Ex-Resort,"*Riverside Press-Enterprise*, Apr. 13, 1980.

175 **"He wanted a head":** Interview with Denise (Larry) Brennan.

176 **"She was a sweet":** Interview with Jim Dincalci.

176 **"You got to be kidding":** Interview with John Brousseau.

177 **"It was a do or die":** Interview with Jesse Prince.

177 **"We had fallen in love":** David Yonke, "Scientology Story Sparks Heated Response,"*Toledo Blade*, July 2, 2005.

178 **"core sense of identity":** Tony Ortega, "Scientology's Crushing Defeat," *Runnin' Scared* (blog), *The Village Voice*, June 24, 2008.

178 **An undercover campaign:** Affidavit of Vicki Aznaran, June 29, 1993.

179 **"I was followed":** William W. Horne, "The Two Faces of Scientology," *American Lawyer*, July/August 1992.

179 **setting up his son:** Affidavit of Vicki Aznaran, June 29, 1993.

179 **fifteen hundred Scientologists:** "Scientologists Scramble to Keep Secrets," *Los Angeles Times* [via the *San Francisco Chronicle*], Nov. 7, 1985.

179 **"A major cause of":** Joel Sappell and Robert Welkos, "Scientologists Rush to Protect Basic Beliefs Released by Judge,"*Los Angeles Times*, Nov. 5, 1985.

179 **Julie Christofferson Titchbourne:** John McCoy and S. L. Sanger, "Travolta and Other Scientologists Swarm into Portland to Protest," *Seattle Post-Intelligencer*, May 21, 1985.

180 **"bull-baiting":** John Painter, "Witness Describes Scientology Drills," *Oregonian*, July 25, 1979.

180 **The jury awarded her:** Tony Ortega, "Scientology's Crushing Defeat," *Runnin' Scared* (blog), *The Village Voice*, June 24, 2008.

180 **"I don't care if I get the chair":** Interview with Dan Garvin.

180 **As many as 12,000:** Affidavit of Andre Tabayoyon, Aug. 19, 1994.

181 **Stevie Wonder:** www.forum.exscn.net/showthread.php?16875-The-Battle-of -Portland.

181 **"I've been something of an ostrich":** Nancy Collins, "Sex and the Single Star," *Rolling Stone*, Aug. 18, 1983.

181 **"Once in a while":** Holly Danks, "Film Star Joins in Scientology Verdict Protest,"*Oregonian*, May 21, 1985, www.forum.exscn.net/showthread.php ?16875-The-Battle-of-Portland.

181 **He ruled that Christofferson Titchbourne's:** Atack, *A Piece of Blue Sky*, p. 349.

182 **"If you had an automobile":** Hubbard, "Death," lecture, July 30, 1957.

182 **"between-lives":** Hubbard, *Scientology: A History of Man*, pp. 109–10.

182 **"The baby takes":** Hubbard, "Death," lecture, July 30, 1957.

182 **Contrarily, when a body:** According to Karen de la Carriere, these instructions were part of Hubbard's secret directives. He also opposed autopsies because the thetan might still be inhabiting the body at the time of the procedure.

182 **"It's very confused":** Hubbard, "Aberration and the Sixth Dynamic," lecture, Nov. 13, 1956.

182 **he had been pronounced dead:** "L. Ron Hubbard, biographical cover note, 'Dianetics: The Evolution of a Science,' " 1972. Hubbard, "Case Analysis—Rock Hunting," lecture, Aug. 4, 1958, question and answer period.

182 **"death assist":** Reitman, *Inside Scientology*, p. 144.

182 **who received $1 million:** Hubbard, Amended Trust Agreement, Jan. 23, 1986.

182 **"Let's get this over with!":** Interview with Steve "Sarge" Pfauth.

183 **"I'll be scouting the way":** Hubbard, "The Sea Org & the Future," Flag Order 3879, Jan. 19, 1986.

183 **Dr. Denk had given him:** Tommy Davis told *New Times* that Hubbard took the medication for allergies. Colin Rigley, "L. Ron Hubbard's Last Refuge," *New Times*, May 28, 2009.

183 **Late that night:** Robert Vaughn Young, "RVY Update by RVY," Sept. 2, 1998.

183 **The site was so secret:** Steve "Sarge" Pfauth, personal communication.

183 **"dropped his body":** Ibid.

184 **"any grief bullshit":** Declaration of Vicki Aznaran, March 7, 1994.

184 **more than two thousand:** Church of Scientology responses to queries.

184 **"He has now moved on":** "LRH Death Event—02 of 16—DM Tells of LRH's Death," www.youtube.com/watch?v=YUXhJtRWRYM&feature=relmfu

184 **Missionaires had been sent:** Hubbard, "Flag Order 3879," Jan. 19, 1986. Robert Vaughn Young, "RVY Update by RVY," Sept. 2, 1998, www.xenu-directory.net /accounts/youngr19980902.html.

185 **"twelve down":** "LRH Death Event 09 Pat Broeker D," www.youtube.com/watch ?v=F2jG7adsPzc&feature=relmfu
185 **"People think I'm trying":** Interview with John Brousseau.
186 **Uzi machine gun:** Reitman, *Inside Scientology*, p. 150.
187 **Mark Rathbun:** Interview with Mark "Marty" Rathbun.
189 **She told the chaplain:** Interview with Aerial Long.
189 **"John Colletto!":** www.factnet.org/Scientology/jesse_tapes.html.
190 **Three days later, John:** State of California death certificate for John Joseph Colletto. Scientology's magazine, *Freedom*, mistakenly asserts that Colletto poisoned himself. "The Rathbun Family: Madness, Mayhem, and Mysterious Death," *Freedom*, undated, unsigned.
190 **special uniform:** Interview with Mark "Marty" Rathbun.
190 **He justified the alteration:** Lauren Wolf interview with Mark "Marty" Rathbun.
191 **targets of an IRS criminal investigation:** The CID investigation ended in November 1987.
192 **a former cop:** Interview with Mark "Marty" Rathbun. Joe Childs, Thomas C. Tobin, and Maurice Rivenbark, "Spying on Pat Broeker," video interview, *Tampa Bay Times*, Sept. 30, 2012.
193 **supervised personally by David Miscavige:** Plaintiff's First Amended Petition, *Paul Marrick and Greg Arnold v. Religious Technology Center, Church of Scientology International, Church of Scientology of Texas, and David Miscavige.*
193 **"He lived a very quiet, normal life":** Joe Childs, Thomas C. Tobin, and Maurice Rivenbark, "Spying on Pat Broeker," video interview, *Tampa Bay Times*, Sept. 30, 2012.
193 **Happy Valley:** Robert Vaughn Young, "RVY Update by RVY," Sept. 2, 1998.
193 **an order of nuns:** Interviews with John Brousseau and Mareka James.
193 **An armed guard:** Peggy Daroesman, personal correspondence.
193 **Dogs were trained:** Interview with Guy White. Happy Valley was closed down in 2000 when a German documentary crew revealed its location. Reitman, *Inside Scientology*, p. 331.

6. IN SERVICE TO THE STARS

194 **"He is one of the few":** "Celebrity Interview: Executive Producer—Paul Haggis," *Celebrity*, unnumbered, undated, p. 7.
194 **"What excited me":** Ibid.
195 **deserved a Nobel Prize:** *Church of Scientology of California vs. Gerald Armstrong*, p. 1503.
195 **The Purification Rundown:** International Association of Scientologists, 21st Anniversary event, Impact 112, 2006.
195 **"the most effective rehabilitation":** *What Is Scientology?* p. 412.
195 **"the heart and soul":** Vernon Scott, " 'Narconon Salvaged My Life'—Kirstie Alley," UPI, May 3, 1990.
196 **"Hubbard Detoxification Day":** "New York Rescue Workers Detoxification Project," undated Scientology publication.
196 **"Starting in the schools":** Celebrity Interview: Kelly Preston, *Celebrity*, #376, undated, p. 13.
196 **The church claims that:** Tommy Davis on *Today*, Jan. 8, 2009.
196 **Hubbard himself denounced:** Hubbard, "Expanded Dianetics Lecture No. 2," April 7, 1972.
196 **"With Jett, you started him":** "Kelly Preston: A Mother's Crusade," *Montel Williams Show*, Mar. 12, 2003.
197 **"thought, life, form, matter":** "Classification Gradation and Awareness Chart of Levels and Certificates," Issue 1, *Flag*, June, 1970.

197 **"I love the fact that you guys"**: Interviews with Ed Zwick and Marshall Hersko-vitz.

198 **He agreed to teach**: Interview with Larry Anderson.

198 **B. Dalton ordered 65,000**: Interview with Bill Dendiu. The church disputes the sales figures but does not provide alternative numbers. By 1990, more than twenty of Hubbard's books—both novels and nonfiction—had become national best sellers, most of them after his death four years earlier. At one point, Hubbard had fourteen consecutive books on the *New York Times* best-seller lists. There were allegations that the church was sending members to buy massive quantities of Hubbard's books to drive up the sales figures. The *Times* investigated those charges but failed to find any instances where large numbers of Hubbard books were being sold to single individuals. In any case, the booksellers were happy to sell them.

199 **"He has had a string"**: Tommy Davis denies that Miscavige met Haggis at the race. "Indeed, we cannot find any record that Mr. Haggis ever met Mr. Miscavige." Both Bill Dendiu and Haggis recall the conversation, however. Jefferson Hawkins has written that Miscavige and other Scientology executives were at the race; *Counterfeit Dreams*, p. 174. David Miscavige refused many requests to speak to me.

199 **Travolta himself at the controls**: Interview with Paul Haggis. Travolta's attorney agrees that his client was at the race.

199 **RPF running program**: Interview with Guy White.

199 **"Have you ever been"**: Ibid.

199 **"People could see"**: Ibid.

200 **"Is he? Is he?"**: Ibid.

200 **His vehicles are still**: Interview with Marc Headley.

200 **On his nightstand is**: Sue Lindsay, "Studio's Ready for Man Who Never Came, Never Will," *Rocky Mountain News*, Feb. 16, 1986; interview with Tom De Vocht.

200 **"for the next 20–25 years"**: David Mayo, "An Open Letter to All Scientologists," www.freezone.org/reports/e_mayool.htm.

200 **Arthur blew**: Interview with Guy White.

201 **"a functional illiterate"**: Morton, *Tom Cruise*, p. 41.

201 **an amateur troupe**: Ibid., p. 9.

201 **We felt like fugitives"**: Ibid., p. 18.

201 **a year in seminary**: Ibid., p. 25.

201 **Cruise's first wife . . . introduced**: Rogers denies this, although her father, Philip Spickler, confirms this often published account.

201 **Using his birth name**: Reitman, *Inside Scientology*, p. 273.

202 **Rogers's close friend**: Ibid.

202 **Cruise would later credit**: Luchina Fisher, "Celebrities with Dyslexia Who Made It Big," *ABC Good Morning America*, Sept. 28, 2012, abcnews.go.com /Entertainment/celebrities-dyslexia-made-big/story?id=17338379#2.

202 **But Mimi's parents had**: Interview with Philip Spickler.

202 **When Miscavige learned**: Morton, *Tom Cruise*, p. 138.

202 **Cruise arrived wearing**: Interview with Sinar Parman.

202 **"I told her"**: Interview with Mark "Marty" Rathbun.

203 **"He thought he had to be celibate"**: Michael Angeli, "Screaming Mimi," *Playboy*, March 1993.

203 **After two years, Annie**: Interview with Jim Logan. Headley, *Blown for Good*, pp. 98–99; and Thomas C. Tobin and Joe Childs, "Caught Between Scientology and Her Husband, Annie Tidman Chose the Church," *St. Petersburg Times*, Nov. 14, 2009.

203 **church funds were used to purchase:** Affidavit of Andre Tabayoyon, Aug. 19, 1994.

203 **Surrounded by a security:** Interviews with Claire Headley, Mark "Marty" Rathbun, and Jesse Prince.

203 **"like one would find in a convent":** Church of Scientology responses to queries.

203 **continuously under guard:** Thomas C. Tobin and Joe Childs, "Caught Between Scientology and Her Husband, Annie Tidman Chose the Church," *St. Petersburg Times,* Nov. 14, 2009. Tidman's lawyer denied to the newspaper that she had been held against her will.

204 **"non-enturbulation order":** Interview with Jim Logan.

204 **"They can't make me divorce you":** Thomas C. Tobin and Joe Childs, "Caught Between Scientology and Her Husband, Annie Tidman Chose the Church," *St. Petersburg Times,* Nov. 14, 2009.

204 **"doomsday machine":** Interview with Mark "Marty" Rathbun.

205 **Those who had cell phones:** Declaration of Robert V. Levine, *Marc Headley vs. Church of Scientology International,* and *Claire Headley vs. Church of Scientology International, et al.,* updated, Jan. 21, 2010.

205 **they would use force:** Interview with Gary "Jackson" Morehead.

206 **The Riverside County Sheriff's:** Sergeant Joe Borja, personal communication.

206 **no one who escaped ever returned:** Gary "Jackson" Morehead, personal communication.

206 **"Oh, we already have you":** Interview with Gary "Jackson" Morehead.

206 **As soon as an escapee:** Tony Ortega, " 'Tom Cruise Worships David Miscavige Like a God': A Scientology Insider Gives First Full-Length Interview to the *Voice*," *Runnin' Scared* (blog*), The Village Voice,* July 28, 2012.

207 **He never saw her again:** Interview with Jim Logan.

207 **A special bungalow was:** Karen Pressley interview on *One Day One Destiny,* a French documentary produced by Magneto Presse, 2009. Affidavit of Andre Tabayoyon, Aug. 19, 1994.

207 **When the couple longed:** Interview with Marc Headley.

207 **Miscavige heard about the:** Affidavit of Andre Tabayoyon, Aug. 19, 1994. Also, interviews with Amy Scobee and Marc Headley.

208 **When a flood triggered:** Affidavit of Andre Tabayoyon, Aug. 19, 1994.

208 **At Thanksgiving, 1990:** Interview with Sinar Parman.

208 **Cruise's investments:** Mark "Marty" Rathbun, personal communication; also, Rathbun blog post, *Moving on Up a Little Higher,* markrathbun.wordpress.com, April 12, 2010; and Rathbun, *The Scientology Reformation,* p. 25. Interview with Sinar Parman. In 1992, having suffered massive losses, the Feshbach brothers dissolved their investment fund.

208 **He was thrilled when:** Reitman, *Inside Scientology,* p. 279.

208 **He modeled his determined:** Interview with Mark "Marty" Rathbun.

208 **Just before Christmas, 1990:** Sinar Parman, personal communication.

209 **she had reached OT 11:** Interview with Bruce Hines.

209 **"Hello, I am Tom":** Headley, *Blown for Good,* pp. 116–18.

210 **"Look at the wall":** Hubbard, "Training and CCH Processes," HCO Bulletin, June 11, 1957, reissued May 12, 1972.

211 **Miscavige's wife, Shelly, interviewed:** Interviews with Amy Scobee and John Brousseau; Mike Rinder, personal correspondence; Mark "Marty" Rathbun, personal correspondence with Lauren Wolf; Reitman, *Inside Scientology,* p. 282.

211 **Miscavige offered the couple:** Scobee, *Abuse at the Top,* p. 70. David Lingerfelter told me he installed the satellite system for the Cruise home, and two other Sea Org members installed the audio and video equipment.

211 **helped design the kitchen:** Interview with Sinar Parman.

211 **"A little singing"**: Interview with Alissa Haggis.
212 **Nearly everyone they knew:** Interview with Lauren Haggis.
212 **"study tech"**: Hubbard, "Barriers to Study," *Word Clearing Series 3*, HCO Bulletin, June 25, 1971.
213 **"Too Steep a Gradient"**: Ibid.
213 **The "Undefined Word"**: Hubbard, "How to Use a Dictionary," *Word Clearing Series 22R*, Board Technical Bulletin, Sept. 4, 1971 R, revised Dec. 15, 1973, revised July 20, 1974 as BTB.
213 **"gives one a distinctly blank feeling"**: Hubbard, "Barriers to Study," *Word Clearing Series 3*, HCO Bulletin, June 25, 1971.
214 **"have him go back"**: Church of Scientology International, *Assists for Illnesses and Injuries*, p. 10.

7. THE FUTURE IS OURS

217 **Miscavige hired Hill & Knowlton:** Hill & Knowlton letter of agreement with the Church of Scientology, International, quoted in Memorandum Opinion and Order, *Church of Scientology, International, v. Eli Lilly & Co., Hill & Knowlton, Inc., et al.* US District Court for the District of Columbia, March 18. 1994.
217 **Robert Keith Gray:** Susan B. Trento, "Lord of the Lies: How Hill and Knowlton's Robert Gray Pulls Washington's Strings," *Washington Monthly*, Sept. 1992. Trento, *The Power House*.
217 **"They took the babies"**: Ted Rowse, "Kuwaitgate—Killing of Kuwaiti Babies by Iraqi Soldiers Exaggerated," *Washington Monthly*, Sept. 1992.
217 **The propaganda operation was:** Tara Weiss, "NPR Insists Funding Doesn't Influence News," *Hartford Courant*, March 15, 2001.
218 **"mindless actor"**: Interview with Mark "Marty" Rathbun.
218 **Ted Turner's Goodwill Games:** Behar, "Scientology: The Thriving Cult of Greed and Power," *Time,* May 6, 1991.
218 **There were full-page ads:** Hawkins, *Counterfeit Dreams*, p. 170.
218 **"part storyteller, part flimflam man"**: Richard Behar, "Scientology: The Thriving Cult of Greed and Power," *Time,* May 6, 1991.
218 **"Those who criticize the church"**: Behar, "The Scientologists and Me," *Time,* May 6, 1991.
219 **He rehearsed for months:** Interviews with Mark "Marty" Rathbun and Mike Rinder.
222 **"I was up in the Van Allen Belt"**: *Nightline*, Nov. 18, 2006.
223 **"I got Ted the Emmy"**: Marty Rathbun, personal communication. Marc Headley, personal communication.
224 **"increase happiness and improve conditions"**: Douglas Franz, "An Ultra-Aggressive Use of Investigators and the Courts,"*New York Times*, Mar. 9, 1997. According to *60 Minutes*, "Now, when you call looking for information about a cult, chances are the person you're talking to is a Scientologist." Leslie Stahl, "The Cult Awareness Network," *60 Minutes*, Dec. 28, 1997. Garry Scarff, a former Scientologist, told me (and has testified) that he was instructed to learn how to sever the brake line on Cynthia Kisser's car; he says that if the resulting accident failed to kill her, he was to pretend to be a good Samaritan, then reach into the car and strangle her. The plan was never put into action, however.
224 **a $3 million campaign:** David Miscavige on *Nightline*, Nov. 18, 2006. Hawkins, *Counterfeit Dreams*, pp. 208–9.
224 **annual litigation budget of $20 million:** J. P. Kumar, " 'Fair Game': Leveling the Playing Field in Scientology Litigation," *Review of Litigation*, Summer 1997, vol. 16, pp. 747–72.

225   it cost *Time* more money: John Huey, personal communication.

225   "to harass and discourage":" Hubbard, "The Scientologist, A Manual on the Dissemination of Material," *Ability*, ca. 1955.

225   "If attacked on some": Hubbard, Hubbard Communications Office Policy Letter, "Dept of Govt Affairs," Aug. 15, 1960.

225   "NEVER agree to an": Hubbard, Hubbard Communications Office Policy Letter, "Attacks on Scientology," Feb. 25, 1966.

225   "virtually incomprehensible":" Douglas Frantz, "The Shadowy Story behind Scientology's Tax-Exempt Status," *New York Times*, Mar. 9, 1997.

225    $1 billion in arrears: Interview with Mark "Marty" Rathbun.

225   Miscavige accused the: David Miscavige, Speech to the International Association of Scientologists, Oct. 8, 1993, http://www.xenu.net/archive/oca/speech.html.

226   the church upped the ante: Reitman, *Inside Scientology*, p. 163.

226   "They didn't even have money": David Miscavige, Speech to the International Association of Scientologists, Oct. 8, 1993, www.xenu.net/archive/oca/speech.html.

226   "All of America Loved Lucy": Ibid.

226   A ten-thousand-dollar reward: Interview with Mark "Marty" Rathbun. Reitman, *Inside Scientology*, p. 165.

226   phony news bureau: Douglas Frantz, "The Shadowy Story behind Scientology's Tax-Exempt Status," *New York Times*, Mar. 9, 1997.

226   Some government workers: Reitman, *Inside Scientology*, p. 166.

227   religious cloaking: Interview with Denise (Larry) Brennan.

228   "A truly Suppressive Person": Hubbard, HCOPL, "Cancellation of Fair Game," Oct. 21, 1968.

229   "I was an Irishman": Interview with Frank Flinn.

230   "Marty and I are just going to bypass": Interview with Mark "Marty" Rathbun.

230   "Is he expecting you?": David Miscavige, Speech to the International Association of Scientologists, Oct. 8, 1993, http://www.xenu.net/archive/oca/speech.html.

230   The level of distrust: Garrison, *Playing Dirty*, p. 101.

230   "Am I lying?": Interview with Mark "Marty" Rathbun.

231   Final Solution document: David Miscavige, Speech to the International Association of Scientologists, Oct. 8, 1993, http://www.xenu.net/archive/oca/speech.html.

231   Two hundred Scientologists: Reitman, *Inside Scientology*, pp. 167–88.

232   Instead of the $1 billion bill: Elizabeth MacDonald, "Scientologists and IRS Settled for $12.5 Million," *Wall Street Journal*, Dec. 30, 1997.

233   "I'm only doing this": Interview with Mark "Marty" Rathbun.

233   began to strangle him: Interview with Stefan Castle. "He did not hurt me physically," Castle told me. "More psychological." Rathbun witnessed the incident.

233   "You just want to get rid": Interview with Amy Scobee.

234   "You know the kind of pressure": Interview with Mark "Marty" Rathbun.

234   "cease acting like a madman": markrathbun.wordpress.com/2009/09/21/the-joe-howard-paradigm-tech-outside-the-wall/.

234   "Because you did this": Interview with Mark "Marty" Rathbun.

234   It was a title that: Hubbard, "Kha-Khan," HCO Policy Letter, May 25, 1982.

234   "I finally know who": Interview with Mark "Marty" Rathbun.

235   Then, on December 5, 1995: Thomas C. Tobin and Joe Childs, "Death in Slow Motion: Part 2 of 3 in a special report on the Church of Scientology," *St. Petersburg Times*, June 22, 2009.

235   "a gopher being pulled": Reitman, *Inside Scientology*, p. 201.

235 *"Aaaaaah! Yahoo!"*: Interview with Mark "Marty" Rathbun. Thomas C. Tobin and Joe Childs, "Death in Slow Motion: Part 2 of 3 in a special report on the Church of Scientology," *St. Petersburg Times*, June 22, 2009.

235 **the case supervisor who pronounced**: Reitman, *Inside Scientology*, p. 227; Headley, *Blown for Good*, p. 181; Thomas C. Tobin and Joe Childs, "Death in Slow Motion: Part 2 of 3 in a special report on the Church of Scientology," *St. Petersburg Times*, June 22, 2009.

236 **When church members decided**: Detective Ron Sudler interview with Dr. David Minkoff, Florida Offense/Incident Report, April 15, 1996. Thomas C. Tobin and Joe Childs, "Death in Slow Motion: Part 2 of 3 in a special report on the Church of Scientology," *St. Petersburg Times*, June 22, 2009.

236 **She was one of nine**: Ina Brockmann and Peter Reichelt, "Missing in Happy Valley," 1999. *Missing in Happy Valley*, video.google.com/videoplay?docid=274250583105142451 7.

236 **"Why aren't you all over"**: Thomas C. Tobin and Joe Childs, "Death in Slow Motion: Part 2 of 3 in a special report on the Church of Scientology," *St. Petersburg Times*, June 22, 2009.

236 **"Lose 'em"**: Interview with Mark "Marty" Rathbun.

237 **Embarrassing details emerged**: Thomas C. Tobin and Joe Childs, "Death in Slow Motion: Part 2 of 3 in a special report on the Church of Scientology," *St. Petersburg Times*, June 22, 2009.

237 **"silent enforcer"**: Interviews with Mark "Marty" Rathbun and Mike Rinder.

238 **"This is the most severe case"**: *Inside Edition*, Jan. 21, 1997.

238 **loss of its tax exemption**: Interview with Mike Rinder.

238 **unflappable witness**: Andrew Meacham, "Lisa McPherson Scientology Case Drove Joan Wood from Medical Examiner to Recluse," *Tampa Bay Times*, July 30, 2011.

238 **"into the Stone Age"**: Mark "Marty" Rathbun video, "Knowledge Report," https://whyweprotest.net/community/threads/wtsp-federal-suit-scientologist-spent-30-mil-to-cover-up-death-of-lisa-mcpherson.106523/page-3#post-2223487. Goodis recalls that there was a suggestion of "legal jeopardy" for his client, but he doesn't remember the quote.

238 **changed her ruling**: Goodis claims that he merely provided all the information he received from the church to his client, and that she made her own decision.

238 **suffered panic attacks**: Andrew Meacham, "Lisa McPherson Scientology Case Drove Joan Wood from Medical Examiner to Recluse," *Tampa Bay Times*, July 30, 2011.

239 **Repper was invited**: Interview with Mike Rinder.

239 **hosting a series of dinners**: Interview with Mike Rinder, Mark "Marty" Rathbun, and Tom De Vocht; Mark "Marty" Rathbun deposition, *Kennan G. Dandar and Dandar & Dandar v. Church of Scientology Flag Service Organization, Inc., et al.*, Nov. 9, 2012.

239 **Tom Cruise**: Interview with Mark "Marty" Rathbun; Times Staff Writers, "Leftovers Again? Mayor Iorio Not Tom Cruise's Only Dinner Partner," *St. Petersburg Times,* June 27, 2003.

239 **Repper held a brunch**: Interview with Mark "Marty" Rathbun.

239 **"This guy is really going"**: Ibid.

239 **change the climate**: Mark "Marty" Rathbun, "David Miscavige the Cheater," http://markrathbun.wordpress.com/2011/08/03/david-miscavige-the-cheater/.

239 **$20 to $30 million**: Mark "Marty" Rathbun deposition, *Kennan G. Dandar and Dandar & Dandar v. Church of Scientology Flag Service Organization, Inc., et al.*, Nov. 9, 2012.

239 **In Hamburg, in 1992**: www.guardian.co.uk/world/us-embassy-cables-documents/135450wikileaks.

240 **The youth wing of the:** Testimony of John Travolta, "Religious Intolerance in Europe Today," hearing before the Commission on Security and Cooperation in Europe (Helsinki Commission), Sept. 18, 1997.

240 **The city of Stuttgart:** Testimony of Chick Corea, ibid.

240 **Seventy percent of Germans:** David Hudson, "Scientology's 'Holocaust,' " *Salon Daily Clicks*, Feb. 25, 1997.

240 **Journet had been influenced:** Clarke, *Encyclopedia of New Religious Movements*, pp. 472–73.

240 **A year after these:** Katherine Ramsland, "The Order of the Solar Temple," www.trutv.com/library/crime/notorious_murders/mass/solar_temple/1.html.

240 **Aum Shinrikyo:** Lifton, *Destroying the World to Save It*, p. 6.

241 **Isaac Asimov's *Foundation Trilogy*:** Kaplan and Marshall, *The Cult at the End of the World*, pp. 30–31.

241 **the source of Aum Shinrikyo's crimes:** Nick Broadhurst, *Aum Supreme Truth*, 2000, web.archive.org/web/20070928161556/http://www.cultawarenessnetwork.org/AUM/preamble.html.

241 **receiving guidance from the television show:** George D. Chryssides, " 'Come On Up, and I Will Show Thee': Heaven's Gate as a Postmodern Group," in Lewis and Petersen, *Controversial New Religions*, p. 361; and Lifton, *Destroying the World to Save It*, pp. 320–21.

241 **Aum's membership:** Lifton, *Destroying the World to Save It*, p. 6.

241 **with resources close to $1 billion:** Ibid., p. 37.

242 **"Hitler was thinking":** Russ Baker, "Clash of the Titans," *George*, April 1997.

242 **friends or clients of Fields:** Bertram Fields, response to Lauren Wolf queries.

242 **"fact-finding mission":** David Hudson, "Scientology's 'Holocaust,' " *Salon Daily Clicks*, Feb. 25, 1997.

242 **"Individuals and businesses throughout":** Testimony of John Travolta, "Religious Intolerance in Europe Today," hearing before the Commission on Security and Cooperation in Europe (Helsinki Commission), Sept. 18, 1997.

243 **"He said he wanted to help":** Josh Young, "Bill Clinton's Grand Seduction," *George*, March 1998.

243 **"Scientology point person":** Ibid.

243 **The Germans were puzzled:** Stephen A. Kent, "Hollywood's Celebrity-Lobbyists and the Clinton Administration's American Foreign Policy toward German Scientology," *Journal of Religion and Popular Culture* 1 (Spring 2002).

243 **"This is not a church":** Jennifer Tanaka, "Hollywood versus Germany over Scientology," *Maclean's*, Jan. 20, 1997.

8. BOHEMIAN RHAPSODY

245 **"mother school":** Interview with Lauren Haggis.

245 **"I guess I'm not supposed":** Ibid.

246 **"Oh, yeah":** Interview with Alissa Haggis.

246 **Miscavige was hopeful:** Interview with Mark "Marty" Rathbun. Anna Schecter, "Tom Cruise's Former Scientology Auditor Speaks about Cruise/Kidman Divorce," *Rock Center with Brian Williams*, July 11, 2012. The church issued a denial that Kidman was considered a Suppressive Person; see Maureen Orth, "What Katie Didn't Know: Marriage, Scientology-Style," *Vanity Fair*, October 2012.

247 **"He was not in good shape":** Interview with Mark "Marty" Rathbun.

247 **She had suffered a miscarriage:** Meryl Gordon, "Nicole Kidman Tells It Like It Is," *Marie Claire*, Nov. 11, 2007.

247 **"Nic knows exactly":** Dickerson, *Nicole Kidman*, pp. 146–47.

247 **He paired Cruise with:** Interview with Jason Beghe. Cruise's attorney says, "Mr.

Cruise may have had a chance encounter with Jason Beghe at the Celebrity Center, but had no meeting with him."

248 **He had known Cruise:** Interview with Tommy Davis.

248 **reporting directly to Shelly Miscavige:** Interview with Claire Headley.

248 **Rathbun assigned Davis to:** Interview with Jason Beghe.

248 **One of the issues:** *One Day One Destiny*, French documentary produced by Magneto Presse, 2009.

248 **"Tommy told them over and over":** Dana Kennedy, "Katie Holmes 'Biggest Nightmare' in Scientology History, Say Experts," *Hollywood Reporter*, July 4, 2012.

249 **Rathbun's auditing sessions:** Interview with Tom De Vocht. Marc Headley told *Vanity Fair* that there were cameras behind a piece of furniture and in a lamp recording Cruise's sessions: "There were two views—one close-up of the E-Meter dial and the other a long shot over Marty's shoulder, showing Tom Cruise holding the cans." Maureen Orth, "What Katie Didn't Know," *Vanity Fair*, Oct. 2012.

249 **"I think I'm done":** Interview with Mark "Marty" Rathbun.

249 **"I have never met":** 2004 International Association of Scientologists Freedom Medal of Valor Ceremony.

249 **Cruise poured millions:** Reitman, *Inside Scientology*, p. 290.

250 **"would understand the details":** Interview with Mark "Marty" Rathbun; www.themortonreport.com/celebrity/notables/exclusive-bill-clinton-tom -cruise-plotted-to-use-tony-blair-to-gain-tax-breaks-for-scientology/.

250 **Later, Cruise went to:** Interview with Mike Rinder.

250 **In 2003, he met:** Reitman, *Inside Scientology*, p. 286.

250 **"Bush may be an idiot":** Interview with Mark "Marty" Rathbun.

251 **"They don't die easily":** Interview with Paul Haggis.

252 **"I think you'll discover":** Ibid.

252 **"You'll win an Academy Award":** Interview with Deborah Rennard Haggis.

253 **"That's great":** Interview with Paul Haggis.

256 **While he was still editing:** Haggis would share screen credit with William D. Broyles, Jr.

256 **"It's really remarkable to me":** Interview with Paul Haggis.

256 **He accompanied the star:** Headley, *Blown for Good*, p. 118.

256 **"It was a joke":** Interview with Tommy Davis, who said Haggis "apologized profusely."

257 **funded a school:** Jana Winter, "Will Smith Funds Private Scientology School," FoxNews.com, May 30, 2008.

257 **Cruise called a meeting:** Reitman, *Inside Scientology*, p. 289.

257 **Erika Christensen:** www.zimbio.com/Erika+Christensen/articles/3/Surprising +Celebrity+Scientologist+9+Erika.

258 **No one had been more instrumental:** Reitman, *Inside Scientology*, p. 266.

258 **"Have a good show":** Interview with Allen Barton.

259 **"Scientological McCarthyism":** Allen Barton letter to Jenna Elfman, June 1, 2004.

259 **After Cruise rallied the:** Interviews with Tom McCafferty and Art Cohan.

259 **Katselas refused:** Interviews with Art Cohan and Allen Barton.

259 **Miscavige even wondered:** Morton, *Tom Cruise*, p. 337.

259 **"He'd say that Tom Cruise":** Jeff Hawkins, quoted in Reitman, *Inside Scientology*, p. 290.

259 **"Miscavige convinced Cruise":** Rathbun, *The Scientology Reformation*, p. 77.

260 **"He didn't have":** Interview with Marshall Herskovitz.

261 **"Well, John, if you have powers":** Interview with Josh Brolin. Travolta, through a lawyer, agreed that the incident with Brando occurred, but characterized it as "tabloid-esque."

261 **The cook was summarily sent:** Lana Mitchell, personal correspondence.

262 **"At Flag":** Interview with Mark "Marty" Rathbun.

262 **showed him how to shoot:** Ibid.

262 **"I am writing this public announcement":** Marty Rathbun, "Public Announcement," Sept. 28, 2003. *Freedom*, "The Posse of Lunatics," undated.

263 **forty or fifty people:** Mariette Lindstein, personal communication.

263 **the Hole:** Joe Childs and Thomas C. Tobin, "Ex-Clearwater Scientology Officer Debbie Cook Testifies She Was Put in 'The Hole,' Abused for Weeks," *Tampa Bay Times*, Feb. 10, 2012.

263 **"Org Board":** Lauren Wolf interview with Mike Rinder.

263 **nine hundred positions:** Ibid.

263 **for four years:** Mariette Lindstein, personal communication. Reitman, *Inside Scientology*, p. 340.

263 **The entire base became paralyzed:** Mariette Lindstein and Tom De Vocht, personal communication.

264 **Mike Rinder was in the Hole:** Interview with Mike Rinder; Rathbun, *The Scientology Reformation*, p. 88.

264 **open scabs:** Mark "Marty" Rathbun, personal communication.

264 **"he's just an SP":** Interview with Tom De Vocht.

264 **When another executive spoke up:** Joe Childs and Thomas C. Tobin, "Ex-Clearwater Scientology Officer Debbie Cook Testifies She Was Put in 'The Hole,' Abused for Weeks," *Tampa Bay Times*, Feb. 10, 2012.

264 **"Pie Faces":** Interview with Tom De Vocht.

265 **"punch you guys out":** markrathbun.wordpress.com/category/debbie-cook/; also, Rathbun, *The Scientology Reformation*, p. 81.

265 **"homosexual tendencies":** http://markrathbun.wordpress.com/category/debbie-cook/; Debbie Cook testimony, *Church of Scientology Flag Service Organization, Inc., vs. Debra J. Baumgarten, AKA Debbie Cook Baumgarten, AKA Debbie Cook, and Wayne Baumgarten*. Joe Childs and Thomas C. Tobin, "Ex-Clearwater Scientology Officer Debbie Cook Testifies She Was Put in 'The Hole,' Abused for Weeks," *Tampa Bay Times*, Feb. 10, 2012. When Cook later complained to other Scientologists about the relentless fund-raising of the church, despite what she said was a $1 billion cash reserve, the church sued her for at least $300,000 in damages. Like many former Sea Org executives, Debbie Cook and her husband, Wayne Baumgarten, signed nondisclosure agreements with the church when they left the staff. They were paid $50,000 each to remain silent in perpetuity. In return, they waived their First Amendment rights to free speech, agreeing to pay a minimum of $50,000 for any such remark made in private and $100,000 for every disparaging statement they might make in any medium. If such a statement happens to be published in a newspaper, or a magazine, they are required to pay $20 for each copy printed—i.e., more than $20 million each if they spoke to *The New Yorker*. They also relinquished any claim to ownership of their preclear folders. "Agreement and General Release," signed by Debbie Cook and Wayne Baumgarten, Oct. 19, 2007. Cook was in the Sea Org for twenty-nine years. In her seventeen years as Scientology's top executive at the Clearwater base, she oversaw an operation that brought in more than $1.7 billion. Joe Childs and Thomas C. Tobin, "Church of Scientology Sues Longtime Clearwater Leader over New Year's Eve Email," *Tampa Bay Times*, Jan. 31, 2012. Cook and Baumgarten settled with the church, agreeing not to speak about it in the future, and moved to the Caribbean island of Guadaloupe. Joe Childs and Thomas C. Tobin, "Ex-Scientology Leader Debbie Cook Moving to Caribbean Island," *Tampa Bay Times*, June 20, 2012.

265 **"Once on a phone call":** "The Rathbun Family: Madness, Mayhem, and Mysterious Death," *Freedom*, undated, unsigned.

266 **"Get away with murder"**: Interview with Mark "Marty" Rathbun.

266 **abortions were common**: Interview with Dan Garvin.

266 **pushed to have two abortions**: Joe Childs and Thomas C. Tobin, "No Kids Allowed," *St. Petersburg Times*, June 12, 2010.

266 **"It's a constant practice"**: Interview with Claire Headley.

266 **Worried about pillow talk**: Interviews with Tom De Vocht and Janela Webster. Hubbard also imposed divorces on Sea Org members at times, according to Gerald Armstrong, who says that Hubbard ordered his wife, Terri, to divorce him in 1979 if she wanted to continue as a Commodore's Messenger. Gerald Armstrong, Complaint Report to the US Department of Justice.

267 **were billed more than $150,000**: Claire Headley, personal communication.

267 **"Marty, I don't want"**: Interview with Mike Rinder.

267 **"musical chairs"**: Interviews with Mark "Marty" Rathbun, Mike Rinder, Mariette Lindstrom, Tom De Vocht, Marc Headley; Joe Childs and Thomas C. Tobin, "Scientology: The Truth Rundown, Part 1," *St. Petersburg Times*, June 21, 2009.

268 **"Is it real to you now?"**: Interviews with Mike Rinder, Mark "Marty" Rathbun, Noriyuki Matsumaru, Mariette Lindstein, Marc Headley, and Tom De Vocht. Headley, *Blown for Good*, pp. 225–31; www.tampabay.com/specials/2009/reports/project/rathbun.shtml.

269 **"I am the ecclesiastical leader"**: Declaration of David Miscavige, *Church of Scientology International vs. Steven Fishman and Uwe Geertz*, USS District Court, Central District of California, Feb. 8, 1994.

269 **"Now here I am, being beat up"**: Interview with Tom De Vocht.

9. TC AND COB

270 **There are cottages built for**: Affidavit of Andre Tabayoyon, Aug. 19, 1994.

270 **salute Cruise when he arrived**: Interview with Noriyuki Matsumaru.

270 **directed not to speak to Cruise**: Reitman, *Inside Scientology*, p. 290.

271 **Miscavige's life began to reflect**: Ibid.

271 **He normally awakens**: Interviews with Tom De Vocht and Mark "Marty" Rathbun.

271 **The coffee is fresh-ground**: Information about David Miscavige's diet comes from his former chefs, Sinar Parman and Lana Mitchell.

271 **"three squares and a snack"**: Interview with Sinar Parman.

271 **"get ripped"**: Ibid.

272 **between 2000 and 2004, the food costs**: Interview with Claire Headley. The church disputes this figure without offering an alternative number.

272 **drinks Macallan Scotch**: Reitman, *Inside Scientology*, p. 319.

272 **his favorite films**: Interview with Mark "Marty" Rathbun.

272 **He usually turns in**: Interview with Tom De Vocht. Lana Mitchell, "Hot and Cold Running Servants," June 27, 2011, www/scientology-cult.com/hot-and-cold-running-servants.html. Sinar Parman says that when Miscavige is in Clearwater, he generally rises at nine a.m.

272 **Miscavige enjoys shooting pool**: Sinar Parman, personal communication.

272 **He collects guns, maintains**: Interview with Mike Rinder; John Brousseau, personal correspondence.

272 **Richard Lim**: richardlimtailoring.com.

272 **His shoes are custom-made**: Interviews with Janela Webster and Mike Rinder; Mariette Lindstein, personal correspondence.

272 **His wardrobe**: Lana Mitchell, "Hot and Cold Running Servants," June 27, 2011, www/scientology-cult.com/hot-and-cold-running-servants.html.

272 **Cruise admired the housecleaning:** Interview with John Brousseau.

272 **Until 2007, when he:** Ibid.

272 **at a cost of thirty to fifty thousand dollars:** Ibid.; Marc Headley, personal communication; interview with Noriyuki Matsumaru.

272 **He brings along his:** markrathbun.files.wordpress.com/2011/11/transcript_of _bryan_seymour_interview_with_lana_mitchell_17b1u9r-17b1u9t.pdf.

273 **He loves underwater photography:** Mike Rinder and Mariette Lindstein, personal correspondence.

273 **issued two sets of pants:** Dan Koon, personal correspondence.

273 **as little as thirteen or fourteen dollars:** Interview with Janela Webster.

273 **Married couples at Gold Base:** Mariette Lindstein, personal communication. Lana Mitchell, markrathbun.files.wordpress.com/2011/11/transcript_of_bryan _seymour_interview_with_lana_mitchell_17b1u9r-17b1u9t.pdf.

273 **Every personal phone call is:** Interviews with Mike Rinder and Lana Mitchell; John Brousseau, personal communication; markrathbun.files.wordpress.com/ 2011/11/transcript_of_bryan_seymour_interview_with_lana_mitchell_17b1 u9r-17b1u9t.pdf.

273 **Bank records:** John Brousseau, personal communication.

273 **They may not know:** Interviews with Daniel Montalvo and Sandy Kent Fuller.

273 **Many Sea Org members:** Mariette Lindstein, personal communication.

273 **On April 30 of each year:** Interviews with John Brousseau, Marc Headley, Mike Rinder, Janela Webster, and Mark "Marty" Rathbun.

274 **Miscavige keeps a number of dogs:** Interviews with Marc Headley, Claire Headley, and John Brousseau.

274 **A full-time staff member:** Interview with Marc Headley; Claire Headley, personal correspondence.

274 **a charge of attempted rape:** Jason Nark, "From Here to Scientology: Worldwide Leader David Miscavige's Philly-Area Roots," *South Jersey News*, Jan. 3, 2012.

274 **church resources were used:** Lawrence Wollersheim Interviews Jesse Prince, Tape 3, Aug. 25, 1998. www.factnet.org/Scientology/jt3.txt.

274 **She worked as an accountant:** Mary Jacoby, "High Profile Couple Never Pairs Church and State," *St. Petersburg Times*, Dec. 13, 1998.

274 **"court jester":** Interview with Mark "Marty" Rathbun.

275 **"She was sick":** Interview with Jenna Miscavige Hill.

275 **women became physically aggressive:** Interview with Mariette Lindstein.

275 **break Cook's finger:** markrathbun.wordpress.com/category/debbie-cook/; Debbie Cook testimony, *Church of Scientology Flag Service Organization, Inc., vs. Debra J. Baumgarten, AKA Debbie Cook Baumgarten, AKA Debbie Cook, and Wayne Baumgarten.*

275 **"The only thing I want":** Interview with Jefferson Hawkins.

276 **"in ignorance and darkness":** Ibid. Hawkins is now affiliated with Anonymous, a hacktivist collective that has targeted Scientology. They often picket church offices, sometimes wearing Guy Fawkes masks. The group pugnaciously opposes any form of censorship, and became hostile to Scientology after the church invoked copyright claims in order to remove from the Internet the video of Tom Cruise extolling "KSW." The church terms Anonymous a "cyber-terrorist" group. Two Anonymous members pled guilty to participating in a 2008 attack on a Scientology Web site.

276 **"He smelled of body odor":** Yael Lustgarten affidavit.

276 **"I gathered all the buttons":** Interview with Amy Scobee. Scobee says she was used to Scientology's methods of resolving internal conflicts. Twice, when she was fourteen and had just become a part of the church, she was sexually abused by an older man in Scientology. She never called the police. "We're taught that

'we handle our own,' " she told me. Because she failed to report the incidents of abuse to her auditor, after her abuser had confessed them, she was consigned to manual labor. Her abuser later became an Ethics Officer in the church.

276 **He said that all of the abuse:** Deposition of Thomas Davis, *Marc Headley vs. Church of Scientology International* and *Claire Headley vs. Church of Scientology International,* US District Court, Central District of California, July 2, 2010.

276 **"He had a weird":** Interview with Tom De Vocht.

277 **"gold bullion":** Ibid.

278 **"You're the biggest":** Ibid.

278 **Donors are accorded higher:** Interview with Mark "Marty" Rathbun. A former Sea Org executive, Debbie Cook, confirmed the $1 billion figure in an e-mail she sent to other Scientologists. Tony Ortega, "Scientology in Turmoil: Debbie Cook's E-mail, Annotated," *Runnin' Scared* (blog), *The Village Voice,* Jan. 6, 2012.

278 **Nancy Cartwright:** David K. Li, "The Church of $impsontology," *New York Post,* Jan. 31, 2008.

278 **The IAS now holds:** Interview with Marty Rathbun; Joe Childs and Thomas C. Tobin, "In Letter, Former Scientology Leader Debbie Cook Renews Concerns about Church Fundraising," *Tampa Bay Times,* Jan. 7, 2012. Rathbun has since doubled his estimate to "nearly two billion dollars—all offshore, out of the reach of tax authoritities or civil lawsuits." Rathbun, *The Scientology Reformation,* p. 50.

278 **Scientology coursework alone:** Urban, *The Church of Scientology,* p. 136.

278 **ranges in price:** Interview with Bruce Hines. According to the church, "there are no 'prices' for auditing," there are "fixed donations." Karin Pouw, personal correspondence.

279 **Services sold in Clearwater:** Joe Childs and Thomas C. Tobin, "Former Scientology Insiders Describe a World of Closers, Prospects, Crushing Quotas and Coercion," *St. Petersburg Times,* Nov. 13, 2011.

279 **"Bluntly, we are the":** Joe Childs and Thomas C. Tobin, "Scientology Amped Up Donation Requests to Save the Earth Starting in 2001," *St. Petersburg Times,* Nov. 20, 2011.

279 **a $1 million gift:** Interview with Mark "Mat" Pesch.

279 **at least $145 million:** Joe Childs and Thomas C. Tobin, "Giant 'Super Power' Building in Clearwater Takes a Pause, Yet Millions Keep Flowing In," *St. Petersburg Times,* Nov. 21, 2011.

279 **Ideal Orgs:** Interview with Guy White.

279 **A number of the Ideal:** "Xenubarb, Scientology: Attack of the Ideal Orgs!" *Daily Kos,* Jan. 28, 2012.

279 **Daniel Montalvo:** Interview with Daniel Montalvo.

280 **According to Florida child labor:** "Child Labor Laws," State of Florida and the Federal Fair Labor Standards Act.

280 **According to California child labor:** "California Child Labor Laws," State of California, 2000.

281 **it was simply impossible:** Joe Childs and Thomas C. Tobin, "Church of Scientology Runs Afoul of Widely Accepted Best Practices for Fundraising," *Tampa Bay Times,* Nov. 20, [year tk].

281 **who was a bank teller:** Interview with Garry Scarff.

281 **Stephen E. Brackett:** *American Safety Casualty Insurance Company and National American Insurance Company of California v. Nancy Cartwright and YO NANCY, INC.,* Superior Court of the State of California, County of Los Angeles, Sept. 21, 2010.

281 **The biggest financial scandal:** Notice of Lodging of the Reporter's Transcript

of Proceedings of the Sentencing Hearing in *United States v. Reed E. Slatkin*, United States Bankruptcy Court, Central District of California, Northern Division, Sept. 25, 2003.

282 **Anne Archer and . . . Greta Van Susteren:** Rathbun, *The Scientology Reformation*, p. 26.

282 **pay back $3.5 million:** E. Scott Reckard, "Scientology Groups to Pay Back $3.5 Million," *Los Angeles Times*, Nov. 8, 2006.

282 **Valeska Paris:** www.youtube.com/watch?feature=player_embedded&v=XWJ lEWWLvLM; markrathbun.wordpress.com/2010/06/20/keepin-it-real-on-fathers-day/.

282 **Shortly before Cruise arrived:** Tony Ortega, "Scientology's Cruise Ship as Prison," *Runnin' Scared* (blog), *The Village Voice*, Nov. 29, 2011, blogs.villagevoice.com/runninscared/2011/11/valeska_paris_chris_guider_scientology_freewinds.php.

282 **"the most dedicated":** www.youtube.com/watch?v=dh2uS-Om-Bs.

283 **Lana Mitchell, the cook:** Lana Mitchell, personal communication.

284 **paying a significant portion:** Interview with Roger Christian.

284 **"I told my manager":** Glenn Whipp, "The Battle for 'Earth': Travolta's Scientology Ties Raise Controversy over New Film," *Los Angeles Daily News*, May 12, 2000.

284 **His critiques would then be:** The head of Author Services International, Barbara Ruiz, was constantly with Travolta. Interview with Roger Christian.

284 **He predicted it was:** Interview with Mike Rinder.

284 **Even at the premiere, Sea:** Interviews with Spanky Taylor and Noriyuki Matsumaru.

284 **" 'Battlefield Earth' may well":** Elvis Mitchell, "Earth Capitulates in 9 Minutes to Mean Entrepreneurs from Space," *New York Times*, May 12, 2000.

284 **There were false accusations:** Interview with Roger Christian.

284 **Miscavige responded that it:** Interview with Mark "Marty" Rathbun.

284 **"Why didn't anyone watch":** Mark McKinstry, personal communication.

285 **Shelly Miscavige had been:** Interview with Claire Headley.

285 **Penélope was suspect:** Interview with Mark "Marty" Rathbun. The church denied that they objected to Cruz's religious beliefs; see Maureen Orth, "What Katie Didn't Know: Marriage, Scientology-Style," *Vanity Fair*, October 2012.

285 **"I want you to look":** Interview with Tom De Vocht.

285 **Miscavige then assigned Greg:** Headley, *Blown for Good*, p. 279.

285 **Shelly Miscavige, the leader's:** Interviews with Claire Headley and Noriyuki Matsumaru.

285 **Wilhere, who was actually in the Hole:** Ibid. According to *Vanity Fair*, Scientology denies that any clothes were purchased or that Wilhere was sent to New York "for this phantom project that never existed."

285 **Nazanin Boniadi:** Boniadi's story comes from four off-the-record former Scientologists, in addition to the published sources.

287 **"was a military commander":** Hubbard, "The Responsibilities of Leaders," HCO Bulletin, Feb. 12, 1967, corrected and reissued Sept. 4, 1979.

288 **Then came the shopping spree:** According to *Vanity Fair*, "Scientology denies that any such clothes were purchased or that any such trip took place 'for this phantom project that never existed.' " Maureen Orth, "What Katie Didn't Know," *Vanity Fair*, Oct. 2012.

288 **She spent that first night:** Ibid.

289 **"He needs to get his ethics":** Rathbun, *The Scientology Reformation*, p. 85.

289 **Naz had embarrassed Miscavige:** Maureen Orth, "What Katie Didn't Know," *Vanity Fair*, Oct. 2012. The church told *Vanity Fair*, "Mr. Miscavige doesn't remember any girlfriend of anyone, in his entire life, insulting him."

290 **"You don't get it":** Interview with Mark "Marty" Rathbun; also, Rathbun, *The Scientology Reformation*, p. 86. Tom Cruise's attorney, Bertram Fields, denies that this exchange took place. "He's never said anything like that, and he doesn't think that. This is vicious rubbish."

290 **Naz's last glimpse was:** Maureen Orth, "What Katie Didn't Know," *Vanity Fair*, Oct. 2012.

290 **The search for a new mate:** Morton, *Tom Cruise*, pp. 261–66.

290 **The names included Kate Bosworth:** Morton, *Tom Cruise*, p. 270; "Katie Holmes' Missing Days," FoxNews.com, June 21, 2005, http://www.foxnews.com/story/0,2933,160192,00.html.

291 **Holmes was an ingénue:** Sara Stewart, "Katie Loves Her Cruise Control," *New York Post*, June 12, 2005.

291 **"I think every young girl dreams":** Jeannette Walls, "No 'Risky Business' for Cruise, Holmes," MSNBC.com, May 2, 2005.

291 **"I was in love from":** Ibid., p. 271.

291 **nighttime helicopter ride:** Interview with Noriyuki Matsumaru.

291 **"best friend":** Robert Haskell, "Holmes, Sweet Holmes," *W*, Aug. 2005; "Katie Holmes' Missing Days," FoxNews.com, June 21, 2005, www.foxnews.com/story/0,2933,160192,00.html.

291 **"Something's happened":** *The Oprah Winfrey Show*, May 23, 2005.

291 *Today* **show:** *Today* show, June 25, 2005.

291 **"At this stage":** Ibid.

293 **"five billion years ago":** Hubbard, "Aberration and the Sixth Dynamic," lecture on Nov. 13, 1956.

294 **"place Scientology at the absolute":** David Miscavige speech, International Association of Scientologists, Copenhagen, Oct. 6, 1995.

294 **The Citizens Commission on:** www.cchr.org/quick-facts/real-disease-vs-mental-disorder.html.

294 **"Whatever type of drugs that Zawahiri":** Larry Byrnes, *The Know Drugs Show, Freedom* magazine video, video.google.fr/videoplay?docid=4437051883726295326.

295 **more than twenty percent of children:** *Mental Health: A Report of the Surgeon General*, www.surgeongeneral.gov/library/mentalhealth/chapter3/sec1.html.

295 **About ten percent of Americans:** Marcia Angell, "The Epidemic of Mental Illness: Why?" *New York Review of Books*, June 23, 2011.

295 **"I identified":** Interview with Paul Haggis.

295 **Kirstie Alley and Kelly Preston:** Alisa Ulferts, "Scientologists Push Mental Health Law," *St. Petersburg Times*, April 9, 2005. Katherine Mieszkowski, "Scientology's War on Psychiatry," *Salon*, July 1, 2005. Retrieved from http://www.salon.com/2005/07/01/sci_psy/.

295 **"None of these children were psychotic":** Alisa Ulferts, "Panel Waters Down Limits on Student Mental Services," *St. Petersburg Times*, April 20, 2005.

296 **Eli Lilly . . . suppressed data:** Marilyn Elias, "Prozac Linked to Child Suicide Risk," *USA Today*, Sept. 13, 2004.

296 **were twelve times more:** Tom Watkins, "Papers Indicate Firm Knew Possible Prozac Suicide Risk," *CNN Health*, Jan. 3, 2005.

296 **One of the killers was:** Joel Achenbach and Dale Russakoff, "Teen Shooter's Life Paints Antisocial Portrait," *Washington Post*, April 29, 1999.

296 **"can experience nervousness":** W. Alexander Morton and Gwendolyn G. Stockton, "Methylphenidate Abuse and Psychiatric Side Effects," *The Primary Care Companion to the Journal of Clinical Psychiatry* 2, no. 5 (Oct. 2000).

296 **Several studies have found:** Thomas P. Laughren, "Overview for December 13 Meeting of Psychopharmacologic Drugs Advisory Committee (PDAC)," memorandum, Nov. 16, 2006.

296 **saving 33,600 lives:** Michael S. Milane, Marc A. Suchard, Ma-Li Wong, Julio Licinio, "Modeling of the Temporal Patterns of Fluoxetine Prescriptions and Suicide Rates in the United States," *PLoS Medicine* 3, no. 6 (June 2006), pp. 816–24.

296 **Jeremy Perkins:** "Scientology: A Question of Faith," *CBS News*, May 7, 2009.

297 **she came close to jumping:** Affidavit of Hana Eltringham Whitfield, Mar. 8, 1994.

297 **It was only when she:** Interview with Hana Eltringham Whitfield.

297 **"It has changed my":** "Prozac Frees Ex-Scientology Leader from Depression," *Psychiatric Times* 8, no. 6 (June 1991).

297 **The Los Angeles County:** www.whyaretheydead.info/flo_barnett/coroner.html.

297 **In 2007, Kyle Brennan:** Plaintiff's Supplement to Response to Defendants' Motion for Summary Judgment, *Estate of Kyle Thomas Brennan vs. Church of Scientology Flag Service Organization, Inc., Denise Miscavige Gentile, Gerald Gentile, and Thomas Brennan*, US District Court for the Middle District of Florida, Tampa Division.

297 **costs approximately $25,000:** Ibid.; and Tony Ortega, "Jamie De Wolf, L. Ron Hubbard's Great Grandson, Gaining More Notoriety for His Views on Scientology," *Runnin' Scared* (blog), *The Village Voice*, July 26, 2012.

298 **suit was dismissed:** Joe Childs and Thomas C. Tobin, "Appeals Court Upholds Dismissal of Wrongful Death Suit Against Church of Scientology," *Tampa Bay Times*, Sept. 21, 2012.

298 **"It is irresponsible for Mr. Cruise":** www.rickross.com/reference/scientology/psychiatry/psychiatry7.html.

298 **But at the 2005 annual:** Morton, *Tom Cruise*, p. 292.

298 **"If someone wants to get off drugs":** "Spiegel Interview with Tom Cruise and Steven Spielberg," *Spiegel*, Apr. 27, 2005.

299 **"a movie of intense fascination":** Roger Ebert, "Crash," *Chicago Sun Times*, May 5, 2005.

299 **"frustrating movie":** A. O. Scott, "Bigotry as the Outer Side of Inner Angst," *New York Times*, May 6, 2005.

299 **most powerful actor:** "The Power List," *Premiere*, June 2006.

299 **most powerful celebrity:** "Tom Cruise Ranked 1 among the Top 100 Celebrities in 2006," *Forbes*, May 1, 2007.

299 **"Cruise was drooling":** Interview with John Brousseau.

301 **"It was a half-million-dollar beauty":** Ibid.

301 **"Oh, J.B.":** Tony Ortega, " 'Tom Cruise Worships David Miscavige like a God': The John Brousseau Story, Part Two," *Runnin' Scared* (blog), *The Village Voice*, July 29, 2012.

302 **"None of the Church staff":** Church of Scientology responses to queries.

302 **reincarnations of Simón Bolívar and Manuela Sáenz:** Interview with Tom De Vocht. Mark "Marty" Rathbun, *Moving on Up a Little Higher; Commemorative Edition*, p. 106.

302 **"The bulldog was gone":** Interview with John Brousseau.

303 **Former Sea Org members say:** Ibid.; Mark "Marty" Rathbun, personal communication.

303 **Miscavige sent Shelly:** Interview with Noriyuki Matsumaru.

303 **Among the celebrities attending:** Morton, *Tom Cruise*, pp. 307–8.

10. THE INVESTIGATION

307 **"The sexual pervert":** Hubbard, *Dianetics*, p. 103.

308 **"the most dangerous and wicked level":** Hubbard, *The Science of Survival*, p. 88. Hubbard's remarks about homosexuality don't appear in later editions of the book.

308   "This is the level": Ibid., p. 89.

308   "to dispose of them quietly": Ibid., p. 157.

308   "Homosexuality is about as serious": Hubbard, "The Resolution of the Second Dynamic," lecture, Oct. 1952.

308   "sacked for homosexuality": Hubbard: HCO Executive Letter: Amprinistics, Sept. 27, 1965.

309   "It has never been any part": Hubbard, "Second Dynamic Rules," HCO Policy Letter, Aug. 11, 1967.

309   Gays in the church: Interview with Guy White.

309   "to make go away": Interview with Mark "Marty" Rathbun.

309   In 2003, a gay artist: Interview with Michael Pattinson.

309   "I was just floored": Interview with Lauren Haggis.

311   In 1996, the church sent: Tony Ortega, "Sympathy for the Devil," *New Times L.A.*, Sept. 27, 2001. The church explains, "In 1996, the Church had in place a program to assist members to post websites about their activities as Scientologists. The Church included in the program a spam filter that these parishioners could use to modulate the inquiries they received as a result of placing their personal stories as Scientologists on the Internet. This program lasted about a year." Karin Pouw, personal communication.

311   "The worldwide interest in Scientology": www.youtube.com/watch/v=OfbLn9xPW4.

312   "Hana told us": Interview with Mary Benjamin.

313   "I was PTS, but I": "Celebrity Interview: Kelly Preston," *Celebrity*, #376, undated.

313   "It was that": Interview with Deborah Rennard Haggis.

313   "Until then": Ibid.

314   "We tried to do": Letter from "Mom and Bob" to Deborah and Paul Haggis, Sept. 14, 2006.

315   "You don't have any money": Joe Childs and Thomas C. Tobin, "The Truth Rundown," *St. Petersburg Times*, June 21, 2009.

315   "It was immensely tender": Joe Childs and Thomas C. Tobin, "Scientology's Response to Church Defectors: 'Total Lies,' " *St. Petersburg Times*, June 20, 2009.

315   "At the top of the church": Interview with Paul Haggis.

316   "We ran ourselves completely": Interview with Jenna Miscavige Hill.

316   These stories reminded him: The church says that it adheres to "all child labor laws," and that minors can't sign up without parental consent; the freeloader tabs are an "ecclesiastical matter" and are not enforced through litigation.

316   "They were ten, twelve": Interview with Paul Haggis.

316   "He turned off all women": Bryan Burrough, "Sleeping with the Fishes," *Vanity Fair*, Dec. 2006.

316   "Being a Scientologist": "Tom Cruise Scientology Video—(Original UNCUT)," www.youtube.com/watch?v=UFBZ_uAbxSo.

317   "When somebody enrols": Hubbard, "Keeping Scientology Working," HCO Policy L, Feb. 7, 1965.

317   "We were a bunch of kids": Interview with Gregg Housh.

317   "We shall proceed to expel": Anonymous, *Message to Scientology*, video, Jan. 21, 2008.

318   the star had a favor: Haggis remembers the show being *Larry King Live*. A former professional associate of Cruise's says it was *Oprah*, although both shows may have been approached.

318   "Yeah, I get that it sounds crazy": Paul Haggis, personal communication.

318   "I came across": Matt Lauer interview with Tom Cruise, *Today*, Dec. 15, 2008.

319   "a rocket ride": Interview with Jason Beghe.

320 "Nobody tells me": Interview with Paul Haggis.

321 "Tommy": Paul Haggis, e-mail to Tommy Davis, Aug. 19, 2009.

325 "If you audit somebody": Interview with Marc Headley.

325 "I just left": Interview with John Brousseau.

325 "Hey, J.B.": Ibid.

326 "seashells and butterflies": Interview with Mike Rinder.

328 "No clearer than when": Interview with Anne Archer.

328 "it was like reading": Interview with Mark Isham.

328 They showed up at his office: Interviews with Michael Nozik and Gian Sardar.

329 "Tommy, you are absolutely right": Interview with Paul Haggis.

329 "You're a journalist": Interview with Paul Haggis.

330 "Paul, what the hell!": Ibid.

11. TOMMY

331 "It made little difference": Interview with Tommy Davis.

331 "I want our time": Tommy Davis, personal correspondence.

332 "Maybe Paul shouldn't have": Interview with Jessica Feshbach.

332 "I saw this girl": Interview with Terry Jastrow.

332 "We were friends": Interview with Anne Archer.

334 "I remember walking": Ibid.

335 He would wander around: Interview with Tommy Davis.

335 "I am a really good dad": Interview with Terry Jastrow.

335 His father, William Davis: Christopher Wood, "The CenterPort Partners," *Denver Business Journal,* Nov. 29, 1991.

335 "a sweet and bright boy": Interview with Paul Haggis. Tommy Davis told me in one instance that he didn't meet Haggis until 1991, but on another occasion he said he has known Haggis since he was eighteen years old.

335 Archer had taken him: William Shaw, "The Cult of Personalities," *Details,* Feb. 1996.

336 "You can either go to college": Interview with John Peeler.

336 Davis would arrange for: Interview with Tiziano Lugli.

336 "Miscavige liked the fact": Interview with Mike Rinder.

337 "When we told Tommy": Interview with Amy Scobee.

337 Davis was disappointed: Interview with Tommy Davis.

337 When Miscavige found out: Interview with Amy Scobee. Davis admits that he has the tattoo.

337 Davis had been called Tom: Ibid.

337 "I made the decision": 20/20, Dec. 20, 1998.

338 "Somehow dealing with Katie": Interview with Mike Rinder.

338 "He complained about": Interview with Donna Shannon.

338 Archer was also at the Clearwater base: Interview with Daniel Montalvo.

339 "You're Tommy Davis's servant": Interview with Mike Rinder.

339 "gaunt, hollow-eyed": John Sweeney, personal communication.

340 "sadistic cult": "The Secrets of Scientology," *Panorama* (BBC), May 14, 2007.

341 Are you a member of a sinister, brainwashing cult?" www.youtube.com/watch?v=BRfMrvpDzj8.

341 "Who's the witness?": BBC footage, Mar. 31, 2007.

345 "That's not his temperament": Thomas C. Tobin, "The Man Behind Scientology," *St. Petersburg Times,* Oct. 25, 1998.

345 "That's the biggest lie: www.tampabay.com/specials/2009/reports/project/rathbun.shtml.

345 Marc Headley, one of: www.blogtalkradio.com/glosslip/2008/04/25/glosslip-from-our-lips-to-your-ears.

345 **Rinder says he witnessed:** Mike Rinder, personal communication.
345 **Lana Mitchell, who worked:** Interviews with Marc Headley and Mike Rinder; Lana Mitchell, markrathbun.files.wordpress.com/2011/11/transcript_of_bryan _seymour_interview_with_lana_mitchell_17b1u9r-17b1u9t.pdf.
345 **"You get very hardened":** Interview with Mariette Lindstein.
347 **"She'll be out of sight":** Interview with John Brousseau.
347 **"I was unable to make":** William H. Patterson, Jr., personal correspondence.
347 **The book reveals that:** Patterson, *Robert A. Heinlein*, p. 538 n.
348 **Sara Komkovadamanov:** Hubbard, "Intelligence Actions Covert Intelligence Data Collection," Memo to "The Guardian," Dec. 2, 1969. In the same memo, he spells it "Komkosadmanov." Karin Pouw writes, in a personal communication, "Sara Northrup Hollister's death certificate dated December 18, 1997 lists her mother's birth name as Olga Malakhan-Casadominov, born in Russia. The information was provided by her widower, Miles Hollister. This is the name that was being referred to. All of the spellings are phonetic, of course, since the actual name would have appeared in Cyrillic." Sara herself recounted that her mother's father had been named Malacon Kosadamanov, but changed his name to Nelson when he moved to Sweden. Sara Elizabeth Hollister (formerly Sara Northrup Hubbard) tapes, Stephen A. Kent Collection on Alternative Religions.
348 **"I'm not interested in revenge":** Sara Elizabeth Hollister (formerly Sara Northrup Hubbard) tapes, Stephen A. Kent Collection on Alternative Religions.
350 **Hubbard applied for a pension:** "Report of Physical Examination," Dec. 6, 1945. Hubbard medical records, Department of Veterans Affairs.
351 **"NOT a palm":** John E. Bircher, personal communication.
352 **There was a fire in:** According to the National Archives website, only records of the Army and the Air Force were affected.
352 **"there was no Howard D. Thompson":** Charles Pellegrini letter to Dr. Jan Willem Nienhuys, May 9, 2000.
352 **"The United States has never":** Erik Voelz interview with the *New Yorker* fact checkers.
353 **Davis blew:** Anonymous former Sea Org member, personal correspondence.

EPILOGUE

354 **"the old religion":** Hubbard, "Routine 3 Heaven," HCO Bulletin, May 11 AD13 (1963).
356 **This fraud has been:** Lawrence Wright, "Lives of the Saints," *The New Yorker*, Jan. 21, 2002.
356 **Like Hubbard, Mary Baker Eddy:** Wallis, in *The Road to Total Freedom*, p. 98, compares the origins of Dianetics to the rise of Christian Science.
361 **"I really wish I had":** Interview with Paul Haggis.
362 **It had the misfortune:** Interview with Eugenie Grandval.
362 **earning $1 billion:** Matt Peckham, "Bye-Bye Avatar: Modern Warfare 3 Takes $1 Billion Record," *PC World*, Dec. 12, 2011.
362 **"It wouldn't stick":** Interview with Mark "Marty" Rathbun.
363 **"It was one of those sudden":** Interview with Stephen "Sarge" Pfauth.

ACKNOWLEDGMENTS AND A NOTE ON SOURCES

368 **he was spied upon:** Russell Miller, "See You in Court," *Punch*, Feb. 19, 1988; Miller, "The True Story of a False Prophet," *Night & Day, The Mail on Sunday Review*, March 30, 1997.
368 **Wallis was spied upon:** Lamont, *Religion, Inc.*, p. 87.

Bibliography

MANUSCRIPT COLLECTIONS

Karen de la Carriere, Private Collection, Los Angeles.

James Free Papers. Manuscript Division, Library of Congress.

Russell Randolph Hays Collection. Kenneth Spencer Research Library, University of Kansas Libraries.

The Robert A. and Virginia Heinlein Archives. The Heinlein Prize Trust and the UC Santa Cruz Archives.

Stephen A. Kent Collection on Alternative Religions. The University of Alberta, Edmonton, Alberta, Canada.

Gloria Swanson Papers. Harry Ransom Humanities Research Center, The University of Texas at Austin.

SCIENTOLOGY SOURCES

Church of Scientology International. *Assists for Illnesses and Injuries*. Los Angeles: Bridge Publications, 1994.

———. *What Is Scientology?* Los Angeles: Bridge Publications, 1998.

Hubbard, L. Ron. *Advanced Procedures and Axioms*. Los Angeles: Bridge Publications, 2007.

———. *All About Radiation*. Los Angeles: Bridge Publications, 1979.

———. *Clear Mind, Clear Body*. Los Angeles: Bridge Publications, 2002.

———. *The Creation of Human Ability*. Los Angeles: Bridge Publications, 2007.

———. *Dianetics: The Modern Science of Mental Health*. New York: Hermitage House, 1950.

———. *Dianetics and Scientology Technical Dictionary*. Los Angeles: Bridge Publications, 1975.

———. *Dianetics: The Evolution of a Science*. Los Angeles: The American Saint Hill Organization, 1950.

———. *Dianetics 55!* Los Angeles: Bridge Publications, 2007.

———. *Electropsychometric Auditing Operator's Manual*. No publisher listed, 1952.

———. *A History of Man*. Los Angeles: Bridge Publications, 2007.

———. "An Introduction to Scientology." Taped lecture. Los Angeles: L. Ron Hubbard Library, 1966.

———. *Introduction to Scientology Ethics*. Los Angeles: Bridge Publications, 2007.

———. London Congress on Dissemination and Help and the London Open Evening Lectures. Lectures 1–7. Los Angeles: L. Ron Hubbard Library, 1978.

———. *Mission into Time*. Los Angeles: American Saint Hill Organization, 1968.

———. *The Organizational Executive Course*. Vols. 1–7. Los Angeles: Bridge Publications, 1991.

———. *The Original LRH Executive Directives*. Series 1–3. Los Angeles: Bridge Publications, 1983.

———. *Philadelphia Doctorate Course Transcripts*. Vols. 1–8. Los Angeles: Bridge Publications, 1982.

———. *The Phoenix Lectures*. Los Angeles: Bridge Publications, 1968.

———. *Science of Survival*. Wichita: The Hubbard Dianetic Foundation, 1951.

———. *Scientology: 8–8008*. Los Angeles: Bridge Publications, 2007.

———. *Scientology: A History of Man*. Los Angeles: Bridge Publications, 2007.

———. *Scientology: A New Slant on Life*. Los Angeles: Bridge Publications, 2007.

———. *Scientology: The Fundamentals of Thought*. Silver Spring, MD: Hubbard Association of Scientologists International, 1956.

———. *A Series of Lectures on the Whole Track*. Los Angeles: Golden Era Productions, 1984.

———. *Technical Bulletins of Dianetics and Scientology*. Vols. 1–16. Los Angeles: Bridge Publications, 1991.

———. *The Way to Happiness: A Common Sense Guide to Better Living*. Glendale, CA: The Way to Happiness Foundation International, 2007.

L. Ron Hubbard Library. *L. Ron Hubbard: A Profile*. Los Angeles: Bridge Publications, 2012.

———. The *Ron* magazines: *Adventurer/Explorer: Daring Deeds and Unknown Realms*. 1996.

———. The *Ron* magazines: *Letters and Journals: Early Years of Adventure*. 1997.

———. The *Ron* magazines: *Letters and Journals: Literary Correspondence*. 1997.

———. The *Ron* magazines: *Letters and Journals: The Dianetics Letters*. 1997.

———. The *Ron* magazines: *The Humanitarian: Education*. 1996.

———. The *Ron* magazines: *The Humanitarian: Freedom Fighter, Articles and Essays*. 1997.

———. The *Ron* magazines: *The Humanitarian: Rehabilitating a Drugged Society*. 1996.

———. The *Ron* magazines: *The Humanitarian: The Road to Self-Respect*. 1995.

———. The *Ron* magazines: *The Philosopher: The Rediscovery of the Human Soul*. 1996.

———. The *Ron* magazines: *The Photographer: Writing with Light*. 1999.

———. *The Story of Dianetics and Scientology*. Los Angeles: Golden Era Productions, 2002.

BOOKS AND ARTICLES

Amis, Kingsley. *New Maps of Hell: A Survey of Science Fiction*. New York: Harcourt, Brace, 1960.

Anderson, Kevin Victor. *Report of the Board of Inquiry into Scientology*. State of Victoria, Australia, 1965.

Andrews, Nigel. *John Travolta: The Life*. London: Bloomsbury, 1999.

Asimov, Isaac. *I. Asimov: A Memoir*. New York: Doubleday, 1994.

Atack, Jon. *A Piece of Blue Sky*. New York: Carol Publishing Group, 1990.

Behar, Richard. "Scientology: The Thriving Cult of Greed and Power." *Time*, May 6, 1991.

———. "The Scientologists and Me." *Time*, May 6, 1991.

Berle, Milton, with Haskel Frankel. *Milton Berle: An Autobiography*. New York: Delacorte Press, 1974.

Bornstein, Kate. *A Queer and Pleasant Danger: A Memoir*. Boston: Beacon Press, 2012.

Campbell, John Wood. *The John W. Campbell Letters*. Franklin, TN: AC Projects, 1985.

Carter, John. *Sex and Rockets: The Occult World of Jack Parsons*. Venice, CA: Feral House, 1999.

Childs, Joe, and Thomas Tobin. "The Truth Rundown." *St. Petersburg Times*, June 21, 2009.

Clarke, Peter B. *Encyclopedia of New Religious Movements*. UK: Routledge, 2006.

Clarkson, Wensley. *John Travolta: Back in Character*. London: Piatkus Books, 1996.

Cooper, Paulette. *The Scandal of Scientology*. New York: Tower Publications, 1971.

Corydon, Bent. *L. Ron Hubbard: Messiah or Madman?* Fort Lee, NJ: Barricade Books, 1996.

Dickerson, James. *Nicole Kidman*. New York: Citadel Press, 2003.

Epstein, Daniel Mark. *Sister Aimee: The Life of Aimee McPherson*. Orlando: Harcourt Brace, 1993.

Eshbach, Lloyd Arthur. *Over My Shoulder: Reflections on a Science Fiction Era*. Hampton Falls, NH: Donald M. Grant Publishers, 1982.

Freud, Sigmund. Translated by Jas. Strachey. *Introductory Lectures on Psycho-Analysis*. New York: W. W. Norton & Co., 1966.

Garrison, Omar. *Playing Dirty: The Secret War Against Beliefs*. Los Angeles: Ralston-Pilot, 1980.

Grant, Kenneth, and John Symonds. *The Confessions of Aleister Crowley: An Autohagiography*. New York: Arkana, 1989.

Gruber, Frank. *The Pulp Jungle*. Los Angeles: Sherbourne Press, 1967.

Hawkins, Jefferson. *Counterfeit Dreams*. Portland, OR: Hawkeye Publishing, 2010.

Headley, Marc. *Blown for Good: Behind the Iron Curtain of Scientology*. Burbank: Blown for Good, Inc., 2010.

Hubbard, L. Ron. *Battlefield Earth: A Saga of the Year 3000*. Hollywood: Galaxy Press, 2002.

Kansa, Spencer. *Wormwood Star: The Magickal Life of Marjorie Cameron*. Oxford: Mandrake of Oxford, 2010.

Kaplan, David E., and Andrew Marshall. *The Cult at the End of the World: The Terrifying Story of the Aum Doomsday Cult, from the Subways of Tokyo to the Nuclear Arsenals of Russia*. New York: Crown, 1996.

Klein, Naomi. *The Shock Doctrine: The Rise of Disaster Capitalism*. New York: Picador, 2007.

Lamont, Stewart. *Religion, Inc.: Church of Scientology*. London: Harrap, 1986.

Lewis, James R., and Jesper Aagaard Petersen. *Controversial New Religions*. New York: Oxford University Press, 2005.

Lifton, Robert Jay. *Destroying the World to Save It: Aum Shinrikyo, Apocalyptic Violence, and the New Global Terrorism*. New York: Henry Holt, 2000.

———. *Thought Reform and the Psychology of Totalism: A Study of "Brainwashing" in China*. Chapel Hill: University of North Carolina Press, 1989.

———. *Witness to an Extreme Century: A Memoir*. New York: Free Press, 2011.

Malko, George. *Scientology: The Now Religion*. New York: Delacorte Press, 1970.

McWilliams, Carey. *Southern California: An Island on the Land*. Salt Lake City: Gibbs-Smith Publisher, 1973.

Miller, Russell. *Bare-Faced Messiah*. London: Penguin Books, 1987.

Morton, Andrew. *Tom Cruise: An Unauthorized Biography*. New York: St. Martin's Press, 2008.

O'Brien, Helen. *Dianetics in Limbo*. Philadelphia: Whitmore Publishing, 1966.

Oufkir, Malika, and Michele Fitoussi. *Stolen Lives: Twenty Years in a Desert Jail*. New York: Talk Miramax Books/Hyperion, 2001.

Parsons, John Whiteside. *Freedom Is a Two-Edged Sword*. Las Vegas: New Falcon Publications, 2001.

Patterson, William H. *Robert A. Heinlein: In Dialogue with His Century.* Vol. 1, *1907–1948: Learning Curve.* New York: Tor Books, 2010.

Pendle, George. *Strange Angel: The Otherworldly Life of Rocket Scientist John Whiteside Parsons.* New York: Harvest Books, 2005.

Quinn, Anthony. *The Original Sin: A Self-Portrait.* New York: Bantam, 1974.

Rathbun, Mark "Marty." *Moving on Up a Little Higher,* Commemorative Edition. N.p.: July 4, 2011.

———. *The Scientology Reformation: What Every Scientologist Should Know.* N.p.: 2012.

———. *What Is Wrong with Scientology?: Healing Through Understanding.* N.p.: CreateSpace/Amazon.com, 2012.

Reitman, Janet. *Inside Scientology: The Story of America's Most Secretive Religion.* New York: Houghton Mifflin Harcourt, 2011.

Rojek, Chris. *Celebrity.* London: Reaktion Books, 2001.

Rotberg, Robert I. *The Founder: Cecil Rhodes and the Pursuit of Power.* New York: Oxford University Press, 1988.

Sappell, Joel, and Robert W. Welkos. "The Courting of Celebrities: Testimonials of the Famous Are Prominent in the Church's Push for Acceptability." *Los Angeles Times,* June 25, 1990.

Scobee, Amy. *Scientology: Abuse at the Top.* Puyallup, WA: Scobee Publishing, 2010.

Spence, Richard B. *Secret Agent 666: Aleister Crowley, British Intelligence, and the Occult.* Port Townsend, WA: Feral House, 2008.

Trento, Susan B. *The Power House: Robert Keith Gray and the Selling of Access and Influence in Washington.* New York: St. Martin's Press, 1992.

Urban, Hugh. *The Church of Scientology: A History of a New Religion.* Princeton, NJ: Princeton University Press, 2011.

Vosper, Cyril. *The Mind Benders.* London: Neville Spearman, 1971.

Wallis, Roy. *The Road to Total Freedom: A Sociological Analysis of Scientology.* New York: Columbia University Press, 1977.

Whitehead, Harriet. *Renunciation and Reformulation: A Study of Conversion in an American Sect.* Ithaca, NY: Cornell University Press, 1987.

Winter, Joseph A. *A Doctor's Report on Dianetics: Theory and Therapy.* New York: Julian Press, 1951.

Wright, Lawrence. "The Apostate: Paul Haggis vs. the Church of Scientology." *The New Yorker,* February 14, 2011.

Zablocki, Benjamin, and Thomas Robbins, eds. *Misunderstanding Cults: Searching for Objectivity in a Controversial Field.* Toronto: University of Toronto Press, 2001.

Zaretsky, Irving, and Mark P. Leone. *Religious Movements in Contemporary America.* Princeton, NJ: Princeton University Press, 1974.

BROADCAST MEDIA

"L. Ron Hubbard." *Secret Lives.* Channel 4, UK. Originally broadcast November 19, 1997. Available online.

Index

Page numbers in *italics* refer to illustrations.

PHOTOGRAPHIC CREDITS

Grateful acknowledgment is made to the following for permission to reprint photographs:

Associated Press: 300
Phillip Caruso V: 319
Curtis / Camera Press / Redux: 7
Deborah Haggis: 215
Paul Haggis: 11
Frazer Harrison / Getty Images Entertainment / Getty Images: 253
Scott Lauder, *Evening Standard* / Hulton Archive / Getty Images: 87
Los Angeles Examiner, USC Libraries Special Collections: 76
Pierre-Philippe Marcou / AFP / Getty Images: 186
Sinar Parman: 175
Private collection: 98, 115, 129
Robin Donina Serne, *The Tampa Bay Times*: 339
Chris Ware / Hulton Archive / Getty Images: 85, 88
All other photos are courtesy of the author.

A NOTE ON THE TYPE

The text of this book was set in Sabon, a typeface designed by Jan Tschichold (1902–1974), the well-known German typographer. Based loosely on the original designs by Claude Garamond (c. 1480–1561), Sabon is unique in that it was explicitly designed for hotmetal composition on both the Monotype and Linotype machines, as well as for filmsetting. Designed in 1966 in Frankfurt, Sabon was named for the famous Lyons punch cutter Jacques Sabon, who is thought to have brought some of Garamond's matrices to Frankfurt.

Composed by North Market Street Graphics,
Lancaster, Pennsylvania

Printed and bound by Berryville Graphics,
Berryville, Virginia

Designed by Cassandra J. Pappas